Eighty Years in the Highlands

Inverewe Garden
3 May 2010
Best wishes
Pauline Butler.

Eighty Years in the Highlands

The Life and Times of Osgood H. Mackenzie of Inverewe

1842–1922

Pauline Butler

Librario

Published by

Librario Publishing Ltd.

ISBN: 978-1-906775-13-1

Copies can be ordered via the Internet
www.librario.com

or from:

Brough House, Milton Brodie, Kinloss
Moray IV36 2UA
Tel/Fax No 00 44 (0)1343 850 178

Printed and bound in the UK

Typeset by 3btype.com

Setting the Scene

1. Beinn Aridh Charr, Osgood Mackenzie's favourite stalking ground.
Painting by Finlay Mackinnon, 1912

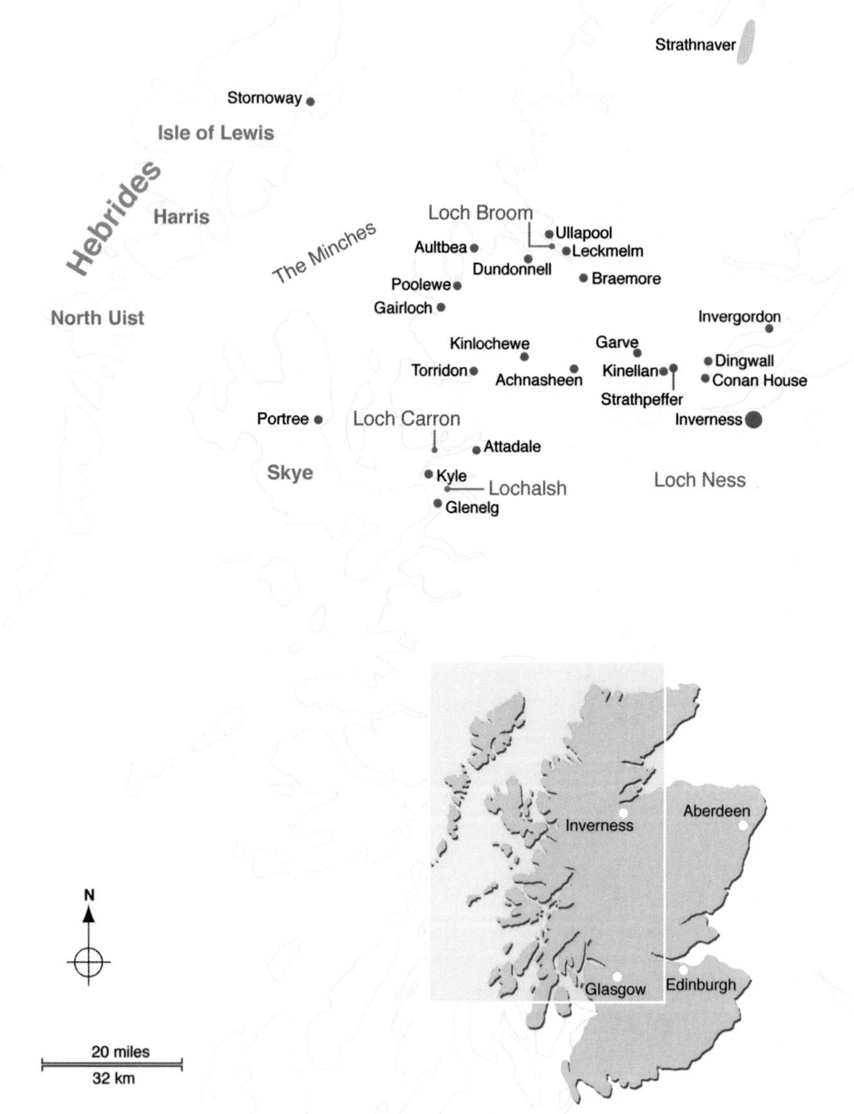

2. Map 1: Northern Scotland

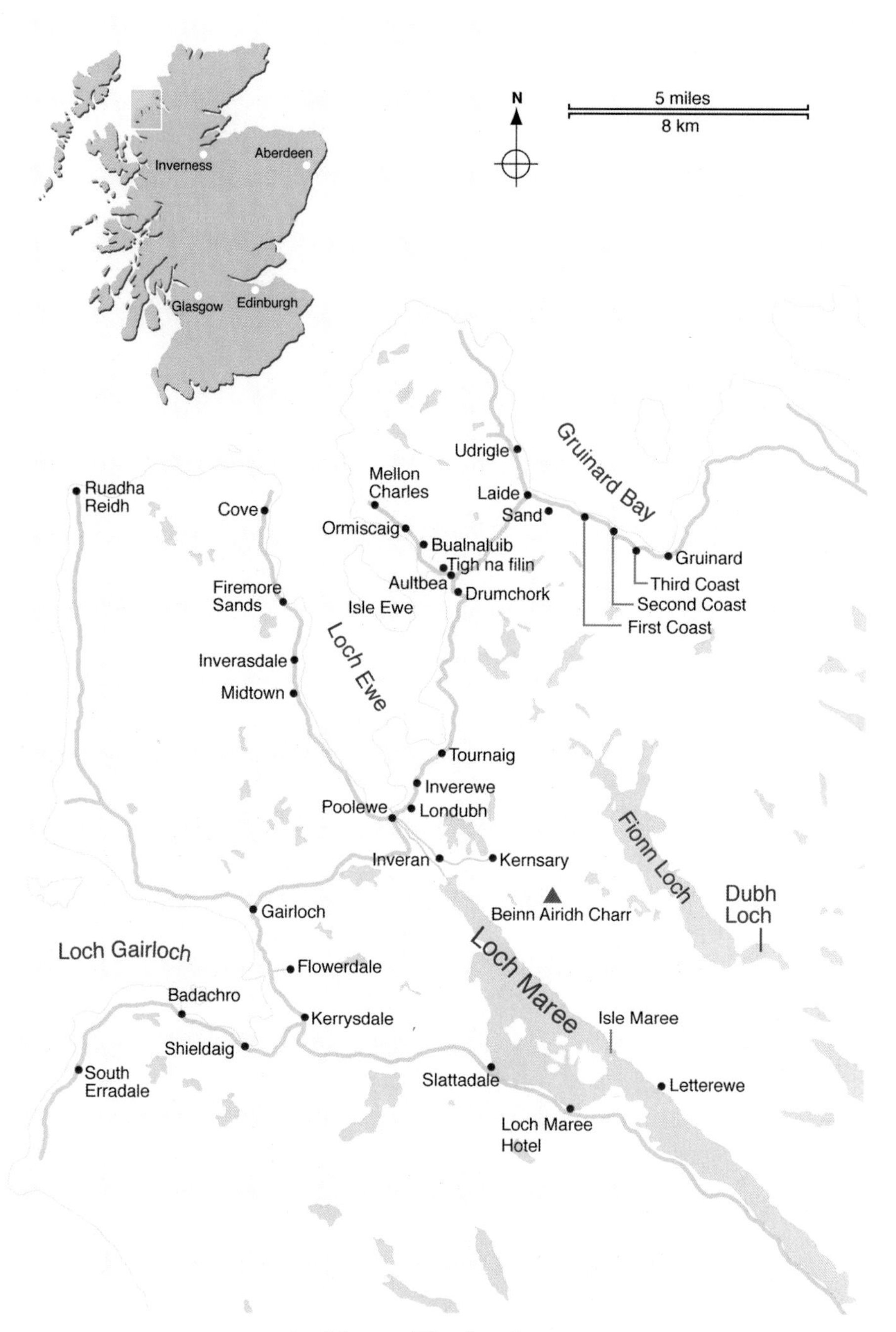

3. Map 2: The local area

4. Sands at Mellon Udrigle, Ross-shire. Watercolour by Mairi Mackenzie

5. Sunset at the Big Sands, Gairloch, from under the grave yard. Watercolour by Mairi Mackenzie

6. The Dubh and Fionn Lochs, looking west to Loch Ewe

Contents

Picture Credits

Jim Buchanan: Book cover design, both maps (illustrations **2** & **3**) and, most especially, for his infinite patience and support in providing the technical help which made it possible to include many of the old photographs and illustrations

National Trust for Scotland, Inverewe House Archive: illustrations **4, 5, 7, 11, 12, 13, 15, 16, 20, 21, 28, 29, 33, 35, 36, 37**

Gairloch Heritage Museum: illustrations **1, 8, 10, 14, 17, 18, 23, 24, 26, 27, 30, 34**

George Washington Wilson collection, University of Aberdeen: illustrations **9, 25**

Peter Hanbury's family albums: illustrations **31, 32**

Bruce Jeffrey: illustrations **6, 39, 40**

E.R.C. Mouat: illustration **38**

Cathy Thomson: illustration **22**

June Miller, by kind permission of her family: the book spine drawing of Osgood Mackenzie.

We believe we have the appropriate permissions to publish these images. If you think we have inadvertently used your copyright material without permission, please contact us.

List of Illustrations

People

Foreword

'I, having reached the age of seventy-nine, it has occurred to me that I might make a book of reminiscences which would give pleasure to those who reverence ancient customs and love the West Coast Highlands'

On 15 April 1922 Osgood H. Mackenzie died at home in the Gate Lodge at Inverewe. One obituary told of the passing of the 'Veteran Highlander':

> Mr Mackenzie recently had a fall while in his garden, from the effects of which he was confined to bed under medical treatment. He seemed to be making good progress towards recovery, but on Saturday he had a heart seizure and passed away.[1]

In 1921, a year before he died, Osgood had published *A Hundred Years in the Highlands*. This was, in his own words,

> a book of reminiscences which would give pleasure to those who reverence ancient customs and love the West Coast Highlands. [...] The reader must be kind enough to imagine that he is sitting on the opposite side of a peat fire listening to the leisurely memories of one who has lived a great number of years, observant of the customs of his neighbours, attentive to things of the passing moment, and who finds an increasing pleasure, after a life of the open air, in dwelling on the times that are gone.[2]

He had dictated his memoirs to a publisher's ghost-writer who had to sort out his ramblings and incorporate much information that came from the memoirs of his uncle, Dr John Mackenzie, (with considerable liberty taken, according to Christina Byam Shaw, who studied nine of the ten volumes of manuscript and published an annotated selection). There are other lengthy extracts from the writings of his mother, such as a description of an adventurous fishing trip to Skye. For those hoping to find out about the life and times of the founder of the world-famous Inverewe Garden it is a somewhat frustrating book. There is some reference to Osgood's childhood and a great deal about his commitment to the country pursuits of hunting, shooting and fishing, as boy and man. Perhaps there came some appreciation that he had helped to destroy the wild life he loved so much.

The chapter on the creation of his house and garden at Inverewe was almost a postscript. Several sections were lifted directly from previously published articles that he wrote for Scottish newspapers and a talk to the Royal Horticultural Society. The chapter on 'Peat' was originally a report sent to the Inverness Scientific Society. His depth of knowledge showed through. He was credited with being 'a skilled, philosophic horticulturalist and botanist, [...] he wrote with a facile pen and an inward knowledge which expert scientists might envy'.[3]

However, in 'dwelling on the times that had gone', he made no mention of many significant aspects of his life: his work as chairman of the Gairloch Parochial Board for twenty-five years; his involvement in the local community, for example as a member of the Gairloch School Board; his part in a long-running dispute over the proposal to divide the medical duties of the parish doctor for paupers into work for two men; his role in the local economy through his management of the Inverewe and Tournaig lands. He did comment on the crofting reforms initiated by his mother and his uncle, (on behalf of his half-brother, Kenneth, laird of Gairloch, a minor on inheritance), which made the area rather untypical of the crofting landscape and practice of nineteenth-century Scotland, but without comparison. Only rarely did events beyond the local area, even those as tumultuous as the First World War, seem to impinge on his life. In particular, though he told of some of the adventures of his childhood, there was relatively little on his family life, nothing on his short-lived marriage (which resulted in a bitter, contested and ultimately unsuccessful, divorce case) and, surprisingly, almost no detail of travels with his mother and daughter.

His obituarists seemed confused about the significance of his life. We read that he was 'one of the leading country gentlemen on the West Coast. [...] He was a deputy lord lieutenant and a JP for the County of Ross and in his native parish he was a prominent and active member of all the local public bodies'[4] and, contradictorily, 'Mr Mackenzie took no part in public life. He wrote to the Press at intervals chiefly on nature subjects but at times, as in these columns on public affairs'.[5]

So, even though *A Hundred Years* was a 'valuable and lasting contribution to the history of life and conditions in the Highlands', which 'secured for its author a permanent place in the ranks of those who have added materially to our knowledge of the social and economic life of the Highlands',[6] and was claimed to be 'a classic autobiography of a Highland Laird', in the review by Sir James Fergusson in the *Glasgow Herald*, it failed to enlighten on much of his life-story and character. In our environmentally conscious time, it even serves to discredit its author.

The purpose of this book, therefore, is to fill the gaps, as far as is possible, in our knowledge of the often troubled life of Osgood H. Mackenzie. At the same time, it aims to place him in the contexts of the age and place in which he was living, using contemporary evidence, much of it previously unpublished. Explanation is given of the wider Highland/Scottish 'background' where this illuminates events in the parish of Gairloch and the activities of Osgood and his close family members.

The result is a still incomplete jigsaw. It is hoped that it succeeds in giving insight into, and a fuller understanding of, a man who must surely, by the end of his days, have found solace in the tranquil woods and grounds of Inverewe. By then (1922) his garden was recognised to be 'famous all over the country'. This enduring legacy has since been appreciated and treasured by hundreds of thousands of visitors, from across the world. Osgood's only daughter, Mairi, 'WHO LOVES THE GAELIC, AND KEEPS TO OUR SIMPLE HIGHLAND WAYS, AND FOR WHOSE STRONG, UNCHANGING LOVE I AM FOR EVER GRATEFUL'[7], was nearing the end of her life and without direct heirs when she bequeathed the Inverewe estate to the National Trust for Scotland in 1952.

References and Notes

1 *Northern Chronicle*, 19 April 1922.

2 Osgood H. Mackenzie, *A Hundred Years in the Highlands* (London: Edward Arnold, 1921), p. VII.

3 *Ross-shire Journal*, 21 April 1922.

4 *The Scotsman*, 18 April 1922.

5 *Ross-shire Journal*, 21 April 1922.

6 *Inverness Courier*, 18 April 1922.

7 As written in the dedication of *A Hundred Years in the Highlands*.

Notes on Key Sources and Support

Three publications were the backbone to, and constant reference points for, the research which resulted in this book. As indicated in the Foreword, it was the *failure* of *A Hundred Years in the Highlands* to answer the questions I was asking about the personal and public life of Osgood Mackenzie which led me to search more widely. Though Osgood as an individual is only briefly mentioned, *Pigeon Holes of Memory*, by Christina Byam Shaw, a distant descendant, was invaluable for providing both the family context and for structuring Dr John Mackenzie's reminiscences on the transformation of local life through the crofting reforms he instituted during his years as factor – the years of Osgood's childhood. John H. Dixon's *Gairloch and Guide to Loch Maree* is essential for anyone interested in this area's *'Records, Traditions, Inhabitants and Natural History'*. At the time of its writing (1885/6) Osgood and he were good friends. Osgood contributed several sections personally, (his mother, the Dowager Lady Mary also). Inverewe was one of the 'Gairloch Estates' and many of Dixon's chapters, such as those on the local 'Ecclesiastical History', 'Ways and Means', 'Fisheries'. 'Living Gairloch Bards' and 'The Poolewe Artist' shed light on aspects which have proved elusive in other resources. 'Gairloch of the Present Day' pointed to areas which could be further explored through newspaper trawling.

So, the microfiche facilities of Inverness Reference Library provided hours of absorbed scrolling through the *Inverness Courier, Inverness Advertiser, Scottish Highlander* and other local papers from the period. Having a date to start from was always useful but random browsing also unearthed unexpected snippets – though surely there is more to find. Conveniently, the County Council archives, then in the adjoining room, produced the Valuation Rolls and County Council meeting minutes. The staff of both resources were always more than helpful. The digitisation of *The Scotsman* and *The Times* enabled me to pinpoint further newspaper information in home comfort.

The meticulous recording of three official investigations – Sir John McNeill's 1851 *Report to the Board of Supervision on the West Highlands and Islands, The Napier Report into the Conditions of the Crofters and Cottars in the Highlands and Islands of Scotland*, 1884, and that of the Royal Commission for the Highlands and Islands, 1894 – provided verbatim evidence from both landowners and local people which shed much light on the management of farming interests and of the stresses and strains of daily life. In the days before 'live recording' the characters were revealed through their own words. A local doctor had unearthed the *Enquiry into the State Medical Services for the Poor in the Highlands and Islands* instigated by the Royal College of Physicians of Edinburgh in 1850, which provided fascinating evidence.

Thirty years of teaching nineteenth-century British History, both political and social, had given me a useful background understanding to many issues of the day, such as the Poor Law, education reforms, 'Medicine through Time' and national politics. This needed to be supplemented by an appreciation of the 'Highland' dimensions. Chapter end-notes and the bibliography give an indication of the debt I owe to many historians and scholars. However, there seemed never to have been any specific coverage of the 'local' focus for the themes I had in mind. It was an unexpected bonus to discover the log books of the local elementary schools. Their entries, from the early 1870s on, provided much important incidental evidence.

Very significant to this study were the range of sources which detailed the sad story of Osgood's marriage and his three efforts to bring it to an end. The interest of Roderick Paisley, (Professor of Commercial Law), in the boundaries of the Pool House Hotel led to documents archived at the University of Aberdeen; the newspapers of the day reported comprehensively, but never salaciously, on the daily proceedings in the various courts as the divorce proceedings progressed and John H. Dixon, a solicitor by background, collected and bound together legal reports from 1892 into a volume entitled *The Mackenzie Case* which was on the library shelves in the Gairloch Heritage Museum.

Unreserved thanks are owing to those who gave crucial personal encouragement and opportunities: to Duncan Donald, then Property Manager at Inverewe Garden (National Trust for Scotland), who, from the day I expressed an interest in the historical issues connected with Osgood Mackenzie, allowed me to access the archive evidence stored in Inverewe House and led eventually to my role as 'Volunteer Archivist' there; to Osgood's Hanbury relatives, who invited me to visit and produced some wonderful photographs and the invaluable *Game Book* of Robert Hanbury, Osgood's son-in-law; to Mr John Mackenzie, of Gairloch and Conan Estates, who allowed me to work through the original manuscripts written by his namesake ancestor, Dr John, finding thereby additional references to Osgood and his mother which had not been selected for *Pigeon Holes*; to Nicola Tayler, curator of the Gairloch Heritage Museum, 2005–2009, whose professional support and friendship made every one of my frequent visits a pleasure; and, most of all, to Bruce without whose 'invitation' in 2001 I would never have come to the Highlands for a 'new life', enabling me to put into practice the theory of local history research, which I had been teaching for so long in my previous one.

Pauline Butler
2009

CHAPTER I

Young Osgood

'She found solace in her devotion to her son, Osgood, concentrating upon him all the love of which she was capable, and receiving as much in return.'

Thirty years after the event Osgood Hanbury Mackenzie met the French piper who had been hired to celebrate his birth on 13 May 1842 in the imposing Chateau de Talhouet. Osgood's father was Sir Francis Mackenzie, 12th laird of Gairloch, in the north-west highlands of Scotland. His mother Mary, daughter of Osgood Hanbury of 'Holfield Grange, Essex, [...] who held 3,392 acres of land in the parish of Coggeshall',[1] was Francis' second wife.

The reasons behind the family's stay in France were not happy ones and within a few months of their return to Britain Francis was dead and his wife was left facing a challenging future, in very difficult circumstances, as she took on the responsibilities of raising three young children and managing the entailed Mackenzie estates.

Osgood's father, Francis

Born in 1798, Francis' education had been carefully structured to prepare him for his future life as laird of Conan and Gairloch.

> It was thorough, and he was intelligent. His tutor's teaching was supplemented in Edinburgh by classes at the University and by private masters. He studied Latin, Greek, French, botany, writing, elocution, mathematics, music, drawing, logic and moral philosophy. He played the fiddle, learned fencing, attended the Riding School, and skated. There followed a period of law study at the University (intended by his father to teach him never to go to law) and there was then, for this eldest son, two years travelling alone in France, Switzerland, Germany, Italy and Austria. After that he returned home to live with his parents in the Highlands, where he was set to learn how to run the estates that he would inherit.[2]

He had evidently been a very lively and sociable young man. In 1814 he danced, at the Northern Society balls, with Elizabeth Grant of Rothiemurchus, whose writings tell much of the life of the higher echelons of Highland society.[3] His Grand Tour, 1820–1822, was recorded in a lengthy Journal and he apparently had a very good time of it, with alcohol not lacking. He also seemed, as a young man, to have had a taste for beautiful women. His brother recalled:

> When I was an Edinburgh student [early 1820s] Frank had taken a trip abroad and got acquainted at Geneva with a celebrated beauty, Miss Georgiana Brummel, niece of the very celebrated, unwise 'Beau Brummel', for years George iv's great ally and companion. On my father's hearing of their attachment, he persuaded Frank that he must wait till he (our Father) died, which would not be long. But that did not suit Miss Brummel, and their engagement ended.[4]

In 1825 Francis contemplated standing for parliament and canvassed his neighbour, Kenneth Dundonnell, for his vote. He didn't get it and appears not actually to have stood for election.[5] When Francis inherited the Mackenzie estates in 1826 he continued to enjoy the pursuits of the gentleman. He went hunting and steeple-chasing in England and became engaged, against her father's wishes, to Miss Kythé Smith Wright, whom he had met in Nottinghamshire. Her father objected to their marriage, because, even with £4000 per annum on paper, Francis' income was 'little enough'. He was also known for being rather generous with loans to friends that were not always repaid. Nonetheless, in 1829 Kythé became the first English bride of a laird of Gairloch. He was 31, she was 18.[6]

However, marriage and the birth of two sons, Kenneth and Francis, in quick succession do seem to have settled him down. The charming Kythé adapted quickly into her Highland life, split between Easter and Wester Ross, and was accepted readily by her new family and tenants alike. Her husband dedicated himself to management of his estates but still found time for social events. In the 1830s he was chair of the organising committee of the Northern Society. This club had been formed in 1788 for 'pleasure and innocent amusement' by the gentry of north Scotland, organising a week of dinners, balls, Games and piping in each August or September in Inverness. One year Francis won the musket shooting competition aiming at a 36 inch target at 100 yards, with young Kenneth third.[7]

But the happy marriage was not destined to last long. In 1834 Kythé died giving birth to her third child, a girl. The baby also died. Francis was distraught. Although he married again, just two years later, this was perhaps to provide a mother to his two boys. Mary Hanbury, also English, was some sixteen years younger than he at twenty-three.

The estates which Francis had inherited from his father in 1826 were not a great asset. In 1823 Sir Hector had reported:

> The farms and estates in the hill country are ruined past retrieve, the rocks and hills only remaining to the starving population. [...] Crops are not in, nor well got what is taken home and the price offered for cattle is worse every fair. My man could not sell a dozen of Gairloch cows and a Bully yesterday in Culbocky, though very good. Money was not offered for them and here they are back again.[8]

Fortunately for the crofters, according to Hugh Miller, then a young stonemason who was working on the new manse, the laird 'was a humane sensible man, comfortable enough in his circumstances to have, what Highland proprietors often have not, the complete command of his own affairs'.[9] But he struggled to meet the demands of maintaining an estate deep in debt. Although on paper he had sufficient income, '£4,144 or thereabouts', he had to pay out the ministers' and schoolmasters' salaries and a number of pensions. He was very anxious, and overworked. The 1840s were a time of agricultural depression and 'creeping famine'. The local population was increasing rapidly, poverty was endemic and rents not being paid. He could not sell his entailed estate to raise cash, and, unlike so many of his contemporaries, refused to evict.

Francis was seen to be a 'good landlord and a progressive farmer',[10] determined on 'improvement'. In 1838 he published a book, *Hints for the Use of Highland Tenants and Cottagers: by a Proprietor*. Nearly three hundred pages long, it had English text on the left hand side and Gaelic on the right. He hoped it would be used by his cottagers to improve their 'wretched hovels'. In particular, he did not approve of animals and people sharing the same entrance doorway. He was unimpressed by the efforts he had observed:

> The management of the native farmers is most destructive. The soil of one field is dug away to be laid upon another, and crop succeeds crop until the land refuses to yield anything. It is then allowed to rest for a season, and the weeds get time to multiply.
>
> The time, however, has at length arrived when the people must shortly change their habits, or quit the country. The labour which is required for small farms occupies but a small portion of the time of the tenants; but they are so perversely indolent and careless.

The laird gave advice as to how farming techniques could improve to become more efficient and effective. He recommended new houses with porch, kitchen and bedroom; a quarter acre garden with fruit trees; planting of oats, clover and turnips, rather than barley (used for distilling!); the land should be drained and trenched with the spade; ploughs take the place of the traditional *cas-chaibe* hand tool; and liquid manure applied (made from animal dung).[11]

Francis did follow the farming trend to some extent when he established 38,000 acres of deer forest at Gairloch in 1842. Four families had to be moved to other parts of the estate (two of crofters and two of cottars) but there were no evictions. Arguably, if he had evicted his hundreds of crofter tenants and replaced them with large-scale sheep farmers he would have doubled his income: there would then have been no need to collect hundreds of separate rents. Osgood Mackenzie later recognised how conscientious the laird was in trying to provide for the welfare of his tenants:

> Even prior to the destruction caused by potato blight, when the potatoes usually grew so well, there was hardly a year in which my grandfather and my father did not import cargoes of oatmeal to keep the people alive, and these cargoes were seldom, if ever, paid for by their poor recipients.[12]

Perhaps Francis was not tough enough. He might even have averted his own personal crisis. His brother believed that he was too kind to his tenants who resisted the introduction of new ways. Even though he went to some effort to ensure Gaelic as well as English text in his *Handy Hints* he failed to take into account that most of his eight hundred tenants could not read and were not persuadable. Some were clearly deliberately awkward – but still paid their rent. So, little progress was made. Though Francis' efforts were admired by the educated public, the crofters of Gairloch did not change their ways. The lack of profitability of his estates almost certainly contributed to his stress and ultimate breakdown.

One additional, somewhat unusual, aspect of 'improvement' advocated by the laird was that of abstinence. 'He laboured assiduously to inculcate habits of sobriety among the people, particularly on his own estate. We remember the enthusiasm with which he used to describe a rent day in Gairloch where no beverage stronger than coffee was drunk, yet all seemed happy and contented'.[13] Dr John confirmed how 'Sir Francis Mackenzie of Gairloch was one of the first Highland proprietors who discovered that smuggling was injurious both to proprietors and tenants' and he suppressed it on his estates.[14] His 'exertions in the cause' were 'most meritorious and unceasing'. In early

January 1840 he chaired two meetings of the Total Abstinence Society in the Northern Meeting Rooms in Inverness. 500 people attended the one on New Year's Day, paying 1s 6d each.[15]

But his financial problems were overwhelming. In 1841 he had a breakdown and the decision was made that he should take his pregnant wife and young family to Brittany, to try to find some peace away from his responsibilities. His brother was willing to take on the role of factor of his estates. Osgood explained a little about that year in Brittany in his memoirs. The focus was on allowing his father to enjoy the opportunities for fishing and hunting. An Aberdeenshire salmon-fisher accompanied the family for 'the capture of the salmon in the River Ellé' and 'my father had a big extent of chasse to shoot over' but 'there was no game to speak of, and the bags consisted chiefly of squirrels, which it was the fashion there to eat'.

The family left France the following year. After a short stay in Jersey, where they dined with 'a friend of my father, a Colonel Lecouteur' and were offered thirty different pear dishes for desert, they went to England.[16] On 7 December 1842, 'Sir Francis Mackenzie of Gairloch was present at a meeting of an agricultural society in Essex and suggested the establishment of model and experimental farms'.[17]

However, in London, his mental condition deteriorated rapidly. At the end of April Lady Mary sent a letter to her brother-in-law, pleading for help: 'I have never seen him so bad before. [...] I can do nothing, yet perhaps you might be able. [...] What a comfort it would be to have you with Francis now'.[18] But Dr John could do nothing either, other than to have Francis certified insane by two of the principal 'mad' doctors in London and to arrange for him to be admitted, on 5 May 1843, to a private asylum in St John's Wood, where he died on 2 June, aged just forty-four. Osgood never acknowledged the full extent of his father's illness, writing only that he 'became very ill, and according to the stupid practice of doctors in those days, he was bled in the arm, erysipelas set in, and he died in the course of a few days'.[19]

The body was returned by sea to Scotland. The funeral service took place in the old, ruined, roofless priory of Beauly: 'The deceased baronet was an Episcopalian, the beautiful service of that Church was read and listened to with a deep and thrilling interest and solemnity'.

> Sir Francis, being a member of the Temperance Society, the funeral was conducted in strict conformity with what might be supposed to have been his own wish and desire. A handsome collation was provided for the better classes

> in the mansion house but without wine or spirits, while meat and bread were abundantly supplied to others on the grounds. This was very different, we need hardly say, from the usual arrangements of great Highland funerals which were formerly marked by wild excess, and a sort of frantic enthusiasm. Even the bagpipe was here dispensed with. [...] The chief mourners were the two youthful sons of the deceased, arrayed in the Highland dress, and their uncle, Dr Mackenzie, Kinellan. The private carriage of Sir Francis followed, containing Lady Mackenzie and her sister, Miss Hanbury.[20]

Osgood's mother, Mary

Osgood's mother was the dominant influence in his life as boy and man. Her father, Osgood Hanbury, was a member of a wide-flung family whose fortunes had been made through the brewing industry. It is not known how Mary met her husband. From 1836, as wife of the laird of Gairloch, she had to adapt to the Highland way of life, be 'mother' to two young step-sons and support a husband who was suffering from considerable stress. On account of this, six years later and expecting her first child, she moved the family to Brittany. Her possessive attitude to the new-born manifested itself immediately. On the first night after his birth she was unhappy with the *accoucheuse* who was sleeping, rather than listening out for a crying infant, and took him to her own bed. 'No-one else was allowed to have charge of him from that day forward'.[21] There was indecision as to the naming of the newly born. Originally he was to have been Hector, a Mackenzie name, but, much to Osgood's regret, (he later expressed a clear preference for a Gaelic first name), and one of the rare occasions on which he disagreed with his mother:

> My father, recollecting that the eldest son of my Uncle John Mackenzie was called Hector, thought two of the same name in the family might be confusing, so, when we reached England and I was christened, the name of Osgood was given me, after my maternal grandfather, Osgood Hanbury.[22]

The next two years must have been devastating for Mary. Having moved from Brittany to Jersey and then on to London, her husband was soon incarcerated in a mental institution. Widowed at only thirty-one, she was left to cope with three young children and the responsibilities of being the trustee of a distant and almost bankrupt estate in the remote Highlands. Her annual allowance was just £900.

Perhaps influenced by her Quaker upbringing, the Dowager showed great dedication to estate duty. She decided to settle in Gairloch, but the tenants and crofters on the estate there 'never showed towards her the warmth they had customarily felt for the laird's wife. She decided that it was her duty to make her life among them, to learn Gaelic and to work hard for their welfare. She thought highly of her brother-in-law, Dr John, and supported his social and agricultural reforms. Parsimonious in her own way of life, she was nonetheless energetic in charitable good works'.

Nor, despite all this, did her step-sons 'grow up to love her'. Young Francis was nine when his father died and Kenneth eleven so it would be another ten years before he could be 'laird' in his own right. It was to her only child that Mary was most committed: 'She found solace in her devotion to her son, Osgood, concentrating upon him all the love of which she was capable, and receiving as much in return'.[23]

Tigh Dige – the Gairloch family home

The Mackenzie family owned two estates, one at Conon, (just outside Inverness)[24], where they traditionally spent the winter, and the second, of 170,000 acres, on the Atlantic coast at Gairloch, seventy or so miles distant. The Tigh Dige, also known as Flowerdale, was the customary summer retreat. The expedition there, in May each year, required considerable strategic planning given that, until the late 1840s, no road existed beyond Kinlochewe along Loch Maree.[25] Retainers from the estate met the convoy and carried all to Gairloch, first by boat to Slatadale and then along rough tracks.[26] Often horse-drawn sledges worked better than carts to move the family's belongings and the provisions necessary for their stay.

The Gairloch house was not immediately available for use by the recently bereaved family:

> Very soon after my father's death, my uncle, as factor for the estate, had occasion to come up to Gairloch, and took along with him my two half-brothers, aged twelve and ten. The Tigh Dige and the sporting rights of the whole Gairloch property had been let to an Irishman, Sir St. George Gore, for £300 a year on a lease, so my uncle and the boys put up at the small Ceann-t-saile Inn.

Sir St. George was given notice to quit.[27] The Dowager Lady Mary 'came to reside permanently at Flowerdale in June 1844', a year after her husband's death.[28]

The recorded history of the Mackenzies of Gairloch went back to a protocol of 1494 giving them title to land from the River Ewe and Loch Maree to Loch Torridon. It was added to in 1671 and 1743.[29] The house the family built just south of Gairloch had been its west coast home through the centuries:

> The old Tigh Dige and its gardens and outbuildings stood in the field below Flowerdale House. The Tigh Dige itself was, as its name implies, a house in a ditch or moat. [...] This was the Gairloch home of Hector Roy Mackenzie, the founder of the family in the latter part of the fifteenth century. The Tigh Dige is said to have been originally a turf hut, with a roof made of sticks and divots. Kenneth Mackenzie, the sixth laird of Gairloch, erected on the same site, within the same moat, about the middle of the seventeenth century, a more substantial building, which was called the Stank House or Moat House.[30]

In 1738 Sir Alexander Mackenzie, aged three, became the ninth laird. His trustees

> pulled down the Stankhouse, which stood in a marshy situation on the site of the old Tigh Dige, and built the present Flowerdale House on a raised plateau surrounded by charming woods and rugged hills, and with a southern aspect. The glen here was a perfect jungle of wild flowers before the introduction, long after this time, of sheep farming, and so Sir Alexander appropriately gave the name of Flowerdale to his new chateau.[31]

It created a very favourable impression on visitors. In 1813 artist William Daniell arrived at Flowerdale by sea, and wrote, in 1825, of a 'beautiful and picturesque domain' of 'sylvan luxuriance', an 'Arcadia', contrasting with the 'steril grandeur of these maritime highlands'.[32] Nine year-old Evander Maciver, who visited in 1820 from Lewis, commented that there were all sorts of fruit trees and soft fruit in the garden, 'well trained and kept'. Black's Tourist Guide (1851) described it as 'a commodious old-fashioned chateau [...] surrounded by extensive and thriving plantations, its lawn also presenting some ancient and large-sized oak, pine, ash, chesnut, and sycamore trees'.[33] Osgood spent much of his childhood at Flowerdale. The tradition for the family to spend the winters at Conan, their family house on the east side of Ross-shire, was not maintained, his mother saying she lived permanently at Flowerdale for the ten years she was the trustee for her step-son's estate.[34]

The other house which was important to Osgood during his childhood was that of his Great-uncle Kenneth, (already well over seventy years old when Osgood was born), and Aunty Flora. Captain Kenneth had served in India during the French Wars of the early nineteenth century and, on his return, had been given the farm of Kerrysdale,[35] a mile or so south of Tigh Dige. He built there 'a small farmhouse, with very picturesque surroundings, but it is placed rather low'.[36] He lived there for seventy years.

Home tuition

Francis' brother, Dr John, was one of the three family members managing the Gairloch estate during Kenneth, the heir's, minority. His diaries indicated that he took considerable interest in the fatherless boys. In 1848 he moved his family, (wife, two sons and five daughters), to live on Isle Ewe so as to be able to support his nephews and Lady Mary more effectively. He aimed to ensure that they were brought up prepared for the lives they were destined to lead. Osgood, putting together his reminiscences in old age, acknowledged a great debt at a personal level to his uncle. There were, for example, many lengthy accounts in *A Hundred Years* of the family history, the journey from Conan to Flowerdale, smuggling and lunatics, which were quoted from his uncle's handwritten memoirs. Certainly Osgood spoke warmly of his contribution to a happy childhood in the Tigh Dige.

Dr John must have helped the young lad to develop a love of the West coast and its way of life which determined him to make his own home there when he was old enough to decide. During the early years of his childhood Osgood did not generally go far from Gairloch, though he did once make a 'horrible voyage' when he was 'four or five years old', travelling for nine days from Invergordon to London 'in a kind of paddle-boat'. On the return journey the party became stuck in a snowdrift at Blair Atholl on the stage-coach leg and was forced to return to Perth. They completed their trip by the newly opened railway to Aberdeen and then steam-boat to Inverness.[37] Otherwise, 'my mother never left Gairloch, not even for a day, for three long years when the famine was at its height'.[38] Osgood was brought up to be aware of the way of life of the local people, he wrote of their tools of bone and wood, he learnt of their poverty and their food shortages and he appreciated the family responsibility to support them in their times of need.[39]

Neither Uncle nor Mother held much truck with sending children away to school. They clearly had similar principles on the education of the three boys, though perhaps John had more say with respect to the elder two and Mary took her own decisions about Osgood. As John commented with reference to his own daughters:

> In nothing do I see more need of improvement than in the absurd cost of education of 'genteel' children, compared with the value received. The world would say our children had no regular education; yet, except in a sprinkling of girls now bred in college studies of every kind, I have not met with any women trained in most expensive boarding schools, who were better educated than our daughters, or more able to hold up their heads in any society – and they were educated at a mere nominal expence by their Mother and very ordinary helps.[40]

As for his nephews: at the time of his father's death in 1842 Kenneth was attending preparatory school at Rugby but was brought back to Scotland and tutored at Flowerdale and then in Edinburgh.[41] To broaden their experience 'I even had them bred to carpentering and turning, and sent Kenneth to the Edinburgh Town Architect (a cousin) that he might understand all about country buildings'.[42] It was arranged that he go abroad to study 'under the famous Professor Liebig, the founder of agricultural chemistry, at the University of Giessen, in Germany, where he took his doctorate. There in the years following the abortive Revolution of 1848 he imbibed Liberal ideas'.[43] His diploma, in chemistry and natural science, was awarded in 1851. Osgood wrote in complimentary words about these sons of his father's first wife, Kythé: 'I do not think it could be possible for any two young men to turn out greater successes than my two half-brothers, the late Sir Kenneth S. Mackenzie and his brother'.

Osgood was fully convinced that the family tradition of education at home was to his benefit:

> Nor was my education being neglected. [...] It is surely better that a Highlander should be something little different from an Englishman. When they are sent to English schools as small boys of eight or nine years old, and their education is continued in the south, they lose all their individuality. They may be very good, but they have nothing Highland about them. [...] Why should the present chiefs and lairds call themselves Highland if they can't speak a word of the language of their people and country?[44]

His English mother, dismissive of school clones, encouraged her son to learn Gaelic from his nursemaid, Janet MacMillan: 'Life for me, living in the west as I have done, would not have been worth living without the Gaelic. No servant on the place, inside or outside, was ever allowed to speak English [...] under pain of being dismissed'. He claimed to have been perfectly fluent by the age of seven. Kenneth and Francis were equally competent. On his death-bed Kenneth 'went out of this world and entered his eternal rest repeating verse after verse of the Gaelic Psalms, which had been taught him by my mother in his childhood'. Francis did not lose his Gaelic language, even whilst in the Navy for some years, and, when he 'took a big farm in Orkney, where no Gaelic is spoken by the natives, he had so many Gairloch workmen there with him that Gaelic was the order of the day'.[45]

When Osgood was seven, a 12 year-old Protestant boy was brought over from an orphanage at Arras, 'to come as a sort of page, and to go out with me, and I never had any trouble in learning French, which seemed to come to me quite naturally'. 'When I was about eight years of age a tutor was got for me, and I had one with me from then till I was eleven, when I left Gairloch for Germany'.[46] Yet, though he always spoke highly of his upbringing, it must have been a rather solitary, detached childhood. His half-brothers were that much older and the crofter children could not really be his friends and companions. It was his mother who proved to be his soul mate.

Hunting, shooting and fishing 1852–1862

Much of the youthful Osgood's time was spent out of doors. His memoirs are full of tales of expeditions undertaken in the mountains and on the moors, organised for him by his mother: 'I started fishing, both on sea and loch, and took up ornithology and egg-collecting, in which she encouraged me in every possible way'.[47] He began young:

> When I was not more than seven or eight years old, I was already quite a keen collector of eggs, and greatly coveted a clutch of those of the sea-eagle, which were always rare in this district, whereas the golden eagles were comparatively plentiful. [...] But, on our arrival we found we were just a day too late, for a south-country shepherd [...] had taken them the previous day. However, a good Caledonian bank-note [...] was fairly powerful in those days.

So Osgood acquired the 'two, big pure white eggs'.[48] Ospreys nesting on Loch Maree islands were also considered to be fair game. From the age of eight he had his own gun. There were sporting trips to the Shiant Islands, St Kilda (in May 1853) and the Lews.

> Some wise folk thought my mother was making a great mistake by letting me start shooting so early, one of the chief reasons brought forward being that I should soon become quite blasé and should not enjoy sport when I grew up to manhood. But all these prophecies were completely falsified, as I was the keenest of sportsmen all my life, until I gave up the gun when I was over seventy. Few men have done more shooting in the course of their lives than I have.[49]

Once the worst years of the famine were over these outdoor pursuits on the Ross-shire moors were interrupted by quite lengthy spells away from home. Osgood referred to a trip to France in 1851, staying in Normandy and Paris and, in the same year, a visit to the Great Exhibition.[50] When his mother was freed from her trusteeship responsibilities she relinquished her role in the young laird's household. Tigh Dige (Flowerdale) was rented out to shooting tenants and she chose to travel abroad with her son, rather than live elsewhere in the area. Osgood wrote of 'having been brought up a great deal on the Continent'.[51]

> I left my home for Germany in the autumn of 1853, when the Crimean War was in full blast. My mother's intention was to remain abroad for perhaps three years, but the first summer at Heidelberg proved too hot for me, [...] so we had to go to Switzerland for three months. Ross-shire saw us back again (at least, for a good long holiday) in 1855, because I was beginning to get very homesick, and in consequence was not thriving quite to my mother's satisfaction.[52]

They returned to Germany the next year. When in Wester Ross Osgood and his mother now stayed at the estate fishing lodges of Pool House, Poolewe or Inveran on the shore of Loch Maree.[53] This gave the lad renewed opportunities to develop his hunting skills on the Gairloch properties. His game books detailed many an expedition to Mellon Charles, Isle of Ewe and the inland moors.

> How distinctly I remember my first day out on the hill in August 1855! I was armed with my little gun, which weighed only three pounds; but I had a real licence to shoot game, and this made me feel very important and quite a man.[54]

> I soon became a good shot. [...] I got fifty or sixty snipe in a week, which I was proud of being able to send to friends in England. [...] I did perfect

> wonders with my little three-pounder, and was the cause of the death of two wild swans and several roe.[55]

There is much in his memoirs on this joyous pursuit of game. He was taken to the lovely islands of Loch Maree where he distinguished himself by shooting 'black game and woodcock, and just enough roe and wild ducks and geese, and even wild swans, to raise one's expectations and make it exciting'.[56] He explored many of the lochs looking for duck, snipe and grouse. It was on his return to Scotland in 1855 that he first rented his own hunting grounds. Sir Alexander Mackenzie of Coul asked only '£10 per annum for something like 7,000 or 8,000 acres, on condition that we put on a good keeper, who would stop poaching and destroy the vermin'. So Osgood benefitted from sporting rights over the lands of Inverewe, 'then just a neglected outlying sheep-farm', and began his acquaintance with the moors that were to become his own a few years later.

At the same time he acquired that essential for successful shooting expeditions, 'a good dog of some kind', selecting "Shot" a curly retriever, 'who made himself quite at home in front of the kitchen fire or under the kitchen table, along with various terriers'. When Osgood was sixteen he 'began rather to look down on Shot, and aspired to getting a brace of properly broken pointers or setters'. He purchased two of an 'unusual colour for pointers–viz., black and tan', walking all the way to Loch Broom, via Dundonnell to collect them.[57]

As he became a more ambitious young hunter he extended his rented land, and the weight of his annual bags, by 'hiring from my brother the Isle of Ewe, the extensive hill grazings of the Mellan, Ormiscaig and Bualnaluib crofter townships, and the small farm of Inveran'. He would stay in the schoolhouse of the Bualnaluib school where he would remain

> for two or three nights at a time and shoot over the crofter hill grounds, which made three good beats. This I did chiefly in November and December, and delightful shooting it was. [...] I used to get from twelve to fifteen brace and sometimes over twenty brace of grouse a day to my own muzzle-loader, and always a few woodcock or teal, snipe or ducks. As for golden plover and rock pigeons, there was no place like it for them; and there were besides a good many coveys of partridges and many brown and blue hares. In short, on Mellan and the Isle of Ewe there was everything a boy sportsman could possibly desire. How constantly do I still dream of those happy days even now in my old age.[58]

Osgood at sixteen was no longer content with birds and hares. He became very enthusiastic about deer stalking and arranged with the wealthy English owner of the 'famous Strath na Sealg' ground to stalk fifty thousand acres for a whole season for the sum of £5. 'Perhaps that was among the happiest days, if not the very happiest day, of my long life'.[59] He devoted a whole chapter in *A Hundred Years* to his exploits on these lands. Nor was the accompanying social life neglected:

> I remember as a lad of fifteen or sixteen starting on foot from the castle [Lews], and on the home beat shooting thirty-six brace of grouse over dogs with my muzzle-loader, and after my return dancing all night at a ball given in the castle to the townspeople.[60]

Whilst away from home on foreign travels Osgood and his mother ('Auntie') kept in touch with Dr John Mackenzie. Dr John had left Scotland in October 1858 for a lengthy trip to Europe of his own, with his wife and two of his children, spending several months in each of France, Italy and Germany. He recorded, almost incidentally, that he had received a letter from 'Auntie' on 8 January 1859. The two family parties met up on 3 February in an unpromising Naples: 'Everything unfavourable. Constant rain, rubbishy houses and streets all mud, sky like gruel, a howling wind [...] but welcoming Auntie and Osgood, and good *coal* fires, good food, rooms etc'. Though Osgood and his mother went with Dr John to see the Town Palace, the Botanic Gardens and Campo Santo, mostly the two groups went their separate ways. Dr John eventually travelled north to Florence via Verona, where Osgood and his mother joined him 'at dinner in 6 days from Rome by Perugia' and attended 'High Mass at L'Annunziata church' on 25 March but on the 31 March 'they left us [...] going north through the fascinating Tyrol'.

On 3 May they met up again, this time in Heidelberg, Germany. Osgood and his mother were already there: 'At 1.30 found Osgood waiting us at Heidelberg station and soon had Auntie's Hooray from 3rd story of Muller's family hotel'. During the three days Dr John stayed in Heidelberg he recorded how 'a nightingale sang his best in a tree having probably got his nest in a safer place than the one Osgood showed us he robbed of 2 dark green unspotted eggs. [...] Osgood employs the police who are set to watch and protect all nests to bring him the eggs he wants and is promised in a day or two eggs of the rare Golden oriole'.[61]

In 1862, now aged 20 and back in Scotland, Osgood established his proprietorial independence. On his behalf his mother initiated the purchase of 'the larger part of Kernsary, which adjoined and lay right into Inverewe'. The fishing banks of the River Ewe were, not surprisingly, specifically excluded from the sale. Nonetheless, Osgood acquired several valuable miles 'of the shores of the famous Fionn Loch, sharing with the Earl of Ronaldshay the joint right of fishing in all its waters'.[62] In 1863 Lady Mary added Lochend (or Inverewe) and Tournaig from Sir William Mackenzie of Coul, another branch of the family.

> The Mackenzies of Lochend, or Kinloch (now Inverewe), sprang from John Mackenzie of Lochend, third son of Alexander, the seventh laird of Gairloch, by his second wife. They were tacksmen of Lochend, which belonged to the Coul Mackenzies, by whom it was ultimately sold to Mr Osgood H. Mackenzie in 1863. The old Lochend House stood where the walled garden of the present Inverewe House is.[63]

As the Inverewe 'laird' Osgood was now master of his own estate, ready to take his place as a 'heritor' of the parish of Poolewe and to play his part in local community issues, great and small. His name, as it turned out, was often to be in the headlines, frequently to the detriment of his reputation.

References and Notes

1 Mackenzie, pp.4, 3.
2 Christina Byam Shaw, *Pigeon Holes of Memory* (London: Constable, 1988), p.109. This book of selections from the manuscript diaries of Dr John Mackenzie (with in-depth annotation and explanation) has been invaluable in understanding the context of family and circumstances during Osgood's childhood years, though there is relatively little direct reference to him and his mother.
3 Angus Fairrie, *The Northern Meeting 1788–1988* (East Lothian: Pentland, 1988), p.14.
4 Byam Shaw, p.205.
5 Byam Shaw, p.69.
6 Byam Shaw, p.212.
7 Fairrie, p.23.
8 Byam Shaw, p.85, quoting a letter Sir Hector sent to his son, John, in 1823.
9 Hugh Miller, stone-mason, geologist, later pamphleteer and editor of *The Witness,* writing in *My Schools and Schoolmasters*, quoted in Byam Shaw, p.86.
10 Byam Shaw, p.218.

[11] J.B. Caird, *The Making of the Gairloch Crofting Landscape* in Ed. John R. Baldwin, *Peoples and Settlement in North-West Ross* (Edinburgh: The Scottish Society for Northern Studies, 1994), p.142.
[12] Mackenzie, pp.180–181.
[13] *Inverness Courier*, 14 June 1843, summarised in James Barron, *The Northern Highlands in the Nineteenth Century, Newspaper index and annals*. Vol. 3, 1842–1856 (Inverness: Carruthers and Sons, 1913).
[14] *Inverness Courier*, 29 August 1866, summarised in Barron.
[15] Byam Shaw, p.314.
[16] Mackenzie, pp.2–3, 5–6.
[17] *Inverness Courier*, 7 December 1842, summarised in Barron.
[18] Byam Shaw, p.221.
[19] Mackenzie, p.6.
[20] *Inverness Chronicle*, 14 June, 28 June 1843. Byam Shaw, p.230, mentions that the Estate accounts included twenty-eight items under 'Sick Bed and Funeral Expenses'. The cost of the 'Mournings' for Lady Mackenzie were '£40. For her son Osgood – £9.'
[21] Mackenzie, p.2.
[22] Mackenzie, pp.2–3.
[23] Byam Shaw, p.230.
[24] To general confusion, the place is spelled Conon (Conon Bridge) and the house/estate is Conan – but not always consistently!
[25] See maps
[26] Mackenzie, pp.8–9.
[27] Mackenzie, p.179.
[28] John H. Dixon, *Gairloch and Guide to Loch Maree* (Edinburgh: Co-operative Printing Co Ltd, 1886), p.148.
[29] Caird, p.139.
[30] Dixon, p.102.
[31] Dixon, p.54.
[32] Byam Shaw, pp.45–46.
[33] George & Peter Anderson, *Guide to the Highlands and Islands of Scotland* (Edinburgh: Adam and Charles Black, 1851), p.477, www.books.google.com accessed 10 November 2008.
[34] Dixon, p.148.
[35] Mackenzie, p.60.
[36] Dixon, p.309.
[37] Mackenzie, p.7.
[38] Mackenzie, p.29. See Chapter III for detail of these destitution years.
[39] Mackenzie, p.181.
[40] Byam Shaw, p.195.
[41] *Inverness Courier*, 13 February 1900.

[42] Byam Shaw, p.226.
[43] Stated in an article on *The Napier Commission*, by I.M.M. MacPhail, in the *Transactions of the Gaelic Society of Inverness* Vol. XLVIII, 1972–1974, p.440.
[44] Mackenzie, pp.58–59.
[45] Mackenzie, pp.34–35. Osgood was a member of the recently formed (1871) Gaelic Society from 1872/3 until 1886/7 (record of members in its *Transactions*). It is not known why he ended his affiliation.
[46] Mackenzie, pp.37, 63.
[47] Mackenzie, p.37.
[48] Mackenzie, pp.156–157.
[49] Mackenzie, p.63.
[50] Mackenzie, pp.72–73.
[51] Mackenzie, p.247.
[52] Mackenzie, p.113.
[53] Inveran Lodge was later to be the home of Mr John H. Dixon, renowned for his *Gairloch and Guide to Loch Maree.*
[54] Mackenzie, p.115.
[55] Mackenzie, pp.69–70.
[56] Mackenzie, p.119.
[57] Mackenzie, pp.113–116.
[58] Mackenzie, pp.121–122.
[59] Mackenzie, p.143.
[60] Mackenzie, p.104.
[61] The manuscript diaries of Dr John Mackenzie are in the archives of Conan House and were kindly loaned by John Mackenzie. The references here, to the travels of Osgood Mackenzie and his mother, were not included in Christina Byam Shaw's selected and edited extracts published as *Pigeon Holes of Memory.* The information can be found in Volume VIII, pp.699, 737, 740, Volume IX pp.807, 809, 821 and Volume X, pp.862, 865. Any doubts as to whether the Osgood mentioned was 'Osgood Hanbury Mackenzie' were dispelled once this mention of collecting the eggs of rare birds was discovered.
[62] Mackenzie, p.154. See Chapter VII for more details of these land purchases. Throughout his book Osgood wrote, erroneously, 1862 for Inverewe and 1863 Kernsary.
[63] Dixon, p.58. The development of 'Osgood's Inverewe' is the subject of Chapter XIII.

CHAPTER II

The Crofting Life

'There is, indeed, very little rest for crofters or their families from one year's end to the other, and any who know how hard they work must consider the remuneration the whole yields scanty in the extreme.'

Osgood Mackenzie was brought up, and lived all of his life, in the north-west Highlands. The area was considered to be remote and wild:

> A region of mountain and bog, scarcely passable by pedestrians. [...] The only approach to the country was by means of boats, and to all intents and purposes the people were wholly excluded from intercourse with the civilised world. [...] They raised potatoes for themselves, caught fish in Loch-Ewe, reared the sheep from which they procured wool, manufactured clothes and stockings, made their own shoes, and were in fact a self sustaining community.[1]

The traditional cultivation by tenant and cottar was based on a small area of arable land and black cattle. Both Osgood's father and uncle tried valiantly to improve the agricultural methods used. It was recognised that the land alone could never provide a full occupation or income. The soil is but thin and peaty, with rock never far from the surface, the climate wet, with severe snow possible in a hard winter and short, often damp, summers though with long hours of daylight. The crofting settlements or townships tended to be close to the sea as fish were a crucial supplement to the diet. Seaweed was a most valuable mulch and fertiliser, and, early in the century, had been a valuable source of income on the Western Isles and coasts, through making kelp (a product of seaweed ashes to provide an alkali which had been used in making soap and glass). This manufacture had come to an end soon after the Napoleonic Wars. Osgood, as a child, was aware of the living conditions and circumstances of the poorer people through the benevolent work of his mother and the experience of his uncle during the famine years.

Houses

Little more than simple huts, the poorest houses were usually circular with stone bases and turf or wattle walls and thatched roofs, generally of bracken. These served essentially as shelter from the storm, having one room but no windows. By the nineteenth century those who could would have constructed stone houses, with thick walls, perhaps a double skin filled with rubble and soil, and often a rounded end. Any windows would be tiny. These 'Black Houses' were usually two-roomed, the 'but and ben'. Sometimes a kiln, necessary to dry the corn, was built onto the end of the house but, more likely, there would be a separate communal one. Stone querns were used for small-scale milling.

A thatched roof was laid over a layer of overlapping sods. Heather was considered better than bracken or straw and was kept in place by ropes, also made of straw or heather, weighted down with large stones. Roof timbers were always the biggest challenge and a good landlord would provide the necessary trees. Otherwise driftwood spars were a possibility.[2] The destruction of the roof timber, during Clearance operations, was considered despicable. If possible the crofters would take their roof timbers with them, given that they counted as 'wealth' as much as their livestock. The roof did not overhang. The floor was likely to be trampled mud and the walls might be mud-plastered and lime-washed. The peat-burning fire would probably be on a raised slab in the middle of the living room, with smoke rising into the rafters. Only later was a fireplace built into the gable end, with a proper chimney.

Livestock and people might well share the same accommodation: 'The houses of the people in general have but one outer door, and as they and their cattle go in by that one entrance [...] it cannot be expected that a habitation common to man and beast can be particularly clean'.[3] Manure was likely to accumulate in the dwelling until needed for the fields. Sir Francis Mackenzie, Osgood's father, wrote a book of *Hints* in 1838 for the benefit of his tenants and cottagers. He protested at 'human beings and cattle entering together in the present fashion at the same doorway', and suggested that dirt was the result of laziness. Sir George Mackenzie of Coul, from whom Dr John leased his first farm at Kinellan, had very forthright thoughts about the living conditions of the Highland tenantry. They 'live in the midst of smoke and filth; that is their choice. [...] As to *sties*, there is seldom such a thing to be seen about the habitations of the common people. The same house, which may indeed be called a stie...'.[4]

Some improvements took place in the mid-nineteenth century on the Mackenzie lands despite, rather than because of, the efforts the crofters made themselves. Dr John, as factor of the Mackenzie estates, and Lady Mary Mackenzie, Osgood's mother, initiated a rebuilding and re-settlement programme in the 1840s which brought about rather slow and patchy progress.[5] Forty years on it would seem that most of the turf houses had been replaced:

> The present cottages have their walls of stone, the better ones cemented with lime; the roofs of timber, thatched with heather, rushes, or straw; divots are also still frequently used in roofing. Some few superior crofters' houses have slated roofs, and modern grates with flues and regular chimneys. But many of the crofters still have their byres under the same roof; still have no chimney in the living room, whence the smoke from the peat fire escapes only by a hole in the roof; and still have the heap of ashes, slops, manure, and refuse just outside the door. [...]
>
> The houses of the crofters are certainly undergoing gradual improvement but the majority cling tenaciously to the type of dwelling their fathers occupied before them. Perhaps the villages of Strath, Poolewe, and Port Henderson contain the most improved houses in the parish.[6]

Furniture, until the last decades of the nineteenth century, would have been hand-built and limited, at best, to a box-bed, dresser, chests, tubs and chairs or stools. A spinning wheel might have pride of place.[7] Light would come from a *cruisgean*, a shallow pan filled with fish oil into which the tail of a wick of dried pith of rushes was dipped. Furthermore, 'very few of the crofters have gardens worthy of the name, so that, of course, they lose the advantage of green vegetables and fresh fruits. Still more rare is it to see trees planted about their dwellings, though pleasant shade and shelter might thus be had, and though, it is understood, saplings might be obtained for the asking from the proprietors'.[8]

Diet

Cooking was a challenge. Wood was not easily available, coal expensive, so 'peats are the only fuel used by the crofter population. [...] Each tenant has a portion of a convenient peat-moss allotted to him'.[9] Very few would have had more than an open fire on which to cook. In any case, the food of most crofters and cottars would be at little better than subsistence level. The Rev. William Macrae, contributing to the *Statistical Account of Scotland* in 1845, reported that their 'domestic economy is frugal, beyond conception, [...] the produce of foreign soil, as tea, coffee and sugar, and the common conveniences of art, as knives and forks &c. are to them altogether alien. Their ordinary food consists of oat and barley meal, potatoes and milk, variously prepared'.[10]

The daily porridge, made of oatmeal, was thus a staple food, along with potatoes. Oatcakes would be baked on the iron griddle or girdle. The coastal crofter's 'piece' might well be a bannock which was oatcakes sandwiched with fish liver.[11] The repeal of the salt tax in 1817 had encouraged the salting of fish such as herring. However, the herring shoals were fickle. Haddock, ling, saithe and cod were possible alternatives but they could not be caught from rocks. Shellfish also were an important part in the diet, particularly in lean years. Evicted tenants elsewhere were often despatched to the coast by their lairds on the assumption that they could survive on mussels alone, scraped from the rocks. Dairy produce was usually regularly available but meat from the croft's own animals would only be in good supply after the autumn killing, though there might be opportunity for 'fresh' occasionally by illicit poaching.

The dependence on potatoes by those on the most marginal land was to be near-catastrophic in the 1840s. One official noted how 'Those who are habitually and entirely fed on potatoes live upon the extreme verge of human subsistence, and when they are deprived of their accustomed food there is nothing cheaper to which they can resort'.[12]

The famine years lasted well into the 1850s but thereafter there was, for most people, a greater prosperity and an improved menu. So, by the early 1880s, 'shop' items such as tea, sugar and jam were no longer considered luxuries.

> The chief articles of diet of the crofter population are fish, either fresh or cured, oatmeal, potatoes, and milk, with a little butcher meat occasionally. Eggs are not much eaten, but are exported to Glasgow in considerable quantities. None of the crofters keep pigs, which they consider to be unclean beasts; it is singular they should entirely neglect a source of food and profit so universal among their Irish congeners. [...] The principal intoxicating beverage in Gairloch is whisky. Very little beer is consumed by the natives.[13]

Fishing

Many crofting families depended on fishing to supplement their income and their diet. However, they did not have the capital to purchase boats and equipment for open sea fishing so they were hired by East coast contractors. From June to September young men, both single and married, were likely to be away from home, leaving children and women to look after the beasts, potatoes and peat in their absence. The Gairloch crofters were mostly employed by boat owners based in Wick, Peterhead, Fraserburgh and Aberdeen who needed extra hands during the peak season of July and August. 'It became the custom, therefore, and one which was firmly established by the 1840s, for each crew to be strengthened by the addition of one or two 'strangers'.[14]

In a bad fishing year, when the herring catches were poor, there was poverty. In 1836 the Poolewe minister reported, in a bid for support at a time of near-famine, that 'for the last 8 years it has been unproductive. [...] There has not been a good fishing here since 1811. The season 1835 was a total failure'.[15] Dr John Mackenzie was convinced that too much reliance was put on this supplementary source of income by 'amphibious crofters'.

> A successful herring fishing turns £10 to £12 into his pocket and satisfies him that ... by a few weeks' toil he can pay his rent and live in all but utter idleness, till it is actually necessary next Spring to commence cutting sea ware to dung his potato land. ... It is all very well pointing out to him that, say three years ago, the fishing failed. [...] Such an argument will no more convince him that his pursuit is a precarious one and not to be depended on for permanent support, than the gambler's unlucky throw convinces him of the danger and ruin attending his hazardous employment.[16]

Fortunately, during the early famine years, the east coast fishing proved resilient so was credited with having saved the Gairloch and Loch Broom areas from the worst of destitution. Those who stayed locally also depended on fishing to help the family diet, particularly during the Hungry Forties. The *Inverness Advertiser* reported 'First rate fishing, [...] boats averaging 15–20 crans of excellent quality' for 28 July 1846 and 'Great quantities of herring of very fine quality being caught' on 7 August 1849.[17]

Fishing continued to be an important aspect of the crofting life until the 1880s. There were opportunities for cod and ling fishing in the winter months and herring dominated the summer. With the improvement of both road and steamer transport it was easier to get to the lucrative markets. The east coast fishing companies would take on west coast crofters each May for a six to eight week season in the Minch and then migrate to the Northern Isles and back to the east coast. Lobsters and crab were an important export from the Gairloch harbours, cod fishing was good and the salmon fishery was leased out to an Aberdeen man, Mr Hogarth, who 'sends a manager each spring to the principal station at Poolewe. [...] In the early part of the season the salmon are boiled and packed in vinegar in kegs. [...] In summer, when the salmon are most plentiful, Mr Hogarth employs fast sailing smacks or cutters, which come twice a week from Aberdeen to Poolewe and take away the fish packed in ice. From Aberdeen they are sent to the London market as fresh salmon'.[18]

It was not always a worthwhile enterprise. In 1868 there was a bad herring season and 'a great many of the hired men came home from the east coast pennyless' and, in 1886, the fishing season was very unsuccessful.[19] The wages did remain relatively high until the decline of the late 1880s.

Arable farming

Prior to the 1840s, the traditional 'runrig' system of cultivation prevailed in the Gairloch area. The small tenants held the arable land in common; in many cases an oversman was responsible to the proprietor for the whole rent. The lower level arable land, growing mainly oats and potatoes, was divided using a system by which township elders would share land between the families. Often lots were drawn. The crofters might well end up with different land from the previous year which gave them no incentive to improve and often led to disputes about fairness. As late as 1875 Queen Victoria, writing in her Journal, was uncomplimentary about these runrig methods: 'This very rude system is quite incompatible with any improved culture, but it is an extremely ancient one'.[20]

The pressures on the land were exacerbated by the rapidly growing population. The population of Gairloch parish almost doubled, from 2,437 to 4,445 people, in the first thirty years of the nineteenth century.[21] But there were benefits in the co-operative community approach and the traditional implements, though basic, had their uses. There was no metal for tools, hooks, or nails so bone and wood were used. Heather and birch twigs made rope. The traditional *cas-chaibe*, or *cas-chrom* (the 'crooked foot', which had a six foot shaft of ash with a long head bent at an angle and tipped with iron) was the foot plough used well into the twentieth century. Osgood Mackenzie had some sympathy with the adherence to the old tools: 'In the old *cas-chrom* days every inch of ground was cultivated even among boulders, where the best soil is often to be found and which no plough can go near'.[22] Though some landowners forbade the crofters the right to keep horses, or even the tough, tiny garrons to pull a plough, there is no evidence for this in Gairloch. A lack of purchasing power was the more usual reason for the primitive methods. Often there would be additional cultivated ground, higher up, for hay, or perhaps for potatoes. Such a marginal area of crop growing was called an *achadh*.

Whether on high or low land the 'lazy beds' system proved a useful way of cultivating small patches of land, particularly for potatoes. The ground was cleared of turf and stones which were used to make the enclosing dykes. Animal dung and seaweed were used where possible to fertilise this small enclosed area. Guano might also be used, or even bracken if far from the coast. The beds were dug by trenching to either side of a strip and throwing the earth between. Once they were exhausted the old beds were allowed back to nature and the next patch cultivated. Outlines of such ridged 'strips' can still be observed in the landscape today.

Inevitably, the weather played the major part in the success, or otherwise, of the harvests. A terrific hurricane in September 1886 meant that the crop, 'the most promising within the last twenty years is almost wholly destroyed'. The potatoes were now black, leafless stalks.[23]

'Women's work'

The women were required to take an arduous part in the cultivation of the crops:

> And how the women used to work among the potatoes, weeding them by hand so carefully, putting all the chickweed and spurry into creels, carrying it to the nearest burn, and there washing it to give to the cattle for supper, much to the benefit of the milk-supply! Also how beautifully they earthed up their potatoes.[24]

Their efforts were vital to supplement the income from the croft: they 'carry home heavy creels of peats for the household fire, [...] they herd the cow, and manage the house. But, more than all, it is the women who are mainly instrumental in producing the only manufactures of the parish. [...] They card and dye and spin the wool, they knit the Gairloch hose, and they prepare the various coloured worsteds which the weaver converts into tweeds of different patterns. Large numbers of the stockings are sent to Inverness, Edinburgh and London. [...] Some of the tweeds are worn in the parish, and some are sold to strangers'.[25] Even when a 'wifie' was bearing home the traditional square creel on her back 'she is also engaged in spinning with the distaff and spindle'.[26]

The Dowager Lady Mackenzie, who had developed this home industry during the destitution years, continued to encourage and support it throughout her life.[27] In 1889 the Countess of Roseberry formed the Scottish Home Industries Association to improve the marketing and sale opportunities of home crafts. This helped the Gairloch hosiery to expand further, with the *Inverness Courier* reporting that Lady Mary had organised an exhibition of yarns and stockings to promote the Gairloch home industry. An article by E. F. Mackenzie, probably of 1894 or 1895, reported on the quality of this hose: 'Stockings that are hand-spun as well as hand-knitted are only produced in the Highlands, and the best of these are made in Gairloch'. Reference was made to how it had all started during the potato famine of 1846–1848, under the guidance of a skilled woman who superintended the knitters. Then the local shops took the stockings in barter for goods.

So the hose became famous. For a while coarse imitations of inferior quality were made and sold under the name of 'Gairloch stockings':

> It seemed so important to check this downward tendency, if the industry were to survive, that six years ago local shows and competitions were instituted, prizes were offered and patterns given, and by these and other means Gairloch has in a great measure regained its former good name; at any rate every prize for homespun and hand-knitted stockings given at Inverness at the last three exhibitions has been carried off by the Gairloch workers. They have also gained all the prizes for 'stocking-hose' at Inverness, Stirling, Dundee, Edinburgh and Aberdeen. [...] The women knit very quickly. [...] Great ingenuity is shown in varying the dice. [...] When there are more than two colours, a number of different threads have to be used – in tartan hose sometimes as many as eighteen – and only a few women have the patience and skills necessary for such laborious work. [...] Nothing can beat *good* Gairloch stockings.[28]

The obituary of the Dowager Lady Mary in 1901, more than fifty years after its beginning, reminded its readers that 'so well was the enterprise managed that in a short time the industry needed no fostering care, as Gairloch stockings became and still are famous'.[29] It continued after her death. In 1907 the Poolewe School log book mentioned that 'several of the pupils are knitting hose and socks for the *Fail* to be held in Glasgow in October and November 1907 for the furtherance of the Gaelic involvement'. The knitting of hose, which had initially been a response to the potato harvest emergency, had now become strongly associated with the revival of Gaelic culture. In 1920 it was still flourishing.

Black cattle and sheep

The traditional cattle were shaggy, surefooted and hardy, 'short in the legs, round in the body, straight in the back'.[30] Properly known as *kyloe* they were capable of being fattened to fifty stone, though the natural weight of a heifer was twenty-four to thirty stone. Those with black coats were reckoned to be the hardiest, proof against rain and storm all year round, though some were dark brown or reddish-brown. They were described by Sir John Sinclair in 1812:

> His general appearance should combine agility, vivacity and strength, and his hair should be glossy, thick and vigorous, indicating a sound constitution and perfect health. [...] The general properties of this breed are great hardiness of constitution, which, as they are driven to distant markets, is an essential one, being easily maintained and speedily fattened on pasture where large animals could scarcely subsist. Their milk is rich, but small in quantity, and they produce beef of fine grain.

Dixon, looking back from the vantage point of the 1880s, explained the routine:

> Before the great sheep-farms were established, the Gairloch people always took their black cattle to the shielings on the hills to feed on the upland pastures. [...] They went up to the shielings when the spring work of the crofts was finished, about the end of May, and remained to the end of August. [...] The shieling bothies, of which many remains are left, were indeed miserable dwellings.

The whole family would help to move the animals to the higher grassy hollows of the hill corries. They carried all the equipment necessary to camp out until Autumn in the turf walled and roofed shieling huts. There might well be a group of bothies clustered together for different families. Milking stools, churns, bowls and jugs were needed for the cheese, crowdie and butter making; spades, ropes and axes to cultivate the lazy beds; pots and griddles for cooking and even sticks to repair the roofs. The older girls, and some children, would then be left to guard the flocks, do the milking and establish the dairy. They might make occasional return trips to deliver the produce and collect more provisions if other family members did not come up to them, but essentially would stay in the hills until the late summer when the stock would be taken down to graze lower pastures before being slaughtered. Very few animals would be kept through the winter because of the lack of fodder. How strongly they felt any 'air of romance' on their summer excursions would depend, no doubt, on the weather and the midges!

Cattle had also contributed to the diet in the early spring when the stored potatoes, fish and meat were running low:

> The practice of drawing blood from living cattle was universal in the Highlands. [...] In Gairloch the practice continued to the beginning of the 19th century. [...] At Tournaig also a place is still pointed out where the natives used to bleed the cattle landed here from the Lews. This barbarous

> mode of obtaining blood as an article of food, affords striking evidence of the miserable poverty of the old days.[31]

Black puddings could then be made of blood, oatmeal and onion. Another older custom, when times were bad, was to 'rent out' cows to others for butter and cheese-making, though this could mean that the cow's calf was semi-starved as a result.

The old drovers' roads were taken when it came to the annual sending of the five hundred or so Mackenzie cattle to market. Estate stock would join those from the Outer Hebrides which were landed, or had even swum ashore from their vessels, in Poolewe. From Poolewe and Gairloch the traditional route was along the north side of Loch Maree to Kinlochewe, Glen Docharty and through to Garve. From Aultbea the cattle would go north towards Gruinard then follow the drove road through the Strath na Sealga to the Ullapool/Inverness road. These drove roads were customary rights of way and no landowner, however much he might improve the original tracks, could levy tolls on them as Meyrick Bankes, notorious landowner of Gruinard, discovered to his cost in a court action against his neighbour, Mackenzie of Dundonnell, in 1886.

By the nineteenth century the main cattle tryst was in Falkirk and merchants gathered from across Britain. In 1850 150,000 head were sold there. The money from the cattle was crucial in paying the rent. Stock might even be confiscated if dues were not met. Mr Charles Macleod, manager of the Gairloch crofts, admitted to Sir John McNeill that he had done this to recover rent in 1850, though the cattle seized were, apparently, in excess to the number permitted.[32] (Each crofter had a specific 'quota' allowed him as part of his common grazing rights). Often the landowner would wait for the annual sale or perhaps take cheese or butter in lieu. Any surplus left to the crofter would pay for meal to tide the family over the spring until the next harvest, or buy necessities such as iron and fishing hooks.

Cattle prices proved to be very volatile throughout the nineteenth century. This contributed considerably to the uncertainties of a crofting life. From the high levels achieved during the Napoleonic War period they dropped to two pounds, or even only thirty shillings (£1.50p), a head by 1852, then recovered considerably in the later 1850s for several decades, reaching four or five pounds in 1883. The price then collapsed once more in the later 1880s, down below two pounds, as steam ship transport enabled much cheaper stock to be brought in from other continents. The quality of the animals, less well-fed, would also be adversely affected in poor harvest years so intensifying the problems.

Evictions and clearances

Until legislation was passed in 1886 crofters held no legal right to the land they worked. Each was a tenant, paying rent on a year to year basis. It made no difference if he had been in the township for a year or for a century. There was no legal contract which gave any security for home or acreage, the laird did not need to give any cause for changing a tenancy or even for ending it. Compensation was not required for any improvements that the crofter might have carried out. All the landowner needed to do to terminate a tenancy at the end of any year was to give forty days notice.

The tenants paid rent to their landlords according to the size of their croft. Cottars, who did not have rights to the land, paid a lesser rent. They were usually allowed to put a cow on the pasture, to have a kail yard and a potato patch by their huts. Cottars might well be the village herdsman, blacksmith, weaver, tailor and shoemaker.

It is likely that the Judicial Rental for Torridon, an estate adjacent to Gairloch, showed a typical situation. It was held in 1824 as part of the process of selling the land to Mackenzie of Seaforth. Just about every tenant was in arrears, often owing three years' rent or more. Crofters depended on the benevolence of the landowners if they were to stay on their lands. The Mackenzie lairds and the Seaforths seem to have been flexible, often tolerating partial arrears or payment in kind but this was not the case with all their relatives. On 4 April 1838 Sir George Mackenzie of Coul, (from whom Osgood was to acquire much of his own estate 25 years later), applied to the Sheriff Court in Dingwall for Decreets (sic) to evict several tenants from Slaggan and Mellon Udrigle and 'tenants of the farm and lands of Pluckhart, Tournag and Inverewe' and against the deceased Roderick MacGregor and his tenants

> and hereby decerns and ordains them instantly to flit and removes themselves their wives Bairns families Servants, Subtenants Cottars and dependents. [...] Cattle goods and gear furth and from the said whole lands of Inverewe, Pluckhart, Tournag and others, with the Houses biggings Yards parts pendicles and pertinents thereof, and the said Murdoch MacGregor for himself and as heir and representative foresaid from the said house of Inverewe with the pertinents all lying as aforesaid and to leave the same void.

The reason being that they owed one full year's rent plus legal expenses plus the cost of extracting this decreet![33]

He was not unusual in this. Other local landowners, such as MacBarnet in

Torridon in 1838 and Meyrick Bankes of Gruinard, after 1835, applied to the Dingwall court for evictions, using the failure to maintain rental payments as a legitimate reason for removal. The intended evictions of nine or ten smaller tenants in 1860 at Gruinard aroused much press anger because the crofters were able to prove that they were fully up to date with their rents. It was only the quasi-legal demand that rents plus interest be paid in advance that enabled the landowner to enforce the decrees of eviction the following year.

Landowners often spoke in very derogatory terms about their tenants. When the same Sir George Mackenzie evicted crofters on his Coul estate in 1838 his justification was the need for large efficient farms. As far as he was concerned, crofters were 'people useless to the community. Their whole system is devoted to keep themselves from starving, and they can neither spare food for others, nor apply themselves to any art. In short, as crofters merely, they can be of no earthly use whatever. [...] The true value of land is to be found, not in the number of ignorant and idle people, who can contrive to live upon it, but in the number of cattle and sheep, and in the quantity of corn it can produce. [...] The present race of tenantry is universally allowed to have an aversion to active employment, and therefore it is neither for the interest of the proprietors, nor of the public, to retain it'.[34]

Such an attitude had led to some landowners justifying the removal of tenants from their rented crofts without quibble or hesitation. Patrick Sellar, the factor for the Duke of Sutherland, expressed the unequivocal view that his master and mistress 'were pleased humanely to order the new arrangement of this country. That the interior should be possessed by Cheviot shepherds, and the people brought down to the coast and placed in lots of less than three acres, sufficient for the maintenance of an industrious family, pinched enough to cause them to turn their attention to the fishing. A most benevolent action, to put these barbarous Highlanders into a position where they could better associate together, apply themselves to industry, educate their children, and advance in civilisation'.[35]

It was the changes in sheep-farming that initiated a long-lasting process of eviction in the Highlands.

> In those olden times there were but few sheep kept, and they were all of the *Seana chaoirich bheaga* (little old sheep) breed, with pink noses and very fine wool [...] accustomed to be more or less housed at night. [...] At night at the shielings the sheep and the goats were driven into bothies and bedded with bracken or moss.[36]

But, by the end of the eighteenth century, the fashionable and 'efficient' Cheviot sheep had been taken 'over the Highland line'. In 1790 they were across the Cromarty Firth into Ross, and two years later they reached Caithness in the far north. Much to the amazement of the sceptical Highlanders they not only survived the winter but 'not one of the flock died from cold, disease or hunger'.[37]

From then on, in many parts of the Highlands, evictions of the crofting tenants were carried out in order to establish much larger-scale and, it was assumed, more profitable sheep farms on upland grazing land. To make the new sheep farming economically viable it was believed that the grazing lands needed to be cleared of the inefficient crofters, with their tiny flocks, to be replaced with extensive sheep farms managed, often, by factors brought in for their experience in England or the Lowlands. Throughout the Highlands from the end of the eighteenth century, including on estates in the vicinity of Gairloch, clearances were undertaken whereby the tenants were forcibly removed, often with the necessity of engaging the police and/or militia. Now the landowners could turn the scattered crofts into wide-ranging sheep farms stocked with the new 'wonder sheep'.

The first significant removals of crofters to make room for Cheviot sheep took place in Strathcarron, to the north of Dingwall and the Mackenzies' Conan estates. 1792, the so-called 'Year of the Sheep', saw spirited, but ultimately futile, resistance by the crofters and their families against the forces first of their landowner, then the local constables and, ultimately, British army red-coats. Five of the leaders were rounded up and put on trial in Inverness in September. One was sentenced to transportation to Botany Bay for seven years, two others banished for life from Scotland, others fined and/or imprisoned. But, mysteriously, the door of the jail was left open. They were able to escape and were never seen again.

The pattern was set. The lairds could claim the law of the land was being undermined by sedition and rebellion. Threats to their property rights could not, and would not, be tolerated. It was clear that landowners could depend on the army and the law whenever required. The story of the 'Year of the Sheep' was repeated time and again throughout the lands north of the Great Glen. The Marquess of Stafford and his wife became notorious for their evictions and clearances, culminating in the 'Year of the Burnings' in 1814. They had commissioned their agent, James Loch, to clear Strathnaver in Sutherland so it could be rented out to Patrick Sellar for sheep pasture. The crofters were summoned in December 1813 to hear that they had until Whitsun to leave and move to allocated coastal sites. They did not want to go. They stayed put until the middle of June when Sellar brought in four Sheriff-officers and twenty men. 'The burning of the house-timbers began as soon as a cottage was emptied and even before if the occupants were laggardly'. No pity was shown to any who were frail or infirm.

> For days after the burning was over the homeless people remained in the glen. They sat on the hillsides among what they had been able to salvage from the ruins. They put canvas over their heads for protection against the night rain. [...] At last the people left for the coast. 'When they came down from the strath to the sea-shore,' remembered George Macdonald, 'they suffered very much. [...] Some people were removed three or four times, always forced farther down until at last the sea-shore prevented them from being sent any farther unless they took ship for the Colonies, which many of them did'.[38]

Close to the Gairloch lands, clearances to establish sheep farms were implemented on the neighbouring estates of Gruinard with Letterewe and Torridon. The lands extending from Drumchork north and east to Little Gruinard River had belonged to the Mackenzies of Gruinard since before 1655 but were bought by Henry Davidson of Tulloch near Dingwall in 1795. James Hogg's *Tour of the Highlands*, written in 1803, tells that one of the estate tacksmen, John Macintyre, rented the lands of Glen Gruinard and cleared them to form a sheep run. He also was the tacksman, it seems, of the Letterewe estate. His evictions gave him a sheep farm stretching from the sea at Gruinard to Kinlochewe. The inhabitants were moved to Little Gruinard and First, Second and Third Coast. About 1835 Davidson sold the Gruinard estate to a wealthy Englishman, Meyrick Bankes, whose family had made their money through coal mining and who held land throughout England, particularly in Lancashire but in counties as far as Dorset. The Letterewe estate was purchased and added soon after. The family held their Wester Ross lands until the first decade of the twentieth century. Bankes lost no time in clearing Little Gruinard and Badentluig for sheep farming, evicting often the same people as had already been moved out in 1803. He reduced the crofts at Sand and evicted crofters at Drumchork. He also took hill grazings from people at Sand, First and Second Coast.[39]

The Mackenzies' neighbours to the south also carried through evictions and clearances. In 1826 Torridon was sold to James Stewart-Mackenzie of Seaforth. He rarely visited the area and left the management of the estate to his factor who started by threatening to evict tenants in arrears with rent. Many did manage to pay off sufficient to keep their lands. Then, because of financial problems on other estates, Torridon was sold to a Colonel Alexander C. MacBarnet in 1838 for £12,150. His fortune had been made in the West Indies. With no Wester Ross background he did not feel he had any obligations to his tenants. When he died within a year the trustees of his estate, a group of Speyside landowners, decided they could improve their profits by subdividing the estate into farms and advertising these for sheep letting. The existing tenants were offered their land at increased rents but if they could not pay it was taken from them, and stock bought also, at the factor's valuation. The remaining crofters were each allowed only one cow and one calf. Their houses would be searched to ensure a second calf was not hidden. As this did not justify the use of shielings most of the hill pasture could now be appropriated for the landowner's sheep. To add further insult to injury, the ex-crofters, now but cottars, might well even be charged for taking seaweed.[40]

The first sheep-farm in the Gairloch area was started about 1810 in Letterewe. It did not seem to have been accompanied by 'any noticeable friction. If one or two small townships were abolished to make way for the sheep-farmer, the inhabitants had other more desirable quarters provided for them. The population of Gairloch steadily increased from the date when sheep-farming began'.[41] In fact, according to his Uncle John, Osgood's grandfather was not at all enamoured of sheep. The Tigh Dige was in 'as lovely a spot in a wild Highland glen as any lover of country scenery could desire to see. I mean *then*, for then no sheep vermin had got hoof in it, as ere long they did. Then only cattle ever bit a blade of grass there, and the consequence was that the braes and wooded hillocks were a perfect jungle of every kind of loveable shrubs and wild flowers, especially orchids. [...] Till my Father's death in 1826, no sheep's hoof defiled the glen unless passing through it to the larder. But very soon after, an offer of a trifling rent for sheep pasturing let these horrid brutes into the glen, and every wild flower, and every young seedling bush or tree was eaten into the ground'.[42]

Despite the cost to the landscape, 'progress' was unavoidable:

> Sheep, unlike cattle, cause a rapid deterioration in the quality of pasturage, so that the number of sheep any particular ground will maintain in health is said to diminish annually. [...] In Gairloch it generally requires ten acres of hill pasture to support one sheep. [...] In the present day the sheep in Gairloch are of the black-faced and cheviot breeds (with some crosses), probably in almost equal portions.[43]

However, the general pattern of clearances to establish large-scale sheep farms was not implemented on the Mackenzies' Gairloch estates. The family was, in any case, unusual in that it had maintained its ancestral ownership of Flowerdale since the late fifteenth century. Perhaps the commitment to their long-serving tenantry was so engrained that they could not contemplate breaking the almost feudal relationship. So, throughout the first half of the nineteenth century, the Gairloch lairds took a different approach to the problems of sustaining the local agriculture. They committed themselves to farming reforms. They encouraged, and even enforced, alternatives to the traditional practices but continued to support the tenant farmer cultivating his own land.[44]

Emigration from the Highlands

One way for the enterprising to escape the poverty of Highland farming was to leave for the virgin lands of the New World. The first ships of emigrants had sailed between 1763 and 1775, decades before people were displaced by Cheviot sheep. Two hundred people of Wester Ross were on board the *Hector*, hoping for a life free of crippling rents, harvest failure and disease, when it left Loch Broom in 1773, with the promise of a farm for every family and a year's free provisions on arrival. They had a terrible journey in a rotten and leaking ship. When they landed in Canada in October, led by their own piper onto Pictou harbour in Nova Scotia, there was nothing for them and they were too late to plant any crops that season. This disastrous voyage was made infamous by the writing and lecturing of Alexander Mackenzie, author of *The Highland Clearances* (1883). However, it proved to be rather the exception than the rule.

Highland memories have it that the journeys were invariably miserable: the emigrants were the victims of speculators and ship-masters in overcrowded and un-seaworthy vessels; they were not provided with edible food on board; typhus, cholera, smallpox and dysentery were rife; travellers were not landed where they were expecting to. Yet, recent research has concluded that these tales of woe, unhappy though they undoubtedly were, were not inevitably the case. Many emigrants went willingly and voluntarily, encouraged and excited by the prospect of becoming independent farmers. They travelled in sea-worthy ships, with some captains donating food to supplement meagre rations.

> The *Lloyd's Shipping Register* thus gives us unequivocal evidence that emigrants were not offered the worst ships as is generally believed. Most emigrants actually sailed in top-quality ships. Shipowners could have cut their costs by

> offering inferior vessels but if they had done so, they would have had no repeat business.
>
> A picture of a continuous nightmare of suffering on filthy, leaky and ill-managed ships can be conjured up, but it is totally unrepresentative. Contrary to popular depiction, emigrant Scots were well served by the men of the transatlantic passenger trade. Lurid descriptions of 'slave trade' conditions and rotting ship hulls may titillate readers, but they bear little relation to the facts.[45]

It has been calculated that in the period 1768–1775 about 9,500 Highlanders left for the British Colonies in North America. There was a lull during the 1775–1783 War of Independence and again during the 1790s, when Britain was at war with Revolutionary France. During the truce of 1801–1803, it was reckoned that 20,000 Highlanders were potential emigrants.[46] A disproportionate number of those moving from Britain to Canada were from the Highlands and Islands. They were not the desperate and poor, but able to pay their own way, having sold their stock or belongings. Often they were re-joining relatives and friends who had pioneered the journey. The pattern was for large family groups from the same area to arrange to leave together, and, once arrived, they stayed as identifiable communities. Six hundred people went from Lewis in 1803 to Pictou, Nova Scotia, leaving Stornoway on three ships, for example.[47]

Initially, rather than being pleased that problem tenants had removed themselves, the landowners and government were concerned that they were losing valuable members of their farming and military establishment. Very few proprietors would help crofters on their way, seeing the trend as 'a rapidly progressive increase of the evil'. In 1802 Thomas Telford (of road and bridge-building renown) was sponsored to undertake a 'survey of the coasts and central highlands of Scotland', with the brief to enquire into 'the causes of emigration and the means of preventing it'.[48] The resulting 1803 Passenger Act was welcomed by the landowners as a deterrent. Whilst ostensibly a humanitarian and safety measure, limiting the number who could be carried on the basis of one person for every two tons burthen, it effectively doubled the cost of the voyage from three to six pounds or more, making it just too expensive for many would-be emigrants. But it proved too restrictive. They were used to overcrowding and usually even accepted that children were not counted in the passenger tally. Once the French wars were over, and kelping had become uneconomic, the landowners had far less reason to retain their 'redundant population', particularly if it had become a barrier to the 'improvement' of sheep-farming. In 1817, as a result of pressure from ship-owners and agents, the space requirements were relaxed to one and a half tons.[49]

Emigration continued to attract able men and their families throughout the first decades of the nineteenth century. In 1828 alone, thirteen hundred people from North Uist and Harris, having paid their own costs, landed in Cape Breton. They soon prospered. Governments consistently rejected calls to assist the process even when it was recommended by their own committee, as in 1826–1827.[50] In 1837 four thousand Highlanders took advantage of a one-off scheme to assist emigration to New South Wales.[51]

Emigration from Gairloch

The New Statistical Account of 1836, with reference to Gairloch, suggested a government grant to convey one third of the people to Upper Canada would be 'most desirable' as a way of relieving the prevailing poverty. Mr Macrae, minister in Poolewe, agreed that this might resolve some of the problems but was not so sure that people would want to go unless they could be enabled to leave as families, and even then would only be willing to go to places where friends or relatives had already settled. The Gairloch schoolmaster, Mr Fraser, 'conversed frequently with the people on the subject of emigration and found them anxious to emigrate if they had the means, most of them would prefer going to Nova Scotia, but some of them would not be indisposed to go to Australia, having received favourable accounts of that colony'.[52]

Some people did emigrate from the area. In 1805 two ships, the *Albatross* and *Sir Sydney Smith*, sailed from Stornoway. With the exception of one family from Lewis these were all friends and relatives sailing together from Gairloch. After nine weeks on board they arrived in Pictou, and established the settlement called 'Gairloch'.[53] By 1820 the north side of Lake Ainslie (Cape Breton) had acquired its 'unbroken line of families chiefly from the district of Gairloch [Ross-shire] in the Highlands of Scotland'. Some forty families in all, they were said to 'exhibit those features of industry, sobriety and decorum which peculiarly distinguish emigrants from this district'.[54] Further:

> The Middle River settlements at the northwest end of Bras D'Or continued to grow as colonization continued up the river valley. More Ross-shire families, from Kintail, Applecross, and Lochalsh, joined earlier groups who came from these same regions, reinforcing the strong Ross-shire presence in

> this part of Cape Breton. By 1828 Middle River had a large Presbyterian congregation having 'upwards of fifty families' who were 'pretty compact together, and some in very independent circumstances'. [Binnington]. Later arrivals from Gairloch in Ross-shire established themselves on high ground to the west of Middle River, naming their settlement Gairloch Mountain after their local parish.[55]

Perhaps some of these were passengers on the *Atlantic* of Stornoway which went from Lochalsh in 1823. But many other ships went from Stornoway during the decade.[56] The 1841 Census showed that another one hundred and fifty people left between 1831 and 1841 but it was not a huge exodus, nor an enforced one. The *Inverness Courier* of 13 July 1842 recorded that 'a vessel sailed from Gairloch in Ross-shire with 215 passengers, voluntary emigrants from Gairloch and Torridon, and a few from Skye. They were bound in good spirits for Canada'.[57] They timed their departure well.

A somewhat different aspect of 'emigration' is illustrated by the story of Malcolm Macdonald, born in 1809, whose father, Colin, was the tenant innkeeper of Pool House from 1812–1820. The family spent some time in Stornoway and then returned to the Poolewe area as tenants of the Seaforths. In 1827 Colin was a tenant at Inverewe with two cows, one stirk and no sheep. In 1837 his son, Malcolm, with a reference from the local clergyman, signed on to work for five years with the Hudson Bay Company as a boat builder at £25 pa. The diaries and records of his time there, based in the Mackenzie River district, have survived. Two years after his return he married and returned to live in Poolewe. In 1848 he emigrated with his wife and two children to Sydney, Australia. No reason is given but clearly he had a sense of adventure. There he spent the rest of his life, had a further seven children and died in 1876. Some of his many descendants have traced their ancestry back to the Gairloch heritage.[58]

Postscript 1920

In 1920 a new tourist guide of Gairloch suggested that almost nothing had changed with respect to the way of life of the crofter people in the almost eighty years which had passed since Osgood Mackenzie was born. Perhaps, though, the attitude to them had altered somewhat.

> By far the greater proportion of the people are crofters and fishermen. There are altogether about four hundred crofts in the parish, with an average area

of about four acres, for which the occupants each pay nearly four pounds annually as rent. In addition to the arable land each crofter has the right to graze a considerable number of sheep and cattle on the hill pasture in connection with the township.

It is usual for people who are in the north for only a week or two in summer to consider crofters a lazy lot, but if they knew what work they do in a year they would probably think they do more for their livelihood than almost any other class in the country. Towards the beginning of March they begin to turn over the land with the footplough – the caschrom, which has not yet here been ousted by the spade and plough, and the amount of ground a family can turn over in a few days with this primitive implement is simply marvellous. By the middle of April, if the weather is anything like favourable, Spring work is completed. The peats then have to be cut, fences have to get an overhaul, and all must be ready the beginning of May, as then many of the able-bodied men set out for the West Coast fishing. During this month between two and three hundred men leave the parish, if not for the fishing, then for 'season' places in the south. From the West Coast, the men proceed to the East Coast fishing, and it is towards the end of September ere they return. Then the crops have to be reaped, potatoes lifted, houses and outhouses prepared for the winter. Sheep have to be looked after, drains have to be opened, nets mended, and, in fair weather, fresh fish have to be got for the household. Peats are taken home, and this, during the winter, is largely done by the men, as the women are then busy at their household work, when not carding, dyeing, spinning, or knitting, as during summer they could do none of these things as, in addition to their many household duties, they had to see the peats dried and the croft kept clean. There is, indeed, very little rest for crofters or their families from one year's end to the other, and any who know how hard they work must consider the remuneration the whole yields scanty in the extreme.[59]

References and Notes

1 'The Laigh of Gruinard', an undated, unattributed newspaper article. Gairloch Heritage Museum Archives.

2 Francis Thompson, *Crofting Years* (Edinburgh: Luath Press, 1984), p.53.

3 Revd. Donald M'rae, *The New Statistical Account of Scotland. Parish of Gairloch, September 1836,* quoted in Dixon, p.406.

4 Byam Shaw, p.201, quoting from the writings of Sir George Mackenzie, 7th Baronet of Coul.

5 There is more detail on this in Chapter III.

6 Dixon, pp.132, 133.

7 A 'crofters' room' can be seen at the Gairloch Heritage Museum.

8 Dixon, p.133.

9 Dixon, p.134.

10 Quoted in Dr Morrice McCrae, 'The Case for State Medical Services for the Poor. The Highlands and Islands 1850'. www.rcpe.ac.uk/library/history, accessed 03 March 2006.

11 Thompson, p.106.

12 James Hunter, *The Making of the Crofting Community* (Edinburgh: John Donald, new ed. 2000), p.93.

13 Dixon, pp.133–134.

14 T.M. Devine, *Clanship to Crofters' War* (Manchester: Manchester University Press, 1994), p.141.

15 Undated letter from the Rev. Mr D. M'crae. Gairloch Heritage Museum Archives.

16 Article by Dr John Mackenzie in the *Industrial Magazine The Great Highland Famine* (Edinburgh: John Donald Publishers Ltd, 1988), pp.306, 308.

18 Dixon, p.146.

19 *Inverness Advertiser*, 23 October 1868 and *Scottish Highlander*, 16 September 1886.

20 Quoted in Byam Shaw, p.260.

21 *New Statistical Account, Parish of Gairloch.* Entry by the Rev. James Russell, Vol. XIV, 1836 p.99.

22 Mackenzie, p.185.

23 *Scottish Highlander*, 16 September 1886.

24 Mackenzie, pp.185–186.

25 Dixon, p.132.

26 Thompson, p.99.

27 See Chapter III.

28 E.F. Mackenzie, *Scottish Home Industries,* undated article, reporting on exhibitions in Inverness, 1890–1894. Gairloch Heritage Museum Archives.

29 Obituary in the *Northern Chronicle*, 13 March 1901.

30 Thompson, p.84.

31 Dixon, pp.136–137.

32 Evidence included in Sir John McNeill's *Report to the Board of Supervision on the West Highlands and Islands, 1851*. Gairloch Heritage Museum Archives.

[33] William MacRobbie, *Gruinard and Letterewe: Lairds and Clearances* (Laide: private publication, 2001), pp.53–54.

[34] Byam Shaw, pp.201, 202.

[35] Quoted in Cliff Hanley, *History of Scotland* (New York: Gallery Books, 1986), p.160.

[36] Mackenzie, pp.189–190.

[37] John Prebble, *The Highland Clearances* (London: Secker and Warburg, 1963. Reprinted by permission of the Random House Group Ltd), pp.26, 27.

[38] Prebble, pp.78, 83, 84.

[39] MacRobbie, pp.18, 23.

[40] Murdoch Macdonald, *Old Torridon* (*Notes on the History of Torridon*) (Evanton: Torridon, 1997), pp.106–107.

[41] Dixon, p.137.

[42] Byam Shaw, quoting Dr John Mackenzie, pp.22–23.

[43] Dixon, p.137.

[44] Developed in Chapters III and IV.

[45] Lucille H. Campey, *After the Hector. The Scottish Pioneers of Nova Scotia and Cape Breton 1773–1852* (Toronto: Natural Heritage Books, 2004), pp.166–167, 181. Context information and direct quotes with permission from Dundurn Press Ltd. Copyright 2004, 2007

[46] Devine, *Clanship to Crofters' War*, p.178.

[47] Campey, p.78.

[48] Hunter, pp.60–61.

[49] Campey, p.179.

[50] Campey, pp.120–121, 116.

[51] Devine, *Clanship to Crofters' War*, p.186.

[52] Letter from Mr M'crae, minister in Poolewe. Undated copy in Gairloch Heritage Museum Archives. Probably 1836 or 1837.

[53] Marjorie Hawkins, *Gairloch, Pictou County, Nova Scotia* (Pugwash, N.S: J.R. MacQuarrie, 1977), p.35.

[54] Campey, p.113 quoting from *Missionary Journey* in Binnington '*The Glasgow Colonial Society and its work in the development of the Presbyterian Church in British North America 1825–1840*'. (Toronto: Unpub PhD, 1960).

[55] Campey, p.114 quoting from Binnington op cit + John Nicholson et al *Middle River: Past and Present History of a Cape Breton Community 1806–1985* (Cape Breton, 1985) pp.245–70.

[56] Campey, p.105.

[57] *Inverness Courier*, 13 July 1842, summarised in Barron. The *Inverness Journal* named the ship as the *John Kerr* of Greenock and identified Cape Breton as its destination.

[58] Colin Graham Macdonald, *Malcolm and Christina's Family* (Australia: Private publication, 2006). Copy donated to the Gairloch Heritage Museum.

[59] Alexander Polson, *Gairloch* (Dingwall. Souter, 1920), p.26.

CHAPTER III

The Destitution Years

'The surveying, measuring, planning and mapping near five hundred crofters' lots was very expensive and the trouble of having this change effected was very great, but it has proved of great benefit to the crofters themselves.'

Dr John as factor 1841–1853

In 1841 Dr John Mackenzie had agreed to be factor of the Gairloch estate, to enable his brother, Francis, to leave his trials and tribulations and take a break in France, in the hope that he would there regain his health. John had never anticipated that his duties would last for over 12 years. The terms of Francis' will were that his wife, Mary, and another relative, Thomas Mackenzie, the laird of Ord, would be the trustees of the family estate until Kenneth should be of age to take control of his inheritance. John declined his nomination as the third trustee, given his possible inheritance rights.[1] The other two were more than happy that he took on the responsibilities of managing the farming and tenancies of the Ross-shire estate. This he continued to do until 1853, despite only being paid but the wages of an 'ordinary factor' of £300 per annum.[2] It is difficult to know how well Mary got on with her brother-in-law. In the context of the time no doubt it was thought inappropriate for a woman, and an English woman at that, to represent the laird, though she testified in 1892 that 'I am a farmer's daughter, and my father was a great farmer, and I am quite up to farming'.[3] Mackenzie of Ord resided in Inverness, and seems to have been 'merely ornamental except when paper required signatures'.[4]

Dr John's factorship coincided with the years of potato famine and destitution, thwarting many of his ambitious plans to continue the farming reforms his elder brother had initiated. Osgood regarded him as 'all round the most intelligent and best educated man I ever came across'.[5] He had not been brought up to be a farmer, (unlike Francis), but trained as a doctor, serving first at army barracks in England, then practising as a physician in Edinburgh. He discovered, though, that this was not likely to 'earn more than a homoeopathic loaf. Because, when a patient asked me what was wrong, I was often obliged to say that I could not tell him then, or for a day or two. A pretty Doctor, indeed, who did not know and name every malady as soon as he saw the patient'. So his patients went elsewhere to doctors who held that 'health depended on lots of draughts and medicines'[6] and he returned to the north of Scotland in 1832, taking on the lease of Kinellan, near Strathpeffer, a farm close to the Conan estates.

Given his training, Dr John considered himself partly to blame for the death of his brother's first wife, Kythé, in 1834, believing that it would not have happened if she had not left Conan to give birth to her third child, or if he had accompanied her to Tigh Dige. He also took it extremely badly when Francis died in a private mental institution in London in 1843. John had gone south in response to the plea for help from his sister-in-law but, soon after, had to return to Scotland as his paralysed child, John Inglis, aged five, had died after a fall at home. Having organised this funeral, he returned to London to find that Francis had passed away just four days earlier, on 2 June, and that his coffin was already on its way north.[7] The pages about this painful period have been removed from his diaries. Thereafter he committed himself wholeheartedly to his nephews. He moved his own large family to live on the West coast, took on the responsibilities of supervising the upbringing of the three boys, Kenneth, Francis and baby Osgood, and threw himself totally into the unenviable job of factor for the estate.

As a practising farmer himself, albeit on the east side of Ross-shire, he claimed to be so successful that he 'never failed any year to make my bread by farming'. The key, he believed, was very careful accountancy and close control. He 'soon found out that farmers only became bankrupt from being above their work, not looking into trifles'.[8] The Edinburgh accountants for the Gairloch lands did, however, call him to task on a number of occasions. They wanted more detail and justification for expenditure, not just for the estate but also the parish costs. Subject to scrutiny were 'income tax, assessed taxes, minister's stipends, Poor's money, Rogue money, Roads and Bridges, County rates, schoolmaster's salaries, sundry burdens, salaries and wages, repairs to farm houses, expenses of collection and management, annuity to Lady Mackenzie (£900) and interest on debts'.[9]

Crofting reforms

As a landowner, Dr John saw his interests to be morally bound up with those of his tenants and he was convinced that both could be prosperous without emigration or eviction. He had travelled widely and studied cultivation methods in Sussex and Armagh and particularly 'la petite culture' of the intensively farmed smallholdings in Holland, Belgium and France. A four-to-five acre croft would be adequate, since 'a man and his family, if industrious, can properly cultivate with the spade alone without aid from a horse but with occasional aid from his cows in carting out dung and carting home crops'.[10]

Echoing Francis, he believed that the tenants must be persuaded to drain their land, stall feed their cattle, use the dung as liquid manure to apply to the field, introduce a rotation of crops which included turnips, and, most crucially, work hard. Agricultural teachers would be employed to give instruction. All this would enable the crofter to live well by the land and to pay his rent punctually and without difficulty. In 1842 Dr John produced a pamphlet, *The Improvement of Highland Crofts*, which was published in the *Industrial Magazine* of the Scottish Patriotic Society. He intended to put theory into practice when he moved across to the Gairloch estate in 1843.

Quite evidently, to Dr John, the existing 'runrig' system was unsustainable:

> Almost every one was discontented. [...] Under such a system, no wise man would be an improver [...] as what he improved would probably be cropped by another next year. A more ingenious plan of preventing improvement of the waste land could not be devised. [...] Each crofter had a fixed number of sheep and cattle allotted to him for his share of the pasture, and those who had not sufficient stock were allowed to hire in as many as they were short.[11]

So he set about organising a comprehensive redistribution of the land. Fortunately for him, most leases for the existing farms were due to expire in 1846. He wanted to give ten-year leases to allow time for improvements but, legally, he could only set them up until Kenneth came into his majority in 1853. With the permission of the Trustees he appointed an experienced land surveyor, George Campbell Smith of Banff, to draw up plans based on the complete re-creation of crofts and townships. The published *Atlas of the Townships of Gairloch 1848* showed the existing arable land in runrig and houses, outbuildings and stockyards. Superimposed on this were the proposed new lots within straightened township boundaries, with numbered crofts. 'The plans are in colour and are quite the finest plans of any crofting estate'.[12] Dr John was directly and personally involved in deciding who went where:

> A lot of from two to five acres given to every family in the rental book, and to many others whom I found jammed in with their parents, unnoticed as tenants and merely eating up the little crop grown, tho' helping otherwise in food and rent by their wages for herring-fishing labour. [...] My first

alteration was to divide the arable land in each township into, say, twenty portions to suit the lie of the land, from five acres down to about one, and then to put a rent on each portion. Then the first choice was given sometimes to the crofters who had for years been most punctual in paying rent, and when these (few) were served the others drew lots for their choice.

And as I never evicted a family, [...] the surveyor had to make room for every family. [...] Then came the fearful cruelty of insisting on every house being removed to its own lot, roads being laid out for access from every lot to the hill. [...] I supplied them gratis with larch trees for the roofs etc.[13]

New crofting areas were created, for example in Ormiscaig where fourteen crofts were established, six of them on improvable moorland with no existing arable. But most people did not have to move far. Three-quarters of the 364 small tenants on the Gairloch estate in 1843 were allocated crofts where they resided, the remainder moving to crofts on other farms. Almost one hundred new tenants were added to the rental, one-third being the sons of existing tenants, the others cottars who could now tend their own crofts.[14] The rent for these new crofts worked out at one shilling per acre. As part of this relocation process the seven crofters of Tollie and six from Kernsary were moved to other parts of the estate in 1848, which meant that Osgood had no crofters when he bought his land in the early 1860s. Perhaps this explains his detachment from the crofter debates which continued throughout his lifetime.

Osgood's mother, the Dowager Lady Mary, provided an account in 1885 about these improvements, but made no reference at all to the role of her brother-in-law in the process.

The surveying, measuring, planning and mapping near five hundred crofters' lots was very expensive to the proprietor, Sir Kenneth Mackenzie, and the trouble of having this change effected was very great; but it has proved of great benefit to the crofters themselves.[15]

Osgood, a further forty years later, explained how his mother took on her full share of estate management, staying in Gairloch all year round, rather than migrating, with household, back to Conan each autumn, as had been the established pattern. She was 'engaged in abolishing the old runrig system, under which the wretched hovels of some five hundred crofters had been built in clusters or end on to each other like a kind of street, so that when typhus or smallpox broke out there was no escape. All the new houses had to be built each one in the centre of the four acre croft'.[16]

But Osgood was also willing to recognise Dr John's contribution:

> When she and my uncle were ruling these five hundred to six hundred families of crofters it was an extra hard time for them, for first of all there was the potato blight – and want generally brings out the bad and not the good qualities of a people; then there was the great upheaval caused by the trustees deciding to do away with the runrig system and dividing all the arable land into crofts of about four acres. They forced the people to pull down their unsanitary houses, where the cattle were under the same roof as human beings, and where the fires were on the floor in the centre of the dwelling room, with only a hole in the roof to let the smoke out, and made them build new and rather better houses on their crofts, the proprietor providing the timber. My mother told me many a time that, with very few exceptions, the one desire of the whole population seemed to be to learn how they could please the young laird, and how they could best fulfil the wishes of those who were managing this huge estate for him to the best of their abilities.[17]

Once the physical movement had taken place, Dr John's aim was to change the farming methods used so as to make the crofters far less liable to poverty. The first priority was to drain and trench to reclaim the land. The loans fortuitously available from the Destitution Committee to help potato famine sufferers came in very useful. A grant of from three pounds to thirty-three (for the most difficult moorland bogs) was available for each crofter. Tenants were then required to introduce rotations of crops and grass. According to a Royal Commission *Report* (1893) they were to grow 'cabbages and carrots, Jerusalem artichokes and numerous other vegetables of which they had never heard before so as to enable them to feed their cattle indoors and to have plenty of green vegetables for their own consumption'.[18]

To show strong leadership, Dr John ran his Isle Ewe farm (where he lived from 1848) in the model way: he drained bogs; found clean running water to avoid having to bring it over in casks from the mainland; built cottages for his ploughman and shepherd, also a threshing and meal-mill; planted trees; cut peats; constructed roads, dykes, a pier and boats for livestock and carriages; kept his cows under cover; fished (for oysters, clams, skate, cod, ling); grew cabbages and produced butter and cheese, sending tons to market in Inverness, Glasgow and Liverpool. 'The wool of my sheep and lambs paid all my rent'. On the island he employed, amongst others, his own school mistress, a grieve and a dairymaid. The family crossed regularly to the local church in Aultbea.

Dr John also offered positive encouragement, rewards and awards to those who conformed with his wishes. In November 1848 the *Inverness Courier* reported on the Crofters' Dinner at Gairloch, which had been preceded by an agricultural show. The prize-giving proceedings were in Gaelic and crofters spoke in support of the new regime, even those with moor and bog land. The event was repeated the following year. But, despite these sterling efforts, his tenants did not follow his example: 'It ought to have given good lessons to the tenants; but they merely sucked the finger of astonishment and stuck to their old ways'.

Dr John was not surprised. One, to him crucial, aspect of the reforms was not allowed him on the ground of cost. In order to persuade the tenants to change their farming methods he very much wanted to provide practical agricultural instruction, believing that prosperity would only come by putting them 'under the charge of a sufficient number of gardeners whose bread will depend on their making the crofters crop their land like rational beings, year after year'. The estate auditors, however, only permitted Dr John to appoint an instructor for each of the six estate districts for two days each week, totally inadequate in his view.

> I had to employ a crofter in nearly every township, at a mere nominal pay, every one as prejudiced against the changes as his neighbours. [...] Yet even with such helpers, and an old sheep-manager who knew as much of astronomy as of agriculture, I went to war with my five or six hundred 'enemies', [...] tho' I only got a fraction of what I had planned carried out.[19]

He even tried to use the potato famine to argue his case for proper funding for advisers, writing to the *Inverness Courier* in November 1848 to explain how the 'current destitution' was 'undoubtedly the consequence of a bad system (or rather the want of a system) of agriculture'. If only the relief funds could have been used to appoint full-time instructors to teach 'improved modes of cultivation'. In a lecture, *Pauperism and its Cure*, given in Inverness in 1870, he was still convinced that this would have been the solution to the problem.

Dr John threatened to evict the tenants who would not co-operate and were passively resisting implementing any new ways:

> I would be quite plain with my crofters – letting them understand that I could know no peace and happiness unless they were doing well, and unless they were able to pay their rents I would have to be hungry or shut up. Therefore they must obey my cropping rules or else emigrate. [...] Such firm carrying out of clear, wise rules would be true charity to crofters as ignorant and prejudiced as ours were in 1846.

There is no evidence that he actually carried out any such sanctions. He also continued to be tolerant about his tenants' failures to pay the full rental. He once, but only once, took the advice of a Government Inspector, Captain Elliott, to insist on the full remittance:

> When the next man, who owed £10, put down only £7, I pushed it back to him, saying, 'I would not take it – he must pay down £10'. The old gent took a look at me, and quietly pocketing the £7 said, 'No one knows where the other £3 are to grow, and it's you that's foolish not to take the £7. Who knows where they will be tomorrow?'[20]

The famine years

The ability of the crofters to pay their rent was to become one of the most pressing issues of Dr John's years as estate factor. Osgood's childhood was a time of considerable famine and poverty in the country and district. The situation was not unprecedented. In April 1837 the minister of Poolewe had written a letter expressing gratitude to those in Edinburgh who had sent one hundred bolls of meal to be distributed in the parish.

> 318 families including 1539 individuals have been relieved by the supply sent. [...] I can safely say that few or none of the families so relieved had anything whatever to eat at the time the meal was distributed. As soon as the supply distributed is consumed the same families will again be perfectly destitute as well as almost all the families that have not been relieved. [...] We are perfectly satisfied that there is no parish in the whole Highlands or Islands more destitute than the Government Parish of Poolewe.[21]

In the early 1840s the people of Gairloch had had to supplement their diet by purchasing two thousand bolls of meal, paid for by selling the precious black cattle. However, major destitution resulted when potato blight, which devastated the crops in Ireland in 1845, spread to mainland Scotland the following year after a damp, warm winter. By the middle of the eighteenth century potatoes had become the basic subsistence crop for the Scottish crofter. It was reckoned that an acre of potatoes provided three times more calories an acre, and was ready for harvest much earlier, than oats. Sir John Sinclair, a contemporary Caithness agricultural 'improver', estimated that four times as many people could be supported by an acre of potatoes compared to oats.[22] 'Even marginal and inhospitable land could be made to yield good returns', and they tolerated the high rainfall. So potatoes had become essential to help feed the rapidly growing population. Though there was initially optimism that the Highlands had escaped the worst of the blight it soon became clear that disaster was imminent, given the over-dependence on this single crop. The repercussions were to last well into the 1850s. By the autumn of 1846 the impact of the crop failure was a major issue throughout lowland Scotland and England.

Relief schemes

The lowland response to news of the impending famine was not always sympathetic. An attitude of contempt towards the backward Gaels was often evident in articles written in the influential *Scotsman* and *Glasgow Herald.* They needed to be 'taught the lesson of industry' and change their 'habitually indolent' ways.[23] The recently established Free Church of Scotland blamed 'the hand of the lord'. Nonetheless, it sent 'schedules of enquiries' to its ministers, asking about food supply, crop failure, number of people at risk and availability of employment in the distressed districts. The replies provided unchallengeable evidence. Not all places were hit equally badly. Glenelg had lost nine-tenths of its crop whereas in Ullapool it was less than half.[24] A committee to organise charitable relief was immediately set up and showed itself remarkably free of sectarianism when providing for even the Catholic communities of Moidart and Arisaig.[25] Gairloch, however, did not receive any of their supplies.[26]

The winter of 1846 set in early. It was cold and stormy, with gales and snow. Typhoid and cholera broke out in several places. Scurvy reappeared after a century. Reports came in of people forced to scavenge shellfish as their only food. Emotive newspaper campaigns, both in England and Scotland, provided graphic descriptions of the sufferings. James Bruce, of *The Scotsman*, sent 15 long 'letters' from Mull, Skye and Ross-shire entitled 'Inquiry into the Distress in the Highlands and Islands' between the end of January and 10 March 1847, but he had little positive to say about the native people.[27] *The Times* showed greater concern. Charitable relief committees were set up in Glasgow and Edinburgh.

Very soon the three separate committees, those of Glasgow, Edinburgh and the Free Church, merged into one Central Board of Management of the Fund for the Relief of the Destitute Inhabitants of the Highlands. It first met in February 1847 and established two sections, one based in Edinburgh and the other in Glasgow. Each worked with specific districts, taking responsibility for raising funds and distributing supplies. These might be wheatmeal, oatmeal, peasemeal or Indian maize. Gairloch, having received some ninety bolls of meal from the Glasgow section,[28] was then put under the auspices of the Edinburgh committee. Captain Elliott, Royal Navy, was the General Inspector for the Edinburgh section and its secretary was William F. Skene. He was certainly to be kept busy in his correspondence with Dr John Mackenzie of Gairloch.

Very generous donations came in from church congregations, expatriates in Canada, India and the East Indies, Highland regiments and the inmates of a lunatic asylum in Dumfries, amongst many others. A national day of fasting was proclaimed by Queen Victoria with proceeds being allocated to help both Irish and Scottish victims of famine. For a while public attitudes to the Highlanders changed. The mood became more generous, tinged with a benevolent 'romanticism' with respect to the clans and their way of life, much influenced by the writings of Sir Walter Scott and others.[29]

The government in London also mobilised its resources. It had learnt from recent experience in Ireland, realised that the Poor Law legislation would never be able to meet the demands for relief and was absolutely determined that there should be no comparable death rate: 'The people cannot, *under any circumstances,* be allowed to starve'.[30] Sir Charles Trevelyan, Under-secretary of State at the Treasury, was given the task of dealing with the crisis and he immediately (September 1846) sent Sir Edward Pine Coffin (sic) north to investigate the situation and manage teams of relief agents. Pine Coffin's military career had begun during the Peninsular War at the beginning of the century, he had worked in Mexico and China and just completed duties in charge of famine relief in south west Ireland.

He proved to be efficient and effective, 'a kindly, painstaking man of marked ability'. He spent a month touring the Highlands and Islands, did not underestimate the scale of the problems and made his recommendations.[31] Depots were set up at Portree and Tobermory to supply meal from Glasgow or Liverpool at 'market', not subsidised, prices because his superior officer, Trevelyan, considered it wrong to disrupt or influence 'natural' commerce and private trade. Pine Coffin, though, recognised that this would discourage those in need from purchasing the government grain until they had exhausted their reserve seed supplies. Two steam ships were borrowed from the Royal Navy to take stocks to the isolated coastal and island townships. Bad weather would no longer hamper aid.[32]

The destitution years in Gairloch

The Gairloch area offered fishing to contribute to both diet and income and, with crofters still living on productive land, was not as dependent on potatoes as, for example, Skye and Loch Carron. However, there was considerable hardship and seed had to be bought by the trustees to tide their people through the spring of 1847.[33] In addition, Murdo M'donald, Convener for Gairloch, reported that there were about '450 Families or upwards of 2,000 individuals depending for subsistence till the middle of August next on the Control Board'. About 80 families in the district of Poolewe had not received a single pound of the supplies sent 'owing to a palpable mistake on the part of Mr McKay'. He recommended that the Poolewe District 'be separated into two districts viz Tynafilin having a population of 1,800, Poolewe and Inverasdale having a population of 700'.[34]

One inevitable result of this increased poverty was that 'in 1846 twenty-two percent of all tenants were in arrears. Two years later the proportion had risen to sixty per cent'.[35] Most were of the crofter class, whose rental was worth £5 per year or less. In fact, the overall income of the Mackenzie estate was not as seriously affected by the famine as might have been anticipated since the wealthier tenants maintained their rent payments.

Duties of the laird

Government officials put considerable pressure upon the local landowners to take responsibility for their tenants. Trevelyan made it clear:

> It is by no means intended to afford relief in such a way as would relieve the landowners and other persons of property from the obligations they are under to support the destitute poor. [...] Any assistance contemplated would be rather in the form of giving a proper organisation and direction to the efforts of the proprietors. [...] It is part of the duty of the landlord to give his small tenants the necessary assistance in provision of food and seed. In every country the party entitled to receive the rent, or surplus produce of the soil, is expected to remit a portion of his ordinary demands when that produce fails, and in extreme cases he is likewise expected to make advances of seed and other necessary means of enabling his underholders to carry on the cultivation – his outlay in the last mentioned case being returned to him in the produce of the next harvest, which must otherwise fall short.[36]

If the landowners were not deemed to be taking full responsibility for providing for their needier people then the government officers would write strongly worded letters. Meyrick Bankes, proprietor of the neighbouring Letterewe estates, received one such in the winter of 1846. He seemed to have taken the message seriously. By June of the following year it could be reported that Mr Bankes had 'generously transmitted £20 to the Rev. Mr Campbell of Gairloch for the benefit of the able-bodied poor on the estates of Uldrigill and Gruinard'. Further, 'when leaving the country last season he left unlimited authority with the manager to give employment to as many as might avail themselves of it. Great numbers did so, and are now, after returning home, cultivating their crofts, laying down the seed and preparing for the fishing season'. He had also improved his own estate, 'changing the appearance of what was formerly almost a barren waste into the appearance of fertile fields and fruitful gardens'. Most impressive of all, 'Mr Bankes' own yacht has arrived from Liverpool, with large quantities of barley, turnip, carrot and other seeds for the tenantry, so that, in the event of a failure of the potato crop, they may have something to fall back on'. He organised regattas at Aultbea and Gruinard, followed by a 'substantial and hearty supper' soon after, advising his tenants to 'devote every spare hour to fishing on the coast'.[37]

The laird of Gairloch did not receive any such letters to remind him of the commitments he should make to his crofters. The trustees of Sir Kenneth, reckoned to be one of the twelve biggest landowners, (and, perhaps not coincidentally, one of the few whose family had owned his estate before the turn of the century), were, rather, praised for their positive attitude and diligent efforts to mitigate the effects of the famine.

The government was not prepared to give meal for free, nor to hand out cash: 'Next to allowing the people to die of hunger, the greatest evil that could happen would be their being habituated to depend upon public charity'.[38] It was considered to be detrimental to the moral welfare of recipients to get something for nothing. They could work to earn money to buy food. The Drainage Act 1846, intended for Ireland, would be used to benefit the Scots also. Landowners could apply for grants to drain, ditch and fence land. From 1847 this became an important source of funding to create employment and was well exploited by Dr John.

> Few of our thousands of people would have survived had not the Trustees borrowed £10,000 from Government for drainage which I invested chiefly in cargoes of oatmeal and Indian corn meal.[39]

The Gairloch estate received £5,000 as a result of his applications 1846–1847.

> In Gairloch [...] a form of truck operated. The crofters were paid a daily wage of from 1s. to 1s. 6d. from the drainage grant. They were supplied with meal on a weekly basis on account of their wages. The residue of their wages went to pay arrears of rent and the balance was then given in cash.[40]

The tenants were expected to repay the loans granted under the Drainage Act and it was added to their rent, payable over twenty years. Those most in arrears might find their cattle sold on their behalf. Dr John was remembered for 'taking away the cattle'.[41] A claim was made in 1850 that he 'sent forth his officers, armed with authority, first to mark the cattle of the cotters in arrear, for the laird, [...] then the Doctor's stout-hearted men were sent to remove and take possession of the cattle. [...] Does this lifting of the cattle display either good feeling or good management? [...] I am assured that there were some who had their only cow, which gave milk to the poor starving children in a family, taken from them'.[42] This was explained at the time as a necessary action and the consequence of the crofters not having sent the cattle, which usually paid the rent, to market. Apparently they deemed the price they were likely to receive too low to warrant the effort. As a consequence they had excessive stock on their land and it was these animals which were confiscated and sold, to help reduce the arrears. Many were still paying their debts in 1885, a matter of some discontent.[43]

The destitution test

By the summer of 1847 the government was claiming that the crisis was over and it withdrew from direct intervention and provision of aid. However, the need for relief was not so quickly resolved. Bad autumn weather, with several weeks of gales and storms, spoilt much of what harvest there might have been.[44] With no seed potatoes to sow and low prices for cattle because they, inevitably, had deteriorated given the lack of fodder, the suffering of the poorer crofters and cottars was of much longer duration and the Central Board of Management for Highland Relief continued to provide aid, with expenditure carefully supervised by the same personnel. Efforts to suspend relief operations again in the autumn of 1848 were thwarted by snow falling before the green corn had been harvested from the fields. The misery was compounded by a poor herring fishing that year and a downturn in the demand for labour from the railway builders in the south of Scotland.[45]

Increasingly influential by now, and joining Trevelyan in a 'grand plan for moral revolution', was Sir John McNeill, Chairman of the Board of Supervision of the Scottish Poor Law from 1845 to 1868.[46] He was most concerned to read in Sir Edward Pine Coffin's final report, at the end of 1847, that those on relief were better fed than they had ever been. Relief, always very limited, had been stopped once the harvest was in. Its renewal, in early 1848, may have been unavoidable but it was going to be much more stringently regulated. On Trevelyan's insistence inspectors were appointed to supervise. He recommended a number of Royal Navy officers on half pay for the role, intending much greater vigilance.[47] Captain Rose took on the Wester Ross area. The increasing bureaucracy was not welcomed. In Skye there was now one inspector, together with thirteen relief officers and a dozen overseers, all being paid a good salary, doing the job of the original voluntary committees.[48]

The rules for food relief were considerably tightened. A new 'destitution' or 'labour' test was introduced which paid only a pound of meal (a much reduced quantity) in return for at least eight hours' work, six days a week: 'The meagre allowance provided but a bare subsistence and only those with no food resources of their own or who did not have the possibility of obtaining gainful employment would endure such a harsh regime for so little in order to avoid starvation'.[49] It was pointed out that this was only half what a prisoner would get. Women had to knit and spin to get assistance. Children under twelve must attend school before they were permitted to receive their daily three-quarters of meal. The old and infirm were to receive but half a pound a day. All food rations were distributed fortnightly to teach the recipients how to budget their resources. The able-bodied men of Skye were taken off the relief registers and told they must go to Gairloch or Ullapool to get work.

There were many instances where, after long months of poor nutrition, people were simply not able to meet the work requirements. The Lochalsh inspector reported that 'the people are very willing to work, but so much are they weakened by insufficient food that much work cannot be got out of them'.[50] A journalist, Thomas Mulock, was outspoken in his criticism of such harsh treatment, inflicting 'further misery on a people already ravaged by famine' and 'systematised starvation', but to no avail.[51] If it was found that their houses were dirty then they might not get anything: 'Rule 8th: The house must be clean, and the pool of water and dirt removed from before the door, or else their meal will be stopped'.[52] The lowland press were now widely unsympathetic. That 'the great cause of the destitution is not the failure of the potato crop but the intense and abominable idleness of the inhabitants'[53] confirmed the views expressed earlier that 'they preferred their habitual mode of life, their few days of desultory labour intermingled with weeks of lounging gossip, their half clad condition, to regular well paid toil'.[54]

McNeill saw a providential opportunity to teach the Highlanders to be more industrious, thus bringing about their moral and material regeneration. He wished to discourage the 'cancer of pauperism'. His principles complemented those of Trevelyan very neatly: 'The object [...] is to prevent the assistance given from being productive in idleness and, if possible, to make it conducive to increased exertion'.[55] To end the Highlanders' 'moral disease' work must be provided at home or away. Thousands were helped to move from the north of Scotland to build railways in the lowlands.

Road building

So, in addition to direct relief, a new approach was developed to widen the scope of the kind of works which would qualify for grants. Now road and bridge building could be included as well as land improvements. The sum available equalled that which would have been necessary for poor relief, provided this was matched from the landowner himself, and the money used to employ poor people who would otherwise be requiring said Poor Relief. It was argued that this 'support from proprietors was not purely charitable. It was cheaper for a landowner, particularly a non-resident one, to give generously in an emergency rather than find his estate permanently rated for poor relief'.[56]

The Gairloch area was the first where this 'co-operative scheme' was trialled. In February 1848 the Relief Board agreed to provide 'a Wester Ross estate management with half the £2,500 required for the construction of a road along the southern shore of Loch Maree – the sum in question being made available on condition that the landlord benefiting from it provided his crofting tenants with work on his road construction project'. It was approved because 'it involved the proprietors in famine relief projects, allowed the board to reduce its staff and, theoretically at least, helped to develop the Highlands' natural resources'.[57]

Osgood Mackenzie, aged eight, proudly recollected cutting the first turf on the extension of this road from Kinlochewe to Gairloch: 'How well I remember it, surrounded by a huge crowd, many of them starving Skye men, for the famine was more sore in Skye and the islands than it was on our part of the mainland'.[58] In 1885 the Dowager Lady Mackenzie wrote of her key role in the projects through close contact with the government:

> For 10 years from June 1843 I was trustee for the Gairloch property with Mr Mackenzie of Ord. There was no road then between [...] the upper end of Loch Maree and Slatadale. The potato disease commenced in August 1846, and this road was begun the following spring. When the government steamers called in at Gairloch, inquiring as to the distress and poverty caused by the potato disease, I did not advocate the sending of supplies of meal, &c, but urged continually, in speaking and by letters, both to the Destitution Committee and to the Home Secretary (Sir George Grey) and to Lord John Russell, that money might be granted to make the road from Rudha 'n Fhomhair to Slatadale, and thus to open up the country, I, on my part, as trustee, guaranteeing to support the people who could not work on the road. [...] Though mentioning my own name throughout this transaction, I could not have done anything without the indefatigable assistance of Captain (now Admiral) Russell Elliott of Appleby Castle; he was at the head of the Destitution Committee. [...] Also I was much indebted to Sir Charles Trevelyan, at that time Secretary to the Home Secretary. By the aid of such good and able friends, the Destitution Committee was induced to advance in all two or three thousand pounds, the district road trustees undertaking to advance equal to what was advanced on the Loch Maree road; and money was afterwards received from the Destitution Fund to carry on the road to Badachro. [...] Lord John Russell sent me £100 out of a fund he had from the receipts of a ball or concert for the destitute Highlanders, and I had several large sums sent me by strangers, besides some from my own relations. Money also was granted from Edinburgh to assist in making the road from Poolewe to Inverasdale. After I received money from the Destitution Committee several other proprietors [...] received grants on the same terms. The road from Poolewe to Aultbea was thus made, and also, I think, the road from Dundonnell, by Feitheann, to the Ullapool road.[59]

As a result the Central Board Inspector, Captain Rose, found Gairloch 'already provided for' but he tried to encourage proprietors in Letterewe, Torridon and Loch Broom to follow the Mackenzie example.[60] This they did as such a 'co-operative scheme' 'was of great assistance to the people, who were supplied with meal while working, and were also enabled in that manner to pay off part of their arrears'.[61] By 1850 the area's landlords were in possession of a network of ninety miles of new roads, linking Ullapool, Poolewe and Gairloch to Dingwall. These 'destitution roads', as the highways in question became known, were the Central Relief Board's greatest practical accomplishment.

Dr John, as factor for the estate, went to considerable effort to arrange the contracts and ensure the men who worked on the roads and transported materials were properly paid over three years.[62] He believed that many of the estate tenants would have died, or, at the very least, been forced to move away, during these famine years had the Trustees not successfully solicited grants to provide them with employment.

> I lost all my natural modesty and never rested till I saw my way to money from the Highland Committee and the Bank [...] and got an engineer and some sappers from Woolwich to line out the road along Loch Maree, so as to make it capable of bearing wheels; thus we employed our starving people [...] to turn out the present road.[63]

In a final contract Dr Mackenzie agreed to 'relieve the Committee from all responsibility for the relief of the population on his estates in Ross-shire during the season ending 30th September 1850'. In return:

> The Committee agrees to set apart for the purposes of this agreement the sum of £900 being the sum which would otherwise have been expended on affording relief to the destitute portion of the population. Dr Mackenzie [...] binds himself to expend the money allotted by the Board on the construction of the following public and useful works, viz:
>
> I The road from the Badochro harbour westwards to Port Henderson
>
> II The Road from the Lonemore line to the large Township of Sand, on the north side of Gairloch Bay
>
> III The road from Poolewe to Inverasdale on the south side of Loch Ewe.[64]

'Co-operative' fishing

Not only roads were built under these 'co-operative' projects. Jetties and piers were also constructed and harbours improved. Good use must be made of them. In 1847 Dr John had already explained what was needed:

> A supply of 'Long Lines' hooks, and baskets for the Lines would be much valued. Also 'hand lines'. The people have a good supply of small boats but few or none fit to go with out to the Cod and Ling banks in 'the Minch' where crews from the East Coast are now killing great quantities of the finest Cod and Ling.[65]

In February 1849 the Committee had commissioned five boats, with their crews and all the requisite fishing materials, including nets, to go from Cellardykes in Fife to Skye, Soay and Badachro near Gairloch to instruct the natives in deep-sea fishing techniques. The Fife fishermen had negotiated a good deal for their contract, which was to last from 12 March until the end of June. The Board would provide furnished house accommodation, fuel and the salt necessary for the curing and send cured fish to market, gratis. In addition:

> We shall take a woman along with us in each boat for the purpose of cooking, washing etc and to teach the Highland women the proper way of baiting lines and these women to be allowed 2/6d a day, or whatever the Board shall think proper in manner of wages. We should require at least four women for baiting the lines etc for each boat in addition to the one that goes along with us [... and] to undertake if desired to put two of their men into a smaller boat to be furnished by us for the natives [sic] and to take four natives into it so as to form a crew of six. Also to take four natives into the larger boat so as to form a crew of ten.[66]

The Committee's final report did give credit to the Badachro fishing station with its curing sheds and pier. The Inspector General expressed his 'confident anticipation' that, together with the new road, 'this excellent harbour would become an important fishing station'.[67] But Dr John was sceptical. In March 1851 he was party to an 'interrogation' by Sir John McNeill, Chairman of the Poor Law Board. Dr John was quoted in his *Report*:

> I have also furnished several persons with boats and fishing-gear, to be paid for from the produce of the fishing, and have engaged a curer who will purchase the fish as they are brought ashore. [...] These advances have been made to about ten crews of five men each in Lochewe about three months ago. [...] They have not prosecuted the fishing with diligence and some of the boats have not yet delivered above 10s worth of fish. Similar advances have been made to the people at Gairloch. There, there are about 20 crews. [...] They have been extremely remiss, and although Gairloch is considered a much better fishing station than Lochewe, the twenty boats have taken only about the same quantity of fish caught by the ten boats employed here.[68]

Though unimpressed with the poor productivity of the local schemes, Dr John continued to take advantage of the subsidies until they ended in 1850. So, the tenants were working (to their advantage) which helped them to pay off arrears of rent (to his!).

'Co-operative' knitting

A further grant-aided 'co-operative' enterprise which was generally highly regarded, without controversy, was that of the Dowager Lady Mackenzie's continuing endeavours to teach hosiery skills to the women of Gairloch. In 1847 Dr John informed the Destitution Board, when asking for 'Materials for Female Employment', that she 'has got above 100 women employed spinning wool who work up about 35 stones pr week which is then knitted into stockgs [sic] or woven into coarse cloth'. A supply of wool 'to keep these people employed and enable us to give them some new clothing when their present is worn out (& they cannot afford soon to buy new) would be of much value. Also a few looms of better make than those now used by our weavers'. He added thoughtfully, 'if wool is to be given it would be convenient if granted before July 8th, the day of the Invss wool market, so that we might buy it from our sheep farmers in the district'.[69]

In January 1850 the *Inverness Advertiser*, not a friend to landowners in general, carried a lengthy article, based on the final *Report* of the Highland Destitution Board, which gave much praise for the efforts of the Dowager Lady:

> The hosiery department has been managed under Mr Hogg, to whom Lady Mackenzie of Gairloch has handed over the trade she originated, and has carried on with so much consideration for the females of that estate. Her ladyship took very great pains to produce the best coloured yarns, and the finest-shaped stockings. The patterns were novel and pretty and Gairloch stockings had acquired a name in the market. We can only hope that Mr Hogg will do his best to continue the liberal treatment displayed by her ladyship to her dependents.[70]

He did, and the hosiery skills of local women were to contribute to the income and renown of the Gairloch parish well into the twentieth century.[71]

References and Notes

1 Caird, p.145.
2 Byam Shaw, p.279.
3 *The Mackenzie Case,* p.105. Gairloch Heritage Museum Library.

[4] Dr John's diaries: manuscript book VI (Conan House Archives), p.474.
[5] Mackenzie, p.60.
[6] Byam Shaw, p.179.
[7] Byam Shaw, p.222.
[8] Quoted in Byam Shaw, pp.193–194.
[9] Byam Shaw, p.262.
[10] Caird, pp.143–144.
[11] Byam Shaw, p.247.
[12] Caird, p.146.
[13] Byam Shaw, pp.246–248.
[14] Caird, pp.147–148.
[15] Dixon, p.138.
[16] Mackenzie, pp.29, 36. Typhus was known as the 'famine fever' but, fortunately, there were no epidemic occurrences in the Highlands at this time, unlike in Ireland.
[17] Mackenzie, p.180. His chronology of events is rather awry, as the changes actually began before the potato blight arrived.
[18] Caird, p.150, using evidence from the 1892 *Royal Commission, Highlands and Islands of Scotland*, enquiring into whether land, now used for deer forest, grouse moor or other sporting purposes could be 'advantageously occupied by crofters'.
[19] Byam Shaw, quoting Dr John, pp.226–229, 257, 247, 248.
[20] Byam Shaw, pp.398, 257, 249.
[21] Letter of 27 April 1837 from D. M'rae, Poolewe Minister. Gairloch Heritage Museum Archives.
[22] Devine, *Clanship to Crofters' War*, p.49.
[23] Krisztina Fenyo, *Contempt, Sympathy and Romance* (East Linton: Tuckwell Press, 2000), p.49.
[24] Hunter, p.96.
[25] Hunter, p.107.
[26] Return of 28 April 1847 from Gairloch parish to the Highland Destitution Committee.
[27] Fenyo, p.60, 93.
[28] Return of 28 April 1847 from Gairloch parish to the Highland Destitution Committee.
[29] Devine, *The Great Highland Famine*, pp.116, 117, 119 and *Clanship to Crofters' War*, p.155.
[30] Devine, *The Great Highland Famine,* p.120.
[31] Hunter, pp.99–100.
[32] Devine, *Clanship to Crofters' War*, p.161.
[33] Devine, *The Great Highland Famine*, p.110.

[34] Return of 28 April 1847 from Gairloch parish to the Highland Destitution Committee.
[35] Conan House rental papers quoted in Devine, *The Great Highland Famine,* p.51.
[36] Devine, *The Great Highland Famine*, pp.84, 92.
[37] *Inverness Courier*, 15 June and 22 June 1847.
[38] Devine, *Clanship to Crofters' War,* p.164.
[39] Byam Shaw, p.246.
[40] Devine, *The Great Highland Famine,* pp.312, 102.
[41] Byam Shaw, p.280.
[42] Letter from Colin Munro in the *Inverness Courier*, 28 November 1850.
[43] They shared their grievances with the Napier Commission investigating the state of crofting in Scotland. See Chapter v.
[44] Hunter, p.109.
[45] Hunter, pp.112–113.
[46] Devine, *Clanship to Crofters' War*, p.164. More on the local workings of the new Poor Law is explained in Chapter IX.
[47] Devine, *Clanship to Crofters' War*, p.171.
[48] Hunter, p.112.
[49] Devine, *Clanship to Crofters' War*, p.170.
[50] Hunter, p.112.
[51] Devine, *Clanship to Crofters' War*, pp.173, 174. In December 1849 Mulock had taken on the editorship of the *Inverness Advertiser*, after the unexpected death of James M'Cosh. The *Advertiser* was a politically independent paper, founded in June 1849, with a 'Free Church' adherence. It saw its roles as to 'expound Highland grievances', and to serve the public good. It asserted that 'the interests of all classes are inseparably bound up together. The prosperity of one is the prosperity of all and only measures just to all shall receive our support'.
[52] Fenyo, p.75.
[53] *Fyfeshire Journal*, 11 February 1847 quoted in the Report of the Royal College of Physicians of Edinburgh, *The Case for State Medical Services for the Poor: the Highlands and Islands*, 1850.
[54] *The Glasgow Herald,* 9 June 1845, quoted in the Report (1850) of the Royal College of Physicians of Edinburgh.
[55] Devine, *The Great Highland Famine,* pp.125–126.
[56] Thomas Mulock, quoted in Devine, *Clanship to Crofters' War*, p.174.
[57] Hunter, p.113.
[58] Mackenzie, p.30.
[59] Dixon, pp.148–149.
[60] *Inverness Courier,* 13 June 1848.

[61] Devine, *The Great Highland Famine,* p.105.

[62] Dr John Mackenzie, 'Letters to the Edinburgh Destitution Board 1847'. Gairloch Heritage Museum Archives.

[63] Byam Shaw, p.246.

[64] Minute of Agreement between William T. Skerne Esq., Secretary to, and on behalf of, the Edinburgh Section of the Highland Destitution Committee and Dr Mackenzie on the part of Sir Kenneth Mackenzie, 22 March 1850. Gairloch Heritage Museum Archives.

[65] Correspondence from Dr John to the Edinburgh section of the Destitution Committee. Gairloch Heritage Museum Archives.

[66] National Archives of Scotland. 16/132 February 1849. Gairloch Heritage Museum Archives.

[67] *Inverness Advertiser,* 17 January 1850.

[68] Sir John McNeill, *Report to the Board of Supervision on the West Highlands and Islands,* reference to his interrogation of Dr John Mackenzie Esq. at Isle Ewe 21 March 1850.

[69] Letter from Dr John Mackenzie to unknown recipient. Gairloch Heritage Museum Archives.

[70] *Inverness Advertiser,* 17 January 1850.

[71] The ongoing significance of this 'Women's work' has been considered in Chapter II.

CHAPTER IV

The Destitution Years – continued

'A deal of absurd ink was spilt in the newspapers about the new crofting system at Gairloch, its great success, its utter failure, etc, etc.'

The final *Report* of the Highland Destitution Board in January 1850 looked back with self congratulation on the work which it had undertaken. The funds were now exhausted but so was the necessity, they believed. In the previous year only 1,393 people had required relief, compared with over 3,000 in 1848. However, the Board's objective, 'to improve the condition of the people and to develop the resources of the country; to prevent the recurrence of so great a calamity and convert the sufferings of the people into the germ of their future amelioration', had not provided a long term solution to the endemic problems of the crofting way of life. With respect to the Gairloch estates, views of the effectiveness of the schemes to relieve the effects of the potato famine were inextricably entwined with commentary on the crofting reforms, which had been initiated before the blight arrived.

Improved crofts? The debate

There was considerable contemporary debate about their success. The *Inverness Courier* reported rather sceptically on Dr John's improvement plans as early as October 1844: 'Whether our inferior soils and climate will suit as well as the richer lands of Sussex for the small allotments may be doubted but the experiment, under benevolent guidance and support, is at least worth a trial'.[1]

In October 1849 an MP and economist, Mr Poulet Scrope, praised Dr John's efforts. He had recently undertaken a tour of the Highlands to compare the relief efforts there with those in Ireland and was most impressed with the results in the Lochbroom and Gairloch areas:

> But there are some who, led no less by humanity than, as I believe, an enlightened consideration of their true interests and duties, are endeavouring, by an improved distribution of their small tenantry (or crofters), by instruction and assistance, to retain and enable them not merely to support themselves, but to improve greatly their own position and the value of the estate at the same time. In this beneficent and patriotic work the lead has been taken by

> Dr Mackenzie of Eileanach. [...] The principle has been to abolish entirely the old run-rig or common tenancy, with the clusters of wretched hovels which usually accompany it, and to locate every tenant on his separate lot, on which he is required, with assistance from the landlord, not exceeding £5 each, to build a new house, with proper offices. Draining, trenching and a due rotation of crops, especially green crops, enriched by the saving of every particle of manure, both liquid and solid, and the stall-feeding of cattle in the winter, are not only taught, but insisted upon. The average area of each holding is not quite 5 acres with, however, a run on the mountain for cattle. More than this would, in Dr Mackenzie's estimation, be beyond the means of the occupier for that garden system of cultivation by the spade alone. [...]
>
> The result of the system, which was begun on the Gairloch estate early in 1846, and the benefits of which have been extended to nearly 500 crofter tenants is that a population of between 4,000 and 5,000 folk, whom the failure of the potato would, under other circumstances, have reduced to absolute destitution, have been enabled, with comparatively little extraneous aid, not merely to maintain themselves during the last four disastrous years, but greatly to improve their original positions, and they are now in a fair way of obtaining one of positive comfort and prosperity. The improved crofts which I went over exhibited flourishing crops of turnips, carrots, mangel, beet, cabbage and clover as well as of potatoes and oats, and this in a district which never till the last few years grew anything beyond the two last.
>
> The difficulties, however, with which Dr Mackenzie has to contend are not slight. These consist not only in a wet and stormy climate, but still more in the almost incredible ignorance and prejudice of a people who have been hitherto cut off from all communication with the civilised world, without instruction in the means of advancement, whether by precept or example. This is now being afforded them in schools and model farms.

Poulet Scrope concurred with Dr John that the current law was an impediment to further progress until it allowed security of tenure: 'For one acre that is now improved without a lease, one hundred would be improved with proper leases'.[2] The *Scottish Highlander* was even more convinced of the need to change the law, though did not credit Dr John with seeing the necessity for lease reform:

> All who are personally acquainted with the wants of the Highlands, attribute much of the present distress to the little encouragement which has been given

> to crofters, producing, with other evils, hopeless apathy of mind and habits, a wretched stationary agriculture, a ruinous sub-division of the family croft among its dependents, little regard for education and the usual consequence of deficient education-restricted views of social responsibilities evidenced in early and improvident marriages. It is of little consequence now to inquire how this neglect of the crofter-class arose; the time has now come when a new course of policy must be adopted. [...] Dr Mackenzie, of Gairloch, is now the only improver who holds that the desirable amelioration of the small tenant's condition can be brought about on the tenant-at-will system.[3]

Journalists came from afar to view the experiments on the Gairloch estates for themselves, with differing conclusions. The *Inverness Advertiser*, a more liberal, Free Church paper, tended to be quite supportive. In contrast, the editor of the *Inverness Courier*, Robert Carruthers, held no truck with small farms and with pampering small-scale crofters. Dr John engaged in lengthy correspondence with both in 1849–1850, warning the *Advertiser* not to give too much praise to his new ideas and berating the *Courier* for criticising him without valid evidence.

> A deal of absurd ink was spilt in the newspapers about the new crofting system at Gairloch, its great success, its utter failure, etc, etc – tho' there was nothing new in agriculture in any of my plans. I was merely trying to make the poor ignorant people cultivate their crofts as was done all over the world by methods which, till I moved the starving mob, had been utterly unknown in Gairloch and the West Highlands, to the sad loss of people and proprietors.[4]

An *Inverness Courier* reporter eventually, in 1850, travelled the seventy miles to Gairloch to see for himself, having given judgment from afar for several years. A further acrimonious public exchange of views was printed thereafter.

> A representative of the paper visited Gairloch, the estate of Sir Kenneth Mackenzie, to investigate the experiments made in a garden system of cultivation introduced among the crofters by Dr Mackenzie of Eilenach. The reporter thought that Dr Mackenzie deserved credit for his effort to introduce the system, but expressed the opinion that it had proved little less than an entire failure. Its best result was to raise the crofters' idea of comfort and to induce them to erect better houses than the old black bothies. The experiment however was not profitable either to the estate or the small tenants.

Dr John felt the editor had not 'met with those who are competent to give him more correct information on many points than he has received' and that he was jumping to conclusions far too hastily. 'If he knew the extraordinary ignorance of the people in every modern rule of cultivation, he would have been more surprised at the progress they have made in the past four years, than that they fell short of his expectations'. The fact that tenants were no more in arrears with their rent now than before the potato famine 'shows how greatly the partial adoption of our rules has increased the amount of food grown by the people, and the probability, at least, that the abatement of the potato disease would find many, even now, growing more food than they required for the support of their families. That the present arrears, in many instances, are caused by the interest of drainage money'.[5]

In subsequent correspondence a Mr C. Bond, member of the Patriotic Society, (which had consistently supported and published information about the Gairloch improvements), wrote a long letter to the *Courier* agreeing with the positive conclusions of Mr Poulet Scrope's enquiry. He remembered Sir Francis Mackenzie's treatise in Gaelic and English: 'One of the best treasures on improved husbandry that ever emanated from the pen of a benevolent proprietor' and continued:

> The chief recommendation of the Gairloch plan is that the self-relying principle is maintained and great results produced at comparatively trifling cost. Thus a model cottage having been erected at Strath, the occupants of the newly arranged holdings erected their own cottages with the assistance of a mason and a wright. The wood was advanced by the estate, and thus cottages which, from internal arrangements &c, are palaces compared with their old black huts, were put up at a cash cost of about £5. As to agricultural instruction, similar economy was observed. Dr Mackenzie detailed all his plans to Mr Anderson, the late very energetic manager on the property; and to see that his directions were carried out, six or seven young men were appointed to direct and overlook the operations of the crofters. These young men had to be taught themselves, and being only of the class of farm-grieves or ground officers, their salaries could not be large.
>
> My object has been to show that I was justified in publicly adverting to the Gairloch improvements. [...] First, because they are based upon broad principles of true political economy; secondly, because notwithstanding all the disadvantages of soil, habits of the people and the potato failure, they have made such satisfactory progress that I have nowhere seen crofters, as regards their holdings, their dwellings, their comfortable clothing, and the education of their children, so advanced or so creditable to the Highlands of

Scotland. I cannot refrain from expressing my conviction that very much of the improved aspect of Gairloch is due to the enlightened and unwearied benevolence of Lady Mackenzie.[6]

The influential journalist who became involved in the wider debate was Thomas Mulock. This outspoken Anglo-Irish reporter had come over to Scotland in 1849. Described as 'notorious', 'eccentric', 'troublesome and unmanageable' by his opponents, his admirers saw him as the true friend and fearless champion of the oppressed highlanders, striking 'terror in the minds of the ruthless oppressors'. As Editor of the *Inverness Advertiser* from December, he initially attacked the Highland Destitution Relief Board and its new 'Labour Test' then considered the longer term solutions to the underlying problem. What was needed was more land for the people and checks on the 'tyrannical' powers of the landowners. 'I maintain that the people are not too many, but that their holdings are too small – their rents are too high – their oppressions innumerable – their encouragements nil'.[7] If the crofters had sufficient land then they could be self-supporting. Certainly enforced emigration was wrong.

His stay at the *Advertiser* was brief and in March 1850 he moved on to the more radical *Northern Ensign*. Here he used the criticisms of the *Inverness Courier*, with which he rarely agreed, to launch his own direct attack on Dr John's efforts. In an article of 10 April, 1851, headed *GAIRLOCH: THE FAILURE OF A PROJECT FOUNDED ON FALSE PRINCIPLES*, he did not mince his words:

> We think it is now made abundantly manifest that a multitude of dependents, hitherto holders of land on the Gairloch estate, will have to rue the foolish and fatal experiments which the medico-agriculturalist of Eilenach has arbitrarily perpetrated on their humble happiness. [...]
>
> The new plan consisted mainly in the division of the old croft land and the recently reclaimed moor into small independent holdings, averaging four and half Scotch acres each, managed by spade labour on the Belgian system. It was an important feature that the cattle should be stall-fed, and the liquid manure carefully saved and applied to the garden-like fields, and that the dairy should be managed so as to produce a considerable return. [...] To attempt borrowing bodily from populous and prosperous Belgium a system of husbandry suited to that fine country, but utterly inapplicable to the wilds of sparsely-populated Ross-shire, was in the outset an enormous absurdity which stamped Doctor Mackenzie's scheme with all the pre-indicants of failure. [...]

> Doctor Mackenzie's scheme was a vile outrage upon common sense and common humanity; blindness and despotism pervaded all his plans and regulation, and an essentially rotten system has now issued in loss, shame and wide-spread suffering.

Famine relief

In contrast, the concluding *Report* of the Edinburgh Section of the Destitution Committee in January 1850 was very complimentary about the way the managers of the Gairloch estates had supported their tenants during the years of potato famine. Inspector Rose explained, at some length, the agreements made with the Gairloch estate:

> The detail of this co-operation with Sir Kenneth Mackenzie offers some peculiarities. [...] It was agreed that Sir Kenneth Mackenzie would undertake the care of his entire population, amounting to about 4000, and would, in addition, give labour and exhibit work to the amount of £1200, in the construction of a road connecting their fishing station at Badachroe with the low country, and with the adjacent fishing villages, to which scarce the vestige of a land track existed. I have now to report that our mutual conditions have been fully carried out. On the part of Sir Kenneth Mackenzie, as in former years, I have every reason, from the reports of the local officer, and from my observation and inquiry, to be satisfied with the judicious way in which destitution among the people has been relieved. I have also carefully examined and satisfied myself, in various ways, of the amount laid out in trenching, draining and fencing on the estate; and it appears that the amount of money paid for labour on the crofts alone far exceeds the amount of our requirement of £1200, and that the total amount paid for labour during the season, extends [...] to the sum of £2,751 6s 5d. I am happy to be able to add my testimony as to the improved condition of the crofters on this property since I first knew them in 1847.

It judged that, overall, such schemes had effected a permanent improvement and stimulated industry and self-exertion. Road building ensured that 'this large population [was] brought within the range of those benefits arising from facility of communication access to markets, and immediate contact with a more advanced society'. Poulet Scrope MP had also commended Dr John's efforts to improve Gairloch's roads:

> Though inhabited by ten thousand souls, [it had been] absolutely shut off from the rest of the world, possessing no means of communication with the more advanced state of society in the east country. I found several lines of road on the eve of completion [...] by which the two natural outlets of the west coast, Poolewe and Ullapool, will be connected with each other and with the trunk line of road which leads through Strath Garve to Dingwall. It is evident how largely this remote district must be benefited, and the self supporting industry of its inhabitants facilitated, by their obtaining access to the eastern markets. In addition to which they will have the traffic through them of the trade of the isle of Lewis.[8]

Mr Charles Macleod, manager of the crofts on the Gairloch land, reflected back in 1851:

> Last year, under a co-operative arrangement with the relief committee, there were employed on road making from about the 25th of May to the beginning of October about 100 persons on average, [...] many employed who were in good circumstances. These were discharged and such only employed as were poor and largely in arrear of rent. They were employed at day's wages, varying according to their ability, from 1s to 1s 6d. They were regularly supplied with meal every Saturday on account of the wages. The residue of their wages went to pay for such articles as they had obtained from tradesmen on orders from the overseer and to pay arrears of rent where they were due. The balance was paid to them in cash. [...] I am of the opinion that the co-operative work carried on here was more beneficial to the people than it has been, so far as I know, anywhere else.[9]

Thomas Mulock, as usual, disagreed. He was vociferous in maintaining that, ultimately, it was the landowners who benefitted the most from such improvements.

> This styled co-operative [...] is neither more nor less than a monstrous malversation of a charitable fund, by giving largesse to noblemen and gentlemen, who may be truly said to have improved their estates by means of public subscriptions.[10]

McNeill's *Report*

In 1851 Sir John McNeill, Chairman of the Board of Supervision of the Poor Law, undertook a comprehensive review of the *State of the West Highlands and*

Islands of Scotland, taking verbatim and written evidence from a range of local worthies. Fundamentally he had already come to the conclusion that charitable relief was never going to solve the 'Highland problem'. He considered that the Highlanders had, to a very great extent, brought their calamities on themselves.[11]

He arrived at the Poolewe Inn on 20 March 1851 to hear evidence from local people. Although there was no one receiving poor relief at that precise moment there was general agreement that people would need to apply for help before the next harvest and that the ending of the relief schemes was already creating new hardship. The Rev. Duncan Matheson, who had been the Free Church minister in Gairloch since 1844, gave evidence:

> I am of the opinion that the great majority of the crofters will this year be in greater distress than in any previous year. They have gradually exhausted their own resources, and have been purchasing food on credit. Their credit too is now exhausted. [...] The present crofts, since the failure of the potatoes, are too small.

The local surgeon, Charles Robertson, medical officer for the parish for the last four years, testified:

> The circumstances of the people have been deteriorating since the failure of the potato crop in 1846. For three years from that time the crofters on the Gairloch property were employed at trenching and draining under the Drainage Act and thereafter they found employment at road-making under a co-operative arrangement with the destitution committee. [...] During the last winter there has been no such employment for the crofters on the Gairloch property. Within the last week or two, some have been employed at the instance of the factor in cod and ling fishing. [...] I am of the opinion that, on an average, the produce of the crofts will not produce food for a family of five persons for more than from six to seven months.

Charles Macleod, the Gairloch estate manager, was 'of the opinion that the crofts, if cultivated to the highest possible pitch, would not maintain more than about two-thirds of the population now residing upon them'. He told both of the farming reforms and of the lack of commitment shown by many of the local crofters. They did not grow clover as recommended. Nor did they have 'command of sea-weed for manure, although they are allowed to take free all that grows on the coast. It was intended that they should supply themselves with manure by feeding their cattle in the house both summer and winter, and by preserving the liquid manure in tanks – but with one or two exceptions they have not yet fairly tried this system'. Mr Macleod pessimistically concluded: 'Although the people were at first much opposed to the new system, they are now more reconciled to it, from seeing its advantage and would be disposed to carry it out if they were able to do so, but from want of sufficient manure they find it impossible'.

Diligence was not seen to be an attribute of the Gairloch crofters by the Rev. Duncan Mackenzie. The Church of Scotland minister had been in the area for only five months. Whilst admitting that 'the great majority do not belong to my congregation', he had already concluded that 'the people here are of decidedly indolent habits'.

McNeill then went on to talk personally, and in private, with Dr John on his Island of Ewe. The factor took the opportunity to justify his management of the crofters:

> I am of opinion that the crofters on the Gairloch property obtained from their crofts sufficient food to maintain themselves and their families for about eight months of the year on average, that is taking into account the fish they all catch for their own consumption. [...] They now, almost without exception, cultivate sown grasses and turnips which were formerly unknown. I am satisfied that, if they would diligently follow out the system laid down for them, their crofts would suffice to maintain them and their families for the whole year. I am of opinion, that if proper instructors were provided, with authority to enforce obedience to their direction, on pain of ejection, the persons now occupying the crofts on this property might, in three or four years, be made to cultivate their lands in such a manner as would give them, from the produce of their crofts, the means of subsistence for the future and make them altogether independent. [...] I attribute the failure of the Gairloch crofters to carry out completely the system laid down for them to the want of the kind of instruction and authority above described.[12]

He was also not inclined to give credence to tales of distress, being unable to find 'any able-bodied man who will work at trenching and draining', even with the offer of lodging and pay of 1s a day. Dr John was 'of the opinion that the eleemosynary [dependent on charity] relief which has been afforded has been most prejudicial to the character of the people. [...] It has had the effect of relaxing their own exertions'.[13] Sir John McNeill accepted that his host was engaged in 'a spirited and benevolent experiment' through his crofting reforms, but remained unconvinced that it would help him reduce the cost of poor law provision. When McNeill's findings were published Dr John took strong issue with them: 'More utter trash than his report to Government on this subject never crossed a real farmer's eye'.[14] He was particularly outraged by a comment that 'the Gairloch crofters, where much has been done for them, are less contented than they are in Applecross, where nothing has been done for them'.

> Our Gairloch crofters, by honest hard labour on their lands, now produce more than double the amount of food they did four years ago. […] We have neither needed relief officer nor Destitution Committee meal in Gairloch. […] I admit candidly that our people in Gairloch occasionally may not be so "contented" as in Applecross. No true Highland crofter is contented, except when he has just enough daily bread to support life, and is exempted from mental and bodily labour. We aim a little beyond this, although at the risk of "discontent".
>
> Were your readers aware of the hand-gallop at which Sir John McNeill and his clerk passed through the Highlands they would perhaps doubt his ability to write authoritatively on Highland destitution and its remedy as much as does your obedient servant.[15]

The *Report* revived the debate in local newspapers. The *Inverness Advertiser*, 9 September 1851, commented in Dr Mackenzie's defence:

> [He] allows that he may not have been so successful at Gairloch as he wished or even anticipated, but he repudiates the stigma of failure. Has not, he asks, the produce of the crofts there been doubled? Is the period of three years a sufficient period to allot for the achievements of a complete revolution in the habits of a district? Is no account to be made of the drawback which the time of famine entailed? He admits, as dear bought experience has taught him, the difficulty of prevailing on the Highland population to adopt new modes of culture.

Two years later, 20 September 1853, the issues were still thought worthy of its newspaper column inches. Under the title '*Improvements in the West Highlands*' a eulogistic letter was published from a D.G.F. Macdonald of Dingwall.

> A most interesting experiment has been in progress for some years on the estate of Sir Kenneth Mackenzie of Gairloch – an experiment introduced and conducted by Dr Mackenzie of Eilanach and Lady Mackenzie of Gairloch –

> a lady whose kind and benevolent actions cannot be too highly appreciated. The plan consisted mainly in the division of the old croft land, and the recently reclaimed moor into small independent holdings, averaging five acres each, managed by spade labour on the Belgian system. It was probably the most enlarged and liberal attempt that had ever been made to improve the condition of a poor and declining Highland tenantry; and it is no flattering report to say that the system has proved itself worthy of being presented as a model for others to copy. [...] In short, the whole district is completely emancipated from indolence and inattention to husbandry on the part of its people, and now exhibits a lively spirit. [...]
>
> The Isle Ewe, the 'wonderful island' will immortalise its improver. I pulled up a turnip the other day, without picking or choosing, that weighs 5½ lbs in the bulb.

Undoubtedly the Gairloch trustees were more supportive of their tenants than many of their northern land-owning colleagues. Although the blight and its consequences affected them directly, the Mackenzies' crofters seem to have suffered less hardship because of the benevolence of their landlords. Nonetheless, Osgood Mackenzie's formative childhood years were spent in this environment of poverty and distress, which he remembered for the rest of his life and recorded in his memoirs.

Emigration in the destitution years

Despite his disappointments at their failure to respond to his reforms, Dr John Mackenzie always strongly opposed emigration by his tenants. Beyond Gairloch the attitudes to, and imperatives for, emigration changed significantly during the 'destitution years'. In the early 1840s increasing poverty had been making it more difficult for those who wanted to leave. A Select Committee of the House of Commons had suggested, in 1841, that there were 45,000–60,000 excess population in the crofting parishes but had no proposals to make.[16] By the late 1840s this 'excess population' was working out its own solution:

> The most telling illustration of the intense pressures unleashed on the population by the failure of the potatoes was the increase in mass migration as certain districts experienced enormous demographic losses during these terrible years. Uig in Lewis lost an estimated half of its total population between 1841 and 1861, Jura almost a third. [...] In several parishes, the scale of out-migration was so great that it eliminated the entire growth in

> population which had occurred from the early nineteenth century. Over the decade of the famine more than 16,000 people were assisted to emigrate to Canada and Australia through a combination of crop failure, clearance, coercion and landlord subsidy.[17]

It was 'push', rather than 'pull', factors which were now dominant. It was the poorest who were trying to claim land in Nova Scotia and New Breton and, for the first time, they were not made welcome. The Cape Breton authorities successfully requested that the British government, the newspaper press and customs officials let it be widely known that the destitute could not be supported at this difficult period. They themselves were fully committed trying to mitigate the effects of their own potato blight.[18]

However, at the same time, some of the Scottish papers were articulating a strong opinion that the burden of relieving the poor should no longer be borne by the general public. They wanted to remove the problem: 'Collective emigration is, therefore, the removal of a diseased and damaged part of our population. It is a relief to the rest of the population to be rid of this part'.[19] The image of rotting and disease, originally applied to the potatoes during the famine, was now extended to the Highland people themselves. They were perceived as 'useless' and best 'got rid' of in the interest of the 'useful', 'productive' section of society. The *Inverness Courier*, though a great advocate of 'Improvement', did not support forced evictions, clearances and violent attacks to bring about 'an extensive and systematic expatriation of the people', such as were being implemented by Lord Macdonald at Sollas (North Uist) in August 1849.

Not all Highland lairds were as willing as Lord Macdonald to bring in constables from Inverness to impose clearances on the resisting tenantry[20] but all faced the prospect of having to shoulder the burden of relief through the Poor Law system once the immediate relief measures by the Government, and the longer-term help from the Central Board of Destitution, had come to an end. With the price of black cattle slumping, commercial fishing in difficulties and the longer-term effects of blight crippling basic arable farming, a number of the more wealthy landowners were willing to help their tenants emigrate. For example, the Dukes of Argyll and Sutherland, Sir James Matheson, (owner of Lewis) and John Gordon of Cluny, (proprietor of South Uist and Barra), considered this a cheaper option than increasing their Poor Law commitment. As sheep prices were proving quite profitable this seemed the ideal time to implement pasture clearances, with incentives.[21]

There might also be help for some from the Colonial Land and Emigration Commission. Only families with not more than four children qualified. Emigrants had to advance a deposit, provide their own outfits and make their own way to ports but would then be given a free passage to make a new life in the Australian colonies where there was deemed to be an acute labour shortage.[22] It was on record in 1848 that 'a great many from Uist have given in their names, also at Roag and Gairloch'.[23]

However, assisted emigration to escape the destitution was not necessarily approved of. The Gairloch lairds never advocated or supported emigration, either as a response to poverty or the increasing population, and, compared with other parts of the Highlands, the loss of active young families was limited. So, in 1851, Dr John objected vociferously to the conclusions reached by Sir John McNeill when he presented his *Report* to the government.

McNeill had been convinced, even before he undertook his visits to twenty-seven Highland and Island parishes to investigate destitution, that emigration was a valid 'solution' to the problems. He found 'wretched poverty, overcrowding and inertia everywhere, except where the people had been removed and the land returned to its natural possession'.

> If henceforward the population is to depend on the local resources, some fearful calamity will probably occur before many years, unless a portion of the inhabitants of those parishes remove to where they can find the means of subsistence in greater abundance, and with greater certainty, than they can find them where they are now.

The testimony both of Rev. Matheson, the Free Church minister in Gairloch, and of the Parochial Board emphasised this further: 'We are of the opinion that the parish of Gairloch cannot be made self sustaining unless a portion of the inhabitants remove elsewhere. We consider a well-regulated system of emigration as affording the best promise of extrication from the present difficulties'.[24]

Echoing almost exactly the same words, Sir John made a strong case in his *Report* that the poor would be better helped by assisting them to emigrate than by providing charitable relief. Laziness and inherent human weakness were still perceived to be the issues and could be overcome by removing the problem. He endorsed the need 'to afford information, encouragement and assistance to all for whom emigration would be a relief from want and misery'. Dr John was stated to be the 'single exception' to this common attitude. He wrote a strongly worded, twenty-four page *Letter to Lord John Russell on Sir John M'Neill's Report on the State of the West Highlands and Islands of Scotland* to refute these conclusions, based on his experience (and 'misfortune') as chairman or member of ten poor law boards.[25]

As a continuation of the campaign for moral revolution that he and Sir Charles Trevelyan had waged when advising on the immediate famine relief measures McNeill became closely involved in a new organisation, the Highlands and Islands Emigration Society. This developed from the Skye Emigration Society which had been set up, after a meeting in December 1850, to consider 'what remedy should be adopted for bettering the condition of the inhabitants'. Some four hundred heads of families on Skye had indicated that they would be happy to go to Australia, if there were some financial help.[26] Funds collected by the Society would be used to assist those who could not afford the passage.

The H.I.E.S. became a national and imperial body whose committee of management included the Lord Mayor of London, the Governor of the Bank of England, Lord Shaftesbury and many other gentlemen. Lord Charles Trevelyan, now his onerous duties for administering potato famine relief were over, became Chair and Prince Albert was the patron. It was intended to be 'a final measure of relief for the Western Highlands and Islands by transferring the surplus of the population to Australia'.[27] Thousands of Highland poor were helped to leave, once they passed an examination by the Commissioners to determine their 'condition, circumstances and character' to ensure they were deserving cases.[28] Thus:

> They must be sober, industrious and of general good moral character, of all which decisive certificates will be required. They must also be in good health, free from all bodily or mental defects. [...] The candidates most acceptable are young married couples without children. [...] Single women with illegitimate children can in no case be taken. Widowers and widows with young children, persons who intend to buy land [...] or who are in the habitual receipt of parish relief, or who have not been vaccinated or had the small-pox, or whose families comprise more than four children under the age of twelve years cannot be accepted.

Very detailed rules and regulations were laid down. One-third of the cost of passage had to be met by the landowner and would-be emigrants had to guarantee to repay the loan for the remaining two-thirds. They were told what clothes they had to take with them and the amount of space they could take up with their tools.

> FOR MALES: six pair stockings, two pair shoes, two complete suits of exterior clothing
>
> FOR FEMALES: Six Shifts, two Flannel Petticoats, Six Pair stockings, Two Pair Shoes, Two Gowns, with sheets towels and soap. [...] The whole quantity of baggage for each Adult must not measure more than 20 cubic or solid feet, nor exceed half a ton in weight. [...] Mattresses and feather beds will in no case be taken. [...] The Commissioners supply provisions, medical attendants and cooking utensils at their Depot and on board the ship. Also new mattresses, bolsters, blankets, and counterpanes, canvas bags, linen etc knives and forks spoons, metal plates and drinking mugs, which articles will be given after arrival in the colony to the Emigrants who have behaved well on the voyage.[29]

In May 1853 five ships were allocated by the Emigration Commissioners to carry three hundred and twelve people, mainly from Skye, on the first voyage to Melbourne. When the Secretary of the Society, a Mr Haly, went to Glasgow to see the ship leave he was surprised at how few books, hairbrushes, knives and forks the emigrants had. Fortunately there was time to provide Bibles and Psalm books, even in Gaelic.[30] Most of the emigrants got immediate employment on the sheep farms of Australia. Trevelyan had believed that this scheme would be the 'final settlement of the Highland problem'.[31] But in reality only about five thousand people took advantage, not the anticipated thirty to forty thousand. The Society was suspended in 1857.

There were other possibilities of help. As a result of McNeill's 1851 *Report* the government had passed the Emigration Advances Act which gave loans at low interest to proprietors assisting their tenants to leave. Funds from the Drainage Act were diverted, accompanied by the inevitable complaints that state money was being used to fund 'Celtic laziness'. The bankrupt Norman MacLeod, 25th chief of Clan Macleod on Skye, tried to take advantage of this. He had supported eight thousand tenants during the famine years but his own personal destitution eventually forced him to abandon his estate to work for the Home Office at the new Victoria and Albert Museum in London.[32]

To everyone's surprise, journalist Thomas Mulock, scourge of landowners, had changed his views. He had always denounced emigration. However, by 1851, he saw no hope for the crofters of Scotland, be they from Sutherland, North and South Uist, or even from Gairloch. The Gaels must go, to escape for their lives. There was no prospect of the landowners changing their attitudes, they were never going to give land to the people. So, the conclusion of his article on Dr John's attempted reforms had the, from him astounding, recommendation:

> We advise them to think seriously of VOLUNTARY EMIGRATION, renouncing all expectation of having their miseries mitigated by an up-springing of justice and liberality on the part of the proprietors of the soil. *Escape for thy life*, we would solemnly say to every poor Highlander ground down by heartless landlords and fraudulent factors. All the ancestral amenities which bound together the cordial chieftain and his devoted clan are gone – never to return! [. . .] Fly, then, ye poor and needy, from the face of the proprietors who deem you to be nuisances on their possessions, and seek on far distant shores the bare subsistence which is cruelly denied you at home. Yield to the wicked wishes of the arch-designers of desolation, and as they would leave the peasantry without land, leave them a land cursed with the want of cultivating peasantry![33]

Mulock's curse on a land 'with the want of cultivating peasantry' came to pass. One consequence of large-scale emigration had been anticipated when landowners opposed it in the early years of the century, during the wars against Napoleonic France. If all the young men left, where would the doughty footsoldiers of the British Army be found? There had been no conflict requiring recruits for forty years but in 1854 Britain became involved in the Crimean War.

An investigative journalist for the *Northern Ensign*, Donald Ross, had taken up the campaign against tyrannical lairds abandoned by Mulock. He 'tirelessly recorded' cases of abuses and evictions, reporting, for example, on the 'savage butchery' inflicted on Greenyard victims when 'officers and constables handled their batons in breaking the backs and smashing the skulls of defenceless women' in April 1854. Ross, like Mulock, initially opposed emigration of any kind as the solution for either landowner or tenant, though later bitterly accepted that a wise crofter would have to 'leave a country where he is starved and despised'. As early as 1851 he had predicted dire consequences given the shortfall of Highlanders for the army. In December 1854, in an article in the *Northern Ensign* entitled 'Depopulation of the Highlands', he wrote: 'Only a wreck of the population was left behind, the others had been driven across the Atlantic and were now 'feeding the strength of other lands'. There had been up to 30,000 able-bodied Highlanders fit for military service in 1745 whereas now there were not even 3,000 men. Areas which had provided several hundred recruits no longer had 'a single human being in them, but one or two shepherds and a brace of gamekeepers'. By early 1855 it was clear that recruiting attempts in the Highlands had failed. Not only were there not enough men to enlist but even those who were there refused to enrol. How could they be sure that their homes would not be levelled and their families evicted whilst they were away?[34]

Emigration from Gairloch

For all such encouragement to start a new life in the colonies, there is little evidence that many emigrants, assisted or otherwise, left from the Gairloch estates during these blighted years. A letter of 16 March 1849 was sent by a relative of the Malcolm Macdonald who had emigrated to Australia in 1848 to his own son, Hector, also in Australia, commenting that Malcolm and his family were the only ones 'who left this country for that Colony … since you left for Sydney'.[35]

Another letter was written to Malcolm by a cousin, Duncan M'Donald, who was a general merchant at Charlestown, Gairloch. This demonstrated that it was not easy to meet the requirements which would qualify for assistance to leave, and also indicated that the economic imperatives were becoming less compelling.

> 24th October 1853
>
> Dear Cousin,
>
> Your much esteemed letter came to hand a few weeks ago. I was glad to understand that you was well and all your family as this leaves us all here at present which is the best news I can give you from here. We had a pretty good Season here this year good prices for Cattle & Sheep & a good herring fishing and the Potatoes has stood very well this year unless they go in the Pits. They are very plentifull indeed, but after all I do believe that some people would do better in Australia if they would muster the courage to go, but for Angus (Malcolm's brother; ground officer to Mackenzie of Gairloch for many years. […]) I doubt that he is within the regulation of a free Passage and […] I do not think that he could go. They are much stricter now than what they have been when you went. If you have only two children, you will not get away if one is not a girl, and whatever number you have the half must be daughters, and Angus has one of his children that is an object ('a person who is deformed, diseased, imbecile or in some way deserving of pity'– *Scottish National Dictionary*) and that alone would keep him from obtaining a free Passage which I am Sorry for, and to pay his passage would take a large sum of money however you that is making a fortune perhaps would be paid through time. […] You can tell Donald M'Pherson the Smith that his brothers Kenneth

> and Alexr are speaking about going. (Donald had emigrated from Gairloch in 1839 and may have influenced Malcolm to go). The Smith is within the regulation. If he guses to go but no Shoemakers will get away, unless under the capacity of Labourer or Shepherd, the Same as you got yourself altho' a Carpenter. About my going to Australia I cannot say anything about it. It requires a great deal of capital to be in business in Australia and if things turn out to be better at home we may do a little altho' not wonders. I know from experience that it is easier to speak about a fortune than to make one even in Australia, but without talking about fortunes we and plenty in Australia should be content with a comfortable leaving (living??) for ourselves & families and if it at all can be made in the mother country there is of course many comforts both temporal and spiritual that are not to be found with you but I do confess that there are thousands of my fellow countrymen that would do better and leave far more comfortable than they could do here, and they would require it.[36]

Though nine (one family) are known to have left from Loch Carron and thirty-three from the parish of Shieldaig,[37] none chose to depart from Gairloch. Perhaps, despite continuing difficulties, they recognised that they were faring better than many of their fellow Highlanders. Sir Edward Pine Coffin, however, on a return visit to the Highlands in 1852, certainly thought that the condition of the people had worsened since the end of famine relief.[38]

For a short time in the 1850s there was emigration of a different nature. Gold had been found in New South Wales, Australia in 1851. In 1852 news circulated of one Murdo Macgregor from Gairloch and other Highlanders who shared 70lbs of gold between them after less than two months' labour in Australia. The *Inverness Advertiser* on 17 August 1852 reported that the Australian gold rush attracted mainly young, unattached men.[39] But it was soon over.

Dr John's farewell

Though always opposed to emigration overseas as the way to start a new life, Dr John left Loch Ewe in 1856, as his lease expired. He moved himself and his family back east for the next stages of his life. He had resigned his factorship when Kenneth came of age in 1853. No doubt he was a very disappointed man, though not repentant in any way of what he had set out to do. He wrote a farewell letter to the Gairloch tenants:

> Surely your dislike to everything new – which has so sadly hindered, and still hinders, your progress – must soon give way before so many blessings and advantages. [...] As yet you are mere children in farming, and have not the smallest idea of its profit, when skilfully carried on. You often thought me harsh and arbitrary in my plans and rules.[40]

Perhaps Dr John's 'bold attempt' had been unrealistic in its aims and expectations, his standards impossible to achieve, given how different Gairloch was from Flanders. He was self-righteous and unable to get his message across to his tenants in a way they found acceptable. His commitment to abstinence came later but, like his brother Francis, he regarded sobriety as a moral crusade to be imposed on the tenants:

> There is not a single still on the Gairloch estates and Sir Kenneth Mackenzie's tutors will not suffer any individual concerned with smuggling to remain on the property. Since this law of the estate was enforced the small farms have improved rapidly and the cottars, when they view their present comfortable circumstances, compared with their former habits, would on no consideration resume the practice even if the proprietor allowed them.[41]

Ultimately, he did believe that he had made a difference. More land was in cultivation and the housing much improved.

> I let many crofters have the use of my cross short-horn bulls, and I have seen their *year old* stock sold for £5 a head, when £3 was a common price for an average country *milk cow*. [...] And whereas previously to my manoeuvres, no family grew more food than they could *easily* consume, I have seen families selling meal they grew that was more than they needed, and loading ships with potatoes, in Gairloch, from improved crops.[42]

In Inverness he served the community diligently as Provost from 1867–1873. He also returned to his medical roots, becoming Chairman of the Inverness District Asylum and president of the Sanitary Improvement Association. He campaigned tirelessly for a number of causes, including advocating a proper Reformatory School system for delinquent boys, and abstinence. He was rather a late convert to this latter. In about 1860 he recognised that good health was a gift from God so he had no right to endanger it by alcohol,[43] soon becoming President of the Abstainers' Union. Furthermore, he was active in the Free Church.

Amongst all this he continued to defend his farming reforms. Dr John died in December 1886 'at the ripe old age of 83'. He was buried in the family lair at Beauly Priory and his funeral was attended by the 'Provost, magistrates and Town Council'.[44] In 1892 Osgood Mackenzie recalled that Dr Mackenzie was 'a gentleman of a kindly nature, with a good deal of experience of the world'.[45] Dr John would no doubt have been thrilled to find that, in the twentieth century, the need to include gardening instruction and practice in the future crofters' education was at last recognised. The Poolewe School Log Book recorded:

> 10 February 1911: Barrow and garden tools have arrived. Mr. MacDonald gave 2 lectures, to the pupils on Poultry and one in the evening to the pupils and farmers, crofters etc on 'Soils and their treatment'.
>
> 10 May 1911: School supplied with barrow, 3 hoes, 3 spades, 3 graips, 2 rakes and a Dutch hoe in Feby this year for garden etc.
>
> 3 June 1914: Angus Macleod inspected school garden.
>
> 13 July 1917: Gardening class busy weeding and thinning vegetables.

References and Notes

1 *Inverness Courier*, 20 October 1844, summarised in Barron.
2 Mr Poulet Scrope MP, 'Notes on Gairloch', *Inverness Advertiser*, 2 October 1849.
3 *Scottish Highlander*, 24 January 1850.
4 Byam Shaw, pp.268, 250.
5 *Inverness Courier*, 19 September, 26 September 1850, summarised in Barron.
6 Correspondence in the *Inverness Courier*, 28 November 1850.
7 Fenyo, pp.130–135.
8 Scrope, 'Notes on Gairloch'.
9 Evidence included in McNeill's *Report*.
10 Thomas Mulock, *The Western Highlands and Islands of Scotland Socially Considered* (Edinburgh, 1850), p.91 – a pamphlet arguing for liberal aid and support. There is further information on his campaign of opposition in Chapter III.
11 Devine, *The Great Highland Famine*, p.125.
12 Quoted in Byam Shaw, p.274.
13 Evidence included in McNeill's *Report*.
14 Byam Shaw, p.254.

[15] Letter from Dr John Mackenzie to the *Inverness Advertiser*, 5 August 1851.
[16] Devine, *Clanship to Crofters' War*, p.185.
[17] Devine, *Clanship to Crofters' War*, p.147.
[18] Campey, p.160.
[19] From a pamphlet reproduced in *The Scotsman*, quoted in Fenyo, pp.77–78.
[20] Fenyo, pp.78–81.
[21] Devine, *Clanship to Crofters' War*, p.188.
[22] Hunter, p.124.
[23] Devine, *The Great Highland Famine*, using the Macleod of Dunvegan – Skye papers. 2 June 1848, p.204.
[24] McNeill, *Report*.
[25] Byam Shaw, pp.273–274.
[26] From the rules of the *Highland and Island Emigration Society (H.I.E.S)*.
[27] Hunter, p.133.
[28] Prebble, pp.202, 203.
[29] All details from the 'Regulations for the Selection of Emigrants and Conditions which Passages are Granted' of the *H.I.E.S.*
[30] Prebble, pp.204–205.
[31] Devine, *Clanship to Crofters' War*, p.191.
[32] Clan Macleod website, accessed 21 December 2006.
[33] *Northern Ensign*, 10 April 1851. Article entitled 'Gairloch – the failure of a project founded on false principles'.
[34] Fenyo, pp.150–158.
[35] See Chapter II. Hector went to Sydney in 1848 on the *Royal Saxon*, under an Assisted Emigrants scheme. Information from Nancy Booth (descendant) by e-mail, from Australia, June 2009.
[36] Macdonald. Some punctuation modernised but otherwise transcribed as written.
[37] Rodney A.C. Balfour, 'The Highlands and Islands Emigration Society', in *Transactions of the Gaelic Society of Inverness* Vol. LVII, 1990–2, pp.560, 562.
[38] Hunter, p.125.
[39] Devine, *The Great Highland Famine*, p.205.
[40] Dr John's 'Letter to the Gairloch Crofters' (1856). Gairloch Heritage Museum Archives.
[41] *Inverness Courier*, 29 August 1866, summarised in Barron.
[42] Byam Shaw, p.250.
[43] Byam Shaw, p.314.
[44] *Scottish Highlander*, 23 December 1883.
[45] *The Mackenzie Case*, p.45.

House and Home

7. Tigh Dige, the Mackenzie family home at Flowerdale, Gairloch. Painting by Finlay Mackinnon

8. Inveran, a fishing lodge on the shores of Loch Maree and John Dixon's home from 1874 to 1899

9. Inverewe House and Policies, *c.*1877

10. Inverewe Mansion House, *c*.1885

11. Inverewe across the Bay, *c.*1911

12. Inverewe House before the Fire, *c.*1912

13. Tournaig Lodge, built for Osgood's mother, 1878–1879

14. Pool House, Poolewe, another fishing lodge belonging to the Gairloch Mackenzies and Minna Mackenzie's Poolewe base, 1881–*c*.1898

15. Inverewe House on fire, 25 April 1914

16. The ruins of Inverewe Mansion House.

CHAPTER V

The Thirteenth Laird of Gairloch

'Sir Kenneth was far and away the most esteemed man in the county of Ross.'

At the age of 21, in 1853, Kenneth took on the legal responsibilities as laird of his estates. He immediately entered the 'high society' of northern Scotland. In August he attended the Dingwall dinner hosted by Sir James Matheson MP, 'his first public appearance since he attained his majority and he met with a very cordial reception'.[1] He also quickly became a full member of the Northern Society, as his father had been, and was soon one of the organising committee.

In December 1860 he married Eila, the daughter of 'the late Campbell of Islay' and there were great celebrations both at Conan, with bonfires and bagpipes, and on the Gairloch estates, where sixteen bonfires were lit between Poolewe and Gairloch and the Poolewe crofters' houses were decorated with flags.[2] They were to have three children, two boys and a girl. Kenneth's social life extended to London also, where he and his wife spent the 'Season' each year. By the late 1870s the family were only regularly spending about five to six weeks each year at Flowerdale House, from mid-June to mid-August, though they sometimes visited at other times.[3] As with many Highland estates it was increasingly rented out to rich gentlemen for the shooting and fishing rights.

Sir Kenneth, laird, 1853–1900

From the beginning Kenneth demonstrated that he intended to run his West Coast estate in the way he thought best. He was unwilling, or unable, to maintain the momentum of change initiated by his step-mother and uncle. Dr John Mackenzie was not pleased:

> I am sadly disappointed with Gairloch matters, because Frank wisely tried to give his heir a love for rural pursuits, but his son Kenneth has none of his father's wisdom in agriculture, and is quite of the take-it-easy Gairloch or Celtic nature, too soft and good natured for such a job. [...] In 1852, a year before Kenneth came of age, he said to me, 'Uncle, you are too hard on the crofters – you forget that Highlanders may be led but can't be driven'. [...]

> And there was a joyful 'hooray' from Kenneth's troops. The screw taken off! I doubt if one in the hundred of his people ever sowed a turnip or clover seed again, or dreamed of a rotation of cropping, while mine persevered well till I said goodbye to them.[4]

He would also have been saddened that 'the young landlord' was not convinced that his 'natural and happy home, is among his thousands of attached Gairloch tenantry'.[5] Another concern was that Kenneth did not, at first, appoint a Gaelic-speaking factor in order to communicate fully with his crofters, though he did recognise some, if limited improvement after a year or so:

> And very soon, the young laird grew wiser and parting with his ornamental staff, while whisky sent the resident clerk to the church yard, there was at least some appearance of common sense in the Management, and could the laird say 'No' as often as required there might be a ray of hope yet for the people and laird prospering.[6]

As Dr John had anticipated, the crofters were not sorry that the pressure on them to improve was now relaxed. They looked forward to a benevolent laird who would return to the more conventional ways, satisfied with small farms and part-time crofts. One tenant expressed his hopes for the future:

> 24th October 1853
>
> Sir Kenneth is of age now but whether people will be better on that account I cannot say. At this very time about 10 families are turned out of their houses on the open fields which is heard [sic] enough but in justice to him I must say that it is lazy people who will not do anything for paying their Rent, as every country has less or more of these useless people, however things promise to be very hard under Sir Kenneth. However it is to be hoped people will be dealt with more fairly.[7]

Sir Kenneth was fortunate that he came into his majority as the famine years were over and farming was entering a sustained period of growth and higher prices which was to last until the 1880s. Cattle, which had been sold for less than a pound in the late 1840s, were achieving £6–£9 a head in the early 1880s, with three-year-old beasts worth an extra £4–£5. Most crofters were able to say that 'the stirk pays the rent' once again. Sheep were also contributing to increased prosperity: 'the three-year-old wedders most commonly marketed by crofters were usually capable of fetching around 35 shillings apiece'.[8] As well as the ongoing demand for seasonal fishermen there was also the possibility of supplementary work as sporting estates took on local people as stalkers and ghillies.

In 1885 the situation was summarised:

> The principal sources of livelihood of the Gairloch people are their crofts and stock and their fisheries. [...] A number of men have regular engagements, as farm or other servants and gamekeepers; whilst a few carry on trades, as tailors, shoemakers, weavers, boatbuilders, thatchers, dykers, sawyers, carpenters, and masons.
>
> The crops raised by the crofters are almost exclusively oats and potatoes; a little barley and some turnips are also grown. Besides their arable land the crofters have the right of grazing cattle and sheep on specified areas of moorland, or "hill" as it is called. The average stock of each crofter in Gairloch is two or three cows, one stirk, and five to ten sheep; a few horses or ponies are also kept. There are now four hundred and forty-two crofters on the Gairloch estate of Sir Kenneth Mackenzie, who pay an average rent, including a common pasture, of £3 15s 5d, and have on average three and a quarter acres of arable land. [...] Of course, each crofter has a dwelling house, besides byre and barn, mostly very humble structures. The average number of persons residing on each croft is five. The crofters live in communities called townships, and the "hill" is occupied in common by each township; a herd boy is usually employed by the township to herd the cattle and sheep.
>
> Few of the crofters have ploughs; they work their crofts by means of the 'cas-chrom'.[9]

Sir Kenneth was not indifferent to modernisation and some effort continued to be made to change the traditional practices. A pamphlet, *Croft Cultivation by an Old Crofter*, of February 1885, in both English and Gaelic, is believed to have been at his instigation. It stated that 5 acres properly cultivated was sufficient for a family. It endorsed deep pick and spade cultivation, rather than the *cas-chrom*, acknowledged that the hill pastures were generally very poor, recommended liming and manuring the ground, growing rye, comfrey, lucerne, turnips and cabbages for stock and the keeping of poultry. It was critical of poor methods usually used and said that, given proper cultivation, there would be no cry for more land.[10]

The 1880s agitations

After thirty years of relative prosperity the decade of the 1880s was to prove a difficult one for Highland farming. The cause of crofters became a national issue and Gairloch was not immune from the agitation. A radical newspaper, *The Highlander*, published in Inverness, was founded by John Murdoch. It expressed strongly anti-landlord opinions. He had had experience of Ireland, with its not dissimilar agricultural problems – and of the militant activities of the Irish Land League, which demanded a complete change in the law respecting land rights. In 1880 Murdoch was involved in the campaign against intended evictions at Lechmelm, south of Ullapool. He wanted to 'awaken [...] an intelligent and vigorous public spirit and afford opportunity and encouragement to the inhabitants of the Highlands to be heard on their own behalf'.[11]

The opportunities came aplenty. The harvest of 1881 had been poor, crops spoilt by torrential rain in August and September. Blight returned. The East Coast fishing had a disastrous year. Boats were wrecked and gear lost. 1882–1883 saw a bad winter, poor fishing and falling cattle and sheep prices as imports from Australia and New Zealand undercut the European rates. Gladstone's Liberal administration resolutely refused to send in seed oats or potatoes at taxpayers' expense.[12] All this helped to exacerbate the long-standing anger felt by those who believed they had lost land rightfully theirs.

On the not-distant Isle of Skye there had been direct action by the tenants of the Braes, south of Portree, in the form of a rent-strike, because the landowner, Lord Macdonald, had refused to allow them access to their traditional grazing lands. He responded by serving summons of removal. Five hundred crofters seized and burnt the notices in April 1882. The ensuing Battle of the Braes, between crofters (especially their womenfolk) and the sixty Glasgow police reinforcements became a cause célèbre in the crofters' war against perceived arbitrary eviction. When brought to trial in Inverness the leaders of the Braes crofters were penalised only with very low fines. They returned home and drove their cattle back onto the disputed grazings. In the end Lord Macdonald offered to rent it out to them – they thought the price high but agreed and so matters were resolved.[13]

Despite this compromise, unrest spread through and beyond Skye over the next two years. Rent strikes, occupation of sheep farms, destruction of farm fences and buildings, and even mutilation and killing of stock, mirrored the actions of the Irish Land League. Almost all major newspapers took on the story, sympathising with, and promoting, the crofters' cause. In February 1883 the Highland Land Law Reform Association (H.L.L.R.A.) was founded and organised in London. Its membership grew rapidly.

The Napier Commission

The gunboats and marines sent to the Minches could not restore order. The somewhat surprising outcome of the crisis, given the usual Government response to Scottish agricultural unrest, was the setting up of a Royal Commission. Prime Minister Gladstone's Home Secretary, Sir William Harcourt, yachted regularly in the Hebrides and, from his own experience, believed that the crofters had real grievances which should be addressed. So Lord Napier, a Border laird, was charged with investigating the 'condition of the Highlands and Islands of Scotland', in particular the land, fisheries and communications, education, justice, deer forests, game and emigration! Others appointed were the Gaelic enthusiast, Donald Cameron of Lochiel, MP for Inverness Burgh (who had defeated Sir Kenneth Mackenzie in the General Election of 1880[14]), Sheriff Alexander Nicholson from Skye, another Gaelic speaker and a keen mountaineer, and Donald MacKinnon, Professor of Celtic at Edinburgh University. The fifth member of the Commission was 'Our trusty and well-beloved Sir KENNETH SMITH MACKENZIE, Baronet'. A rather unflattering pen-portrait was painted of him at the time in the Glasgow magazine, *Quiz*: 'Sir Kenneth Mackenzie is a half sailor-looking man of dark complexion speaking with the slightest possible suspicion of an aristocratic lisp'.[15]

In the Commission's terms of reference it was explained that

> By the word crofter is usually understood a small tenant of land with or without a lease, who finds in the cultivation and produce of his holding a material portion of his occupation, earnings, and sustenance, and who pays rent directly to the proprietor. The term cottar commonly imports the occupier of a dwelling with or without some small portion of land, whose main subsistence is by the wages of labour, and whose rent, if any, is paid to a tenant and not to the landlord. The crofter is a small farmer who may live partly by the wages of labour; the cottar is a labourer who may have some share in the soil.

But Napier appreciated that 'these definitions are deceptive' and he was willing to be flexible in taking evidence from crofters.[16] He was also well aware that public testimony might make them vulnerable to landowner retaliation and so reluctant to give evidence. He guaranteed that any so doing would not be persecuted or risk eviction. He was conscious of the initial cynicism and determined to give them every opportunity to state their case.[17] The very first session of the Commission was, symbolically, held at Braes in Skye. From the beginning there was considerable uniformity in the witness statements. Alexander Mackenzie and John Murdoch both gave freely of their time in providing 'advice'. Meetings of tenants were organised to elect 'delegates' to state their case. The H.L.L.R.A. produced three pamphlets in Gaelic and English 'highlighting past wrongs and encouraging agitation'.[18] The common themes were that rents were too high given the small acreage of the crofts, that there was no security of tenure and that no compensation was paid for improvements.

When the Napier Commission came to Poolewe in July 1883 Sir Kenneth stood down, so as to ensure no compromising of evidence. His tenants used the occasion to express the common concerns, but added local grievances. These included complaints that sea-ware was taken by farmers and not available, except to buy, to crofters, that they were not allowed dogs or guns and that they had to give sixty days a year labour to the laird. Alex Mackenzie, from Midtown, wished that Sir Kenneth resided more frequently on his west coast estate. Much concern was expressed by several tenants that they were still paying, through their rents, for the trenching and draining of the 1840s, although this ought only to have been for twenty years. Some were careful to avoid personal attack on their current laird. Kenneth Mackenzie, crofter aged 44 of South Erradale, remembered that thirty-six years ago 'the estate was under trustees and perhaps the management was not very good'.

Pressed by the commissioners, many of the crofters had to agree that, relatively speaking, Sir Kenneth was a good landlord who had not evicted any of his tenants, despite their failure to pay full rents for many years. There were other more positive comments: fishing had improved over the last forty years; rents had not been increased since the 1840s; the crofters got free wood for roofs of houses; there were no depredations from deer or game; the estate labour due was very often neither given nor enforced, especially if the crofter worked away part of the year and, though they did pay poor rates, they did not pay road rates. It was even acknowledged that Sir Kenneth was a very kind landlord, as none had been sent away: 'Our present proprietor is a friend of the poor'.[19]

Napier completed his Commission tour later that same year and prepared to write his *Report*. Many had high hopes that he would find solutions to all the problems. Others remained deeply sceptical. In the meantime unrest continued, particularly in the Outer Isles of the Hebrides. On Lewis boulders were put on the landowners' roads and sheep fences pulled down. There was a 'campaign of subversion' and 'agrarian crime'. Renewed troubles on Skye resulted in constables being issued with revolvers and ammunition by the War Office and a gunboat and troopship with three hundred marines arrived in November 1884, together with a civilian steamer, to act as a mobile police station. On one occasion the marines fixed their bayonets to protect the local police. Across the north-west of Scotland there were widespread rent strikes as the market prices for cattle and sheep plummeted. Stirks were lucky to fetch one guinea. Arrears built up. A meeting of more than fifty Highland lairds took place in Inverness in January 1885 to consider lower rents, payment for improvements and some lease arrangements. But it was too late to have much effect. 'We want no concessions. We want our just rights.'[20]

The H.L.L.R.A.

The H.L.L.R.A. was becoming ever more powerful. It set up branches in the Highlands, the first being on Skye, in December 1883, and in 1884 it held its first national conference in Dingwall. The Manifesto demanded security of tenure, compensation for improvements and compulsory land settlements. When a General Election was called for the end of 1885 it was evident that the recently passed Third Reform Act had created an unpredictable electorate of newly-enfranchised agricultural workers. The H.L.L.R.A. made strong recommendations as to which candidates should be supported by them and promised a 'knell of doom for landlordism's long dominance of Highland politics'.[21]

Sir Kenneth Mackenzie of Gairloch stood for election, his second attempt. He had a long record of public service, being Ross and Cromarty's Convenor from the age of 24 (1856), and, like his grandfather, Lord Lieutenant of the County from 1881.[22] Osgood considered him 'far and away the most esteemed man in the county of Ross'[23] but the H.L.L.R.A. and its supporters were not so impressed. In September 1885 the Association held a meeting in Achtercairn Public School (Gairloch) and challenged the claim that Sir Kenneth was 'universally admitted to be one of the best landlords in the Highlands'.[24] The audience was reminded of sessions of the Napier Commission when their landlord 'showed the most determined antagonism to the crofters'. They were told of hill grazings taken without compensation, crofters required to build the new dykes at their own expense and effort and of forced labour to provide the foundations for the Gairloch hotel and a new house for the estate factor. Further, 'there is no district in the Highlands so strictly preserved against trespassers'. Most damaging of all were reports of evictions that Sir Kenneth had allegedly carried out. The crofters were urged to return to Parliament 'men that would look after their interests, and not landlords who had kept them in the chains of slavery for so long. [...] The meeting, which was most enthusiastic throughout, broke up with ringing cheers for Dr Macdonald, the crofters' candidate'.[25]

The campaign against the laird was very public and the *Scottish Highlander* used every opportunity to support the anti-landlord party. On 6 November it published a letter to the Editor, referring to many instances of 'petty tyranny', such as the taking of hill-grazings and the labour required for roads and restrictions on the access to the hills. The question was raised as to why Sir Kenneth had chosen to be the candidate for Inverness rather than his own county of Ross-shire. In the same edition there was a second, much stronger, letter from 'An Old Gairloch Crofter' which added to the accusations by citing not only a number of evictions, including that of a man who had a very sick wife, but detailing how, in enforcing these evictions, the 'houses of some of them were burnt over their heads'. 'I will tell you of more of them if you want it, and about killing the dogs, and hundreds of them too'.

On 20 November the *Scottish Highlander* carried 'Another letter from An Old Gairloch Crofter' repeating the previous allegations, rebutting Sir Kenneth's refutation of the incidents, and quoting further examples 'long before he had management of the estate'. It was also claimed that it was cheaper for Sir Kenneth to allow a widow to have a half croft than to pay for her and her children on the Poor Roll, so this was not an example of the laird's benevolence at all. On 2 December the newspaper published, with evident hostility, the conditions of the Gairloch estate tenancies, under the heading 'The Immaculate Whig Candidate'. The crofters would be evicted, for example, if they broke the rules 'not to carry a gun or keep a dog without permission, nor to commit any act that will injure the proprietor's right in either game or fishing. The government licence to keep a dog or gun was here to be of no account, and when the dogs were kept they were brutally and unceremoniously shot in hundreds on repeated occasions, on the whole of the Gairloch property'. The previous attacking letters were re-printed 'for information'.

Though there were many who thought that 'Sir Kenneth was peculiarly well fitted to represent a Highland constituency in Parliament and there was a strong desire to see him in the House of Commons', once again he failed to win election, the 'circumstances proved unfavourable'.[26] In four of the five crofting constituencies H.L.L.R.A. candidates, the 'Crofters' Party', rather than the traditional tory or whig lairds, won the seat after well-organised campaigns. It could claim to be the first mass-membership political party and social movement.[27]

Shortly after the election the Crofter's Holdings (Scotland) Act was passed. This was based on the work of the Napier Commission, though Prime Minister Gladstone went further than the *Report* had recommended. For example, all crofters were to be given better protection against eviction and not just those who possessed holdings paying between six and thirty pounds rent per annum. 'It was a radical change from the kind of assumptions which had governed external intervention in the Highlands during the famine years of the 1840s and 1850s'. It gave security of tenure as long as the rent was paid; 'fair rents' to be adjudicated by a land court; compensation for improvements to the croft and the right for a crofter to pass his land on to a relation (though not to be sold). The Scottish crofters were deemed to be a social group which had been treated badly in the past and now was being treated as a special case. Landowners believed that a dangerous precedent had been set and their property rights had been undermined. Radicals thought that the new law did not go nearly far enough as crofters still had no right to buy their land.

The arguments continued on the remote West Coast. Three Crofting Commissioners had been appointed, one of whom was, as required, Gaelic speaking. They spent the next three years touring the Highlands as a rent-tribunal. A meeting was organised in March 1888 prior to their scheduled visit to Gairloch. John Dixon gave an address at a 'largely attended meeting, convened by the Secretaries of the Gairloch Branch of the Highland Land League'. He advocated that the crofting people be most careful always to act within the law. He reminded them that they now had the vote and could send whoever they pleased to parliament to represent their views and reform the laws. He wanted landowners, 'regarded with some contempt by land leaguers', and their opponents to meet and discuss their differences. He believed that if 'the Game laws could be abolished and the shooting tenants driven from the Highlands, the burden on the rate-payers would be intolerable. The relief of the poor and the education of children would be paralysed. Grouse shootings were a valuable property if duly preserved. [. . .] He trusted the Gairloch League would not initiate the first conflict with the proprietors by giving their sanction to poaching'. Not surprisingly 'discussion followed' before 'the meeting closed with the usual votes of thanks'.[28]

On 16 and 17 April the Commissioners reviewed the rents of the Gairloch estate. Alexander Mackenzie, reporter of the radical *Scottish Highlander*, represented the crofters as they could not afford their own agent. The old complaints were revived and it was claimed that Sir Kenneth was being allowed to dictate the issues considered, with the tenants' views being ignored and dismissed because they were critical of their landlord. The newspaper did though comment that 'the interest in the proceedings did not appear to be very great, the attendance during the day, as compared with other districts visited by the Commission, being rather small'.[29]

The H.L.L.R.A. continued to make Sir Kenneth's political life difficult. In the late 1880s he found himself challenged for his county council seat, and his reputation. He may have been Convener for many years but the League organised a targeted and strong campaign against him on behalf of their candidate, John Ross. At one meeting of the Gairloch electors, in December 1889, Sir Kenneth found that his opponent, with supporters, had arrived to heckle. Provocative questions were raised, for example about Sir Kenneth's advocating that Aultbea, rather than Gairloch, be the terminus for the railway that was being planned. The experienced Sir Kenneth appears to have responded in very measured terms.[30] The following month John Ross wrote a letter to the *Scottish Highlander* suggesting that the laird was using his factor to canvass and intimidate the crofters and promising them transport to help them get to the poll. Reference was made to 'frail and infirm old women' and illiterate crofters being anxious that it would be known how they had cast their votes.[31] On this occasion, despite the energetic campaign against him, Sir Kenneth successfully retained his seat.

Evictions and clearances

Whilst evictions were relatively isolated incidents on Sir Kenneth's lands, they were more relentless and widespread elsewhere in the area during his lairdship. Through the 1850s and 1860s Meyrick Bankes continued to remove tenants on his Letterewe estate. For example, in the Aultbea and Drumchork area, adjoining Osgood Mackenzie's own Tournaig lands, Bankes 'extracted writs' against:

11.4.1854 Mrs Peggy or Margaret MacKay or MacIver and John MacIver both at Aultbea tenants or pretended tenants of a croft at Aultbea together with the mill at Aultbea

25.4.1862 Removal of Donald Munro, Innkeeper at Aultbea

22.4.1864 Removal of [...] Roderick MacKenzie (Gough) residing at the School House, Aultbea; Alexander MacIver at Slaggan

13.9.1865 [...] Murdo MacAulay [...] son of the deceased Donald MacAulay sometime residing at and Tenant of the Farm and Lands of Drumchork, as Executor of the said deceased Donald MacAulay – to pay £13/15/8d in interest and other expenses on half year's rent of the Farm and Lands of Drumchork, owed by the late Donald MacAulay.[32]

The evictions of 1860 had brought the press out in force in support of the crofters as Meyrick Bankes concentrated once again on the Gruinard and Coast areas. *The Inverness Advertiser*, (19, 23, 30 October and 9 November), *John O'Groat Journal* and the *Invergordon Times* (25 November) all came out in unrelenting attack when, in October 1860, Bankes sent in law agents to evict tenants just as they were about to harvest their oats. He had given due notice of evictions but had then failed to act so the crofters had gone ahead with their usual plantings. For the first time here the crofters resisted and refused to leave their land. Yes, they had planted their crops –

> But their error was venial compared with that of the landlord, who allowed them to sow their land, and then, with all the aggravation that could possibly be heaped upon their misery, turns them out of house and home, and out of the means of subsistence, just as their crops are ready to be gathered in. [...] Need we wonder that the poor creatures resisted. [...] A week or two ago a second attempt was made, and six of the Ross-shire police, headed by the chief constable, were despatched to do the despicable work – all the more despicable that it was not done at the proper time, before the crops were put in – and the policemen met with no better success than the lawyer. One of them, on what provocation we are not informed, struck an old woman with his baton, and this became the signal for a regular battle. [...] The police were driven from the field. It is now reported that, by order of the higher legal authorities, 100 men of the Ross-shire militia are on their way to Gruinaird to enforce the summons. [...] It may be of some satisfaction to the unfortunate people at Gruinaird who are threatened to be turned out amongst the wintry mountains of Gairloch that their case is beginning to attract the attentions of those who are able to do them not immaterial service. [...] The fact remains that not one of the poor people is due Mr Bankes a single penny of legitimate rent.[33]

In the end they were able to stay the winter, but the reprieve was short-lived:

> Under certain circumstances it is illegal to evict tenants more than six weeks after Whitsunday. He would not wish to be found in breach of the law when he was using the law for his own purposes. By the next spring he was able to state that they were in arrears with the rent, as he was charging interest on rents not paid in advance.

Meyrick Bankes seems to have been oblivious to public condemnation. One infamous case was that of Isabella Mackenzie or Gunn, a widow, removed from Drumchork in 1862, then again in 1871 from the cave at Sand to which she moved with her daughter and granddaughter, just nine months old. The 1881 Census suggested she was then living in Achgarve but she lost that home also when the croft was split up. It seems probable that she ended her days as a pauper in Dingwall.

Bankes had to use the more legitimate reasons for eviction – money owing – against his own factor, William Tattersall, who evidently appropriated for his own benefit the rent money he had collected. The Extracts from Decreets included:

> 12.6.1874 Meyrick Bankes Esq. of Letterewe and Gruinard, residing at Letterewe against William Tattersall sometime Factor residing at Laide House and present residing at Dingwall – to pay £1,691/7/8. being the sum appearing due to 16th April 1872 [...] rents [...] belonging to the Pursuer. [...]
>
> 12.6.1874 Meyrick Bankes against William Tattersall [...] to pay £2000 held to be the balance due to the Pursuer, [...] as Factor or Agent to or under the Pursuer, with the rents and others on the Estates of Letterewe and Gruinard belonging to the pursuer and under the manager of the Defender, for the period from 16th April 1872 to 26th May 1874, with the interest thereon at the rate of £5 per centum per annum.[34]

Bankes' successors maintained the same policies. Crofters at Drumchork were evicted to enlarge the sheep farm when a new lodge was built in 1881 (the current Drumchork Hotel). Yet none of this seemed to have had any impact on his neighbour, Osgood Mackenzie. He never used the 'eviction' publicity as a stick with which to beat Meyrick Bankes when in dispute over fishing rights.[35]

Another highly publicised clearance took place within the Wester Ross area on the Lechmelm estates, Loch Broom. In 1879, the new landowner, Mr Pirie, a paper-manufacturer from Aberdeen, gave notice to all his tenants (twenty-three families) that they were to hand over to him all their stock and stop growing crops and grazing ('trespassing') upon the enclosures and hills for which they were paying rent of £3–£12 each per annum. At Martinmas in 1880 he took over every inch of land, arable and pastoral. So, although all but three tenants kept their cottages, they could not sustain themselves, except as cottars or day-labourers. They were not even allowed to keep a hen. These actions were roundly condemned by the Press (except *The Scotsman*) and people had to resort to the Parish. In December 1880 a public meeting about their plight was held in Inverness, organised by Rev. John MacMillan, the Free Church Minister of the parish. Although nothing could be done the outcry contributed to the development of the Land Reform movement throughout the Highlands.[36]

These evictions were related to Mr Pirie's decision to establish about five thousand acres of the higher land at Lechmelm as deer forest.[37] The general move to sheep farming had consistently proved disappointingly unprofitable. Many landowners were persuaded that letting their shooting rights might well bring them a better return. This was not a new idea. Some deer forests were developed locally in the first half of the nineteenth century. Kinlochewe forest was formed in 1842 and part of Flowerdale became forest in 1847.[38] During Kenneth's minority, the Gairloch land was rented out for shooting quite regularly.

The creation of deer forests to replace sheep runs had been given considerable impetus by the 1880s when the advent of steam shipping and refrigeration meant shiploads of frozen carcases could be brought from the New World. The wool imported from Australian sheep was also considered better value than that from the Cheviots. The impact on the local crofters varied from estate to estate.

> On a few occasions crofters were actually evicted to make way for deer forests and, although these evictions were not as numerous as some contemporary critics claimed, they helped to foster antagonism between crofters and sportsmen. This was reinforced by the more frequently adopted measure of appropriating common grazing to create or extend the forests. Deer not only required land for sanctuaries but they also attacked crops on neighbouring arable lands.[39]

Osgood Mackenzie gave testimony to the Napier Commission in 1883 acknowledging that both the Mackenzie lairds and he had deliberately established deer forests to let to wealthy sportsmen, as it brought a welcome addition to the estate income. Further common grazing was taken over in the 1880s at Flowerdale but Sir Kenneth at least made sure there were fences to prevent deer encroachment on the local crofts.[40]

Another area of enquiry by the Napier Commission had been that of emigration. With more settled and prosperous times in farming there had been a lull in the pressure to leave the Highlands for economic reasons. However, the attraction of emigration as a solution to poverty re-emerged when farming went into decline again in the early 1880s. Osgood Mackenzie, who had no crofters of his own, gave his evidence:

Q Can it be considered that the present position of the crofters in this parish, apart from the earnings they make in the south, is satisfactory?

A No, I don't think so. We are always liable to poverty.

A Can you suggest any remedy?

A I should suggest that they should be encouraged to emigrate, and that fishing villages should be made. [Melvaig and Laid being suggested as possible locations].[41]

Kenneth and Osgood

Such evidence showed considerable differences of attitude between Osgood and Kenneth. But the difference in views here was to be nothing when compared with their estrangement, at much the same time, as relations between Osgood and his wife broke down completely. Earlier camaraderie was illustrated in a letter fragment written by Osgood, probably in 1878, from Otterspool near Liverpool, his wife's family home. He was responding to a query over a story dating back to the 1780s concerning local methods of recruitment for the British army. Lilias, wife of 'William of Gruinord' and sister of John Mackenzie of Lochend, was notorious for the method she used to 'press' young men into the army so that her son could obtain a commission. The story further went on to say that no one ever prospered in Aird House (Lilias' home) from that day on. Osgood commented: 'This latter part had better be left out for fear of giving offence to old Bankes!" and was signed 'Your affect brother'.[42]

In proceedings in the divorce courts during the 1890s Kenneth and his wife, Lady Eila, consistently undermined Osgood's testimony.[43] There is no evidence that good relations had been re-established by the time Kenneth died, unexpectedly, of acute pneumonia, at Conan House on Friday, 9 February 1900, aged 67. The previous Sunday he had been 'in usual health and attended service in the Free Church of Maryburgh'. His funeral took place from Conan to the family's traditional burial ground at Beauly Priory. Osgood was one of the six hundred or more mourners, from all levels and interests of society, including representatives from the County Farmer's Club and the Institute for the Blind. There were 'no flowers at his special wish'.[44] His obituary recorded that the 'County of Ross had been deprived of its most distinguished and capable and its most trusted public man'. The many tributes to him after his death referred not just to his roles in public life but also to his concern for ordinary people, his humanity. He 'maintained his high position with dignity' yet was 'most humble and approachable'. His generosity as a laird extended to allowing the widow of a deceased tenant to stay in the croft rent free until another family member attained his majority. As captain of the militia he had 'attended to the wants and comforts of his men and his Company adored him'.[45] A memorial subscription fund was set up in his memory, which resulted in the building of two nurses' homes, one in Conan, his Easter Ross home, and the other in Poolewe on the West coast.

Rather bizarrely, his widow commissioned a portrait to be painted of him using his corpse as the model. The result was, apparently, 'life-like' and was given to the County Council to hang in their Dingwall building. It was presented by his eldest son, also Sir Kenneth. The letter he read from his mother emphasised how her husband had served, presiding over the County meetings for forty-four years, 'sparing neither time nor trouble, nor personal inconvenience in his endeavour to promote the public good'. Though they had not been reconciled at the time of his death, Osgood also did not stint, towards the end of his own days, to praise his half-brother who was 'at the head of everything that was good'.[46]

References and Notes

1 *The Inverness Courier*, 4 August 1853, summarised in Barron.

2 *Inverness Advertiser*, 18 December 1860.

3 *The Mackenzie Case*, p.272.

4 Byam Shaw, p.258.

[5] Dr John's 'Letter to the Gairloch Crofters' (1856). Gairloch Heritage Museum Archives.

[6] From the manuscript diaries of Dr John Mackenzie, Vol. VI, p.509. Conan House Archives, kindly lent by John Mackenzie.

[7] A letter written to Malcolm by a cousin, Duncan M'Donald, a general merchant at Charlestown, Gairloch quoted in Macdonald.

[8] Hunter, p.159.

[9] Dixon, pp.132, 138.

[10] Pamphlet 'Croft Cultivation by an Old Crofter', published by R. Carruthers and Sons, Inverness, 1885. Gairloch Heritage Museum Archives.

[11] Hunter, p.186.

[12] Hunter, p.188.

[13] Hunter, p.198.

[14] Kenneth had stood for election as a Liberal. The county had been solidly Tory since 1837. He lost by just 29 votes to the 'reformer' Lochiel.

[15] Stated in MacPhail, *The Napier Commission*, p.404.

[16] *The Napier Report into the Conditions of the Crofters and Cottars in the Highlands and Islands of Scotland*, 1884.

[17] Hunter, pp.202–203.

[18] Devine, *Clanship to Crofters' War*, pp.225–226.

[19] Evidence to the Napier Commission, Poolewe, 31 July 1883.

[20] Hunter, p.214.

[21] Hunter, p.207.

[22] Sir Kenneth remained Chairman of the Commissioners of Supply and Convener of the County for forty-four years until his death in 1900, and was Lord Lieutenant until 1899. His obituary in the *Inverness Courier*, 13 February 1900, recognised that 'his knowledge of county business has rarely been equalled even by the most skilful officials, and his sound judgement and advice, quietly but clearly given, influenced many an important decision. [...] To attempt to give an account of Sir Kenneth Mackenzie's career would be to write a history of most of the public movements in the North of Scotland during his lifetime'.

[23] Mackenzie, p.58.

[24] Dixon, p.58.

[25] *Scottish Highlander*, 18 September 1885.

[26] Sir Kenneth Mackenzie's obituary in the *Inverness Courier*, 13 February 1900.

[27] Hunter, p.215.

[28] *Inverness Courier*, 23 March 1888. Report on a meeting of the Gairloch Highland Land League.

[29] *Scottish Highlander*, 19 April 1888.
[30] *Scottish Highlander*, 12 December 1889.
[31] *Scottish Highlander*, 23 January 1890.
[32] MacRobbie, pp.46–49.
[33] *Inverness Advertiser,* taken from the *John O'Groat Journal,* 9 November 1860.
[34] MacRobbie, pp.45, 33–34, 51.
[35] See Chapter VII for details of this legal case over the Dubh Loch.
[36] Alexander Mackenzie, *History of the Highland Clearances* (Inverness: A. & W. Mackenzie, 1883. Re-printed Melven Press, 1986), pp.314–326.
[37] Willie Orr, *Deer Forests, Landlords and Crofters* (Edinburgh: John Donald, 1982), pp.60–61.
[38] Orr, appendix v Chronology of Forest Development, p.169.
[39] Orr, p.5.
[40] Orr, pp.119, 133.
[41] Osgood Henry (sic) Mackenzie's evidence to the Napier Commission, Poolewe, 31 July 1883. Paragraphs 29394–29397.
[42] Letter in Inverewe House Archive.
[43] See Chapter VI.
[44] *Inverness Courier*, 13 February 1900.
[45] *Inverness Courier*, 3 May 1901.
[46] Mackenzie, p.58.

CHAPTER VI

'A Painful Case'

'Mr Mackenzie was constantly saying that a wife must be submissive and obedient to her husband.'

On Tuesday 17 May 1892, with Lord Wellwood presiding, a petition was started in the Court of Sessions. Osgood H. Mackenzie of Inverewe was requesting that he be granted a divorce, on the grounds of her wilful and malicious desertion, from his wife, Minna Amy Edwards Moss, or Mackenzie, of Pool(e) House. The case was defended. At the time Osgood was fifty and Minna aged thirty-nine. There was one daughter.

It is through the testimonies of witnesses at, and the newspaper accounts of, this divorce case, which Osgood lost, and reports of the two appeals against this decision, to the Court of Sessions, Second Division in 1893 and the House of Lords in 1895, that the sorry story of his short-lived marriage unfolds.[1] Though what actually took place was rarely disputed, the attitudes, emotions and intentions expressed demonstrated all too clearly why the breakdown was so speedy and so bitter. Witnesses on Osgood's behalf were his mother, his half-brother Francis and a number of Inverewe and Tournaig servants. Minna had the support of her family and servants, doctors and, perhaps surprisingly, Osgood's half-brother Kenneth and his wife, as well as Osgood's erstwhile friend, John H. Dixon.

Courtship and marriage settlement

It was claimed in court that, by the mid-1870s, the Dowager Lady Mary had decided that it was more than time that Osgood, now in his thirties, found himself a wife. Allegedly, lists had been compiled of young ladies who might be suitable, though whether Minna was included was never clear. The matter of money, which played a big part in the relationship problems, was said to have been significant from the very beginning. According to Minna's divorce counsel, the Dean of Faculty: 'At least £5,000 down. These were his sailing orders from his mother. He was in the market looking for a wife with money'.

The couple had first been introduced in the autumn of 1874 when both were guests of Sir Patrick Grant at Moniack, near Inverness. Then, in the winter of 1875, Osgood met Minna, by chance it seems, on the road between Gairloch and Shieldaig and accompanied her home. She was staying with her family at Flowerdale, which her father had rented for the shooting season. She much impressed Osgood by expressing a wish to live in the Highlands, even during the winter. Her family home was at Otterspool, four miles along the Mersey from Liverpool, 'with fresh winds from the Welsh mountains'. Her father, Sir Thomas Edwards Moss, was a very wealthy businessman who had been made a baronet in 1868. Her mother, Amy Charlotte, was the only daughter and heiress of Richard Edwards of Roby Hall, Lancashire.[2] Minna had two brothers, John and Tom Cottingham (Cottie) and a younger sister, Ethel.

In February 1876 Osgood called on Minna several times whilst both were in London and he informed her father how he felt about her. Initially she turned down his offer of marriage, one reason being that she would not live in a family where the mother-in-law was part of the household. He renewed his suit the following year and on a day's outing to Aldershot, in early May 1877, asked her again. This time Minna accepted. Osgood was thirty-five and Minna twenty-four years old.

Osgood always maintained that he married for love and not for money: 'At that time he knew nothing of Miss Moss's expectations. He knew that Sir Thomas was well off but he had no motive for marrying her except his love for her'. But no doubt the £20,000 Minna's father put on the marriage settlement was very welcome to him. She was to have £370 per annum as her personal income, the interest on £10,000. The second tranche would be paid on the death of her parents. There were several suggestions in court that Osgood was disappointed with the outcome of the marriage contract and had hoped for much more. 'He rather gave me to understand that he had rather been a sort of victim of deception', according to Sir Kenneth. This was denied, though Osgood thought 'her father had been stiff' in insisting that he put down £20,000 of his own. It was also considered that he might have exaggerated his own wealth. He disputed this. From his mother he was to receive £600 each year, (of her £900 widow's income), as well as ownership of the Inverewe estate which, bought for £15,000, was, according to Osgood, valued at £70,000 by 1892. Minna commented in court:

> I asked him if he had married me for the money, and he said he would not have married me without it. He said he hoped more money would come. These things, said within two or three days of the marriage, took away all the happiness off my life.

The question of where his mother should live was a moot point from the very start. The Dowager assumed that she would continue to live with her son, at Inverewe. She had, after all, built the house at her own expense. It was, however, agreed, at the insistence both of Minna's father and Sir Kenneth, that she would move out. Dr John wrote a letter in August 1877 clearly, and prophetically, aware of the risks if she were to stay:

> He and his mother have till now been one person, and without his meaning or knowing it, if his mother lives within ten miles, say, of Inverewe, we know that dear Minna will come ere long to be almost third instead of first partner in the concern. There are women (semi-women?) who could endure this, and vegetate through life, but I can't and won't picture Minna as one of them, and if my fears are correct, such an arrangement involves certain sorrow for all concerned where there ought to be nothing but peace and happiness.

In court Osgood stated that this had not been a problem for him at all: 'He thought it not right himself. They were quite unanimous about it. It was quite clear to them all that it would be a very grave matrimonial risk'. He said that his mother was quite amenable to doing whatever he wanted. She had given her son a letter: 'I would live with you, or entirely away, or during the dull time of the year, just any plan that would seem best to please others. If I saw you thoroughly happy I never could be really unhappy'.

The first months of married life

The marriage took place, without delay, on 26 June 1877 at All Saints Church, Ennismore Gardens, the church being close to the Edwards-Moss London residence. The Right Rev. the Bishop of Guiana officiated, together with the Rev. Edmund Warre.[3] Presents were bought for the bridesmaids. Minna's parents and brothers and Osgood's brothers attended, though his mother was 'too ill to go'. The couple first went to stay at Otterspool (her parents were away), then spent a week in Ireland and then returned to Otterspool for another fortnight or so. Osgood claimed that there were very agreeable relations during the honeymoon but Minna saw things differently. She testified that 'during the honeymoon he was not very attentive to me. He seemed to like to go out by himself a great deal and leave me alone. [...] I don't think he treated me as a bridegroom would treat a bride'.

Just two days after the wedding Osgood's will arrived in the post, drafted in his mother's handwriting because, he claimed, his was so poor. He recalled that he had discussed with Minna whether or not, in the event of his death, she would wish to have Inverewe, and hope to raise income from it, or rather have a cash settlement of £800. He said she preferred the latter. So he left his property firstly to his mother and then to a cousin.

After the honeymoon the couple returned to Scotland, staying at Dr John's house at Eileanach, Inverness for two or three days. Once again Minna complained that 'my husband left me a good deal to myself. [...] I did not know where he was or what he was doing'. On their last day there she requested that they go out together. He refused, requiring her to do his packing. They took the train from Inverness to Achnasheen, then drove by dog-cart to the Loch Maree Hotel, where Osgood was re-united briefly with his mother. She had moved out of Inverewe, at Kenneth's insistence, just before the couple returned and was staying with her second stepson, Frank (Francis), at Kerrysdale. The newly-weds completed the journey to Inverewe by boat across the loch to Inveran. From there it was but a short drive to the House.

Minna said she felt uncomfortable in her new home from the very beginning. On the first evening she went to sit on a particular chair in the dining room only to be told by Osgood that she had chosen the dogs'. He justified this in court by saying he did not want her to get dirty. Minna, he added, always felt anxious about his long-haired terriers. 'She thought they were told to snap at her, [...] she was very nervous about dog bites', apparently because a relative had died of hydrophobia following an attack by a rabid dog. Minna had made her feelings clear:

> I have hinted and even spoken seriously to you about my dislike to dogs, more especially small ones, and still you persisted in having three in the drawing-room, until having been flown at, I positively refused to sit in the same room with one, and even then no steps were taken to keep it entirely out of the house.

On the first Sunday of their return, 29 July, Minna went over to Flowerdale to meet the Mackenzie family. They were all to go to the two o'clock 'English' service at the Free Church in Gairloch. Osgood had left his bride at Tigh Dige to collect his mother, still at Kerrysdale, and accompanied her into the church by a side door leading to the family's private pew. Minna went in with Sir Kenneth: 'She thought it strange that her husband took no notice of her but walked on ahead with his mother'. Osgood 'found out later that she had taken offence'. Minna said in court that the Dowager Lady was cold to her and did not give her any welcome. Sir Kenneth corroborated this: 'The Dowager Lady Mackenzie showed no cordiality towards the young wife, was in fact barely courteous towards her and rather took possession'. His wife went further. She considered the attitude of the mother-in-law to be 'forbidding towards Minna', and 'barely civil'. 'The reception was not such as a daughter-in-law was entitled to expect. [...] The pursuer took no notice of his wife and his manner was not that of an affectionate husband, newly married, appearing the first time in the church of the locality and bringing his wife for the first time to his family'.

Osgood's mother then came to Inverewe from Gairloch, 'by invitation', to see the wedding gifts, staying 'no more than three days'. John H. Dixon, their nearest neighbour and friend, came over.[4] He was most concerned:

> I think the first occasion on which I saw the pursuer and defender together was within a day or two of their coming to Inverewe in 1877, when I lunched with them. The party consisted of pursuer, defender, the Dowager Lady Mackenzie and myself. I was rendered exceedingly uncomfortable by the position of affairs. The ladies scarcely spoke at all, and any conversation was carried on mostly by the pursuer. It struck me that this was a very bad beginning. [...] It struck me that the mother-in-law was [...] sitting upon the wife, and that the husband was not taking the wife's part.

Soon after, in early August, Minna's parents arrived, to stay rather than just visit, their yacht apparently having sunk on the coast. They remained until they went to the Northern Meeting about 20 September. The unresolved matter of where the Dowager Lady Mary was to live was raised as a priority by Minna's father. Notwithstanding the pre-marriage assurances, it became evident very soon that both the Dowager and her son were 'desirous of breaking or evading the condition'. Though she 'was engaged for several weeks before the wedding in getting my things collected and packed up for the purpose of removing them' she did not see this as anything but a temporary accommodation. As she wrote in a letter of 13 November 1880, 'no circumstances will ever induce me to give up residing on this property, which I purchased in 1863 as a permanent residence for my son, and a home for myself'. In court the Dowager Lady said 'she did not expect she would be kept to her word', (that she should go to live elsewhere), given how miserable she was not to be living at Inverewe with her son. Being required to keep the promise had the 'effect of kindling very deep resentment in the mind of the Dowager towards the defendant' but Osgood was never prepared to press his wife's case for their exclusive use of the marital home. Suggestions that Lady Mary move into Dr Black's house at Moss Bank in Poolewe, or Inveran, Dixon's home, were rejected as unsuitable, both being too small, (for Osgood's liking), and too close (for Minna and her father). Minna assumed, at the very least, that Lady Mary would be going well away from Inverewe. Sir Thomas Moss anticipated it would be Inverness. They were both wrong. 'Ultimately it was arranged that a house should be built for his mother at Tournay (sic) a mile and a half from Inverewe. Sir Thomas lent £1,500 to build the house at 4%'. Tournaig, so close along the road, was part of the Inverewe estate, with farmhouse and cottages already established there. The loan was repaid.

Osgood and Minna also went to the Northern Meeting. He had been a member of the Society since 1875. They attended the balls, though again she felt 'he did not take such notice of me as I would have expected', then returned to Inverewe for a few days before setting out on a round of visits to the gentry of the area. Sir John Fowler at Braemore was the first of these.[5] Osgood still paid little attention to his wife. In particular, his insistence that they return home to Inverewe, as his mother was expecting them back, though 'the day on which we left was a very wild day indeed and it was not a suitable day for travelling', aroused much comment amongst their hosts. In the event they were not able to complete the journey. The Vaughan Lees at Dundonnell attempted to offer them respite but Osgood pressed on 'in a hired dogcart with one horse. The weather was frightful. It got worse and worse'. When the Gruinard River proved impassable they were forced to stay the night with David Murray, proprietor of Gruinard House. He gave evidence in court:

> During the course of the evening Mr Mackenzie seemed to me to utterly ignore his wife. He never spoke to her. He did not indicate any anxiety to know how she had been affected by exposure to the storm. His demeanour to his wife was the subject of conversation amongst my friends in the smoking room that evening after he had retired.

Although it was still considered unsafe to cross the river, Osgood insisted on continuing the journey the next day. The luggage was put on a 'manure cart', with Minna forced to walk on the very rough track, battling against rain and sleet. Mr Murray added: 'It did not appear to me that Mr Mackenzie's conduct on those two days displayed any ordinary regard for the health or safety of his wife'.

Their next round of visits was to the Torridon area during which time Osgood left his wife to walk over to Gairloch to see his mother for 'several days'. The strong bond between mother and son caused another rift when, soon after arriving at Inverewe, Minna found letters she had written to her husband open in a drawer, together with, in his mother's handwriting, a draft of a letter renewing his suit to her. Osgood acknowledged that he had often shown Minna's letters to his mother.

Whilst her parents were staying Minna had seemed more cheerful, though her mother's maid, Annie Plumridge, did recall her 'sad countenance, so very different from what I had ever seen before'. Once alone together Osgood claimed that Minna 'got very dull, took no interest in country affairs and did not give him that welcome on his return that he expected from his young wife'. By October, having only actually stayed at Inverewe a few weeks, Minna was intent on going south, to her parents, for the winter. Osgood agreed, on condition that his mother looked after both house and farm in his absence, as she had done, on occasion, before his marriage. They left very soon after a visit to the local school in Poolewe on 30 November, Minna's only recorded visit there: 'Tuesday had a visit from Mr and Mrs Mackenzie of Inverewe. Mr Mackenzie examined a class on Geography and appeared well pleased with the answers given'.[6]

So Lady Mary moved back in. Osgood considered that having his mother manage the household, rather than his wife, would be worth £200 to him. Certainly he was confident that his mother could deal with his affairs, even though she had been ill and 'nervous' in the preceding weeks to the extent that she had had to come to stay at Inverewe. Minna was sceptical of such health concerns: 'I was told she was nervous, but she could walk great distances'. One day her husband took his mother to the doctor in Gairloch. His wife 'was very cold on his return and they had no lunch that day'. The couple went to Otterspool together, spending Christmas with the Moss family, though Osgood returned to Inverewe, alone, for two to three weeks during the course of the winter, ostensibly to check on his sheep.

Money and household management

The Mackenzies' stay in England was prolonged and they did not return to Inverewe until July 1878. But, even away from the presence of the Dowager, relations between them continued to deteriorate. One issue that became a never-ending source of complaint was Minna's expenditures. When staying with Dr John, on their return from honeymoon, Osgood had made a special point of instructing her not to accept offers of help from his uncle's servants.

'Do not employ the servants here, they require tipping, and there is nothing so expensive as tipping servants'.

The maid, Annie Plumridge, accompanying Minna's parents when they went to stay at Inverewe, was quite surprised at the rather basic accommodation there. 'It seemed very sparsely furnished and with not much comfort in it'. Giving evidence Minna stated:

> When I came to be mistress of the house I did my best to make some improvements upon the furniture and equipments. My husband did not seem to like any change at all, and anything I suggested he thought unnecessary or inadvisable. He did not even seem to like me rearranging the furniture in the drawing room. I found very little house linen in the place. When I was proposing to get supplies of that kind, he said they had done without them before and thought I was extravagant, but we did get some linen.
>
> He used to complain of my extravagances and remind me that I had brought him little or no money. He said he thought my father being a rich man should have helped him over difficulties better than he had done. There was no justice whatever in that complaint. My father, I thought, was very liberal to him; I think he gave him £100 that Christmas.

Other household 'improvements' also caused problems. Minna moved some Hanbury family pictures and a case of stuffed birds out of the drawing room. She said she was not made aware at the time that this had irritated him.

During the Spring of 1878 Osgood and Minna had travelled to the Isle of Wight, (where Osgood suffered from German measles), and Cheltenham, staying with various members of the Moss family. In March they were with Minna's parents and brother in London. His hosts were surprised that Osgood 'mainly went out by himself'. In June 1878 the Mackenzies were back in London to hear the results of an appeal to the House of Lords by a neighbouring landowner, Meyrick Bankes, who hoped to overturn a judgement, originally given in favour of Osgood in the Court of Sessions, with respect to fishing rights on the Dubh Loch.[7] This time the verdict went against Osgood. He was devastated. The case cost him £1,000. He told his wife that this 'would necessitate some retrenchment' but believed she made no effort to limit her spending. Nor did she appear to be worried about the effect this had on him, seeming cold and indifferent. Minna refuted both points: she 'was very much upset about the matter' and appreciated that economy was necessary in consequence of her husband's financial affairs.

To try to help, though he had not originally intended to go to Scotland that autumn at all, her father took on Inverewe for the shooting season of 1878. Osgood did not express much gratitude for the £600 rental, since it had to be spent 'to keep a company of six at Inverewe and supply them with everything including game-keepers, dogs etc'. As part of the same arrangement Sir John had given Osgood an additional £400 so that Minna could get some furniture for Inverewe. So the couple returned and Lady Mackenzie moved out again, going to England between July and November. She accepted an invitation from Lady Moss to stay with them at Otterspool on the way back north. However, she must have spent some time at Inverewe as a new issue arose. Minna said that her mother-in-law was in the habit of going to the kitchen where she heard her 'talking in Gaelic with the servants, her name mentioned and laughter and Lady Mackenzie certainly spent more time in the kitchen than was necessary to feed the dogs. Minna often spoke to her husband about his mother's interfering with her authority in the house'.

Who was 'mistress' of Inverewe was disputed in court. The judges heard criticism, from Jane McGregor, Lady Mary's parlour maid, corroborated by other Inverewe servants: 'Mrs Mackenzie did not seem to take any interest in the management of the household though the Dowager Lady Mackenzie did not interfere'. Osgood said his wife had full authority over the servants, the keys and the domestic budget. However, he 'had not a farthing to spare' so refused her requests for 'throwing a passageway into the drawing room' and extending the bow windows to the top of house. In a letter of 3 February 1879 Minna expressed her sense of unfairness:

> You have, to please your mother, built her a house at our expense, and have very rightly consulted her whims and fancies on the subject, and spared yourself no trouble to add to her comfort. [...] Have you taken the smallest trouble or done anything, but at most given a most unwilling consent to any alteration which might have added to the comfort of your wife's home?

When Minna's parents returned during the summer they brought with them her Otterspool pony and trap. Osgood regarded this as both an affront to his household proprietorship and an additional financial burden. Minna said he told her she would have to keep it clean herself and she later claimed he did not provide the horse with sufficient fodder. The lack of affection between the two was becoming more and more evident. Osgood's mother noticed Minna's manner to her husband 'and it broke her heart'. 'She wondered at his kindness to his wife who was so cold and numb'. As yet, he had not admitted to her that he was unhappy in his marriage.

Baby Mairi

In court there were suggestions that the only reason the Dowager Lady had encouraged her son to get married was to ensure there was a son and heir to the estate. Lady Mackenzie, Sir Kenneth's wife, recounted a conversation with her to the effect that 'Mrs Mackenzie was no use because she had no child during the first year of her marriage'. Any hope that the birth of a child would improve the situation was soon dashed.

In October 1878 Osgood and Minna went, again, to stay at Otterspool and his mother, again, returned to Inverewe to keep house. Minna was now pregnant but there was no mutual joy in anticipation. Sir Thomas Moss' butler commented on the 'cold and contemptible manner which Osgood used when with his wife' and how, when she almost fainted one evening at dinner, he left it to others to help. He seemed disinterested in her welfare. Dr Fitzpatrick, the family doctor who had known Minna from birth, gave evidence about how Minna was affected:

> They were a united and a most affectionate family. As an infant, a child and a woman, the defender was most amiable, and of a happy disposition, and temperament. She was rather reserved. The relations between her and the other members of her family were most affectionate. [...] When she arrived at Otterspool she did not appear to be in the best of spirits and her health was not good, but her condition might have accounted for some portion of that.

The couple were now hardly speaking to each other and communicated only on paper. Osgood returned to Scotland to deal with his farming affairs in January 1879 and left a letter on the dressing table about his misery. In her reply, three days later, Minna expressed strongly many of her feelings:

> I should like to know what interest you take in me. [...] Nor have you ever interested yourself sufficiently to inquire whether for the coming event I had been able to engage a good doctor that I like or a good nurse. To have fixed upon this month to go so far away by English people is thought queer, to say the least of it.

This correspondence also highlighted their lack of mutual interests. Minna 'did painting and went out driving and visited the poor' according to one of her maids. She had no wish to get involved in sheep-farming, breeding dogs or the buying and selling of a sporting life. Their 'tastes, occupations and interests' were 'diametrically opposite'. During the divorce case Osgood's half-brother, Francis, testified:

> There could scarcely be two people more unlike in their natural tastes than my brother and his wife, and she, unhappily [...] being short sighted, it made her still more shut out from the ordinary pursuits of recognising people in a field or anything of that sort and therefore she seemed to take very little interest in that which was his daily life and interest. [...] Mrs Mackenzie seemed to take little interest in her husband's social life. Mr Mackenzie [...] had a very large circle of friends and acquaintances in the higher ranks of life whom he used to visit. He was a great gardener, botanist and naturalist.[8]

Minna was none of these. A maid in the household, Annie Harris, said Minna took no interest in 'his affairs or to have any regard for his feelings or wishes'.

The financial implications of the pregnancy exacerbated the disagreements. She claimed he was not giving her enough money to run the household:

> For every pleasure or comfort beyond the barest necessaries of one's existence I have enjoyed since I married, I am entirely indebted to the generosity and thoughtfulness of my own family; for what *I* call necessaries in the house, for a pony carriage, for newspapers and something to read, for the very clothes I wear, I am obliged to thank others.

He countered with:

> My whole income was being spent in our house under a household administration guided by herself. I did not bet or spend my money in any way unconnected with the house and household. I had all but given up my shooting, and I did not smoke, drink or gamble.

His sister-in-law, Lady Eila, testified that, as early as 1878, Osgood had begun to talk about his wife in a 'fault-finding, grumbling manner. The matters of which he complained were trifles about the arrangement of his house. He also complained about his wife not wanting his mother to live with them and about her extravagance. [...] There was no ground for these complaints. Mrs Mackenzie took great pains in the management of the house and tried not to be extravagant, though she was not parsimonious'. Not surprisingly, she heard him complain further of the costs associated with the forthcoming event:

> His demeanour did not strike me as that of an affectionate husband expecting his wife's confinement. I remember him complaining of an outlay of £6 which

had been made for the expected baby and he complained very much that his wife had not paid that out of the pin-money which was allowed by her father.

As relations became increasingly acrimonious the parents were drawn in. Minna told her mother about the 'Gaelic in the kitchen' issue. Lady Moss informed Osgood in no uncertain terms that it was totally unacceptable that Lady Mackenzie 'had been in the habit of abusing, or at least discussing, the defendant in Gaelic with the domestics'. In a letter of 3 February Minna had taken Osgood to task over his relationship with his mother:

> Though our form of religion is widely different, we have the same Bible. Can you honestly say that you have 'left your father and mother and cleaved to your wife'? Do you trust and confide in your wife as you do in your mother? Are her wishes looked upon almost as a command by you, as are those of your mother? [...] If you and your mother continue one, and expect me to join you as a sort of inactive partner and form a trio, you will find yourself very much in the wrong. [...] If you don't support your wife as a man should, your mother will have to answer for still further misery than what she has already caused. [...] There is no love lost between your mother and I, but I expect to be treated by her as one lady expects to be treated by another.

His absence in the north with his mother until two days before her confinement on 1 March further alienated Minna from her husband. He did return, just in time, and on the evening after the birth there seemed to be affection between the two, 'she threw her arms round his neck and asked him to forgive her for her past conduct'. But on his next visit she was 'back to her old ways and turned her head away'. Osgood stayed only a fortnight or so before returning to Ross-shire. He was angry that he could not take the baby with him given that Minna was too weak to travel. Mrs Parry, the nurse attending Minna immediately after the birth, told how very distressed she had become at Osgood's indifference to her and then his going away so soon.

Dr Fitzpatrick was 'in almost daily attendance from the 1st March till the 5th June'. He told of how during her confinement, under the influence of chloroform, Minna demanded that Osgood keep his mother away from her because 'she will take the baby'.

> After her husband left I think her sufferings were so great that she felt she was very much neglected by his not coming near during the time. [...] I thought it very careless – a newly-married couple and the first infant. I thought it very cool. What struck me most was that the pursuer took no

> opportunity of enquiring after the condition of his wife from myself. [...] His conduct made witness believe there was something far wrong in his domestic relations.

He did suggest that Osgood might not appreciate 'the delicate health of his wife after confinement' (though one of the Appeal Court judges considered this 'one of the most unsatisfactory features of the case'). But Dr Fitzpatrick did not like the way Osgood tried to stop Minna taking claret by getting him, as doctor, to order abstinence from it.

The issue of a nurse for the baby was to cause another upset for Minna. She and her mother were discussing whether to have a Swiss or French nanny. All seemed agreed that an English one would not fit well into a Highland household, but Osgood, on his own initiative, put an advertisement into the *Inverness Courier* and 'engaged the nurse himself'. Nurse Bain was selected. She was Gaelic speaking (with some English) and, in the opinion of Minna, 'was very unsuitable for the situation. She could neither read nor write nor sew and was rather too fat to carry the baby. She was very kind to the baby but she did not look to me like a lady's servant'. Nurse Bain confirmed, 'I am not very good at reading, but I can read'.

So Minna made the best of her. Osgood did not think this should have been an issue as 'she had said she was happy with locally-born servants when they got married' and 'the nurse whom I selected and my wife were always the greatest friends, and I never heard the smallest complaint. [...] English servants don't stay here very willingly'. Nurse Bain was to be a resolute witness for Osgood throughout the divorce hearing.

Minna made a poor recovery from childbirth. Dr Fitzpatrick reported:

> For the first three weeks she went on fairly well, and then she began to shew symptoms of debility. Later on at the end of the fifth week she showed symptoms of abscess of the breasts, suffering for some considerable time intense pain, sleeplessness and night perspirations. [...] Her sufferings were very great for four or five weeks. [...] About 5th of June I ordered the defender to Buxton. Had it not been for the mental distress I think she would have recovered much sooner. The mental state of agitation in which she was, and distress and reserve – keeping it so much to herself – had a very poor effect upon her health.

Minna's mother paid the bills for the consulting fees and the hotel at Buxton. Osgood said he wrote three times a week whilst he was back home but received no replies. Minna said she was too ill to write. Besides which 'his letters did not seem to be the kind of letters appropriate to such an occasion. He seemed to think very little of my illness. He was generally complaining of the bill he had got for the baby's clothes. There was a great-to-do made about that'. She had been at Buxton about a fortnight when Osgood arrived to take her home. But it was no joyous reunion. She was still weak but he insisted that she rise from her chair and come towards him and give him a kiss. In court he could not remember this.

Return to Scotland

The next day the couple took the train to return home. The maid, Annie Plumridge, remembered hearing Lady Moss say 'that she would rather have followed her child to the grave than bid her adieu to go to Scotland with Mr Mackenzie [...] he was so unkind to her. Lady Moss was in very great distress at the time, weeping'. The journey was strained. Osgood was preoccupied with the expense of the addition to the family and remonstrated with his wife that she had spent too much on the cost of the baby's clothes (£36) as he was near bankrupt at the time. He objected that Annie Harris, Minna's maid, insisted on travelling second class rather than third, that Minna had bought Swiss dried milk for the child, and also that she had been vaccinated (presumably against smallpox as this was compulsory by that time) at Otterspool, rather than waiting until he could get the serum in Gairloch. When the couple stopped overnight in Edinburgh Osgood, as he informed his wife later that journey, went out and consulted his advocate, Mr Adam, about his rights as father to the child. He was pleased to be told that, once over the Tweed, they were absolute.

Minna wanted to break off the journey home, whilst staying with Dr John, to have her child christened in Inverness Cathedral. Osgood utterly rejected the idea, which she could not understand. They had been married in an episcopalian church, he had taken communion in an episcopalian church and 'under these circumstances I took it for granted that the child would be christened in an episcopalian church'. A letter from Lady Moss stating that he would be cut out of her will if the baby was not baptised in Inverness made no difference. Sir Kenneth thought it 'rather cantankerous' of him to refuse. But Osgood was resolute. The ceremony would be carried out by his 'own' Free Church minister once back at Inverewe.

As was usual, Osgood arranged that the last stage of the journey to Poolewe, beyond Kinlochewe, proceed by boat through Loch Maree rather than by carriage along the road. This was both quicker and cheaper. Osgood was keen to catch up on the local news and spent much of the journey talking to the boatmen in Gaelic, thus excluding his wife from the conversations.

Minna had agreed to the boat trip, provided the weather was favourable. However, after a fair start it turned wet. An exhausted Minna fainted as the boat arrived at the Inveran Lodge jetty. Some of Osgood's servants suggested she was shamming. The servants and Mr John Dixon, tenant of the Lodge, tried to revive her. Osgood apparently kept out of the way. Whether or not he showed any genuine concern for his wife was debated at length in the divorce hearings. His gamekeeper, John Matheson, said he 'was much distressed' and he did enquire of her wellbeing frequently. Joanne Mackenzie, a servant at Inverewe, said she had actually seen Osgood kissing his wife whilst she was in a faint, though she would not have known it. The couple were forced to stay at Inveran overnight, Osgood lodging in a little attic as there was no other room for him. Unbeknown to Minna, Osgood's mother had come and taken the baby on to Tournaig.

Soon after their return, on 21 June, the child was baptised in the Free Church Meeting Room in Poolewe. Osgood went, together with his mother, brother and uncle, but Minna refused to attend the service. Nurse Bain said, in evidence, that Minna had expressed the hope that the baby would cry all the time. Minna's response was that she had probably said this because there was an old superstition that it was lucky for a child to cry during the christening. When Nurse Bain told Minna that the minister had prayed earnestly for her Minna replied that he could have saved himself the trouble as she could pray for herself! Following the service Osgood said to Minna that he would very much like it if she were to call him 'dear'. She replied: 'I never will'. They were also unable to agree on the names for the baby. Osgood had suggested she be named 'after the two grandmothers, either Amy Mary or Mary Amy; but my wife said she hated the name of Amy, and that she would choose one name and I might choose the other. Accordingly I chose Mary and she chose Thyra'.

The day of the christening was, said his mother, the first time that Osgood told her of his unhappiness. The Dowager Lady had moved out of Inverewe before the couple returned, and moved into Tournaig in June, 'rather before it was finished'. However, she was not there long as, early in August, she went to England for three months. Her son had, out of financial necessity, let Inverewe to the Duke of St Albans for the shooting season and so Osgood and Minna based themselves at Tournaig for the time being, until Inverewe became available again in October.

Discord and strife

Wherever they lived, it was more than obvious to the Mackenzie family that the couple were further apart than ever. In July 1879 Sir Kenneth suggested where the fault lay: 'My wife and I were very much struck by his roughness and rudeness and bearishness towards his wife, especially after entering into the room. [...] He seldom spoke to her and never looked at her'. Osgood wrote to his brother in August 1879 that 'my love is the same as when I married her and only wants an occasional smile or a kind word from her, or the touch of her hand, to keep the fire going'. Nurse Bain's evidence was that 'Mr Mackenzie was kinder to his wife than she was to him', but, in court, Minna said she did not think these were his genuine feelings, 'he did not love her [...] he was shamming his misery'.

There were wider social implications. Minna very much wanted to go to that season's Northern Meeting. Osgood said he could not afford the expense and only reluctantly agreed when Minna paid the costs. The real reason though, it turned out, was that he found it 'unpleasant going to any place where we were like to meet friends'. Minna was less keen to go to a ball at Inveran held in honour of John Dixon's ghillie so Osgood went with his mother and some of the servants (with whom he danced, as was customary).

Minna had excused herself, being 'unwell'. The Moss family doctor, Mr Fitzpatrick, remembered her to be 'in her youth very healthy and possessed of good spirits', but by the autumn of 1879, back at Inverewe, there was cause for concern. In December Osgood wrote to Minna's father, 'I am very anxious about her as she is no better. She certainly gets up every day, but she is becoming so thin and weak and eats nothing. She is always in very low spirits – never speaks when I come into the room'.

In early January 1880 the Dingwall medical man, Dr Bruce, was summoned. He diagnosed 'nervous diarrhoea with gouty dyspepsia, epigastic pain and pain under left ribs, griping before action of bowels, much furred tongue, pulse weak'. Osgood 'professed to believe that her illness was of her own causing and was due to an excessive use of alcohol and drugs taken contrary to medical orders and advice'. In a telegram sent to Otterspool on 6 January Osgood informed her parents that the doctor said that there was 'nothing serious matter with Minna, only effects of low spirits; forbids wine, brandy, opiates, tea, recommends change, but certainly not for baby'. Dr Bruce protested vehemently that he had done no such thing.

> I did not forbid wine and I allowed Mrs Mackenzie to have brandy by the written dietary which I laid down. I prescribed tea. [...] In this case I was against opiates, but not entirely against opiates. [...] The catalogue of things mentioned by me is a very unfair version. [...] I knew and felt for the prejudice he had against stimulants. [...] I knew he was a man with strong total abstinence views. If I had thought that what Mrs Mackenzie had been taking in the smallest degree affected her health, I should have stopped it entirely and probably given her a lecture besides. [...] I had not the least reason to believe that she was doing what in any reasonable sense could be called taking stimulants to excess.

The judges were appalled that Osgood had sent a telegram through the public system giving, as if a medical opinion, his own views that Minna's diarrhoea was to be attributed to her deliberately taking drugs. They also considered that it was unfairly damaging to Minna's reputation. Several of the Inverewe servants testified that she kept opiates and other medicines in her room. John Matheson, the gamekeeper, seemed to have had ready access within the house. He had been most concerned when he was 'asked, by a servant, to take the stopper out of a bottle labelled opium or opiates. He had said to the girl, having done so, to tell Mrs Mackenzie, that if he saw the bottle again he would tell the minister. He thought no one should take such stuff'. She acknowledged having an unopened phial of laudanum, brought with her in a medicine chest from Otterspool long ago, and had only taken some 'Tamar Indien lozenges recommended by the monthly nurse'.

Perceptively, Dr Bruce had advised that Minna would benefit from a complete break on the continent, 'as the relatives on both sides were probably doing harm'. Osgood maintained 'he was too poor' to do this, but he was not averse to Minna going to her parents. However, on no account was she to take the baby with her. This caused further arguments. Minna absolutely refused, for many weeks, to go south without her baby. Osgood was adamant Mairi was not to leave her nursery, giving as reasons that the air in Liverpool was smoky and unhealthy, the journey too long, the milk would be different so unsuitable. He suggested in court: 'I had another reason – that I had been recommended by several friends to try and get my wife to have a liking for her home. We had spent nineteen months out of the first two years with her people or they with us and I thought it was time we should think of making Inverewe our home'.

He did not appreciate that going to see his mother almost every day, as he had 'occasion to go to Tournaig about the farm', was not likely to be improving matters. It was pointed out by John Dixon that, actually, Osgood's farm manager, who lived there, was quite capable of looking after the Tournaig side of the farm with Osgood checking things at Inverewe. A letter he wrote to his mother at the end of the month, 'I really and truly believe that the reason Minna won't leave the baby is that she fears you will get hold of it in her absence', showed he was well aware of his wife's fears.

It was, apparently, because of her poor sleeping that, as Jessie Macpherson, wife of Osgood's sheep manager recalled, Osgood moved out of the matrimonial bedroom to sleep in the dressing room next door. They never spent another night together. They also went their separate ways during the day. Anne Harris, then an Inverewe maid, was questioned in New York in 1892. She stated: 'During the three months before we left Inverewe to go to Conon the pursuer and defender were not together even at meals. [...] Mr Mackenzie was usually away all day. [...] When the defender was well enough to have her dinner downstairs she would have it upstairs to avoid seeing him'.

Even when she was fit enough to breakfast with him it provoked more complaints from Osgood. In a letter written in November 1879 he listed a number of perceived faults. These included 'breakfasting in bed when she was not ill, shaking out her napkin whilst he said grace, kneeling on the seat of her chair during the prayers, coming to morning prayers in her dressing gown and then being extravagant and lighting too many fires in the house'. Minna responded that the first was untrue, she was unaware of the second, felt faint if kneeling on the floor and wore a padded tea-gown to keep herself warm.

Beyond all this there was the fundamental issue which was judged to have destroyed the marriage – Osgood's attitude to the role of a wife. He disputed that he had spoken in the earliest days about the degree of subjection of a wife to a husband and the ease with which he could get a divorce in Scotland if 'a wife did not obey as a slave'. But he accepted that he had consulted a lawyer on this in Edinburgh as he returned north after the honeymoon. Osgood saw it as Minna's personal and religious duty to obey him to the letter, without question, and his role to teach her what was required when she failed to oblige. Sir Kenneth's wife testified: 'Mr Mackenzie was constantly saying that a wife must be submissive and obedient to her husband. He continually used the expression "I will be obeyed" until it became a joke. Mr Mackenzie was very serious. She never saw him make fun at all'.

Minna did not see it as a joke either. In early December Osgood wrote to his brother: 'His wife had been disobedient and not shown sufficient deference to him. As a punishment she was not being allowed to go to the wedding of Miss Davidson'. Another letter, dated 5 January 1880, was sent to Minna's father:

> The season of the year, the long journey, and teething, and not having been weaned, are the reasons I give to the world for not letting the child go South at present. But though I consider these quite sufficient reasons in themselves, I have other reasons for not letting Baby go. [...] As long as Minna continues to act towards me unlike a wife (I may say unlike a Christian) I cannot and will not trust the child with her and away from myself. A wife who cannot behave properly to her husband is not fit to be trusted by him with her child; and unless Minna turns over an entirely new leaf, expresses sorrow for the past and promises amendment for the future, the child must remain here.

Hurtful letters continued to be exchanged. On her dressing table on 16 January Minna found another, accusing her of having a 'discontented, stubborn, rebellious spirit'.

> I do not believe that in this large parish there is another instance of a wife behaving to her husband in the way you behave to me, or of a wife who shews such utter indifference towards her husband, and treats his advice and his wishes with the scorn with which you treat mine. [...] If you do not amend your ways (sad though it may be), I may see it my duty to arrange that my child be not brought up under such bad influence and example, – That God may avert this by giving you a new heart and a new nature is the earnest prayer of your sorrowful husband.

At this Minna lost her self-control, went to him and shouted, 'How can you be such a brute as to treat me in that way?' but she regretted her anger immediately and followed him to express her sorrow. He ordered her to leave his room and, as he told her father in a later letter, threatened to keep her under lock and key. 'Certainly if she ever attempts the like again I shall do so'.

Lord Watson, summing up his views in the House of Lords in May 1895, commented on Osgood's uncompromising attitude in demanding 'absolute deference' from his wife:

> He appears to have assumed that he was justified in adopting any means that occurred to him for the purpose of enforcing what he deemed to be his rights, and that the infliction of mental distress, even to the aggravation of her bodily ailments, physical restraint or personal violence were, should he think it advisable to resort to them, consequence for which the respondent [Minna] was to blame.

Further, 'he was manifestly acting under the belief that he was entitled to use physical means in order to subdue her will and to reduce it to absolute submission to his own'.

The 'Plot'

There was relatively little that Sir Thomas and Lady Moss could do from a distance, but Sir Kenneth and Lady Mackenzie kept in contact with them and did all they were able to retrieve the situation. After much persuasion Osgood eventually agreed to go with Minna to Conan House for a break on 20 January 1880. The change seemed to be beneficial as far as she was concerned. Her health improved, she became livelier and she went out a little. As usual, Osgood went about his own business without her, keeping in unhelpful, close contact with his mother: 'Snog is more and more devoted to me, and cries every time I leave her, and generally cries every time she goes to her mother. She has an extraordinary craze for music'.[9]

Sir Kenneth and Lady Mackenzie then had to go away unexpectedly at the end of the month and did not return until 9 February, leaving the couple and their daughter, aged fifteen, behind. Allegedly, in their absence, Minna devised a plan to 'abduct' her baby and take it with her when she went to Otterspool, counter to her husband's instructions. The courts heard evidence from Nurse Bain and Ann Harris, lady's maid, that Minna had proposed that they help her in this 'plot', working with her brother, Cottingham, to arrange a 'special train' and an English nanny to take them to England. On 11 February, whilst Minna was in Inverness, meeting her brother and having lunch with Dr John, the Inverewe servants informed Osgood of the scheme. In order to pre-empt it he decided to take the baby himself, straight back to Tournaig. Sir Kenneth and his wife pursued him and Nurse Bain to the train station and, in a very public scene, insisted that he return to their house. This he did, but Mr Smith, the solicitor summoned at once from Dingwall, confirmed that the father had the right of control over the child. Osgood therefore went, with the baby, back to his mother on the west coast.

Minna returned to her parents in great distress, denying that she had ever countenanced any 'plot', rather that she had, after discussion with Lady Mackenzie, recognised that she could not take her daughter with her. Both Sir Kenneth and, later, John Dixon believed the abduction story was 'entirely a fabrication', but the law was not on Minna's side.

Not surprisingly, she became very unwell again. Dr Fitzpatrick was questioned in court about the nature of her illness: 'Typhoid fever, pain over the lower bowel of long standing, and uterine infection, which had probably existed since the birth of the child' and, understandably, 'she was suffering mentally from the separation from her child'. Again, though, 'there was not the slightest indication that Mrs Mackenzie's condition had been brought about by the improper use of drugs. [...] The illness from which Mrs Mackenzie suffered was not sufficient to account for the great state of depression from which she suffered'. Annie Plumridge, Lady Moss's maid, expanded: 'She was very weak and poorly when she arrived and could not get up stairs without assistance. She was very low spirited'.

In retrospect, the episode of 'The Plot' ended any chance of the marriage surviving. Minna spent three weeks at Otterspool and then went to the family home in London. Osgood arranged his affairs, rented out Inverewe and stayed at Tournaig. He claimed in court that he had left servants for a while at Inverewe, should Minna return, but was unable to sustain this once Minna's parents decided to call up a loan which had been part of the marriage settlement so that the interest went directly to her rather than to her husband. Osgood saw this as an 'act of retaliation' and was very angry. In 1893 he claimed that this 'had so crippled him that he had to break up his own establishment and go and live with his mother'. Minna denied that she thought the marriage was over, or that she wanted to embarrass him, or get him to give up Inverewe.

There was no communication between them from the end of February until early June, though locally Osgood 'widely circulated his own version both as to the *plot* and as to his charge against the defender of taking drugs and stimulants to excess'. John Dixon, 'the shooting tenant at Inveran', was still his good friend at the time. Recalling a conversation with Osgood on 23 March 1880, he 'formed the opinion that he had the strongest aversion to his wife and after this often spoke about divorce. He looked forward with satisfaction to the time when he would get a divorce'. Osgood also decided, at the end of May 1880, to send Minna's pony and chaise, by train, to Otterspool. She was not there and had been given no advance notice that it was coming. She assumed that it was his way of telling her he did not want her to return.

Breakdown

Nonetheless, Minna decided to return to Wester Ross. She wrote on 5 June giving her reasons: 'My love for my child impels me, now that I am permitted by the doctor to go north, to return to Inverewe, where you have promised I shall find her'. She was 'offering to return to her home and rejoin her husband and child, and making certain proposals as to the contributions to be made by her out of her separate income – her fortune having been settled on herself'.

'That letter produced the greatest consternation at Tournaig'. Osgood's reply, 8 June, declined the proposed pecuniary arrangements. He offered to receive her in his mother's house.

> Dear Minna, – Having waited nearly four months for some sign from you of sorrow and repentance for your past conduct, I have been the more grieved at reading your letter of the 5th of June, which holds out no hope nor guarantee against a repetition of that line of conduct which has made my married life so miserable, and especially as regards what occurred at Conon.
>
> First and foremost, I am determined to take every possible precaution towards guarding my child; and secondly, not being considered by you as fit to be entrusted with your money [...] I decline allowing any of it to be spent in my house, or on anything over which I have control. [...] Knowing that I could only live by joining my means with those of my mother, and by living in the strictest economy I gave some of the servants warning, and have made entire fresh arrangements, and do not intend returning to Inverewe at any rate till the winter after the shooting tenant has left, and perhaps I may make this permanently my home. [...] Should you like to come here and write to say so, a room will be prepared for you. Baby is quite well. – Your husband.

Despite this unwelcome, and unwelcoming, response Minna wrote again, 19 June, to suggest that there were faults on both sides and they should let bygones be bygones. According to Dixon this letter caused Osgood to weep bitterly – but tears of sorrow not of joy. Lady Moss also wept when her daughter insisted she was going back to Scotland. She was 'anxious as to the defender's [Minna's] condition, health and prospects, [...] she was really frightened about her bodily safety among the people where she was going, [...] she was afraid she might be locked up and not allowed to see any friends'.

When Dixon suggested he should meet his wife at Achnasheen and accompany her on the last leg of her journey to Tournaig Osgood said he could not bear to sit beside her. He had even suggested she should stay at the Loch Maree Hotel and he would bring their daughter to see her there, to avoid her joining him, though in the 1887 'access' court case Osgood claimed he had 'offered to receive [Minna] as his wife at Tournaig and to resume conjugal relations without reference to the past'.

On 1 July Minna arrived at Flowerdale to have tea with Sir Kenneth and Lady Eila. She discovered that Osgood had sent his carriage to collect her. Unfortunately she had, by then, booked one from the Gairloch Hotel and saw no reason to cancel the arrangement, especially as Osgood's chaise was rather too small for herself, her maid, (Annie Plumridge had been lent her by Lady Moss), and her luggage. Osgood was very displeased about this. Their meeting, after so many months, was, on Minna's evidence, very cool. She was allowed to kiss her baby, held in Osgood's arms, but he did not kiss her or shake hands. He was 'cold and repellent'. According to a report from the 1893 Divorce appeal:

> The pursuer received her coldly, and occupied another bedroom during her stay. We find a chronicle of the pursuer's attitude towards her in a series of little notes that he was in the habit of writing to her, and leaving on her table, containing for the most part reproofs and instructions as to her conduct. [...] The defender was in the end completely isolated.

Nurse Bain supported Osgood's claim that a real effort had been made for Minna. 'The best accommodation in the house had been prepared for her that had previously been occupied by Mr Mackenzie. He got old Lady Mackenzie's room and she got the maid's room'. Further, 'the house at Tournaig is quite a small one. There was only one servant's room at that time, in which there were already three servants sleeping'. So Minna was told that her maid could not stay with her at Tournaig, though there was space for a young relative, Duncan Davidson of Tulloch, who was there at the same time. She believed, in retrospect, that 'he did not wish her to have witnesses of the treatment she would get there'. Annie therefore lodged at the Poolewe Hotel and met Minna most days on the road, using a conveyance which Minna had hired and kept at the Hotel 'exclusively for her own use, with a hotel driver'. This upset Osgood greatly. 'I felt it very unpleasant that my wife should be going about in a hired carriage with her maid staying at a hotel. It made a dreadful scandal in a small place like that. She went out every day and took long drives to Gairloch. She seemed to be able to do so without any injury to her health'. He also expressed his anger when the maid brought a telegram directly to her mistress. Furthermore, Minna was not allowed to have the key to the hanging cupboard in her bedroom so had 'no accommodation for her clothes, she was not informed of the time of meals and seldom spoken to'. Communication between husband and wife continued to be almost always by letter. Osgood claimed that he did all in his power 'to regain her affections, without avail' and 'he received her as kindly as he could. It was his wish to conciliate and please her' but 'during that time her manner was colder if possible than ever'.

Lady Eila Mackenzie had promised Minna's mother that she would keep in close contact and she took Minna out on several occasions, for example: 'Monday 26th, she joined me and two cousins of mine and we drove to Inverasdale to sketch'. At Tournaig Minna became resigned to being the pariah. Lady Eila had tried to intercede with the Dowager but was accused of making trouble:

> The Dowager was very excited, very indignant and very abusive. [...] I thought Mrs Mackenzie would have very hard times of it with the Dowager. The Dowager, I think, is a very masterful person. I left the room and went to Mrs Mackenzie's room. [...] It was naturally very unpleasant for her to hear herself abused, and it was very unpleasant for me to listen to it.

When Lady Mackenzie made a further visit, to see an unwell Minna, the Dowager refused to meet her. Worst of all, Minna found it was made very difficult for her to spend time with her daughter, undoubtedly the reason for her return. Osgood and his mother would make arrangements to go out with the child without telling her. Minna was only permitted to see her in the garden or on the private road to Dallan and the fields there. Apparently Osgood was on the watch for a yacht which might spirit the child away. Nurse Bain suggested that Minna 'did not come to the nursery nearly so much as formerly'.

The final scene, involving mother-in-law, baby and the issue of Minna's obedience to her husband took place on 4 August. Both sides agreed the general facts, though not the motivations. Minna had requested that the baby come to her bedroom for breakfast. Osgood, however, sent the nurse to collect Mary who was to be brought to him, as was usual practice, in the dining room. 'That was the time of day [he] had chiefly an opportunity of seeing her, because when he returned at night the child was generally asleep'. He said he then heard Minna tell the nurse that if he came near her she would strike him. He went in to try to reason with her as to why he wanted the child with him for breakfast. 'When he entered the room she hit him once or twice but did not hurt him'. He went out to give her a chance to calm down but then heard the child scream 'most violently'.

He believed that the child 'had either been scalded or pricked with a pin at her mother's breast. He knew she would not hurt the child willingly'. His mother then came into the room, 'frightened because the child was a good-tempered, healthy child and hardly ever cried'. His wife (stated Osgood) threatened to strike her also but Minna claimed that the Dowager Lady was shouting 'hold her down, hold her down. The father has every right. She must obey'. Osgood held down her right hand, his mother the left. She was 'very excited'. She said the house was hers. Minna replied that the house might be hers but the baby was not. The Dowager's evidence was that she held down Mrs Mackenzie's arm to stop her hitting her husband. Bain denied having seen any arm being held. The judges were sceptical:

> The evidence of the nurse Bain was most unsatisfactory, because, although she was standing facing Mrs Mackenzie, and must have seen all that took place, she obstinately refused to admit that she saw either the pursuer or his mother put a hand upon the shoulder. [...] Her evidence in regard to any other matter likely to tell against the pursuer must be received with considerable reserve.

In any case, 'the child scrambled out of the mother's arms and was taken away'.

Minna got up, dressed and left, believing it not safe to remain. She walked nearly three miles in the rain from Tournaig to the Hotel in Poolewe where her maid was staying. Annie Plumridge testified that 'she was heart broken and unable to speak at first and weeping bitterly'. Word was sent to Flowerdale and Lady Mackenzie came to collect her. She and Sir Kenneth saw the bruising on Minna's arm where she had been held down four hours earlier. 'An important part of Sir Kenneth's evidence showed that violence used in taking the child away from its mother was considerable'. The support Sir Kenneth and his wife gave to Minna throughout resulted in the ending of familial relationships. From 1880 until the court case in 1892 'he had hardly seen the pursuer [Osgood] though they had been on close and intimate terms before these occurrences'.

The next day Minna, accompanied by her maid, returned to Tournaig to see her child. Osgood did not welcome her. 'My wife stayed just so long as it took me to go to the hayfield – about twenty minutes or half an hour. Having seen the child, she drove off again. [...] I gave her the child in her arms, but I kept hold of her'. Osgood had, said Annie, 'spoken in an angry tone', refused to allow his wife to hold the baby but did allow her to kiss it. She then left, 'crying bitterly' again. The marks on her arm were still visible on 6 August when Minna met with her elder brother in Conon. He had rented shootings at Coul for the season and took her back to their parents' home at Otterspool.

Minna at Pool House

A year later, in August 1881, Minna returned to Poolewe to be near her daughter. On her behalf her father rented Pool House, the Mackenzie fishing lodge in the village. It was 'formerly the Londubh Inn. It has been enlarged and improved by Sir Thomas Edwards Moss, Bart., who has a lease of it with some shootings. He has erected a stable near the east end of Poolewe Bridge where the smithy formerly stood'.[10]

This meant that she would be living just a few hundred yards away from Inverewe, in full view across the bay. This shocked Osgood. She had her furniture and belongings moved there and set up a 'regular establishment, engaged servants and received visitors'. According to the 1881 Census she employed two women and a boy and a middle-aged married couple were visiting. It's unclear how much of the year she stayed there. In court during an 'access hearing' in 1884 it was stated that Osgood had written to his wife recently: 'though you have at times visited your child here, you have at other times not seen her, nor inquired after her, for long intervals of many months'. At Pool House Minna passed some of the time, it would seem, in carving English roses the length of the stair handrail.[11] One known visitor was the David Murray of Gruinard who had provided lodgings for that night in October 1877 when the newly-wed couple were unable to return home because of appalling weather.

Osgood was horrified by Minna's arrangements, on the borders of his 'march'. Both claimed that each ignored and 'cut dead' the other when they passed in the street. Salt was rubbed into the wound as Osgood could no longer rent out the shootings at Inveran and Isle Ewe which were linked with Pool House and which he had used for twenty five years. 'I felt very much aggrieved'. Major alterations were carried out there in 1889, nominally for Sir Thomas Moss. The architects were the Tain-based company of Andrew Maitland and Sons, ironically the same firm as had designed Inverewe House and the new Poolewe Free Church, completed also in 1889.[12] By 1890 the fishings in the River Ewe were being rented by Minna in her own name, 'Mrs Mackenzie of Inverewe', though her elder brother took on the tenancy of Pool House itself, after their father died in 1890.[13]

'Access' arrangements

Most important of all for Minna, who 'ordered all her life so that she might be near her daughter to whom she was devotedly attached', was the issue of seeing her daughter. As early as 5 March 1881 the Inner House of the Court of Session heard the case: 'A lady who had left her husband presented a petition to the Court praying their Lordships to regulate the terms on which she was to have access to her only child, two years of age, who remained with its father'.

> Her husband stated he was prepared to permit her to see her child for an hour three times a week at his mother's house, on condition of her coming unaccompanied, and of the child being attended by either its nurse or its grandmother. The petition then proceeded,– "The petitioner does not dispute that in law the custody of her child belongs to its father, subject to her right of access to it, but she considers that, taking into consideration her being prepared to isolate herself in this remote part of Scotland, many hundred miles from any of her own relations, where she has taken and furnished a residence and will there keep a suitable establishment for the one object of being able to see her child, from whom she has now been separated for a year, with the exception of a few weeks, the access now offered is insufficient and is hampered with conditions which ought not to be imposed upon her, and she now craves your Lordships to make such regulations as shall seem to you good for securing to the petitioner adequate access to and means for enjoying the society of her only child."

Minna hoped that she could have 'free access to her child, at all reasonable times' and that her baby should be with her, at her own house, for two whole days in each week and, when she went to Tournaig, to be able to be with the child 'outwith the presence of its father, or his mother, or any one on their behalf'. She also stated that she was 'desirous of being reconciled to her husband, and has made overtures more than once with that view, but hitherto without success'.

Osgood rejected any suggestion that he had neglected or been unkind to his wife; told the court how she had plotted to take the child to England 'without his knowledge' and explained how she had 'made calls upon his resources which had so crippled him that he had to break up his own establishment and go and live with his mother'. He offered to receive Minna 'as his wife, at his mother's house, his mother having offered to take up her residence elsewhere in the meantime'.

He convinced the judges: 'Her legal duty as a wife is to return. [...] She is not acting according to her legal duty in absenting herself from her husband and child'.

> The separation has not been of so long duration as to destroy all hopes of the parties coming together again. [...] She has been invited to come and live in her mother-in-law's house, but declines to do so unless she is to be the mistress of the house. We consider that demand not legally warranted. As far as we can judge from the correspondence we are inclined to sympathise to a large extent with the husband, and to hold that the wife is not legally warranted in absenting herself in such circumstances. We know of no authority empowering a wife so deserting her husband and child to apply to the Court for access to the child. [...] The affectionate terms of the husband's letters precludes the idea that he, in any spirit of vindictiveness, or from any other motive not to be commended, will deny access to this child on the part of its mother. This child may eventually be a bond to bring the spouses together again. The petition will be refused.

They were wrong. Osgood had initially allowed Minna to visit the nursery, (usually at Tournaig), for two hours at 10 a.m. three days a week. He had said in court that he would 'give her access to the child [...] at all times when she might choose to come; and further, to arrange that during one or two hours on certain days in each week the child shall always be kept either in or immediately about the house, so that the petitioner might depend upon finding it'. On 14 August 1882 Osgood was 'requested by his mother' to limit Minna's access. It no longer suited her that Minna should be at Tournaig 'after 11 o'clock on the days she visited her'. The time Minna might come to see her daughter was now a much less convenient 9 a.m. and she was still always to be observed when there. Minna tried to work with this, but found it not good for her health, particularly with winter coming. In September she asked to revert to the previous arrangement. Osgood declined as 'it did not suit the Dowager Lady's arrangements'.

So, for the next year or so, when in Poolewe, Minna visited three days a week, 9–11 a.m. But the climate 'prevented her from living there during the winter' and when she was away she was not allowed to correspond with her daughter. Annie Plumridge, who came back to Poolewe with Minna, recalled how difficult it always was. 'I remember Mrs Mackenzie being allowed to see the child twice a week, and taking toys and so on for the child. She always brought them back with her; she was not allowed to make the baby any presents'.

A possible reason for refusing to make the situation more comfortable for Minna was that, in the early autumn of 1882, the shooting tenant of Inverewe intervened in these domestic affairs. Sir James Speight was well acquainted with the Moss family and spoke to Osgood, urging him to 'make it up with his wife', emphasising the advantages of 'living once more at Inverewe together'. Minna's elder brother claimed that they were all very desirous of this. Sir James' advances 'were met with a fair degree of acquiescence at first, and he had great hopes of being able to bring about a reconciliation'. However, on their next meeting Mr Mackenzie, having apparently discussed the matter with his mother, was 'most abusive about his wife, and used very strong language about her', saying 'none of the county families would visit her, as she had two years on the loose'.

Minna heard about this and was very upset. Relations between Sir James and Osgood then deteriorated rapidly. Sir James took Osgood to court, on a charge of 'some fraud about the shootings'. Osgood won initially, but, on appeal, judgement went to Sir James.[14] Matters thus became worse rather than better. The Moss family were banned from going to Inverewe or Tournaig, even to accompany Minna on her visits. Lady Moss was now dead but Sir Thomas dearly wanted to see his grand-daughter.

In May 1884 Minna sent a letter to Osgood, from London, making overtures for reconciliation, 'to live with you as your wife [...] forgetting the past, act so as best to promote and maintain peace and harmony; thus by mutual forbearance on both sides may a happier feeling in time exist between us – Your wife.' Osgood replied from Tournaig. He was prepared to consider this for the sake of the child but required

> contrition, and a hearty desire and determination (with God's help) to endeavour to become henceforward a dutiful wife. But true forgiveness requires deep and heartfelt repentance and I promise that such repentance on your part shall always be met by kindness and forgiveness from me. But [...] you have never asked to see me, nor given expression to any feelings of regret for your past conduct and desertion.

He then listed a number of conditions to which she had to agree in writing. She was not to 'have anything further to do with Pool House, nor ever again enter its doors, or its grounds'. Should she wish to drive out it had to be only with his consent, in his carriage, using his pony and with his servant. Further, 'I shall require you never to associate with persons in the parish of Gairloch who are not on friendly terms with me, without my special permission, nor leave me for long or short intervals without my consent or by the advice of my medical man'. So she was to be debarred the society of her relations and even that of his own brother and sister-in-law.

There was further correspondence. Minna replied that 'the wisest course was for both parties to forgive and, if possible, forget'. Osgood repeated his demand that she accept his conditions (23 May). She (3 June) repeated her desire to return. In November Osgood dispensed with his demands for assurances in writing but clearly intimated that he would enforce the conditions, which he repeated in a letter on 9 December, when he brought up again the alleged 'plot', and reminded her that she was not to bring any maid of her own with her. Minna saw these requirements as a clear indication that he did not want her back.

This exchange was used in the divorce courts later to Osgood's disadvantage: 'His own conduct to the defender was entirely ignored, and no expression of regret made for it'. There was no acceptance that he might have been blameworthy in any way. The impression was that 'the pursuer did not wish the defender to return to him, and that he would have been much better pleased if she had not proposed to do so, because I think he would then have endeavoured to obtain a divorce for desertion'. Osgood justified his stance given that she had 'dishonoured him very much'.

In October 1885 Osgood limited Minna's access to her child even further, reduced to 'two hours on one day a week' (9–11 a.m.) with 'servants always present'. Osgood explained this in court in 1887: 'a more prolonged visit would seriously interrupt the education of the child, which was being regularly and systematically carried on by her grandmother, Lady Mackenzie' and 'the child's learning must not be interrupted'.

The 1886 Guardianship of Infants Act enabled Minna to renew her claim to better access. This new law said that the court must take into consideration 'the welfare of the infant, and [...] the conduct of the parents, and [...] the wishes as well of the mother as of the father', giving Minna hope of having her daughter to live with her, at least some of the time. So she reapplied, in 1887, to the Second Division. Osgood believed she had no right to 'invoke the interference of the court'. The judges found the whole situation 'a great deal too delicate for them to get at the real cause of the difference', afforded them 'anxious consideration' and they took some time to reach any judgements.

There was a fresh round of correspondence between man and wife to consider. The letters Osgood wrote in May 1887 had repeated the conditions of 1884. That of 13 June was completely different.

> My dear Minna, – I write to ask you once more whether you will not still return to live with me as my wife.
>
> If my former letters have seemed to you harsh, I sincerely regret it, and can only say they were not meant to be so. I am quite ready to receive you back

> whenever you choose to come, without further reference to the matters which you have considered difficulties in the way of return. I am now willing to leave these to your own discretion and good feeling. Whatever the differences between us have been, I for my part shall try to forget them, and shall strive by every means in my power to make your life in the future a happy one.

He claimed that now his farming was unprofitable, his shooting rents uncertain and his annual income, after paying the interest on his debts and estate expenses, reduced to about £100 they would have to stay at Tournaig. The accommodation there was limited, but he would permit her to bring a maid with her. Should circumstances change, he hoped to return to Inverewe, without his mother. He understood that this might not be acceptable:

> I am willing that you should come to see Mary as formerly – viz., three days in the week, from ten to twelve o'clock, and that you should have her to yourself during your visits, without the presence of anyone. Perhaps you may see your way to occupy part of the time in helping the child with her studies, as you are so well able to do, but as to this you must yourself judge. I shall be at all times willing to see you when you come, if you will allow me. If you should be at any time unwell and unable to come to Tournaig, I promise myself to bring Mary to see you at Pool House, and to leave her there with you for the usual time.
>
> Anxiously awaiting your reply, which kindly address to me, to the Cockburn Hotel, Edinburgh.
>
> I remain, ever your faithful husband.

In the divorce hearings it was adjudged 'an excellent letter, but it is scarcely the letter of the pursuer. It was revised by his legal advisers, and is absolutely different in tone from any of his letters in 1884–1885. [...] It is an unconditional invitation to his wife to return, even the maid being conceded, and it is expressed in very conciliatory language'. But it had been boxed to the Court even before it was received by Minna. She believed that this 'altered tone' was only after strong advice from his solicitors in the light of the new act. In a letter of 16 September Osgood repeated that he was now 'anxious to let bygones be bygones and begin our married life anew'. She did not believe that he was sincere.

The Appeal Court judges concurred in 1895 'that Osgood would have wanted to see himself presented in a better light in court' and that Minna could be 'excused for thinking that the offer was not written in good faith, but was intended as move in the litigation to influence the Court, or to lay the foundation for an action of divorce'. This was corroborated by Dixon, whom Osgood had consulted: 'He said to me that unless he were to give an unconditional invitation to her to return, he might lose the child altogether. He seemed to be afraid of that. [...] He never contemplated his wife returning at that time'.

The judges in 1887 decided, as an interim order, that it was 'quite in the child's own interests that it should be with the mother in the mother's home [...] during the months of August and September'. Osgood was devastated: 'He seemed to feel very severely the order pronounced by the Court. [...] All his views were that his wife would injure the child's character and so on'. Osgood's request that Minna bring the child to visit him and her grandmother at Tournaig was mocked by Minna's legal counsel. Was he expecting 'Fridays at nine o'clock in the morning'? The decision was made that the child did not have to be taken to Tournaig at all. In Inverewe House there is a Gaelic Bible, with a Gaelic inscription, 'To Mairi T Mackenzie from her loving father at the time of parting from her on the first day of July 1887'.[15] Minna, of course, would not have been able to read this Bible with her daughter.

Osgood would take Mairi to stay with her mother at Pool House and he claimed that he was hopeful that 'there might be an opportunity for conversation between me and my wife, resulting in reconciliation'. He also tried asking her to bring Mary to the garden at Inverewe 'to eat gooseberries', but 'did not succeed in getting an interview with her alone'. Whether this was a genuine change of heart or to prevent Minna gaining more influence over the child was debated at length five years later.

So Osgood offered Minna a return to Inverewe, as his shooting tenants had now left. They met in Pool House on 24 September but Minna refused to send Miss Davidson, 'a second cousin of mine, who was living with my wife', out of the room whilst he was there, and Osgood refused to discuss anything unless alone. 'She refused to kiss him, and he thought she hated him. "He felt quite gulpy"'. Minna's brother, Cottingham, also staying there at the time, tried but failed to bring the couple to talk to each other amicably. Minna wrote back to Osgood in October saying that she did not think they could ever live together again. He replied saying that their child would bring them together, but Minna believed 'they had such different ideas about her upbringing that this would be the first cause of disagreement'. She asked about 'permanent arrangements he was prepared to make that she might have reasonable enjoyment of Thyra's society'.

In December Minna was applying once again to the court for more access to her daughter as she and Osgood could not agree, either over the immediate Christmas holiday or longer term arrangements. He still claimed that the courts had no jurisdiction over the matter. Minna requested a fortnight at Christmas, with permission to take the child to see relatives in England, six weeks in the autumn and to have 'regular and unrestricted access' during the course of the year. She was given custody for three weeks, though seems not to have taken advantage of the court's allowing her to take Mairi away on family visits. She was not required to produce the financial guarantee she had offered against returning the child. Lord Young, one of the judges, stated: 'For my part I think the child would be infinitely better in the custody of its mother altogether', with which the other law lords agreed. They expressed the hope that the parties could now resolve the longer term issues between themselves but compromise proved to be out of the question and all parties were back in court again in March 1888. Osgood offered six weeks in the autumn, two weeks at Christmas and Easter and all visits otherwise to be at the Dowager Lady Mary's house. Minna had hoped for six months each year. Eventually, in May, she was actually granted six weeks during August and September, three weeks at Christmas and every Saturday and Wednesday from twelve to two o'clock. Osgood made a point of saying that he and his daughter were now living at Inverewe, 'her own home' (though he was still renting it out to shooting tenants throughout this period).

This was the final court decision on access. Minna though failed to win the affection of her daughter. She must have been optimistic that the arrangement would have been long-term given the major alterations made to Pool House in 1889.[16] However, in 1891, now twelve, (the legal age at which she could make up her own mind), Mairi wrote to her mother that she was electing to reside with her father alone. To verify that this was genuinely her own decision Minna traced daughter and father to Brighton. She heard the same message from Mairi's mouth. Osgood later claimed, 'I thought that if the child had passed the age of twelve and the regulated access came to an end, my wife would certainly come back, anticipating that the child would make a home for us. I felt so confident of that that I made some changes upon Tournaig, to which I added three or four rooms'. According to Dixon, these changes were so that Mairi could have a governess and nothing to do with any possibility that Minna might return. Minna, testified Osgood, then 'wrote two or three notes to the child. The last was in the beginning of June, and since then she has not spoken to the child or acknowledged her on the road, and has never asked to see her'.

Three Divorce Courts

Minna must have accepted that Mairi's decision was final. Before the year was out Osgood decided he would legally end the marriage which had failed in reality so long ago. He confided in Dixon once again: 'In December last he told me that he was about to apply for a divorce, and I said in reply "Well, I am very sorry to hear it". He said: "Well you see it is this way: if I don't get a divorce and my wife were to survive me, she would have Inverewe"'.

Divorce would 'strip the wife of her name and hand over her fortune to her husband, regarding her, in fact, as dead'. There were only two grounds permitting this, adultery or desertion. Of adultery there was never any suggestion: 'There is no imputation on the character of either of the parents, none whatever. [...] In point of character each parent is irreproachable', so Osgood's plea was that his wife was 'guilty of wilful and malicious non-adherence to and desertion of the pursuer for the space of four years'. He applied for a decree of divorce, and to 'have it declared that the defender had lost the dos and tocher &c', essentially all the financial assets which she had brought to the marriage. He claimed that he had 'all along been willing and ready to adhere to the defender, and he has made repeated attempts, both personally and by letter, to induce her to return and adhere to him as his wife. The defender, however, has repelled all these advances and refused to adhere to the pursuer. She has continued in wilful and malicious desertion from him since said 4th August 1880 or at least for four years prior to the present date'.

Minna's defence was that 'the pursuer never entertained a genuine desire that she should return to his society, and that the offers as made were not such as she could accept consistently with self-respect, and that they were made solely in order to lay a foundation for the proceedings against her. The pursuer has shewn entire want of affection and consideration for the defender and she has suffered very acutely in her feelings from his conduct towards her and her family, and she has no reason to suppose that, if she returned to his house, he would treat her otherwise than in the cruel and tyrannical manner which forced her to leave Tournaig in August 1880'.

Osgood maintained that he had never recognised the separation as permanent and wanted to 'terminate a state of matters which was injurious to the present welfare and future prospects of their child, and was also the cause of public scandal and much suffering in himself'. However, Minna had 'steadily rejected his advances, both in her letters and at personal meetings, and has for long ceased to recognise him when they meet'. He must have been confident of success since, in those days, divorce was extremely unusual and the husband almost invariably seen to be in the right. Surely he would not have exposed himself and his mother to the public and press otherwise? But on three occasions he was to fail and, in the process, be condemned himself for his conduct and attitude.

The first hearing was in 1892. On 24 June

> Lord Wellwood, in the Court of Session, Edinburgh, gave judgement in the action for divorce by Osgood Hanbury Mackenzie of Inverewe against his wife, Miss Amy Edwards Moss or Mackenzie, residing at Pool House, Poolewe, Ross-shire. He found that Mrs Mackenzie's desertion of her husband was owing to his own conduct and that Mr Mackenzie took no reasonable means to try to get her back. He accordingly refused divorce and found the pursuer liable in his wife's expenses.

The second decision came in March 1893, again in the Court of Session, this time the Second Division. One judge, Lord Rutherford Clark, thought Osgood entitled to his divorce. Minna should have had more tolerance of her husband's mother. He saw nothing more 'than the unhappiness of an ill-matched pair due to the fact that their ideas, tastes and pursuits were entirely dissimilar, and that they could not or would not shew any forbearance or make any concession'. He blamed the breakdown of the marriage firmly on Minna:

> From an early date the defender repented of her marriage. She was translated to a new and uncongenial scene. She was, I think, disappointed in the place of her residence, as being different from her former luxurious home. She was disappointed in her husband. She was distressed with the presence of Lady Mackenzie, and with the influence which she possessed over her son. These and other causes produced a great revulsion of feeling, and led her to treat her husband with a sullen coldness. She says she married for love. I believe her [...] but her love very soon died. She made no effort to keep it alive. She did worse. She so acted as to alienate the affection of her husband, [...] she was very prompt in taking offence, and her resentment was manifested in a very marked and disagreeable way.

But he was the only law lord who ever took Osgood's part. The other judges in 1893 showed great sympathy for Minna:

> She might and even perhaps ought to have been more docile and submissive than she was, and to have continued longer to endure the prejudices of her

> husband and mother-in-law and win her way to their favour. [...] She may not always have behaved in the most judicious, amiable and gentle manner. [...] A young wife and mother whose demeanour and conduct under very exceptionally trying circumstances of some duration met with universal unqualified approval would be a marvel.

They agreed that 'the pursuer's conduct to the defender, culminating in the act of violence on his part on 4 August 1880, was sufficient to entitle her to a decree of separation, and afforded more than would have been necessary for a sufficient defence to an action of adherence'. So she had been justified in leaving, she had 'reasonable cause' so to do and for refusing to return to him, 'notwithstanding an offer on his part to take her back', and Osgood was, therefore, not entitled to decree of divorce.

Undaunted, Osgood tried once again. He applied to the highest court in the land for a 'declarator to the effect that the appellant was free to marry again, and that the respondent had forfeited all the privileges of a lawful wife, including her claims as a widow, whether legal or conventional'. The *Inverness Courier*, 8 March 1895, reported:

> In the House of Lords consideration was given to the appeal by Mr Osgood Mackenzie of Inverewe, seeking divorce from his wife, a daughter of Sir Thomas Moss of Otterspool, Liverpool, on the grounds of wilful desertion for four years. The appellant alleged that a plot had been arranged to remove his child from Inverewe.

There were a thousand pages of evidence with detailed accounts of their married life, altogether a 'painful case'. Minna 'objected to the petition being granted pleading that her desertion was justified because of her husband's treatment "which amounted to legal cruelty"'. In Scottish law two kinds of misconduct were recognised as releasing a spouse from the obligation of adherence, (fulfilling conjugal duties), namely adultery and saevitia (cruelty). So there was much re-examination of the evidence of the events of 4 August 1880. Osgood maintained that what had happened on that particular day was an isolated incident, which did not amount to cruelty or 'saevitia, such as would entitle the respondent to a separation *a mensa et thoro*'.

Against this Minna's lawyers concentrated on incidents amounting to cruelty which justified her 'desertion'. On 4 August, when Osgood had removed the child from her by force, 'he was manifestly acting under the belief that he was entitled to use physical means in order to subdue her will and to reduce it to absolute submission to his own'. There was complete agreement with the conclusions arrived at in 1893 that the defender had had 'reasonable cause' to leave him then, as 'she could not with self-respect or safety to health have remained in the house. [...] When a husband, who has habitually treated his wife in such a way as to make her life miserable and impair her health, uses physical violence to her, his previous conduct may at once be appealed to to strengthen and complete the charge of cruelty'.

It was not considered to have been 'an accidental outburst' but rather 'evidence of a settled determination that he would compel his wife to obey him, however trifling and unreasonable his commands might be, and that if necessary he would use force [...] as part of a systematic course of treatment which the defender had to accept and submit to if she remained at Tournaig'. He demanded from her strict obedience and constant acknowledgement of error. 'His manner to his wife from some of the evidence would appear to have been rough, and his brother says on one occasion "bearish"'.

Lord Watson gave his considered view:

> I do not impute to the applicant that his conduct, cruel and reprehensible though it was in my estimation, was dictated by a wilful intention to injure the respondent. That he is a man capable of entertaining strong affection, his attachment to his mother and to his child afford ample proof. But he had some peculiarities, and amongst these was a very exalted sense of the dignity and supremacy of his position as husband, and of the absolute deference which he was entitled to exact from his partner in life. [...] Add to this that it seems never to have entered into the mind of the appellant to conceive the possibility of his being in the wrong.

It was even suggested that Minna might not still be alive, given the medical evidence, if she had stayed, as 'for two of the years she was there she was in great peril'. So Minna 'could not have returned to his house without apprehension that the unjustifiable violence he had used might be repeated'. The mental cruelty of the refusal by Osgood to allow Minna, a 'delicate, sick woman', to take her 'little infant girl' south with her in the winter of 1879–1880 was another aspect. 'It is impossible to conceive a more cruel, harsh and unfeeling threat'.

Osgood's conduct was deemed to be 'misguided and censurable'. Furthermore, the husband had not made any serious effort for seven years to invite Minna to return to him. As Minna's counsel said, 'even the honeymoon exhibited a very peculiar character, and if he (Osgood) was not in a position of actual wickedness, there was a total want of the feelings of one person to another, particularly of husband towards wife. [...] The pursuer was a man who talked of separation in the course of his honeymoon'. When he did ask her back it was to be on the basis of 'absolute submission'. Lord Watson commented that he had never seen a case before where there was no word of affection or penitence from a husband who wanted his wife to return. It was scarcely surprising that his wife regarded his offers with suspicion. 'One of the most remarkable features of the case is that the pursuer withdraws nothing and regrets nothing' and was now following a process of divorce for desertion which would strip Minna of her name and fortune.

Lord Ashbourne stated that Osgood Mackenzie had 'showed by his conduct great recklessness and disregard of her feelings and those of her family', in that he had responded to her genuine efforts at reconciliation 'hardly and harshly and showed no desire to meet her half way'. Osgood's emphasis on 'The Plot' was also dismissed as illustrating the 'proneness of mankind to believe only so much of the truth as will suit their own purposes'. He had 'grave doubt whether the Court ought to be called upon to assist a husband in getting his marriage cancelled if he himself adopted a line of conduct towards his spouse which made it impossible for her to live with him'.

So, although Minna was not 'wholly free from blame', Mr Mackenzie's appeal was dismissed, with costs awarded against him. Though she never asked for it, Minna was judged to have 'ample ground for a decree of separation'.

> Regarding all the circumstances of the case, I arrive at the clear conclusion that the violence of the 4th of August 1880, the mental torture to which she was subjected, the dread of coercion and confinement caused by her husband's threats, would have entitled the wife to ask for a judicial separation, and therefore in any view of the law to resist a suit for adherence.

Osgood had lost his wife, his potential fortune and his relationship with friends and family. John Dixon, with his legal background, had been a convincing witness in court on Minna's behalf. But that had not been his original intention:

> It was upon reading his statement to the effect that he was sincere in making the offer to take his wife back that I was led to offer to give evidence to-day, and I have therefore volunteered to say what I have said this morning. I have come forward entirely of my own accord.

Osgood had often taken him into his confidence and shared his thoughts about his wife's attitudes and behaviours. In retrospect, he now believed that both the 'plots' (Minna planning to take the child to her parents in February 1880 and the 'yacht' fears of August 1880) were 'fabrications'. But it was when he 'formed the opinion that the pursuer had the strongest aversion to his wife and [...] he looked forward with satisfaction to the time when he would get a divorce', that he distanced himself from the situation. He said that he 'had hardly seen the pursuer' since 4 August 1880, 'though they had been on close and intimate terms before these occurrences'. However, there were certainly further discussions about Minna's various applications for access and they had co-operated over many sections of Dixon's *Guide to Gairloch* in the mid-1880s. Only when Osgood actually applied for divorce did his friend take his wife's side as he was not prepared to be complicit in Osgood's claims. Ultimately, Dixon believed it was Minna who was the innocent party in the marriage failure and that Osgood never genuinely wanted to be reconciled with her.

Likewise, Osgood's brother, Kenneth, and sister-in-law, Eila, had impressed the judges with their efforts to sustain the marriage, modify Osgood's behaviour and to support Minna: 'Nothing could be more high minded than the conduct of Sir Kenneth and Lady Mackenzie in defending their sister-in-law from what was a great injustice and breach of faith and they were not afraid to say so'. Osgood's other half-brother, Francis, had spoken out in his support, though he had limited day-to-day knowledge of the circumstances of the marriage, having lived for the past twelve or fourteen years in Serbia. He did return home for about three months each year 'but just as a visitor among friends' and had been at Kerrysdale when Osgood and Minna returned from their honeymoon in 1877.[17]

Most telling of all were the comments on the role Osgood's mother had played in this sad case: 'The Dowager was the dominant power and the pursuer was clay in the hands of the potter'. Minna never had a chance: 'It was perfectly plain that at a very early period Mr Mackenzie had come into the condition of mind that if it came to be a question whether he should lose his mother or his wife, he would prefer to leave the latter'.

The 1893 court had already recognised that, from the early months of the marriage, Minna had a 'growing dread' of the influence of the Dowager, which Osgood did not comprehend. He was 'from first to last blind to the effect [...] upon the defender of the relations between himself and his mother [...] of his own conduct to the defender. [...] The Dowager did, both at Inverewe and Tournaig, monopolise her son; her influence over him was great, and it was not exercised favourably to the defender'.

> We must all sympathise with a mother's love for her only son who had never lived apart from her, and with her strong and perhaps passionate desire that

> they should continue to live together even after his marriage. [...] She seems to have found, on brooding over the thing, that the sacrifice was more than she could bear. The result was that she and her son agreed together to break their pledged word and faith to the defender and her parents. [...] The Dowager assumed the position of head of the house, and in concert with her son acted with the manifest and indeed not concealed determination of subjecting the young wife to a humiliating state of obedient subjection. The evidence shows that the Dowager was of an imperious temper and took but little account of the defender's feelings of wife or mother. I think the design was to break the defender's spirit, and subdue her to be a nonentity in the house of which her mother-in-law was the supreme and indeed only head.

The conclusion reached by the House of Lords was that the origin of the dispute was 'to be found in disagreements with the pursuant's mother. [...] The strong attachment which existed between them and her control over him were altogether exceptional circumstances'. Lord Ashbourne put it in a nutshell:

> The pursuer is a Highland gentleman of good family, of austere mind and exacting nature. He married the defendant some eighteen years ago, she being a young lady of good position, fortune and education. It is most sad to think that but for the existence of his mother their married life might possibly have been unbroken and untroubled. [...] The injury she did was immense and continuous.

One of the Dowager Lady's obituarists recognised the situation, though put it in a positive light: 'His father having died when he was a child Osgood was brought up under the direct influence and inspiration of his devoted mother'. However, this 'influence and inspiration' went beyond natural love and respect and was to dominate his whole life. As his uncle's biographer commented: 'Their obsessive love for each other was a monopoly in which no one could share, least of all her unhappy daughter-in-law, Minna, the daughter of Sir Thomas Edwards Moss, banker, of Liverpool'.[18]

To the bitter end

Minna continued to lease Pool House until 1897.[19] She was never mentioned in any of Osgood's writings. Poignantly, in one of her photograph albums, without comment, Mairi pasted a notice of her mother's death, which took place on 19 August (1909) at Birdingbury Hall, Rugby. She was there for the 1901 Census, as head of the household, with several servants. However, she was not buried in the local cemetery. Now that his wife was dead, Osgood made one last effort to benefit from her wealth. In 1911 he applied to the Chancery Division for judgement that he, as her surviving husband, and Mairi, (now Mrs Hanbury), her only child, were entitled to a large share of her estate, since 'by her will she disposed of this property to the exclusion of her husband and child'. His claim was based on the fact that Minna had still legally been married to him, was therefore domiciled in Scotland and her 'free movable estate' subject to Scottish inheritance laws.

Her executors had two lines of defence against the action. The first was that the marriage contracts had been drawn up in 1877, before the Married Women's Property Act of 1884 (which might, in this situation, have acted against a woman whose cause, in general, it had been intended to improve). These arrangements had given Minna separate and independent rights to her own fortune and the inheritance from her parents. In fact, her younger brother, Tom Cottingham, had also predeceased her, dying of typhoid in 1893.[20] So she was a very rich lady indeed. The second argument was that, although she had never actually gone to court to achieve a decree of judicial separation, the clear statements of the judges of the various divorce proceedings meant she would certainly have been granted such, had she asked. So, she had every right to her own English domicile. 'She was no longer under the power and authority of her husband'.

After much complex legal debate and reference to previous case law the judges ruled, once more, against Osgood, on the basis that the date and terms of the pre-nuptial contracts allowed Minna to dispose of her wealth as she thought fit. She had won the legal arguments again, even in death.

Appendix

Legends of Leading Cases[21]

The Mackenzie Case

I

OSGOOD MACKENZIE a courting would go,
Heigho!
Young men do so,
Whether his mother would let him or no:
And it's O, but the dowager looked right glum,
She's got Master Osgood well under her thumb;
Should he go or come
Without asking his 'mum'–
There'll be ructions which you might consider as rum.

II

To the county of Ross,
Came the fair Minna Moss,
The sweetest young moss-rose you ere came across,
And Osgood's heart was an absolute loss –
Clean derelict,
Although brought up so strict,
The arrows of Cupid his bosom had pricked
(And, whisper it low,
Young Osgood doth know
That Minna has some twenty thousand or so).
So his suit he did press,
With clasp and caress,
And many professions of deep tenderness,
Till the fair Minna Moss was induced to say 'yes'.
But smit with a fear,
That their life might be queer,
In her *fiance's* ear, she murmured 'my dear!
If I wed you the dowager mustn't stop here.'

III

Then out spoke that dowager, wrinkled and grey,
'If I'm going away –
Not one single day,
In the young people's home, do I purpose to stay;
I beg you to note it' –
On paper she wrote it,
And she said it, as plain as a body could speak;
But she said it, I fear, with her tongue in her cheek;
For Minna and Osgood scarce were wed,
And not long had the honeymoon been fled,
When they saw at the door the dowager's head,
With boxes a score,
And trunks galore;
And they've got to endure it, say what they may,
For it's plain the old lady has come to stay.
She had promised she wouldn't, but then 'twas absurd,
So she said, to suppose she would keep to her word.

IV

O, the dowager's crusty, and crabbed, and cross,
And she loathes all the kin of the fair Minna Moss;
She is ready to 'boss'
All the county of Ross;
And for other folks' feelings she don't care a toss.
O, that dowager gaunt and grim,
Osgood bowed to her slightest whim:
He may love his young wife,
But the whole of his life
That masterful matron managed him;
And everyone saw,
With pity and awe,
How poor little Minna was under the claw
Of a most reprehensible mother-in-law.

V

Osgood and Minna a-visiting went;
In the calm, bright days, ere the autumn was spent;
For a fortnight or more
They stayed at Braemore,
A place where young Osgood had oft been before.
But they had to pack
Up their goods in a crack,
Though the lift grew dark, and the clouds rolled black –
For the dowager ordered Osgood back.

VI

Alas! for fair Minna – the wind blew cold,
The lightning flashed, and the thunder rolled,
Deep was the mud,
The rivers in flood,
And the roads impassable, so they were told
In a farm-cart – Good lack!
Up a rough hill-track,
With the luggage piled in a tottery stack,
And poor little Minna must walk beside,
A pitiful plight for a three months' bride,
Mid the elements' din,
Drenched to the skin;
But Master Osgood don't care a pin,
The word hath been said
And, alive or dead,
They must reach Inverewe ere the night close black,
For why? – the dowager ordered him back.

VII

Quoth Osgood, "My wife
Is the bane of my life,
And that is the cause of this trouble and strife.
For, you know, I'm a very superior man,
Built on the old Calvinistical plan;
And grace upstored

On me is outpoured,
I'm a chosen vessel before the Lord;
I stand for a sign,
And brightly shine
Before the Auld Kirk, an example fine:
But that Saxon, Prelatical, wife of mine
For holy example, in nowise cares –
In a godless tea-gown she comes downstairs –
And kneels on the chairs,
When I read prayers;
Or flippantly out of the window stares.
At dinner besides, with a smile on her face,
She shakes out her napkin when I say grace;
And what is worse,
She don't care a curse,
Though I go to visit my elderly nurse."
Quoth the dowager, "Keep it up, my son,
When the web is spun,
And the game is done,
And Minna's fortune for us is won,
The Clan Mackenzie will see some fun.
She's obstinate still, but don't you fret,
We'll put the screw on tighter yet;
As soon as may be
We'll bag her baby,
And that will bring her to book – you bet".

VIII

So, early one morn, as the baby lay
Beside its mother in peaceful play;
Those precious two,
They raised a stew,
And Lord! what a riot and hullabaloo;
For the dowager, and Osgood too,
One on each side,
Seized her, and tried
All they knew

That deed to do,
And pinched poor Minna black and blue;
And succeeded, at last, I grieve to say,
For they managed to carry the baby away.

IX

Now, a lady gets wild
If you steal her child,
And Minna became most uncommonly 'riled',
Such treatment would rouse
The poorest church-mouse,
So she picked up her bag, and walked out of the house.

* * *

And some time after, the Second Division
Heard all the arguments put with precision;
And gravely and solemnly gave their decision –
Without a doubt, and plain as could be,
Gave Minna her baby's custody.
So it was plain
The dowager's reign
Now, at last, was upon the wane,
And Minna had got her baby again.

X

When many a year was come and fled,
And Minna's parents both were dead,
Osgood matured a plan in his head,
And unto himself he softly said;
"My wife has deserted me many a year,
By the old Scottish law she is bound to 'adhere,'
So I calculate now that her hand I can force
By raising an action to crave divorce;
And so her fortune I'll calmly bag,
And, as though she were dead, I'll collar the 'swag.'"

* * *

But the Court they turned him inside out,
And sent him away to the right-about.
No doubt, a reason good they saw
For Minna's flight from the angry claw
Of that grimmest of grim old mothers-in-law.

J.W. BRODIE-INNES

References and Notes

1 Newspapers used:

Paper	1887/8	1892	1895
Ross-shire Journal		20 May 27 May 3 June 10 June 24 June	22 March
Northern Chronicle		20 May 27 May 3 June 10 June 24 June	6 March 13 March
Inverness Courier		24 June	1 March 8 March 17 May
The Scotsman	14 May (1887) 2 June (1887) 8 July (1887) 23 Dec (1887) 2 March (1888) 23 May (1888)		17 March 17 May

Paper	1887/8		1892	1895
Scottish Highlander	19 May	(1887)		
	2 & 9 June	(1887)		
	14 July	(1887)		
	22 December	(1887)		
	8 March	(1888)		
	24 May	(1888)		

A copy of the testimonies of the 1892 court case witnesses was bound together by John H. Dixon as *The Mackenzie Case*. Gairloch Heritage Museum Library.

Legal records of the proceedings of the 1893 and 1895 cases have been made available by Prof. Paisley of Aberdeen University.

All these records have been used to relate the events of Osgood's married life.

2 In 1851 Thomas had assumed the additional surname of Edwards by Royal licence.

3 Marriage notice in *The Times*. This possibly rather unexpected choice of minister is explained by the fact that the bishop was associated with the Edwards-Moss family's West Indies sugar-plantation business.

4 Born in 1838, John H. Dixon told, when a witness in the Divorce Court, that he had been a 'solicitor in Wakefield and held the appointment of Deputy-Clerk of the Peace for the West Riding of Yorkshire and other public appointments until bad health compelled me to retire from practice'. (*The Mackenzie Case* p.279) He had a tubercular arm. He had known Osgood and his mother before he took the lease of Inveran, on Sir Kenneth's estate of Gairloch, in 1874. It still stands, about a mile from Poolewe village, on the shore of Loch Maree. In 1878 Dixon enlarged the house and made it his home, spending nearly all the year there, often joined by his 'amiable sister'. He rented trout fishings and shootings from Osgood, his nearest neighbour, who often used his jetty for the last stage of his journeys home.

5 John Fowler bought the estate of Braemore, about 40 miles from Inverewe (see maps).

6 Poolewe School Log Book.

7 See Chapter VII for more detail on this case.

8 Despite Francis' evidence, there is little support for Osgood having many close friends other than John Dixon.

9 The nickname 'Snog' for the child was only used this once by Osgood. In court he usually referred to her as 'the child'. The judges called her 'Mary' as did Osgood in correspondence. Minna preferred to call her baby, Thyra. 'Mairi' seems to have

been generally used when the family were in Scotland and is the name by which she is known at Inverewe. Her Hanbury relatives called her 'Aunty Mary'.

10 Dixon, p.317.

11 Pool House Hotel staff information.

12 Andrew P.K. Wright, *Inverewe House Conservation Plan* (National Trust for Scotland, 2008), p.24.

13 Ross-shire Valuation Rolls, Highland Council Archives, Inverness.

14 See detail in Chapter VII.

15 The translated month of 'July' is perplexing. Perhaps Mairi had already gone to stay with her mother before the official court decision.

16 Wright, p.24.

17 *The Mackenzie Case*, pp.136, 137, 138–139. In *A Hundred Years* (p.58) Osgood spoke very generously of his 'second brother, Francis' who was, 'quite as great a man' as Kenneth, and 'equally beloved and respected'. There is little to be found about him. Osgood mentioned that he had a farm in Orkney and Dr John, in his manuscript diaries, referred to concerns that he was living his own life in Serbia. According to Wikipedia, accessed 8 December 2008, Francis Mackenzie was a member of the Plymouth Brethren Nazarene group, who travelled to Belgrade to start work for the British and Foreign Bible Society to foster religiousity among the Serbian people. He lived in Belgrade from 1876 till 1895, was a prominent figure in Belgrade society and a friend of many Serbian politicians. He became very wealthy and influential and built a large Peace Hall which was renowned for political events. He was also known for policies, such as not allowing restaurants on his land and forbidding smoking in all public places, which were generally disliked and eventually failed. Mackenzie contributed around eight thousand square metres of his land for the construction of the Temple of Saint Sava. His name was inscribed in the list of Great Benefactors, right after the members of the Royal family and senior church dignitaries. The main street in Vracar was named after him. He never married and died in 1895 in Croydon, near London.

18 Byam Shaw, p.230.

19 Ross-shire Valuation Rolls.

20 *New York Times*, 4 January 1894.

21 This 'poem', provenance unknown, was found pasted inside John Dixon's copy of *The Mackenzie Case*.

CHAPTER VII

Farming and Livelihood

'I can truly say that neither the Hill Lands nor the Arable of these properties will pay any one who farms them.'

The Inverewe property

The General Register of Sasines recorded that on 4 June 1862 Osgood Hanbury Mackenzie became the legal owner of the lands called Kernsary and on 30 June 1863 the Davoch lands of Inverewe were added, together with 'all and sundry houses, biggings, yeards, orchyards, lofts, crofts, outfield lands, infield lands, loanings, grazings, shealings, woods, fishings, as well in fresh as in salt waters, mosses, muirs, marishes, lochs, havens, harbours, privileges, pasturages, annexis, connexis, dependencies, parts, pendicles and universal pertinents pertaining or that shall be known to belong and appertain to the said haill lands and grazings by any manner of way whatsoever excepting the Salmon fishing of the fresh water of Ewe herein no wise to be held as contained in any manner of way and excepting also the Salmon fishing in the Waters of Loch Ewe'.[1]

Osgood's twelve thousand acres of bog, moor and hill, given to him by his mother, included the areas known as Kernsary, Lochend or Inverewe, and Tournaig. The Seaforth family had bought Kernsary in the 1830s to provide a port at Londubh from which they could access the Isle of Lews (Lewis) which they also owned. When they decided to sell this in 1844, having given up their Hebridean interests, it was purchased by the Gairloch Mackenzies. Dr John, as factor, introduced some crofting reforms on these new acquisitions, including moving the three sets of tenants to other parts of the estate. The Lochend and Tournaig property was bought in 1863 from Sir William Mackenzie of Coul to whom it had come after a succession of owners. 'These and Kernsary now constitute Mr Osgood H. Mackenzie's charming estate of Inverewe, about one-sixteenth of the whole parish of Gairloch'.[2] Osgood recalled: 'I think the Inverewe properties were bought by my mother about 1862 at the price of £15,000'.[3]

For the next sixty years these lands were to be his home and provide his income. Early in the twentieth century he wrote, in longhand, an *Account and Statement as to the properties of Inverewe and Kernsary*, explaining the land usage before he bought it and explaining how, and why, he developed the property over the years.[4] According to this *Statement*,

> there were no Crofters on these Lands when I bought them, — each Property being in the sole occupation of a Sheep Farmer.
>
> In the case of Kernsary, the Tenant lived in the near Vicinity, though not actually on my land.
>
> — But in the case of Inverewe, the Tenant was non-resident, — as he had the large Farm of Moy, on the east side of this County, where he resided.
>
> Neither of these Sheep Farmers expended anything in improvements & they only employed two Shepherds each, at low wages. [...]
>
> At the time of the Potatoe Famine, about 1847 — the few Crofters who were then at Kernsary, were shifted to other Townships on the Gairloch Estate where they would have the advantages of Roads & schools where they could get Fish all the year round, — & no longer depend upon Whisky Smuggling & poaching loch fish, — of the latter they used to do a great deal in Nov.m & Dec.br by Torch & Spear in the Kernsary River, when the Salmon were spawning & out of condition, — & these blackfish when smoked were one of the main-stays in the way of food.[5]

In 1854, when the estate of 'Inverewe, Pluckhart and Tournaig in the parish of Gairloch' was advertised to let by Sir Alexander Mackenzie of Coul, it was stated that there was 'a good dwelling house and Garden, and several large, well-enclosed Parks, and it has a coast front of about six miles'.[6]

Livestock

The contemporary view, that the best profits for Highland farmers came from sheep-farming, appeared never to have been the reality on the Inverewe estate. The *Statement* provided insight into the trials and tribulations of sheep farming before Osgood took over:

> Sir George Mackenzie then tried as an experiment the stocking of Inverewe with Blackfaced Sheep, — the Shepherd & his flock tramping it all the way from the Borders, – but these latter (like the stock of the Kintail men) did not thrive, & they in their turn being sold off, the Property was for the third time filled up with Crofters.

> — This time it was made a Club Farm with 8 families at Inverewe, – & 8 families at Tournaig. — This last set of Crofters were all natives of this Parish, a good many of them coming from Melvaig, a township on the Gairloch Estate, — & to show how much even in these comparatively recent times the people of the West Highlands lived on Shell Fish I have often heard tell of how the Melvaig people despised the weaker Mussels, Oysters & Cockles of these Island Seas & longed for the most substantial Whelk & Limpet pots of their former homes on the Stormy Coast of the Rudha Reidh.
>
> — These Crofters or Club Farmers were no sooner in possession than they commenced to get into difficulties, & thinking to make matters easier to themselves they began taking in a number of Subtenants, settling them on different green spots here & there so that the rent might be less to each individual by dividing it over a greater number. — But this only made bad worse, & they ended poor people after 10 years of tenure in complete Bankruptcy & in being evicted. — The Farm was then taken by a Mr Brown of Linkwood who worked Inverewe as a Cheviot Sheep Farm, along with other high grounds in Strath Conan & Low Country Farms in Morayshire. Perhaps Inverewe did better financially in Mr Brown's days, than it ever did before, but even he always declared that he lost by it — & his successor, Mr Murdo Mackenzie of Moy, (from whom I took over the Stock in 1862) declared himself very thankful to get rid of it.

Records exist of a number of transactions of Inverewe sheep stock at market about this time: Cheviots were sold at Inverness sheep and wool fair on 15 July 1863 and at Falkirk tryst on 7 October 1867; Cheviot wethers went to Muir of Ord market in October 1868 and 1869, the latter sent by a Capt Davidson; blackfaced ewe washed wool was marketed in July 1864.[7]

Kernsary also was run as a sheep farm. Again, the tenants struggled to make a living from it, be they the 'Highlander from Kintail with an admirable & energetic wife & a strong family of Sons & Daughters', or Mr Peterkin who 'had the advantage of the Road, & of a good deal of new fencing'.[8] Each relinquished the lease at the earliest opportunity. At the time of his marriage, in 1877, Osgood had informed his future father-in-law that 'the income from the farm was very big at that time; for two or three years I had fully £400 for wool' and that 'sheep farming was very much more prosperous than it has been since. I got nearly four times as much for my wool as I do now, [1892] and the price of sheep was also higher'.[9] However, when he gave evidence to the Napier Commission in 1883, he acknowledged that he was a sheep farmer only 'to a small extent', with about 800 cheviots and that such farming led to deterioration of pasture because 'the sheep feed during the day time and go up and lie on the rocks at night and leave the manure there; whereas cattle always lie on the best places at night'.

Osgood came to the conclusion that 'the Hill Lands of Inverewe & Kernsary are very unsound for sheep & are subject, I think, to every known Sheep Disease'.[10] When the neighbouring Letterewe estate decided to make a deer forest, he abandoned his sheep enterprise. He would have had to create 'miles upon miles of fencing over the top of a Mountain about 2,600 ft high, where, if a Fence were erected, there would be no prospect of its standing'. So, 'For Sale' at the Muir of Ord market on 17 June 1885 was 'the Kernsary sheep stock, belonging to Osgood H. Mackenzie, Esq of Inverewe, comprising 190 blackface ewe hoggs, 70 blackface wether hoggs, 60 cross ewe hoggs, 30 cross wether hoggs, 100 blackface Two-year-old wethers, 90 cross wethers, 60 eild ewes and gimmers'.

Now he was more 'taken to cattle'. He bred pure West Highland animals, being unenthusiastic about shorthorn crosses. They were useful to the pasture, though he did not expect to make much profit from them. He considered it troublesome to be 'constantly buying in fresh Highland heifers'.[11] There were compliments as to their quality: 'The lover of the picturesque must admire the shaggy cattle of the breed now called "Highland", especially those of Mr O. H. Mackenzie of Inverewe, and of Dr Robertson of Achtercairn'.[12] 'A good slice of the low ground alongside Loch Maree' was wired off 'as a summering for my young Highland Cattle, & all the Arable & enclosed green ground as a wintering for the Calves of my fold of pedigree West Highlanders & for the Hoggs of my Inverewe Sheep Farm. — The Calves (of which I had 21 last year) are wintered in a large Cattle Shed & fed on Silage, the whole of the Arable being mowed & ensiled & the Deer being kept out by a 6 ft high Deer Fence'. Though, on reflection, he had to admit that 'the Highland Cattle are not really the "bona fide" product of the Soil but are in great measure produced by a pretty heavy expenditure on Glasgow feeding stuffs.'[13]

Arable and woodland

Similarly, Osgood appreciated the difficulties of establishing successful arable farming, given the challenges of ground and climate. He agreed that 'agriculture was very far behind in the old days of the runrig system. That this system was as bad a one as could be there is no denying. There was no incentive to improve your rig or patch, for what you had this year one of your neighbours probably had next year. There were continual quarrels over the distribution of the allotments'. Nonetheless, based on his own experience, he was 'prepared to prove that far more crop was raised out of the soil then than there is now'. Despite the investment and encouragement of both his father and uncle he concluded 'education has done nothing for agriculture among the crofters on the west coast as far as I can see. Though the people are certainly improving their dwellings, I seldom, if ever, see them use the pick, the spade, and the crowbar, which are so essential for trenching and draining and getting rid of boulders. In fact, many of the crofts are going back, instead of being improved'.[14] He did change his mind about the industriousness of the people between 1883, (giving evidence to the Napier Commission), when he said of the crofters 'I don't think they are very energetic at present', and commenting in his memoirs in 1921, 'there is, I think, a very mistaken idea afloat that these Highlanders of the olden times were a lazy lot, instead of which they were, in my opinion, just the very contrary'.[15]

The issue of 'crofters rights' and of land use was raised again in the 1890s. In September 1894 the Royal Commission for the Highlands and Islands came to Poolewe as part of its enquiry:

> Whether any, and what, if any, land in the counties of Argyle, Inverness, Ross and Cromarty, Sutherland, Caithness and Orkney and Shetland, now occupied for the purposes of a deer forest, grouse moor, or other sporting purposes, or for grazing, not in the occupation of crofters or other small tenants, is capable of being cultivated to profit or otherwise advantageously occupied by crofters or other small tenants.

One Aultbea crofter, Duncan Urquhart, aged 47, had suggested local land suitable for making new holdings including 'Isle of Ewe, Gruinard Island, Kernsary, Strathnasealg, Letterewe, Inverewe'. Osgood gave evidence that Kernsary was part of Inverewe Forest, a deer forest, 'made about nine or ten years ago', (though Mr David Brand, the chairman, said he had failed to find such a place as Inverewe Deer Forest on the 1891 Valuation Roll), but he disputed that it would be feasible to set up six or seven crofting holdings as Mr Urquhart suggested. Osgood claimed that he was productively farming sixteen acres of arable land at Kernsary himself but doubted that creating a number of small crofts would be viable: 'How could you put 5 crofters comfortably on 16 acres?'[16] The Commissioners agreed with him as they did not recommend Inverewe for restructuring.

Despite his evidence to the Commission that his arable land was well utilised, Osgood explained, in some detail, in the *Statement* how he had tried, and essentially failed, to improve it as he would have wished:

> The Arable Land at Kernsary has not, I fancy, ever been measured but I think it is about 16 Acres in extent – out of this 9–10 Acres are constantly liable to be flooded whenever there is heavy rain, & though I have at different times, spent a good deal of money in clearing the Bed of the River, & lowering the level of the Loch by blasting at its outfall, I fear the money has been mostly spent in vain as every fresh flood brings down such masses of shingle that the Bed of the River is raised to the Level of the Land, & the water spreads over the whole flat, which makes it quite unfit for cultivation — Even under Grass laid down most carefully with Manure & Lime & Sutton's best permanent Grass Seeds, I get but the poorest returns, as no Farmyard Manure can be put on the Flat in the Autumn or Winter as it would all be swept into the Loch.

His other land was no more productive:

> The Arable Land of Inverewe & Tournaig is about 70 Acres in extent. – I should be ashamed to tell the amount of money that has been expended on it. [...] With all this expenditure, it is of the most inferior description & after 30 years trial of it, I can truly say – that neither the Hill Lands nor the Arable of these properties will pay any one who Farms them-
>
> — Both Inverewe & Kernsary have down the last 100 years been tried in every possible way that could be thought of.[17]

But Dixon was approving as he drove along through Poolewe: 'On the right is Srondubh, with a few trees, and by it the farm buildings of the home farm in connection with Inverewe House. The roads skirts along well cultivated arable land until the Inverewe plantations are reached'.[18]

These trees were a lifelong interest. Osgood somewhat exaggerated by claiming that, when he bought the estate, there had been 'no cultivation for fifty years at least, not a vestige of wood on 12,000 acres'[19] as he actually acquired 'small natural woods at [...] Kernsary, also a natural wood between Kernsary and Tournaig, called Coille Aigeascaig'.[20] He immediately planted saplings at Inverewe, more as a shelter belt than with any anticipation of making money, a long term proposition at the best of times when his need always was for ready income. Nonetheless, he was genuinely willing to invest in woodland. When questioned by the Napier Commission about its value he responded: 'I cannot say. I have never sold any wood; my wood is all young; but I think it is all low'. There were problems: the bog had to be drained before the trees would grow and all of the higher land was of such poor soil that it was not appropriate to replace deer forest with trees. Most of what he had planted was ornamental rather than utilitarian, to be useful for housing, roofing and fencing posts and he confirmed that 'if I had more money I should like to plant thousands of acres, but it is rather expensive work'.[21]

Marriage and money

It was suggested during the divorce case proceedings that Osgood had been expected by his mother to find a wife with considerable wealth. Although Osgood strongly denied this, financial arrangements undoubtedly played a significant role in his pre-marriage discussions with Sir Thomas Moss, who was clearly aware that his daughter brought with her a dowry that completely overshadowed her future husband's own resources, even given the commitment of the Dowager Lady Mary to provide a substantial annual income to her son. Ironically, this meant that she was unable to pay for the building of her residence at Tournaig, which was made possible only through a loan from her son's new father-in-law.[22]

Osgood maintained later that his 'financial position very much depended on the success of farming' and, unfortunately, such income declined considerably in the next few years. He could not maintain the £2,000 pa. he had anticipated and money continued to be a matter of major concern. The legal costs of the Loch Dubh case in 1878, [see below] were a heavy burden and when Minna first left him, in the spring of 1880, her father called up a loan which had been part of the marriage contract funds, since the interest of it was for her use. Osgood struggled to pay this and was very bitter.

In court in December 1887, when Minna was applying for better access to her daughter, the difference between his 'available income' of about £100 each year was compared with that of his wealthy wife, generously supported by her father. Her husband was said to be 'in such circumstances that he must of necessity live upon the bounty of some other, and he is living on the bounty of his mother, and the only house that he speaks of for his wife is his mother's house – his mother's home and establishment'.[23] His financial security would certainly not have been helped by these ongoing legal bills.

Shooting tenants

Neither livestock nor arable farming produced a satisfactory income for Osgood. However, there was one increasingly popular way in which he could use his 12,000 acres of boggy moorland and lochs to economic advantage and that was by renting it, to wealthy visitors, with his house as accommodation, for the hunting, shooting and fishing seasons.

Hunting as sport had not been usual at the start of the century. Dr John wrote of his father, Sir Hector:

> His income was about £3,000, but shootings were not let in his time, in the Highlands at least. [...] My Father never went out to kill a heavy bag. Such things were never boasted of in those times as they are nowadays, when a man who shoots, say, a hundred brace in a day is looked up to as quite a hero. Except to vary the house diet, and give some game to a tenant, killing more was mere wastery, there being no way to dispose of it – no steamers, no rails, no wheels in Gairloch, to send it fizzing all over the Kingdom.[24]

Thereafter the fashion for game hunting developed rapidly in the Highlands. In 1836 Hugh Snowie, a gun-maker in Inverness, advertised eight shootings to let; by 1839 he had at least 28 deer forests on his books. Once Prince Albert had shot several stags in Scotland in the 1840s, and so bestowed royal approval on the activity, it became both fashionable and prestigious to rent or own a Highland deer forest. The 'new rich' added a seasonal migration to the hills of the north to their annual calendar.[25] Aristocrats from the south purchased islands and mainland estates to create their own 'deer forests', though the planting of trees was rarely included in the enterprise. Those lairds who could afford it would convert some of their own land, with sheep farming and deer stalking co-existing.

> By the middle of the century most of Sir Kenneth Mackenzie's income came from letting his shooting and fishing lodges, with their sporting rights. In 1842 38,000 acres of deer forests had been made at Gairloch; this had involved moving to other parts of the estate (not removing *from* the estate) four families – two of crofters and two of cottars. If the Mackenzies of Gairloch had elected to evict their hundreds of crofter tenants, and replace them with three or four large-scale sheep-farmers, they could have at least doubled their income.[26]

The enthusiasm for this new sport remained strong for the rest of the century, despite it being an expensive undertaking either to sustain or rent a deer forest. Quite why there was such a strong desire to spend weeks lying in the mud, often soaked by the rain and plagued by midges, is a question perhaps not fully answered by the response of a 'good trophy' whereby the hunter 'could display the antlered head in his lobby as a symbol of his manly attainments, and the prestige associated with the possession of a fine head encouraged the practice of killing stags for their heads rather than for their venison'.[27]

Deer stalking was 'an arduous and absorbing sport, its difficulty is its glory. This is especially so in the stag season, for in summer and autumn the deer often keeps to the higher parts of the mountain'.[28] The army even allowed 'sporting leave' as a way to toughen up officers, who were allowed as much sporting leave 'as is consistent with attention to duty':

> The superiority in pluck and endurance of hardship which the British islands have so long held over the other nations of Europe is pretty generally admitted to be in no small degree due to the love and practice of out-of-door recreations.[29]

The actual 'stag-hunting' season was quite short:

> Stags are usually in condition for killing between 15th August and 8th or 10th October. These dates depend upon the season. In the case of a stag with a very fine head, the sportsman will probably not wish to shoot it until the horns are quite free from velvet, which perhaps may not be until well into September. Roaring begins in the last days of September, and a week or ten days later the stags are out of condition.

Given the expense, and the limited period of time when it could be undertaken, it is not surprising how 'fatal to a successful stalk would be the sudden presence upon the scene of a thoughtless rambler upon the mountains, who, quite unintentionally it might be, would thus mar the pleasure and success of the hard-earned and well-paid-for sport of the deer stalker'.[30]

The business grew: 'The demand for shootings in the north is so great this year that there are no places on the market although higher and higher rents are given year after year', Snowie reported in 1872.[31] Rents for shootings were usually fixed on the grouse as a unit of value with a brace worth five shillings. One red deer was reckoned to equal a hundred brace, a roe deer or salmon twenty and a hare one brace.[32] English sportsmen rented the shootings in syndicates of four or six, paying perhaps £125, or more, a month for use of the estate.

As sheep farming became less profitable in the 1870s, with the arrival of frozen meat and quality wool from across the globe, deer forests frequently were seen as the best diversification. They were an aspect of the crofting life that was brought into the Napier Commission equation. Three of the commissioners, including Sir Kenneth, had their own deer forests. They 'rejected most of the adverse criticism of this form of land use and merely recommended that new forests should exclude land below a certain height [...] and land which belonged to crofters' holdings; other recommendations included the obligation on proprietors to deer-fence crofters' lands and the granting of the right to crofters to kill marauding deer. They reminded Parliament that, 'It is of importance to the welfare of the Highlands and Islands not to impair the attraction of property. [...] They depend on the beauty of scenery, the pleasure of sport, repose and exercise'.[33]

In addition to deer stalking, 'grouse and ptarmigan are shot in all the deer forests of Gairloch. There are only three separate grouse shootings in the parish, viz., those attached to Inveran, Poolhouse, and Drumchork'.[34]

Osgood had recognised very early on that sporting rights were a great asset. He had negotiated a rent for the sporting rights over the Inverewe estate, then owned by a relative (Sir George Mackenzie of Coul) and conveniently close to the fishing lodges at Poolewe, where he and his mother stayed on their returns to Scotland from long visits abroad in the 1850s. The opportunity to do likewise once the land was his was probably his salvation financially. Throughout his long life he continued to enjoy stalking and shooting. He was more than willing to share such pleasures, given appropriate remuneration, with prosperous fellow enthusiasts.

His cause was greatly helped by the opening, in 1870, of a branch line of the Highland Railway from Inverness to Strome Ferry. Passengers could now travel on to Gairloch by coach from the station at Achnasheen, thirty miles away. It was a further eight to Inverewe. Some wealthier guests came by steamer up the west coast from Glasgow. His mother was commended in an obituary for inducing 'the late Mr Burns to send a steamer on a trial trip to Gairloch, an enterprise which has since grown immensely'.[35] This was probably that from Oban to Gairloch which began in 1863 as a direct tourist route.[36] Osgood could also offer his own 'splendid anchorage for yachts close to the House'.[37]

The Valuation Rolls, recording who was in residence at Inverewe each year, demonstrated how Osgood exploited the potential of this source of income. The first entry for a shooting tenant was a C.R.M. Talbot in 1872/3. The records for 1875/6 and 1876/7 are missing but in 1877 Osgood reckoned to have an income of '£400 for house, gardens and shooting', together with '£50 from Mr Dixon of Inveran, £25 from Hornsby at the hotel, and the tickets at the hotel for fishing ran from £30 to £50'. Given that Tournaig House was not built until 1878 it is not known where he stayed whilst his house was let at this time. For the first two 'seasons' of his marriage the shootings were unlet which caused problems when it came to paying the bill for Minna's confinement. The doctor was unsympathetic![38] That Osgood was then able to find shooting tenants for Inverewe House might have helped with the later doctor's bills but made it impossible to resolve the conflict between his mother and his wife.[39] In 1892 he valued the Inverewe House income at £1,000.[40]

Thereafter the shootings were rented out every year, except 1898/9, until 1914 when much of Inverewe House was burnt down and became unavailable. Osgood certainly would have agreed with Angus Steward, factor of the Letterewe Estate, who lived at Drumchork, Aultbea. He testified to the 1894 Crofters' Commission enquiry at Poolewe: 'There is no doubt that sporting rents are much higher than you can get from any one who works arable and pasture land as a farm. About double!'[41]

Legal matters

The value of fishing rights was exemplified when Osgood went to court three times in a dispute with his neighbour, Meyrick Bankes of Letterewe. From about 1845 the 'proprietors of Kernsary and their sporting tenants and persons having leave from them' believed that they had 'a joint right or common property in that loch called the Fionn Loch, and particularly in that part of it sometimes called the Dubh Loch, and a joint right of boating, fowling, fishing, and exercising all other rights in or over the loch'. Osgood's land bordered five miles of the Fionn Loch, but did not touch the Dubh Loch, which was completely surrounded by the Letterewe estate. To get from the one to the other it was necessary to take the boat across a causeway of loose stones which had been built about 1830 for sheep to cross the narrow ridge, or 'phait', which separated the two sections of water. If the water was high it was said to be possible to float across but usually the boat would be dragged over.

Until 1876 there had never been any challenge to this fishing of the Dubh Loch but Bankes had then taken possession of 'a boat and oars' belonging to Osgood. It was claimed that the fishermen had, until that time, been allowed access, not as a matter of right but out of neighbourliness, but now 'there was a probability of the deer on the hills round Dubh Loch being scared by fishers'.[42] Osgood wanted a court decree to state that 'the march between [his] lands of Kernsary and the defender's lands of Letterewe lies on the south-west of Fionn Loch, and from that loch in a southerly direction to the stream flowing into Loch Beannochbeag', and that he was entitled to fish the whole loch. He claimed nominal damages of £500.[43] Dixon thought it worth explaining the situation in some detail:

> At the head of Fionn Loch is a smaller loch, called the Dubh Loch, swarming with large trout. In 1876 and 1877 this sheet of water was the subject of litigation. The Lord Ordinary, in the Outer House of the Court of Session, decided that the Dubh Loch was not a separate loch from the Fionn Loch, and that Mr O.H. Mackenzie had a joint right of fishing in it as well as in the Fionn Loch, part of the shores of which belong to him. This decision was reversed by the Inner House, whose judgement was (on appeal) finally upheld by the House of Lords. The issue raised was a nice one, and depended on the determination of several interesting questions.[44]

Whether it was significant that the two lochs were differently named was one such question, whether it mattered that the Dubh Loch was totally surrounded by Bankes' land was another. However, the key one seemed to be whether or not the causeway which separated the Fionn Loch from the Dubh Loch established it as a separate loch, as Bankes claimed, or was an artificial man-made barrier, so the waters were one. Although Osgood won the initial case Bankes appealed and got the decision he wanted, on a majority vote, that there was 'a natural boundary, the waters of the Dubh Loch are appreciably higher than those of the Fionn Loch, there is a […] physical demarcation between two sheets of water. […] The loch is not capable of being used as if it were one loch'.

Osgood decided to take the case further, to the highest court in the land. Unfortunately for him, though Lord Blackburn could see both points of view and 'whichever way the verdict was found I should not have been able to say that I was dissatisfied with it', judgement went against him again. The law lords decided that boats could not cross from one stretch of water to the next without being carried and that 'these two bodies of water are naturally distinct, no part of the waters of Loch Fionn mixing with those of Loch Dubh, while those of Loch Dubh overflow into Fionn Loch'.[45] This failure to establish fishing and shooting access to the Dubh Loch for Inverewe cost Osgood dear.

Nonetheless, according to *The Highland Sportsman* in 1882, Inverewe was still 'one of the most delightful sporting quarters in the whole Highlands':

> The shootings extend to about 20,000 acres and should yield in good seasons 500 to 600 brace of grouse, besides snipe, woodcocks, rock pigeons, plover, roe deer, rabbits and hares. There are upwards of 30 lochs on the ground, containing trout, char and salmo-ferox of great weight. These lochs include the famed Lochs Maree and Fionn.

It was reported in 1886 that 'Mr Ross made a fine basket of 19 lbs on Loch Kernsary'[46] but perhaps the productivity of Inverewe's sporting grounds was exaggerated. Osgood lost another court case in 1884. From 1 August to 10 December of 1882 Sir James Speight was the tenant at Inverewe. He had, during his stay, tried but failed to reconcile Osgood with Minna. He was to be so disappointed in his shooting endeavours at Greenstone Point that he refused to pay the £80 rent 'averring that he was induced to become tenant by the misrepresentation [...] as to the character and value of the shootings [... that] he might rely on getting 50 or 60 brace of grouse, besides any amount of plovers, snipes and hares'. When he actually went shooting there he only secured twelve grouse.

The case of fraud rested on whether Osgood had provided 'a statement of fact' or 'an expression of opinion' as to the potential of the area. Initially the judge, Lord McClaren, decided Osgood was 'entitled to recover the sum claimed with costs', though he thought it 'a matter of regret that that this case should have come into Court. It was just one of those differences that arose from feeling and temper'.[47] No doubt there was more to it than a dispute about game bags but, according to Minna's brother, Sir John Edwards-Moss, the matter was not yet over. He recalled, with respect to the law suit, that 'Mr Mackenzie won it first and Sir James afterwards.'[48]

Community benefits

Osgood was fully cognisant of the benefits the incomers brought for local people, not just for his own pocket. He commented in 1883 on shooting tenants employing villagers 'a good deal for a short time' and of them taking on gardeners. The hotel keepers provided the fishermen with boatmen.[49] He did some calculations a few years later:

> I let my Shootings & Fishings every year, for 3 or 4 months, to the very great advantage of the locality. Some few years ago, out of curiosity, I totalled up some of the payments made in the District by my Shooting Tenant, whilst in occupation of Inverewe & found they amounted to £667.19.3. Of course he spent a very great deal more than ever came to my knowledge, – I only give here the amount which he paid through the Head Keeper, or to other parties who happened to mention to me the sums they had received from him that year. This Tenant was at Inverewe during 2 seasons namely 1891 & 1892.[50]

The Valuation Rolls show this to have been a Col. O. H. Charlesworth who rented Inverewe House and Garden, the associated shootings and fishings and also the Deer Forest, Kernsary. In terms of rateable value the shootings and fishings were assessed at £505 and the next part of the estate in rateable value was Inverewe Home Farm at £160. Osgood continued:

> Before I bought these Properties, the total amount of expenditure by the Owners & Occupiers of them in wages to the 4 shepherds & to a few extra hands at Clipping & Smearing, could not have exceeded about £100 a year. — Now thanks to the Deer Forest & to the great outlays & improvements I have made the expenditure is about 14 times as much being from £1300–£1400 a year. — Previous to 1862 the rateable value of the Properties even when Sheep Farming was at the height of its prosperity, & including shootings, was only about £340. – Last year the rateable value was £942.[51]

The rates payable would have contributed to the parish income, possibly reducing the bills for other smaller ratepayers, though some contemporaries argued strongly that 'the thing that, in this case, helps to sustain the poor is the very thing that causes their poverty', that is they had no access to the land which had been enclosed for hunting.[52] The full valuation was not paid. The amounts shown in the Valuation Rolls were not gross rents as the wages of gamekeepers could be deducted and 'a certain percentage for furniture in the Lodge' – a negotiable amount it seems, with somewhere between 22 and 80 per cent being allowed, 44% being the average. Unlet deer forests were rated as grazing land until 1886 when the Sporting Land Rating Act allocated unlet forest a sporting value defined as £25 per stag shot.[53]

Osgood himself was convinced:

> Never, in my opinion, were these two properties doing as much good generally in the Parish as they are doing under the present system, – viz, with

a resident Laird all the year round & with wealthy Shooting Tenants for 3 months of the year, & with the ground partly under Deer & partly under Sheep & Cattle & Grass. I think no one will deny, that the chief cause of the great progress Gairloch has made during the last half century, is mainly due to the Sportsmen, who have been pouring in English Capital all these years - & if the 10 or 11 big houses in this Parish with their sporting Occupants, were suddenly swept away it would simply land this Parish in bankruptcy.

— The Rental of this Parish last year was £11,639 — out of which £3,690 was paid by Sporting Tenants, & this is but a small portion of the money they spend & which directly or indirectly benefits almost every inhabitant.[54]

As the Poolewe School Log Books showed, the local children sometimes benefited from the generosity of Osgood's tenants:

26 July 1906: All the scholars attending Poolewe school were sumptuously entertained at Inverewe House yesterday by Mr Thornton of Nottingham, lessee of the Inverewe fishings,

and

28 June 1911: Mr. Macleod presented the nice Coronation Bibles gifted to the children by the SB this afternoon. 4 Bibles given away. [...] Mrs Hope Morley, 2 Grosvenor Square, London, kindly presented the Poolewe School with 2 sets of quoits, Dominoes, Draught Bd etc and also some games for Public Hall.

Osgood congratulated himself on his significant contribution, over such a long period of time, to the local employment and economic prosperity:

As soon as I bought the Properties of Inverewe & Kernsary I commenced spending large sums of money in Building, first of all the Inverewe Mansion House, & later on Tournaig Cottage. I built Farm Buildings at Tournaig, & at Inverewe, – Gardeners' & Gamekeepers' Houses, Silos, Sheep Fanks, Cattle Byres & Sheds & Kennels. I made Gardens & I fenced & planted & I made miles of Roads, drained, trenched & removed the Boulders out of all the old land & surrounded & divided it with Stone Dykes. —

This Land hardly deserved the name of Arable when I got it, being mostly a bed of Rushes, with great Stones sticking up through it. I also nearly doubled the cultivated Land by considerable reclamations. —At that time, & for many of the subsequent years, I kept a very large number of Workmen constantly

> employed & even now, when my improvements are mostly finished, – I may say, that besides my own Household my property supports 12 other families all the year round ie 13 Families in all, instead of the four it supported when I bought the place.[55]

Kernsary road

Both for his own benefit and for that of his shooting tenants it was important that Osgood enabled the hunter to reach the moors, mountains and lochs where the prey awaited their fate. Although the 'Destitution Fund' money of the potato famine period contributed greatly to road building locally by connecting the main townships, the fishing interests of Osgood and his guests necessitated an improvement in the estate tracks. The most important was the one to the Fionn Loch, although there is some discrepancy as to when precisely it was completed.

According to Dixon, initially the road was on the property of Sir Kenneth Mackenzie but then, once through a locked gate at Inveran Bridge, entered that of Mr Osgood H. Mackenzie until reaching Loch Kernsary. 'Turning to the right the farm of Kernsary, with its sheltered fields and smiling woods, is reached. The small river is crossed by a frail foot-bridge, below which is the ford for carts and carriages. [...] From Kernsary the almost Alpine road constructed by Mr Osgood H. Mackenzie about 1875 gradually ascends to the height of 600 feet above sea-level. [...] At a distance of about six miles from Poolewe the road terminates at Fionn Loch'.[56]

Osgood, however, wrote in his *Statement*: 'There was never any road to Kernsary, or any means of access except on foot, by fording two Rivers & by scrambling over Rocks & across Bogs — until I made my private Road — 4 ½ miles in length with the Bridges etc in 1890'.[57] Regardless: 'A laborious task it must have been to drag the first heavy sea-boat over five miles of bog and a ridge eight hundred feet high, but they managed it and were rewarded by some first class fishing. In later years many other boats were taken up, and finally Osgood had made the road [...] nine miles of it levelled and roughly surfaced by his men'.[58]

The access to the Fionn Loch was always carefully guarded. Dixon emphasised that an excursion from Poolewe 'as far as beyond Inveran can only be made by special permission of Mr O.H. Mackenzie of Inverewe and that certainly cannot be obtained after July', the road beyond the bridge being 'strictly private, and the gate there is locked'.[59]

Dogs

Essential for any successful hunting expedition, and almost always part of the package for shooting, were good dogs. Osgood built a 'big kennel' as part of the 'steading' at the Londubh farmhouse, where he not only kept those for the use of his guests and himself but also bred black-and-white setters to sell. 'These fifteen or twenty dogs were let out on couples for exercise on the shore twice a day'. They proved to be a useful source of income of which Osgood was proud:

> Indeed, I was never, perhaps, quite as successful with anything else as I was with my setters from 1858 to 1914. For many a long year they had such a good name that I used to sell from £80 to £140 worth every season, and I always had more orders than I could possibly supply. In 1914 we were compelled to give up the setters. My gamekeeper and faithful friend and companion, John Matheson, who was such a wonderful dog-breaker, had, alas! Died, and it was impossible to get food for a kennel of dogs during the war, while the grouse had decreased greatly in number.[60]

It is, perhaps, rather telling of his priorities and interests that this is the only direct reference Osgood made to the First World War!

The last decades

In 1901 Osgood's mother died. Mairi became the named liferentrix of Tournaig House and with Inverewe House, Home Farm and Estate, Tournaig shooting grounds and the deer forest of Kernsary Osgood's financial situation seemed more comfortable. He had sufficient spare income to be able to spend on improving the Inverewe farm steading (1912)[61] and travel abroad.

So, it must have been a devastating blow when much of Inverewe House burnt down in April 1914. In one fell swoop his major source of income had, literally, gone up in smoke. But, now in his seventies, with his daughter married and independently financed, his own needs were much reduced. He made no effort to rebuild the house. By 1915 the Valuation Rolls show that he had put all his property into Mairi's name. For the last seven years of his life he dedicated himself more to his gardening and writing interests, leaving the farming and sporting enterprises to his son-in-law. Photographs in Mairi's albums show Robert hunting and fishing, with a white-bearded Osgood in the background, observing the prize-catches and antler trophies.[62] Tournaig was also often let out to shooting parties and the Hanburys then stayed in the Gate Lodge, where there was room not only for themselves but also for family guests.[63] An important task in the estate management was the spring burning of heather, intended to improve the likelihood of a good grouse season.

Robert took the farming seriously and, during the war years, recorded his successes and failures with oats, barley, potatoes, turnips, swedes and cabbages. The weather, as ever, played a large role in determining the cropping and yield. Getting in the hay dry was an annual gamble. It turned out a 'splendid crop' in 1916. He bought and sold ewes and lambs, reflecting on the high prices until government action was taken in 1917 to fix them. Most problematic was keeping his herd of Highland cattle. It was difficult to buy in enough food for them.[64]

After the First World War there were several instances of extremely 'bad luck' which affected the Inverewe/Tournaig estate. In March 1920 the spring planting was much delayed by appalling wet weather. The flooding brought down many bridges and Inverewe was completely cut off from both main road and railway for several days. Then, in October that same year, the big grain barn burned down. 'In twenty-five minutes there was not a wisp of hay or grain of corn that grew at Inverewe left. There was not even a sheaf for any cattle. The Highland cattle had to be sold'.[65] Most distressing of all, this fire was followed on 14 November by the cyclone which felled 2,500 mature trees.

> By 8 o'clock the wind was fearful and the trees began to go. [...] All the large trees near the Lodge, below the road came down. And all the trees along the Drive. [...] No-one living remembered such a storm here. All this week has been very stormy, the men have been clearing the roads.[66]

Osgood had been quite right when he had testified, so many years earlier, that tree planting was an expensive business and not likely to yield financial reward. Mairi certainly did not inherit a fortune and required the input of Hanbury family money, from both her husbands, to keep the estate going, just as Osgood had always depended on the same source, courtesy of his mother.

Appendix

On going to Law

This undated, unattributed, newspaper article was pasted into one of Mairi Mackenzie's photograph albums, surely because of its relevance to her father's many, and painful, experiences with the judicial system.[67]

ON GOING TO LAW

When you go to law you require a barrister and a solicitor. At least, you don't really require them, but you can't help yourself. The barrister can't work with the client, and the solicitor won't work without the barrister. First you get hold of your solicitor. Then he gets hold of you, and he and the barrister get hold of everything. The difference between the two is that a barrister's charges are high and a solicitor's frequent. The first makes his money out of what he does. We will touch on the solicitor first – before he touches us.

You will notice that when you call on a solicitor he always keeps you waiting. The longer you wait the longer the bill of costs. Having heard your case, he will at once advise you to go to law. Then can you go home and turn up the address of the nearest workhouse.

After the solicitor has seen you several times and taken you to counsel's chambers for consultation, and the case is set down for hearing, you can arrange to take a trip round the world. You will not be wanted for at least a year. It will save you some expense also. Though not much. When your solicitor rings you up, whether you are there or not, he will charge you six-and-eight. Hence arises the saying, "The Law and the Profits".

We now come to the Courts – most reluctantly. First there is the High Court, so called because of its charges. Then there is the Appeal Court. This was invented for the purpose of reversing the decisions of the High Court. There is also the House of Lords. That reverses both. The High Court tries your case. The other two merely try your temper. All three try your pocket. The House of Lords is the highest tribunal in the land – at present by kind permission of John Redmond.

If you win your case in the High Court the loser will appeal. His solicitor will make him. If you lose, then you will appeal; your solicitor will make you. Several years elapse, and if the plaintiff and defendant are long-lived they may have the infinite pleasure of hearing an order for the case to go back to the High Court. Hence they are back where they were about ten years previously.

Several more years elapse. By this time you are – if lucky – in receipt of an old age pension. By this time too, your original opponent is dead. You will probably find you are fighting his executors and five grand-children who have been made parties to the suit. Then the Court gives its decision on a point that has never been mentioned at all before. This reverses all previous decisions. Again the plaintiff and defendant appeal in turn. Before this all the original Law Lords have died of senile decay. Justice Grantham is the solitary surviving judge. He outlives everything and everybody. And as by now you have been made a bankrupt, the suit lapses automatically. So you never get a decision at all.

Seriously, if ever you are in doubt as to whether to consult a solicitor or shoot yourself, don't hesitate, – shoot him!

References and Notes

1 *Search of Encumbrances over Inverewe* from the General Register of Sasines. Inverewe House Archive.

2 Dixon, p.63.

3 *The Mackenzie Case*, p.41.

4 Osgood H. Mackenzie, *Account and Statement as to the Properties of Inverewe and Kernsary*. Copies in Inverewe House Archive and at Gairloch Heritage Museum. Precise date and provenance unknown. He also told a little of how he farmed and derived an income from his estate in *A Hundred Years*. He gave testimony to the Napier Commission in 1883 and to the Royal Commission of 1894. Something is learned from evidence given during the divorce cases of 1892 and 1895.

5 *Account and Statement.*

6 *Inverness Advertiser*, 21 February 1854.

7 All from *The Scotsman* Market Reports.

8 Mr Peterkin was the tenant from 1878–1885. Ross-shire Valuation Rolls, Highland Council Archives, Inverness.

9 *The Mackenzie Case*, p.41.

10 *Account and Statement.*

11 Evidence to the Napier Commission, enquiring into the 'Conditions of the Crofters and Cottars in the Highlands and Islands of Scotland', Poolewe, 31 July 1883.

12 Dixon, p.232.

[13] *Account and Statement.*
[14] Mackenzie, pp.184–185. See Chapters I and III.
[15] Mackenzie, p.190.
[16] Royal Commission for the Highlands and Islands 1894 Vol. II, pp.1403–1405.
[17] *Account and Statement.*
[18] Dixon, p.318.
[19] Mackenzie, p.258.
[20] Dixon, p.221.
[21] Evidence to the Napier Commission, Poolewe, 31 July 1883.
[22] See Chapter VI.
[23] *The Scotsman*, 23 December 1887.
[24] Byam Shaw, p.75.
[25] Orr, pp.29, 4.
[26] Byam Shaw, p.285.
[27] Orr, p.39.
[28] Dixon, p.374.
[29] Orr, p.38, quoting J. Colquhon *Sporting Days* (Edinburgh: 1866).
[30] Dixon, p.374.
[31] Orr, p.33.
[32] Prebble, p.146.
[33] Orr, pp.61–62.
[34] Dixon, p.379.
[35] *Inverness Courier*, 13 March 1901.
[36] *The Scotsman*, 18 August 1863.
[37] *The Highland Sportsman*, 1882.
[38] *The Mackenzie Case*, p.302.
[39] See Chapter VI.
[40] *The Mackenzie Case*, p.41.
[41] Royal Commission for the Highlands and Islands 1894 Vol. II, p.1410.
[42] From a set of papers lent by Roderick Paisley, Professor of Commercial Law, University of Aberdeen: Court of Sessions, November 1877.
[43] *The Scotsman*, 20 December 1876, 1 December 1877.
[44] Dixon, p.365.
[45] Paisley papers: House of Lords, 27 June 1878.
[46] *Scottish Highlander*, 22 July 1886.
[47] *The Scotsman*, 23 January 1884.
[48] *The Mackenzie Case*, p.316.
[49] Evidence to the Napier Commission, Poolewe, 31 July 1883.

[50] *Account and Statement.*

[51] It is not possible to establish exactly which year this was. The Valuation Rolls for Ross-shire show no year with £942 as the rateable value. In 1893/4 it was £910 but then declined considerably until 1906/7 when the total valuation was £915. There is, however, no record for 1905/6.

[52] Orr, p.102, quoting evidence presented to the Deer Forest commission by the Minister of Lochs on Lewis in 1893.

[53] Orr, pp.91, 104.

[54] *Account and Statement.*

[55] *Account and Statement.*

[56] Dixon, p.335.

[57] *Account and Statement.*

[58] Dawn Macleod, *Oasis of the North* (London: Hutchinson, 1958), p.63.

[59] Dixon, pp.335, 388.

[60] Mackenzie, pp.233, 118–119.

[61] Wright, p.24.

[62] The photograph albums of Mairi, Osgood's daughter, are in the Inverewe House Archive.

[63] Pauline Butler, *Memories of Inverewe* (internal booklet for the National Trust for Scotland, 2007), recording the recollections of Peter Hanbury, Mairi's nephew.

[64] Robert Hanbury's *Game Book* (in the private collection of Nigel Hanbury, Mairi's great-nephew).

[65] Alasdair Camshron, *Am Bard*, (Glasgow: Archibald Sinclair, 1926), pp.177, 189, informally translated from the Gaelic by Alice Mackenzie.

[66] Robert Hanbury's *Game Book.*

[67] Given the references to Old Age Pensions and John Redmond it is likely to have been written between 1911 and 1914.

CHAPTER VIII

Outdoor Pursuits

'I was the keenest of sportsmen all my life.'

Game records

'He devoted himself to country pursuits' wrote the obituary writer in the *Inverness Chronicle*, 18 April 1922, as he highlighted the achievements of the recently deceased Osgood Mackenzie. Osgood had been introduced to the skills and pleasures of hunting, shooting and fishing very early in life, given his first gun at the age of eight. Many chapters in *A Hundred Years* told of his commitment to the pursuit of almost any living creature and of exploits on moor and loch. Fishing and shooting were an essential part of his childhood, encouraged by his mother and taught by family servants and relatives. He was immensely proud of his catches and bags and clearly derived great enjoyment from his sporting life.

It is not surprising that, when it came to purchasing his own estate, he considered it essential that there was potential for the pursuit of abundant game. The twelve thousand or so acres of Inverewe and Kernsary seem to have fulfilled his hopes and expectations. He kept Game Book records of the successes of himself and of his shooting tenants. Ironically, some Game Books have survived at Inverewe House though all his plant notebooks have disappeared.[1]

To the modern naturalist the catalogue of his catches indicates a much greater diversity of wildlife than is currently to be found in the area. The birds he shot included snipe, blackcock, grouse, quail, woodcock, teal, duck, ptarmigan and partridge which might be considered 'game'. Several of these he acknowledged to be rarely seen in the area so considered a particularly noteworthy prize. Further, wild swan (including three whooper swans in one day on Loch Kernsary, of which he was very proud[2]), puffins, osprey, golden eagle, rock pigeons, thrush, short-eared owl and golden plover were all indicated as worthwhile targets for his guns. John H. Dixon of Inveran published his *Gairloch with a Guide to Gairloch and Loch Maree* in 1886. His references to Osgood's shooting of birds, particularly the rarer ones, did almost always suggest that this had taken place a long time ago, with dates from his childhood. Most of those in the list Osgood prepared for him, almost one hundred and fifty long, had simply been 'observed'.

As far as egg-collecting went, he certainly sought those of gulls, ospreys, golden eagles and white-tailed eagles, the rarer the better: 'I flattered myself for some time that I was the first to find in Britain, or at any rate in Scotland, a goosander's nest with eggs, and that was on an island in the Fionn Loch'.[3] Outraged at the temerity of a certain Mr Booth, he wrote a letter in 1868: 'As a resident proprietor [...] I am glad that attention has been called to the late raid on the rare birds and their eggs in this neighbourhood by Mr Booth.' Eight greenshank eggs had been found as part of the spoils taken at Gairloch. It could not possibly be true, as Mr Booth had claimed, that he only took eggs from one nest, as 'greenshanks don't have that many eggs'. Osgood believed that not all the story had yet been told as to 'injury done in the county to its rare birds, and to the morality of its game-keepers'. Apparently Mr Booth tried to bribe one of the game-keepers, offering £7 for an eagle's nest.[4]

Osgood's Game Books and *A Hundred Years* illustrate the range of wildlife which it was, in those days, considered legitimate to kill. Animals recorded included roe deer, stags, otters, badgers, brown and blue hares. Of these last few were to be found, 'except as great rarities on the summits of the highest hills'.[5] Rabbits, pine marten and polecat were destroyed as vermin. He noted with pride both the quantity and quality of some of the most impressive shoots. At the end of his life he wrote:

> My stalker, Donald Urquhart, at Kernsary in the winter of 1918–1919, killed twenty-five foxes. He once got two eagles and two foxes in one day. Two seasons running he got ten eagles. [...] One day he went out to shoot hinds and visit traps. First he got a wild-cat in a trap. Shortly afterwards he got a hind; he visited three other traps, getting an otter in one trap and a fox in another, and then he shot a hind on the way home – a useful day's work for a stalker.[6]

Not that this was anything new. Dixon recorded:

> Dr Mackenzie has the following note of a good bag of eagles made in Gairloch in the early part of the present century: He says:- "Our game-killer, Watson, had a good day once with eagles, producing three splendid birds from a day's shooting, besides two young birds also killed. [...] I wait to hear of the gunner in Britain who could shew his two and a half brace of eagles killed in one day, before breakfast!".[7]

Osgood also was very proficient with his gun. Dixon recalled, with reference to short-eared owls, that: 'Mr O.H. Mackenzie once shot five over setters in the Isle of Ewe in the month of November',[8] and Osgood recorded various freak shots such as: 'On two different occasions I have killed a hare and a grouse with the same shot, and another time I shot a woodcock and a stoat with the one barrel!'[9]

It is not surprising that Osgood, once his finances were in better order, travelled abroad to enjoy his sporting interests. In 1903 Compton Mackenzie, aged 20, was invited to dinner by Fournier-Salovèze, Secretary of the prestigious 'Sociètè de Sport, an almost hopelessly exclusive club' at Compiègne, outside Paris, to meet Osgood Mackenzie – a distant relative. Compton was fascinated by the story of the creation of Inverewe but declined an offer to move to live on a croft in Wester Ross when his Oxford studies were over. They did spend the next day together 'following in a chaise a boar hunt in the forest' and discussing whether or not Osgood's daughter would take to 'sitting about in her chemise to play the piano', amongst tales of the old crofters. The author credited his later determination 'to span the great gap more than a century wide which lay between me and my Highland birthright' to the laird of Inverewe.[10]

An essential companion for hunting and shooting was a well-trained dog and from his young days Osgood kept dogs and seemed to have been very fond of them. The first was 'Shot', a curly retriever, which played happily with Osgood's pet otter under the table. He then had two pointers:

> They proved useful dogs, were as hard as nails, and never got tired or gave in, but they required constant flogging, as nothing could ever cure them of running hares or of quarrelling and fighting; and though they were brothers, of the same litter, before very long the one killed the other.[11]

He continued to keep dogs until the First World War when the death of his gamekeeper, John Matheson, and the problems of feeding the animals in such times of shortage, meant that he had to give up his breeding interests. However, he still managed to get out on the moors with his son-in-law, and was last mentioned shooting with Robert and a frequent visitor, Major Regnast, as late as August 1920, at the age of 78.[12]

Fishing

Fishing, to supplement both income and diet, was an integral part of the crofter's work but for Osgood it was essentially a leisure and pleasure pursuit. Again, his initial introductions to the sport were organised by, and with, his mother, who seemed to have enjoyed the boat-trips into the Minch and across to St Kilda and the Isle of Lewis especially. Osgood caught a wide range of sea-fish both by line and net, such as cod, herring (mainly used as bait), ling, congers and halibut (called 'broad salmon' in Gaelic). The salmon in the River Ewe were highly prized and Osgood 'about 1853 killed seven salmon in one day, and five the next. He was only a boy at the time, and was not fishing long on either day'.[13]

Salmon fishing in the Ewe was so highly valued that Kenneth, laird of Gairloch, specifically retained all the fishing rights for himself when he sold Kernsary to his half-brother Osgood. But land on the shores, and therefore fishing rights of the waters, of the Fionn Loch, was included in the purchase,[14] bringing with it a strong reputation for yielding enormous trout.

Osgood rented out fishing rights to paying tenants for many years. It was a valuable source of income for him, separately recorded in the Valuation Rolls from 1874 onwards. The fishing report for Poolewe in *The Scotsman*, 10 June 1907, noted:

> Trout fishing during the month of May was very good in this district, but especially on Fionn Loch, which is considered one of the finest trout lochs in Scotland. Mr Buchanan, Liverpool, who is the leasee of Inverewe fishing during the months of May and June, and party have secured some heavy baskets of excellent trout on this loch.

No doubt Osgood allowed himself a quiet smile when the same report added that 'salmon angling on the River Ewe in May was not so successful'. He was very proud of a Fionn Loch fish he himself had caught 'only a few years ago. [...] This monster was a typical Fionn Loch trout, only quite double the size of any we had ever seen before. [...] Without in the least wishing to exaggerate, I honestly declare that fish to have been a twenty-five pounder.'[15]

Less than a year before he died, Osgood was still actively interested in the fishing on his estate, though he had long passed over the management of it to his daughter and her husband. In October 1921 he and Robert 'saw 16 salmon spawning in the burns nearly as far as the woods, some 12 to 14 lbs. We had no idea so many had come up'.[16] The only mention made of his son-in-law in

A Hundred Years is with reference to the fact that he had caught an impressive twelve-pound trout a couple of years previously![17]

Stuffed and cured

Although, of course, much of the game would have gone straight to the kitchen there were other destinations for some of the animals and birds killed. The most prized might well be stuffed or preserved. For example:

> One day on the Isle of Ewe, in a wet turnip field which was full of snipe, I started a thrush which had a broad white ring round its throat, just like that of a ring ouzel. I promptly shot it. Immediately afterwards old Fan [dog] pointed at something. […] If she could have spoken she would have whispered to me that it smelled like something she had never heard before; and what should it be but a quail, which I also shot. Afterwards I had both thrush and quail stuffed in the one case. […] With the exception of this one on Isle Ewe I had never, until that year, heard of a quail having been killed in Ross-shire in my time.[18]

Dixon corroborated the story of the 'very rare' quail, which he dated to 'about 1860'. Osgood proudly told how he had hunted down a 'grand big royal' (a stag with a head of at least twelve points) in the Slioch mountain area. Initially he had only wounded it, had then tracked it to administer the 'coup de grace' the following day, before taking it to the taxidermist in Inverness for stuffing.[19]

Exactly when one particular expedition took place that resulted in friction between husband and wife is not known. Osgood took umbrage when Minna decided, without consultation, to re-arrange a display: 'In the dining room there was a case of stuffed humming-birds which I had myself shot in Brazil, and which I rather prized: she shifted it to some other part of the house'.[20]

Skins were useful. 'There were plenty of pine martens and polecats and some badgers even in my young days'. 'We still have in use a big rug of badgers' skins in front of our smoking-room fire, all caught on this place' or, even more creatively: 'My mother used to have an average of forty or fifty skins of martens brought to her by the keepers every year, of which she made the most lovely sable capes and coats for her sisters and lady friends'.[21]

Not all the hunted animals were actually killed. Otter kittens were sought to be trained to fish at command and one, after being kept for some weeks, was sent to the London Zoo 'where it lived and throve for many a long year in the otter pond'.[22] Possibly this was the same occasion as Dixon recorded when he mentioned two (sic) young otters which were sent to the Zoological Gardens in Regents Park in 1881.[23] Then there was the

> WHOOPER, OR WILD SWAN – Occasionally visits Gairloch in winter. [...] Mr O.H. Mackenzie broke the tip of the wing of one on Loch Ewe with a bullet, and sent the bird to the Zoological Gardens, Regent's Park, where it still (1886) lives.[24]

Vermin

Throughout his memoirs Osgood's strongly held and eloquently expressed attitude about much of what he killed was that it was vermin. He was doing a public service, as was long the custom:

> There was so much vermin in those days that the so-called gamekeepers were in reality only game-killers, and vermin trappers were only then being started. [...] Until my father and uncles started stalking, not a Gairloch laird had ever troubled himself to kill deer either for sport or for the larder. The vermin consisted of all kinds of beasts and birds, a good many of which are now extinct. The fork-tailed kites swarmed, and I have heard that the first massacre of them that took place was when my father poisoned with strychnine the dead body of a young horse which had been killed by falling over a rock.[25]

So polecats, martens, otters, fox, wildcat were all considered mammals to be exterminated. In the only County Council meeting where Minutes show that he contributed, 20 December 1898, Osgood moved a resolution that 'Bullfinches, Peregrine Falcons, Golden Eagles' should not be added to the list of birds needing protection as there was 'no reasonable apprehension of their becoming extinct; and that being birds which occasion damage, their protection is uncalled for'. However, he did agree that sea-eagles should be included on the County list under the recent Wild Birds Protection Act.[26]

To the end of his life, Osgood continued to advocate the killing of eagles:

> We have had far too many eagles in our country of late, and when one can see seven in the air at once it is about time to thin them out. [...] We never set traps for eagles, but when one is caught I must confess we do not mourn very much. Strychnine is a wonderfully handy drug.

Somewhat on the defensive, perhaps, he questioned:

> I often wonder why some County Councils take the trouble to forbid eagles being destroyed. How can the killing of eagles be prevented? Do the County Councils wish no traps to be set for foxes, wild-cats, ravens, or hoodie crows? And if the traps are to be set for these very destructive beasts and birds, how are the eagles to be kept out of the traps? Is it the wish of the wiseacres of the County Councils that an eagle with both or even one of its feet smashed should be let go to a lingering death of starvation? [...] Eagles are terribly destructive. They tear the live rabbits out of the rabbit-trappers' traps, kill lambs wholesale and the very sight of one scares every grouse off the ground. [...] The Ross-shire County Council very wisely does not forbid the killing of eagles.[27]

Vanishing wild life

So, it was of no concern that many of the so-called 'vermin' of his youth had been eliminated: 'the pine-martens, the polecats and the badgers are all quite extinct with us now, but they were all still in existence when I bought Inverewe'. He did suggest though, with respect to the badgers, that, though they served their purpose as rugs, 'we had no wish to exterminate them like wildcats and foxes; in fact, we should have liked to preserve them, but they would not keep out of the vermin's traps, and so they soon became extinct'.[28]

Sometimes he did express some regret:

> Birds'-nesting expeditions were also made to the islands of Loch Maree after ospreys' eggs. [...] There is an island on which stood one big Scots fir. In it was the ospreys' nest, as large as a wagon-wheel, with three eggs. [...] There was another fir-tree where they bred [...] from which I got two eggs. But alas! the birds have been extinct in that region for at least sixty-five years.

and

> A few pairs of black-throated divers still float about on our lochs, and sometimes rear their young, but sad to say they are diminishing in numbers, and many lochs where they used never to fail to breed are now without these beautiful and most interesting summer tenants.[29]

Rather astonishingly, he does not seem to have linked the extinction of species in the area with his egg-stealing, shooting or hunting:

> Then off we went to the haunt of the black grouse. What a big pile it would make if all the black game I shot there between 1855 and 1900 were gathered into one heap. Now, alas! There are none, and why, who can tell?[30]

The last-but-one chapter in his book was called 'Vanishing Birds'. It had originally been published as an article in the *Scottish Naturalist* magazine, about 1916. He wrote, perplexed, that this was 'a sad subject to take up, but alas! I fear it cannot be disputed that birds of many, if not of most, kinds are far less numerous now on the west coast of Ross-shire than they were fifty or sixty years ago. [...] No one can account for their disappearance.' He quoted from his Game Books to illustrate the scale of the problem. He mentioned black grouse as 'a bird of the past', also partridge, ptarmigan and greylag geese with only a very few snipe, golden plover, greenshank, whimbrel and dunlin. Even birds that he did not shoot had all but gone:

> In 1918 we had about the heaviest crop of rowanberries I have ever seen, and they remained on the trees in scarlet masses right through November and long after every leaf had fallen. In former years huge flocks of Fieldfares and Redwings came from Norway at the end of October and quickly finished them off; this year all I saw was a tiny flock of Redwings, about a score all told, which, with the few Blackbirds, Song Thrushes and Missel Thrushes (also in very reduced numbers) were quite unable to make any impression on the berries, which were nearly all wasted. [...] Can anyone explain what has caused so many of our birds to disappear?[31]

Dixon had implied the reasons thirty-five years earlier. 'Gairloch is not without examples of very rare birds, but those usually seen, though rare in many parts of the kingdom, are mostly the common birds of the Highlands. They are interesting enough to all – to the lover of nature they are delightful; let the gunner spare them; let the bird-nester allow them to rear their young in peace'.[32] But Dixon also had 'trophies', shot and stuffed, including 'a cream-coloured bunting at Inverasdale some years ago: it is in my collection at Inveran' and he was happy to accept specimens, such as the water shrew given to him by Osgood on 13 October 1885.[33]

So, they shared a love of nature. However, he had, by 1885 at least, a somewhat different approach to its conservation. Dixon commented strongly when detailing a visit by an artist friend, William Joly, to the Fionn Loch area:

> On another island [...] the very rare goosander used recently to build, Mr Mackenzie being the first discoverer of its nest in Scotland. On another islet

> close by the opposite shore the white-tailed eagle nested more than twenty years ago. On Eilean Molach, near the pier, the black-throated diver still exists. The peregrine falcon then haunted the scene, having its eyrie on the cliffs of Beinn Aridh Charr, and one flew over our heads, chased close to his nest by two angry curlews; but he has, it seems, now deserted the place. Other still rarer species yet linger in this retired spot.
>
> It is devoutly to be hoped that they will long continue to do it honour, guarded by the proprietors, and all good and true men. Happily none are allowed on the lake unless under the care of sanctioned boatmen; and the whole has now been forested. These means of protection, we trust, will preserve these rare creatures as a beauty and a boast for generations to come. In this connexion, nothing shows the defects of the moral and aesthetic training of our people more than the prevalent desire, in even the so-called cultivated classes, to destroy such unusual visitants, some of them harmless. If individual kindliness and sense will not do it, public indignation and penal enactment should be invoked for their preservation.[34]

The sentiment he expressed at the end of the quotation was not one with which Osgood would concur. Perhaps it was not just Dixon's sympathy with Osgood's estranged wife, Minna, which led to the end of their friendship?

'Life-long ornithologist and observer of nature'

Osgood undoubtedly did develop an extremely wide knowledge of the wildlife and environment over the course of his long lifetime and shared this frequently with the outside world. As early as 1883, reference was made to his sighting of a chough in the *Proceedings of the Royal Physical Society of Edinburgh.* He wrote letters to newspapers informing their readers of unusual birds he had seen at Inverewe such as the 'Great Grey Shrike'[35] and submitted articles for *The Scotsman, Glasgow Herald* and more specialist journals. The *Annals of Scottish Natural History* of 1911 reported that Osgood Mackenzie notified them of having seen a Turtle Dove in October 1895 and another in June 1896. He provided lecture material for the Inverness Scientific Society and the Royal Horticultural Society. A letter published in *The Scotsman*, 30 April 1916, reporting the sighting of a hoopoe at Inverewe, generated some correspondence in its columns.

Dixon's *Guide* made considerable use of the expertise of this 'life-long ornithologist and observer of nature [who] has spent more of his life in his native country than perhaps any other Highland gentleman now alive. He has very rarely been absent even in winter'.[36] Osgood was thus 'mainly responsible' for the section on the one hundred and fifty species of birds, for example,

> GOLDEN ORIOLE *(Oriolus galbula)*.– This splendid bird is very rare here. Mr O.H. Mackenzie, and a friend with him, saw one at Coile Aigeascaig on 25th May 1884.

Unfortunately (for these birds) Dixon frequently recorded that they had been shot, even if uncommon:

> CROSSBILL *(Loxia curvirostra)*. – Not common, but occurs. Mr O.H. Mackenzie shot three out of a large flock, in a larch tree close to the house at Inveran, about 1851.

and

> goldfinch (Corduelis elegans) – Mr O.H. Mackenzie shot several at Charleston many years ago. It has not been observed latterly.

He also noted some of the behaviours of birds as observed by Osgood. 'Mr O.H. Mackenzie has actually seen the woodcock pick up its young one, when nearly full-grown, at his very feet, and fly off with it'. William Jolly's visit to the Fionn Loch was accompanied by 'the proprietor, Mr Osgood Mackenzie, whose unrivalled knowledge of the country, and especially of its birds, completed our enjoyment'.[37] Dixon did add a comment that he 'earnestly hoped that the information used in this Chapter will not be used by visitors to enable them to disturb, destroy or rob any of the interesting birds of Gairloch'.

The list of mammals was also 'prepared with the assistance of Osgood H. Mackenzie of Inverewe and is believed to be complete', with individual animals being mentioned in great detail, such as the killing of 'a true wild-cat measuring 43 inches in length'.[38] There was a further chapter, providing a list of 'flowering plants of Gairloch' compiled with the aid of Osgood Mackenzie and Lady Mackenzie.[39] Once again there was a conservationist comment. Dixon accepted the view of Dr John that 'the larger and more showy of our woodland plants [...] have become rare, and in some cases have altogether disappeared, since the introduction of sheep farming into Gairloch. Not only do the smearing materials applied to sheep poison the ground [...] but the close nibble of sheep deteriorates pasture, and destroys many succulent plants'.[40]

Peat

The final chapter of *A Hundred Years* was a reprint of a paper presented at a meeting of the Inverness Scientific Society and Field Club in 1908. Osgood had written it and it had been read there by Mr Black, solicitor, eventually being published in 1919 by Lorimer and Chalmers before being incorporated into his memoirs. He invited his readers to contribute to the debate through the pages of the [*Inverness*] *Chronicle*. Polson, in his 1920 *Guide*, also included five pages on the topic, explaining:

> Mr O.H. Mackenzie, of Inverewe, who has all his life been a zealous naturalist, has set the ball a-rolling in the matter of investigating the Gairloch bogs, and has, with his customary courtesy, placed at the writer's disposal a paper he wrote on the subject for the Inverness Field Club.[41]

Osgood was certainly not very impressed with the scientists in Edinburgh who queried his samples as a hoax initially and then suggested they were of whin, which he disputed. Peat, he believed, 'deserves to be classed among the most interesting natural phenomena of our land. [...] Still more interesting are the many objects found preserved in it. [...] From the bottom of one of my bogs I take out handfuls of hazelnuts as perfect as the day they dropped off the trees; or, still more wonderful, when I find the peat full of countless green beetle wings, still glittering in their pristine metallic lustre, and which may have been buried in their black, airtight silos before Pompeii was thought of'.

He reflected on climate change over millenia, the date and speed of peat formation, (which he believed to be very slow): 'Can anyone tell when the Bronze Age was up here? We found a perfect bronze spear head in one of the peat bogs', along with a deer's antler and part of its wooden shaft, well preserved. He wanted to know about the retreat of glaciers and whether or not the trees on the top of mountains originally grew at the bottom, having observed white-barked birch and hazel eight feet below the surface of the lochs: 'How were these lochs created to the ruin of thousands of acres of forest?' He had retained a questioning mind well into old age, and had a genuine interest in improving his, and the public's, understanding of the peat which dictated the flora and fauna of the area: 'Can any of my readers help me to fathom some of the many mysteries that lie at the bottom of our peat-bogs and lochs, which have always interested me so much?'

References and Notes

[1] Four of Osgood Mackenzie's *Game Books* are in the Inverewe House Archive. They cover the period 1 January 1878 to 1910. If he were making reference to Inverewe in a comment in his own *A Hundred Years* chapter on 'Vanishing Birds': 'I have a record of all the game killed on a property on the west coast from 1866 to 1916', p.260, then at least one book has gone astray.

[2] Mackenzie, p.127.

[3] Mackenzie, p.158.

[4] *Inverness Advertiser*, 28 August 1868.

[5] Mackenzie, p.64.

[6] Mackenzie, pp.150–151.

[7] Dixon, pp.229–230.

[8] Dixon, p.243.

[9] Mackenzie, p.126.

[10] Compton Mackenzie, *My Life and Times. Octave Three. 1900–1907* (London: Chatto and Windus, 1964), pp.141–142.

[11] Mackenzie, pp.115, 117–118.

[12] Robert Hanbury's *Game Book.*

[13] Dixon, p.371.

[14] Mackenzie, p.154.

[15] Mackenzie, p.165.

[16] Robert Hanbury's *Game Book.*

[17] Mackenzie, p.166.

[18] Mackenzie, p.123.

[19] Mackenzie, pp.148–149.

[20] *The Mackenzie Case*, p.6.

[21] Mackenzie, pp.117–118, 66.

[22] Mackenzie, pp.58, 161.

[23] Dixon, p.238.

[24] Dixon, p.254.

[25] Mackenzie, pp.64–66.

[26] Minutes of the Ross and Cromarty County Council meeting on 20 December 1898, Highland Council Archives, Inverness.

[27] Mackenzie, pp.150–152.

[28] Mackenzie, pp.66, 117–118.

[29] Mackenzie, pp.54, 158.

[30] Mackenzie, p.116–117.

[31] Mackenzie, pp.258–262.

[32] Dixon, pp.230, 241.

[33] Dixon, pp.245, 239.

[34] Dixon, pp.354–355.

[35] *The Scotsman*, 11 December 1903.

[36] This invaluable record of the area is still in print, thanks to the Gairloch Heritage Society. The information on birds comes from Part III, The Natural History of Gairloch, Chapter VI, pp.241–255.

[37] Dixon, p.351.

[38] Dixon, pp.236, 238.

[39] If the Lady Mackenzie mentioned was the wife of the Gairloch laird, Sir Kenneth, one wonders about such collaboration in view of their distinct animosity at the time. However, it may be that it is the Dowager Lady, i.e. Osgood's mother, to whom the reference is being made.

[40] Dixon, p.256.

[41] Polson, p.37.

CHAPTER IX

The Heritor

'He was a deputy lord lieutenant and a JP for the County of Ross and in his native parish he was a prominent and active member of all the local public bodies.'

Osgood's obituary notices gave rather conflicting evidence as to his roles in public life. *The Scotsman,* 18 April 1922, had a somewhat different view from the *Inverness Courier*, quoted above:

> Mr Osgood Mackenzie himself took little or no part in public life but he loved the Highlands with a passionate devotion and passed practically all his days in the west of Ross-shire.[1]

Osgood did not have the high public profile of his uncle, Dr John, who went on to be Provost of Inverness and a leading figure in many reforming, medical and sanitation bodies after he left the Isle of Ewe in 1856. Nor did he emulate his half-brother, Kenneth, who was Lord Lieutenant of the County and stood, albeit unsuccessfully, for Parliament in 1880 and 1885. He was, though, appointed as a Deputy Lieutenant of the County of Ross in 1876,[2] an honorary rather than onerous position, which he held until the end of his life. He was also a Justice of the Peace, (described in the 1881 Census as a 'proprietor-magistrate'), a Commissioner of Supply and a member of the County Council from 1898 to 1916.

At the more local level, as a significant landowner, or heritor, he took a prominent role, as would be expected, in the activities and controversies of the area.[3] Parochial boards had been set up in 1845, bringing together the heritors and the local kirk session to implement the new poor law provisions. In 1896 Osgood claimed to have been chair of the Gairloch Board for twenty-five years. The Local Government (Scotland) Act of 1894 replaced these boards with parish councils. In the first elections of April 1895 Osgood came only fourth, and so was not voted onto the Parish Council.[4] This did not stop him continuing to be outspoken in local matters thereafter. Only by 1911, when he was almost seventy, did the entry in Slater's *Royal National Directory of Scotland* list Osgood H. Mackenzie, DL. JP. as 'private resident at Inverewe', though in 1915 he was still a member of the Parish Council for Poolewe ward.[5]

Poor relief

The responsibilities of the parish council developed rapidly during the nineteenth century. In particular, from the 1840s onwards, it had to take on significant duties with respect to the welfare of its people. In 1834 the Whig Government in London had accepted, for the first time ever, that the state had some responsibility for those unable to maintain themselves and their family. The Poor Law Amendment Act required the parish to provide for the poor and sick. In England this brought about the end of the idea of 'outdoor relief' for the able-bodied poor, the inadequate public welfare help since Elizabethan times. Since the 1790s, in some areas, those unable to find work which enabled them to support their families had been given cash payments to prevent total destitution when the price of corn, and therefore bread, was particularly high, (the so-called 'Speenhamland system'), but this had proved far too expensive for the landowners who paid for it. A deliberately less generous and more 'efficient' way of helping the poor was demanded, though the emphasis was on the moral virtues of the proposed changes: 'Every penny bestowed that tends to render the condition of the pauper more eligible than that of the independent labourer is a bounty on indolence and vice'.[6]

So the new English Poor Law of 1834 established workhouses where the segregation of families, and the labour demanded of them, would discourage all but the most impoverished. The sick, the old and orphans could also be catered for in these poorhouses. Boards of Guardians were set up to administer them with magistrates, Church of England ministers and some parish representatives elected by the ratepayers. In Scotland the poor had been helped in other ways. The *Second Statistical Account* for the Gairloch area reported, in 1836, that 'the number of poor receiving parochial aid in the parish is about 100, each receiving from 2s 6d to 6s per annum. The annual amount for the relief is about £16, principally arising from church door collections'.

There was no organised system. The main providers of life's essentials for the most needy were the Church, charities and the beneficent local landowners.[7] The lairds often accepted that their crofters would run up arrears of rent, particularly in famine years, and they frequently expected to avoid their tenants starving by subsidising cheap oatmeal. However, the support of family and neighbours would often be the crucial factor for survival.

By 1840 the Scottish voluntary system, compared with that now operating south of the border, was being seen as increasingly inadequate. Neither the Speenhamland approach nor the 1834 Amendment Act had been extended to

Scotland. Chadwick, one of the leading officials and advocates of the new Act in England, had visited Glasgow slums in 1840 and the Tory government of Robert Peel established a Royal Commission on the Scottish Poor Law in 1844. Its report, together with the collapse of the existing provision consequent on the Disruption, (which had split the Church of Scotland in 1843, creating the secessionist Free Church), made the establishment of a more formal administration inevitable.

The *Act for the Amendment and Better Administration of the law relating to the Relief of the Poor in Scotland* of 1845 set up a system somewhat different from that in England. It established parochial boards, with a maximum of thirty members, which included representatives of the kirk, heritors and elected representatives of ratepayers (on a complicated basis giving multiple votes to the richest). Though the Church of Scotland had lost its control it was still very influential. There was no mandatory levy to pay for the provision of aid though the parish could choose to impose one on those with £30 or more of 'means and substance'. Initially it was hoped that income from legacies and fees, together with voluntary donations from the kirk and from the local land-owners, would suffice. In practice this proved wishful thinking, especially as the Potato Famine, with its long-term repercussions, pauperised many more almost as soon as the Act was passed. It had not been designed for such natural disasters.[8]

Poor relief in Gairloch parish

A parochial board had to meet twice each year to draw up the roll of the paupers, that is of the old, sick, orphaned and destitute. Each had to appoint an Inspector of the Poor. Quite often the local schoolmaster had little option but to take on the role. In Gairloch Mr James MacIntosh, who had been in post for forty-five years by 1896, was paid to do the work.[9] Although the parish could establish a poorhouse, independently or in co-operation with other parishes, this was totally impracticable for the thinly-populated Highlands. Three workhouses were actually set up in Ross and Cromarty, the first in 1850 at Tain as the Easter Ross Combination, the other two being at Fortrose as the Black Isle Combination (1859) and near Stornoway for Lewis (1894). Lochbroom belonged to the Easter Ross Combination but the Gairloch parish did not subscribe.[10] Fifty years later, on the Parish Council notice of business for March 1902, the item 'To renew the right to use 5 beds in Skye P.H' (poorhouse) was listed.[11] Thus, Gairloch parish itself continued to provide outdoor relief only. There was no requirement to provide support for the able-bodied poor unless they were women with dependent children. In any case, no one was eligible for help unless resident in the parish for at least five years 'without begging, application for relief or receipt of it'. A husband or father who neglected his children or failed to provide for his illegitimate offspring could be prosecuted.

Overall control came from the central Board of Supervision in Edinburgh which was to meet three times each year. However, it was not very tightly regulated. The Board had only one salaried employee with the other eight members being unpaid. This continued until 1894 when it was replaced by the new Local Government Board for Scotland. The parish council then took over from the parochial boards, though in practice this made little difference in remoter areas.[12] The first chairman of the Local Government Board was the same Sir John McNeill, (then of the Board of Supervision), who, in the conclusions of his *Report on the West Highlands and Islands* of 1851, had come into conflict with Dr John Mackenzie by insisting that emigration, rather than poor relief, was the way to relieve pauperism.

Dr John, when factor of the Gairloch estates, certainly had his own ideas about the new Poor Law system. He believed that it was not beneficial as it took away the local sense of responsibility for charity, using church collections and donations of food and clothing from crofters. Now people were unwilling to give anything to the poor, considering that the Poor Rate should provide for all:

> I have seen an old woman force her way into the Gairloch Poor Law Board Meeting and insist on her name being erased from the Poor Roll. Because, she said, 'everybody was kind to me before I was on the Roll, and everybody is cruelly unkind to me now'. [...] Altering the old system in rural parishes was fearful cruelty to the paupers, and meant the extinguishing of all natural, kindly feeling among the lower classes.[13]

In February 1870 he gave a lecture on *Pauperism and its Cure* where, even twenty years on and in the light of his experience on the Gairloch estates, he maintained that his methods of reforming farming practices would have solved the problems of poverty:

> He expounded (with some digressions) his theories on the reclamation of waste lands, and emphasised his conviction that an average family could not consume nearly the amount of food that five acres of average land, properly cultivated, would produce.

He met the same cynical response from the *Inverness Courier* editorial, that his views were misguided, as he had in the late 1840s. It commented sarcastically of the 'good time coming of which the Provost of Inverness is at once the prophet and the Celtic bard, when every man shall have his own pig on his own five acres ... and luxuriant crops, shall be grown from Glen Docharty to Poolewe'.[14]

John H. Dixon, writing in the 1880s, also reflected attitudes of dissatisfaction with the way in which the Poor Law worked. Although he accepted that 'under the old clan system there was no organised method of relieving the poor; indeed it is certain that the mass of the population was then in miserable plight', he did not seem enamoured of its replacement 'which is very thoroughly applied to the parish. [...] Begging is almost unknown, and, though the people have a large measure of Highland pride, they are as a rule callous to the humiliation of receiving relief from the poor rates; nay rather, some few even appear to think that they have a positive right to draw parish pay, irrespective of the state of their purses. The very few beggars seen in Gairloch are generally lowland tramps of the drinking class'.[15]

Meticulous as ever, Dixon provided valuable information on the extent of the poor law register in the Gairloch parish:

> Pauperism is too prevalent in the West Highlands. There are on the Gairloch roll of paupers one hundred and thirty-eight persons receiving parochial relief, viz, forty-six males and ninety-two females, besides fifty-three dependants, such as children, who are relieved along with the paupers. There are also six lunatics boarded at home and nine in the joint-asylum in Inverness. The other paupers are relieved at home. The total outlay on these paupers, dependants, and lunatics was £1172. 14s. 10d for the year ended Whitsunday 1886. The poor-rate is one shilling and ten pence in the pound, half of which is paid by the proprietor and half by the tenant. The poor-rate is administered by the Parochial Board, which includes the proprietors of the parish or their representatives and certain elected members. Mr Mackintosh is the inspector of poor for the parish, and has kindly given me the particulars here stated.[16]

The Roll of Paupers for 14 May 1892 provided details of each recipient, the nature of their pauperism, with the amount paid weekly as an ordinary allowance and any extra payments. Most such folk were old and frail but there were some orphans, some lunatics in the asylum and some illegitimate children. The most common weekly allowance was 1s 3d. The total cost to the parish of each pauper during the year varied from £3 5s to £22. For example, details were provided of two paupers in Londubh, (very close to Inverewe House), and one on the Inverewe Estate:

> Rory Maclean, lunatic aged 68. Weekly payment 3s. Total ordinary and extra payments = £12 0s 1d. "Defective utterance".
> Annabel Urquhart, aged 81. Weekly = 1s 3d. Total £5 8s 6d. Eyesight affected, attendance given.
> [On Inverewe estate] Widow Kate Maclean. Aged 70. 1s or 1s 3d pw. £2 18s 6d in year ordinary allowance. No extras. Readmitted to outdoor relief. Nov 1891.

Other payments were made, including for grave-cloths, or a coffin, for paupers who had died. There was a useful summary of the number of paupers over the preceding ten years:

1883	1884	1885	1886	1887	1888	1889	1890	1891	1892
159	174	171	167	161	166	167	167	161	164

It was reckoned that 3.92% of the parish population in 1892 were dependent on poor relief. The costs were categorised:

Poor at home	£426 10s 11½
Attendance at home	£ 35 3s 0d
Clothing and shoes	£ 24 14s 7d
House repairs	£ 7 13s 8d
Funeral expenditure	£ 8 16s 11½
Pauper education	£ 2 5s 9d
Lunatics in private houses	£110 2s 5d
Lunatics in asylum	£276 9s 1d

All these demands had to be met from the poor rate which was set at 9d in the pound for proprietors and occupiers on rent. The only help from the government was for the medical aid provided. In 1892 this had worked out at £69 19s 0d, with another £120 17s 4d for the maintenance of lunatics.[17]

The *Inverness Courier*, 26 October 1894, stated:

> The half yearly statutory meeting of the Parochial Board of the parish of Gairloch was held on 19th inst. Osgood Hanbury Mackenzie Esq of Inverewe was re-elected Chairman. After revising the roll of paupers the meeting levied the assessments for the year. The amount required for Poor law purposes was £1132 which was on a valuation of £11,000, requiring a rate of 1s per £ on proprietor and tenant.

By 1900 the average number of paupers was 177 and the parish was supporting sixteen lunatics.[18]

Lunatics

This group of paupers posed a particular problem. 'Lunatics' were a constant drain on resources. Unless they were very severe cases they were likely to be placed in lodgings paid for by the parochial board. Treatment was unknown. On 4 November 1852 the *Inverness Courier* reported on the traditional local methods:

> On Friday last, confident in the success of the virtuous properties of the fountain, a woman, accompanied by a young lad and an idiot daughter, were conveyed down Loch Maree in a boat, in order to put to the test the restorative powers of the well in St Mary's Isle. [...] The unfortunate creature was dragged to the well, and having been compelled to drink of its water, was put through the ceremonial of ducking, after which she was towed round the island after the boat, and after midnight bathed in the loch. The result of all this, it is lamentable to add, has been that the hitherto quiet imbecile has become a raving lunatic.[19]

The 1855 Royal Commission on Lunacy in Scotland had published a horrifying report on the conditions in which lunatics were held in hospitals and even in their own (or lodging) homes. One unidentified Ross-shire pauper lunatic was 'looked after' by his sister who tied him with a short chain to his bed of 'filthy straw'. She received 12s 6d a month from the Parochial Board for providing this care.[20] Eventually, after much campaigning and fund-raising, an asylum was opened in Inverness in 1864, with Dr John Mackenzie as District Commissioner. It was considered to be a model institution, particularly noteworthy for its lack of walls. In 1886 there were nine 'lunatic' inmates there from the Gairloch area.

The onus on the parish to look after the poor continued until the early twentieth century when the government took responsibility for the first time. The social welfare reforms of the Liberal government of 1906–1914 made a significant difference, especially the support given to the elderly – from 1908 a regular weekly payment by the state for those with an annual income of less than £31 10s per year, who had no criminal record and who had never received support from the Poor Law. As the *Third Statistical Account* related: 'The aged people were raised to independence by the old age pension of 5s per week'.

Medical issues

Be they old or young, the poor of the parish were likely to suffer considerably from ill-health, particularly during the destitution years, and the Dowager Lady Mary Mackenzie showed a note-worthy commitment to the sick among her tenants during her years as trustee for the Gairloch estate. This was commented on in her obituary notices.

> For three whole years the large parish of Gairloch was without any doctor, and she gladly placed her medical skill, and nursing abilities, at the disposal of the tenantry, and was willing at any hour of the day or night to mount her pony and gallop over the moors to the bedside of the suffering, no matter what the disease. Many a time she had to tend those suffering from typhus – then a much more common ailment than is now the case. Her medical skill was held in great repute.[21]

Osgood echoed these: 'There had never been a doctor in Gairloch and my mother doctored the whole parish for over three years – a population of about 5,400. [...] But after the doctor arrived her work became a little easier'.[22]

In Scotland, much more so than in England, it was believed that there was a strong link between debility (poor health) and poverty. W.P. Alison, the influential Professor of Medicine at Edinburgh University in the 1840s, argued consistently and eloquently that medical help must be available to the able-bodied poor to ensure they, and their families, did not sink unnecessarily into 'destitution, debility, depression and disease' in case of sickness.[23] In other words, he wished there to be a qualified doctor available to help sooner, rather than too late. In Scotland the 1845 Poor Law Act did include the requirement to 'provide for Medicines, Medical Attendance, nutritious diet, Cordials and Clothing for such poor and in such a manner [...] as seem equitable and expedient'. The logical extension of this would be a resident medical officer in every parish, with funds for medicine, paid for by the ratepayers. Sir Robert Peel, then Prime Minister, decided that this was both impractical and unrealistic. It was not included in the Act.

However, in 1848 the Act was extended by making an annual grant of £10,000 to the Board of Supervision which would allow a payment to be made to any parish that did appoint a medical officer, provided that the ratepayers matched the subsidy.[24] His income would be derived from that grant and, possibly, the payments of private patients. What became very clear though, during the famine years, was that few parishes were in a position to make any such appointments. When the Royal College of Physicians of Edinburgh learned of this, from Dr John Coldstream, a Free Church member who had been involved in delivering aid to the stricken Highlands, they enquired further. There was no information available from the Board of Supervision.

1850 Enquiry into the State Medical Services for the Poor in The Highlands and Islands

So, in 1850, the Royal College instigated what became a remarkable survey to discover the availability of doctors in the northern districts of Scotland and 'whether there be much complaint on the part of the people of the difficulty in getting medical aid'. A two-section questionnaire was sent out, one part going to some of the main landowners and the other to ministers of the parishes. Three hundred and twenty copies in all were posted to one hundred and seventy parishes and, additionally, to the seventy-one local doctors who were known to the Royal College.[25]

The subsequent *Report regarding the Existing Deficiency of Medical Practitioners in the Highlands and Islands* was published in 1852. It highlighted the poverty, its effects on the viability of a medical service, the problems for rural doctors and, incidentally, provided insight into some very localised problems. In the Gairloch area detailed responses came from the Parish Minister and Charles Robertson, Surgeon and rather briefer ones from the minister of Shieldaig and Dr John Mackenzie.[26]

All four respondents reported endemic poverty. The Gairloch Minister commented how 'death and every kind and degree of discomfort have ever prevailed' and Dr John corroborated that 'the greatest hardship is the poverty of the people'. So, not surprisingly, Charles Robertson observed that 'the generality of practitioners with just cause complain of the inability of the people in general to pay', which the Shieldaig Minister echoed almost to the word. Robertson continued: 'Private practice has not averaged five pounds per annum' and the Gairloch Minister told the enquiry that 'several kind and generous people give simple medicines both strangers and others'. He also indicated that there was only a doctor for the poor through the generosity of Dr Mackenzie, who thus provided for the paupers and crofters of the Gairloch district.

The provision of a medical service was further hampered by the lack of income which was the consequence of the poverty, the inadequate state of many of the roads, (despite the recent improvements), and the distances to be travelled. The Gairloch Minister expressed gratitude that Dr Mackenzie was available despite the fact that 'he does not commonly practise tho' a very proper person for it', a point picked up in the final *Report*:

> The deficiency of duly-qualified Practitioners is compensated in many Parishes [...] by the Ministers themselves giving advice and medicine; while, in a few places, there are proprietors and factors on large estates, who, having studied medicine in their youth, benevolently exert their skill on behalf of their sick neighbours.

Having received returns from all over the north and west of Scotland – almost all the questionnaires were returned – the Royal College of Physicians collated the information. Ninety-two parishes had no resident doctor, though some could call on one in a neighbouring area. There was a total of one hundred and thirty-three 'medical' men, though not all had appropriate training and qualifications. The consequence was that the Highland people were at risk of 'far greater suffering and fatality' than their 'more favoured countrymen in the south'.

Though it was recognised that emigration was reducing the population of the north it was also realised that many existing doctors were leaving the Highlands because they could not afford to live there any longer. Furthermore, those qualified who were moving in were more likely to depend on their farming than their medical expertise to earn a living. Examples were given of many who were not expecting to stay long. A common theme of the replies from the medical side was that they were rarely able to secure payment for the services they rendered. Even worse, they had often been called in so late that it was impossible to be of any help to the sick and injured.

To improve the shortage of medical doctors the Royal College of Physicians considered a wide, and often radical, range of measures. These included: government grants to supplement the income of medical practitioners; forming benevolent associations to supply medical aid and medicines for those poor not receiving parish relief; locating army and navy doctors now on half-pay in the destitute parishes; providing doctors with small farms or even free houses and land for grazing their horses and cows at public expense. The Duke of Sutherland was complimented for his generosity in such respects. He also gave £40 each year to pay for district surgeons on his estates.

One of the concerns found in many responses had been that, to reach their patients, doctors often had to travel far and wide at their own expense, in severe weather and across rough terrain, then to 'remain for many hours in a miserable hovel without warmth and almost invariably without food'. Often, as they well realised, there was little chance they would be paid. Given the nature of the countryside it was seriously suggested that steamships could be used to get doctors to more remote coastal and island locations! The Marquis of Salisbury had already done this for his medical man on Rum so he could 'move constantly about among the people when they could conveniently assemble to be cured of their diseases. By this plan [they] would more economically and efficiently be brought into contact with the sick and the maimed than by the establishment of stationary practitioners'. It was also proposed that small local hospitals should be established where the sick could be looked after in hygienic conditions, because in the 'filth and wretchedness of the hovels' there was little chance of recovery. Further, local women could be trained as nurses and midwives.

Fundamentally, the Royal College agreed with Dr John's analysis of the problem:

> While the operation of the New Poor Law has, in some measure, improved the condition of the existing medical men and contributed to lessen the evils of deficiency of medical aid, it has also produced the anomaly of the very poor, who are recipients of parish-aid, receiving more attention than those who are in comparatively independent circumstances, although unable to pay for medical aid.

The great majority of the highlanders, irrespective of the potato famine, (which was rarely mentioned in the responses), was too poor to pay a doctor and the situation was not likely to change.

> This destitution is at once a consequence and a proof of the miserably depressed social state of the Highlands. [...] The past history and present circumstances of Highland destitution forbid the hope that any such improvement in the social state of the people will be brought about within the

> present generation, as will enable them to provide medical aid for themselves; and therefore, if relief is to be given at all, it must be from without.

The conclusion which some in the College came to, totally at odds with the prevailing 'laissez-faire' opinion of the day, was that the state would have to intervene to correct 'the evils of deficiency of medical aid' and enable the great majority of the independent working poor to access medical treatment. Charity was not the solution to the problem. At the very least, the Treasury should pay for the medicines and the cost of the doctor's travel when the poor were sick. Parochial boards should not have the option of declining to provide a doctor and a centrally funded locum should be available when needed. State support would enhance the status as well as the income of the medical practitioner. Ideally central government should help to fund 'salaried medical officers to provide free services to all those in need'. Parishes could be combined to make this more economic. However, in its final *Report*, 'keeping in mind that the College should never aim at any object which they are unlikely to obtain', these most contentious recommendations were omitted. They were not to be brought to fruition until well into the twentieth century.

There was another conclusion, showing the advances of medical science:

> The scourge of small-pox may be kept in check by an increase of vaccinators in the Highlands, as it appears that many of the inhabitants are not protected by vaccination, so that when they come into the Lowlands, they are particularly liable to suffer from small-pox.[27]

There was very strong official support for vaccination against smallpox, which was actually made compulsory in 1852. One of the criteria of the Highland and Island Emigration Society, when selecting from the applicants for supported passage to Australia, was that they must have been vaccinated against, or actually have had, the smallpox. However, Scotland did not, in 1848, put into practice the permissive terms of the Public Health Act which had been passed following a major cholera epidemic, even though there had been serious outbreaks north of the border.

Medical dispute in Gairloch Parish (1)

There was a further issue raised in the Gairloch responses which did not merit comment in the national *Report*. Unresolved, it was to rumble on for decades, and erupt into a vociferous dispute in the area at the end of the century and split the north and south of the parish. The Gairloch Minister, the Rev. John Mackay, in his questionnaire replies, told how 'Charles Robertson, surgeon and little farmer, was procured for the paupers and crofters on the Gairloch property and for other inferior purposes. It seems to be an increase numerically speaking but we are worse than wanting a medical man for all I know and hear'.

He fulminated at the lack of respect shown to him by the Gairloch doctor: 'Since I came here Robertson's chief work was to libel the Gairloch minister', and told of 'petty and impertinent mischief' in Robertson's case and his being indifferent to pain. So he regarded the Poolewe side of the parish (the 'north') to be 'quite unprovided now' and 'a feeling of jealousy between the Parishes hurts. The Dr is said to presume on the Gairloch interest and not to regret any harm which Mr Bankes' people may incur on the Poolewe bound'. The only hope for improving the current position, to 'get a Proper Person for Poolewe soon', was one that he indicated was even then being proposed through 'a subscription headed by Mr Bankes [of Letterewe] to get a conscientious and skilful medical man for Poolewe'.[28]

The problem of the competing demands from the two parts of the parish (Gairloch and Poolewe-Aultbea) festered for the next forty years. When it surfaced again in the 1890s it was the southern end of the parish which now felt disadvantaged. The disagreement took up many pages in the county press and many hours of public meeting time. Osgood Mackenzie and his half-brother, Kenneth, the laird of Gairloch, were on opposing sides, at the same time as they were adversaries in Osgood's divorce hearings. Although Sir Kenneth worked mainly through his factor, Donald Mackenzie, there can be no doubt that the laird was a key player in the matter and the press published personal attacks on both men. The Local Government Board in Edinburgh was drawn into the conflict, though clearly not happy to be involved.

Dixon had recorded:

> Dr F.A. M'Ewen, who resides at Moss Bank, Poolewe, is the only general practitioner in the parish. He receives a fixed salary for medical attendance on the paupers of the parish. He is a duly qualified surgeon and physician.

He had arrived in 1882: 'Dr Macewen, physician to the Alnwick infirmary, was elected medical officer for Gairloch in room of Dr. Black who is leaving for a practice in England'.[29] Unfortunately, he does not seem to have fulfilled his duties to everyone's satisfaction. A vocal group from the Gairloch side considered that MacEwen (variably M'Ewen) was providing an inadequate service to the paupers, being unable to cover the whole area effectively. Letters from Donald Mackenzie, (the factor to Sir Kenneth), showed behind-the-scenes preparation for a concerted effort to appoint a separate doctor for Gairloch.[30] One, 8 August 1896, informed that the salary of the doctor was £140. This included £16 for the visitation of lunatics with the £2 rent for his home at 4 Pool Croft being paid for by the parish and an additional £20 from the County Council. So his income was £162 excluding any private fees. Donald recognised the difficulty of 'our Gairloch side [...] to carry anything in the face of the opposition of the north members who are in the majority'. Another letter, 1 November 1896, offered his help in drafting resolutions for the Council.

The Gairloch electorate claimed that they had less than their fair share of the doctor's time, though they paid more in rates. Initially they tried to get additional funding from the Local Government Board, now responsible for the supervision of the Poor Law, but it was not prepared to support two doctors. Osgood Mackenzie (still active in the local community despite his recent failure to be elected to the Parish Council) and Dixon both opposed any extension of the medical service, claiming that the poor rates were already high. So it was proposed, at a meeting of the Gairloch Parish Council in October 1896, with the Rev. Dingwall in the chair, that the salary of Dr MacEwen be increased by £30 p.a. to enable him to employ a qualified assistant to help care for the paupers in this extensive parish, stated to be thirty miles by forty miles. Interestingly, at the same meeting a proposed increase of £10 in the fee paid to the local inspector for the poor law, Mr Mackintosh, in recognition of his increased workload and 45 years service, to help him to employ a clerk, was not approved.[31]

The *Northern Chronicle*, 28 October 1896, told of a public meeting then held in Poolewe in response to the 'medical' issue. Mr Osgood Mackenzie presided. The ratepayers declared their outrage at the Parish Council decision, believing that one doctor based at Poolewe could well cope with the demands of 'only 140 paupers'. Mr Cameron, one of those who had voted against the Council resolution for appointing a second doctor, said that it had no legal right to assess ratepayers for such. 'In a stirring speech' Osgood expressed gratitude to Mr Cameron for bringing the matter to Poolewe.

> He could lay claim, he thought, to a better knowledge of this question than many of them. During the 25 years he had been chairman of the Parish Board he had never heard a single complaint from paupers of want of attendance. The whole thing, to his mind, was absurd. Because a few at Gairloch wanted

> a resident medical officer for themselves, were they going to saddle that parish with such heavy expense? He said no.

The meeting then passed a resolution moved by Mr Finlay Mackinnon, artist, Poolewe, to be sent to the Local Government Board for Scotland, opposing the Parish Council's resolution. Dixon seconded: 'the rates were high enough without adding to them for such a purpose'. He disputed the extent of the area also, claiming it had been exaggerated. The meeting passed the resolution unanimously and accorded 'a hearty vote of thanks to the chairman'.[32]

The dispute then became very public and very personal. The next day the *Scottish Highlander* published a long, strong letter from Dr MacEwen:

> It is simply a proposal to shift the centre for all parochial business from Poolewe, which is the real centre of the population, to Gairloch, which is what may be called the aristocratic centre of a crofting population and where Sir Kenneth Mackenzie, the Lord Lieutenant of the County, has a residence.[...] We live in an age of restless philanthropy, and while one cannot help admiring the good intentions of noodles and nobodies, most reasonable men generally recognise what is fair and just to a public official who has tried to do his duty, however much he may have failed to come up to the expectation of the goody-goody men who too often try to rule the roost in this part of the county.

He rejected the Parish Council request to submit details of fees as against professional etiquette and opposed the idea of £30 being paid for an assistant to be based in Gairloch: 'a proposal so absurd on the face of it that one cannot understand what its intention was'.

Dixon also had written a letter, included in this published correspondence, which suggested it would cost at least £80 to pay an assistant, so Dr MacEwen would be £50 worse off and would still have to keep a horse and trap. It would add ¾d (three farthings) to the poor rate, he claimed, and it 'would be unjust thus to reduce the salary of a medical officer of long standing'.[33]

On 12 November another meeting was held, this time in Gairloch. Some advocated appointing a separate doctor for their area since Dr MacEwen would not accept an assistant. Applecross, with its two medical men, was cited as a comparable example. The Local Government Board would be asked to investigate the plan to bring about better medical provision in this ward of Gairloch, even if 'the Poolewe friends thought they had no right'. Osgood's point that no paupers had complained was explained by suggesting that they were afraid so to do. Dixon's rate increase claims were refuted as exaggeration. The campaigners believed that there was apparently so little demand for a doctor from the people of Gairloch because they knew there was little chance that he would ever arrive in time. To strengthen their case they brought up an apparent refusal by Dr MacEwen to shut the local school when there was an outbreak of measles so necessitating the Dingwall Sanitary Inspector to do so.[34] In December enquiries were made of Dr MacEwen as to the travelling he had undertaken in the course of his duties that year. He provided visit by visit details of 89 journeys across the breadth and length of the parish, to visit 134 paupers, covering 1212 miles. Although mainly on horseback there had been some miles on foot, and one journey by steamer to Kinlochewe.

Matters deteriorated further. The *Scottish Highlander* of 14 January 1897 had a note added by the editor to say they had deleted several remarks of an offensive and personal nature by F.A. Macewen. A Mr Mackinnon of Gairloch had commented that, if he were ill, Mr O. Mackenzie would no doubt call a doctor from Dingwall, just as Mr Dixon had done. Mr Macewen, with reference to the school closure, suggested that Mr Mackinnon learn his Education Board's Code, Article 30, so he would see that he had acted strictly according to the rule book. He also denied that his quoted comment on 'noodles and nobodies' was a direct reference to anyone in Gairloch, 'being just a general statement'.

Sir Kenneth then sanctioned more detailed research into the validity of the Gairloch claims that there was inadequate provision given the extent of the parish and how a second doctor might be funded. In a letter of 1 April 1897 his factor wrote that there were 236 crofters in the ward between Point and Melvaig who had stated they would be willing to contribute four shillings each annually towards paying a fixed salary of £80 to a doctor. This would get them a young man if they guaranteed the salary, with ten shillings for confinements and the opportunity to charge subscribers and tourists. 'I have deputed to advertise for a medical man in *The Scotsman* and *Daily Free Press*', he said. The situation was getting worse it seemed: 'The country is not safe really as it is only with Dr MacEwen living at Poolewe and he is frequently unable to attend owing to illness and this has been the case lately more than ever'. He provided examples to prove his point.

In a further disagreement, in 1897, Dr MacEwen had asked permission of Sir Kenneth, the landowner, to extend his residence at 4, Moss-side, Poolewe. He wanted extra living rooms, a bathroom and wc. The desired extension had been rejected on the grounds of inadequate drainage and concerns that the building might be divided into separate accommodation units in the future.

Two years later a letter from the Local Board in Edinburgh, dated 2 February 1899, showed that they were running out of patience with the intra-parish disputes and correspondence: 'The Board must therefore request that the matter be dropped for the present'. In fact the next month, on 7 March, a Board officer travelled via Loch Maree to Gairloch Hotel to meet with some of the Gairloch council. Here he was given many examples of the inadequate medical provision for paupers, with cases named, and informed of the doctor's absence "off duty" for 25 days, from 26 January until 17 February, without a substitute. The officials were not convinced and wrote on 11 July to the effect that the Local Government board would not support any increase in salary and believed the current provision to be satisfactory.

Four members of the Gairloch Parish Council called a special meeting in Poolewe Hotel to consider the Local Government Board's reply. There were seven members present. D. Mackenzie was elected chairman, though opposed. One reason for the meeting being called was unhappiness that the clerk of the council had not summoned a special meeting and that he had begun the regular meeting (two minutes) before the advertised time! Recent correspondence was considered, especially between D. Mackenzie and the Government Board. Issues raised included the distances to be covered in the area and the time required to attend to paupers, the lack of literacy of these paupers to be able to complain and the frequent absence of death certificates for paupers (indicating that the doctor had not attended early enough to certify the cause of death). There had been some change in the situation as there was now a doctor in South Gairloch but he was not being paid to deal with paupers.

There were more meetings throughout the summer and autumn, putting further pressure on the Local Government Board. It was suggested, in October, that Osgood Mackenzie might have changed his mind: 'Inverewe admitted if he were living at Gairloch that he would be as keen as we are to have a doctor in our midst', and it was proposed that there be a plebiscite on the issue.

However, Osgood stood his ground after all. The *Inverness Courier*, 7 November 1899, printed a letter from "A ratepayer" who wished to bring out the true facts of this matter. He took exception to the rash statement made by Mr Osgood H. Mackenzie that the paupers of the parish of Gairloch were not medically neglected. He wished to prove that very great dissatisfaction had existed for sometime already in the southern ward of that parish in regard to the want of proper medical attention on the poor. He listed several cases of paupers living fifteen miles from the doctor's residence who had not been properly visited and then soundly berated the said Mr Mackenzie.

On 20 October, 1899, the *Inverness Courier* reported the death of Dr MacEwen. He had died of pneumonia, having served the parish of Gairloch for eighteen years. His death gave the opportunity to reconsider the situation and this, together with renewed agitation, at last had some effect. On 10 January 1900 the Local Government Board sanctioned a salary increase, from £150 to £200, for the medical officer of Gairloch in response to his duties under the Poor Law. However, this 'must be subject to reconsideration if, at any time, the parish is divided'.

Medical dispute in Gairloch Parish (2)

Dr MacEwen's successor as parish medical man, Dr MacNaughton, had early cause to believe himself out of favour with the Gairloch laird when, in 1900, he was informed that the laird was withdrawing the concession that he have use of one of the estate fields for his horse – essential to visit his patients across the parish. The complex dispute which blew up in early 1901 again highlighted the north–south divide within the Parish. Dr MacNaughton proposed to sell his recently-purchased house to the Parish Council for dual use as the official 'doctor's house' and as council offices. The existing 'office' was a room in the home of Mr James Mackintosh, the long-serving Inspector of the Poor and Clerk of the School Board. He had a life-rent of the ex-Free Church School building, having been the teacher there. So the office was neither leased nor rented by the Council and, according to at least some of the councillors, it was small and inadequate for the demands of the twentieth century. Given also that Mr MacIntosh was elderly and likely to die or retire soon, there was no security of tenure. So, it was argued, there needed to be a contingency plan.

Osgood Mackenzie was very much implicated in this plan. He was willing to provide the money required to purchase the house, 'on the assurance that the Parish Council would relieve him', that is, pay him back. By a majority vote (6 to 4) the Council decided to apply for a loan of £1000 from the Local Government Board for the purpose. The minority group, all Gairloch parish councillors, was vehemently opposed. Though the vote was lost these four appealed for support from the new laird, another Sir Kenneth. He wrote strongly to the effect that the proposed purchase price of £926 was exorbitant and not a fair imposition on the tax-payers who would have to repay the loan. There was then, again, much correspondence with the Local Government Board as to the legality of the plan and the apparently premeditated purchase of his house by the doctor only weeks before the scheme came to light. As far as the General Superintendant, Alex B. Millar, was concerned, there had been no complaint that business had not been properly attended to in the fifty years since the office was first used (1851) and the Council seemed to function perfectly well from the Poolewe Hotel meeting room. He was 'of opinion that to provide a House for the Medical Officer in the guise of purchasing premises for the conduct of Parish Council business is illegal and is an evasion of the Act'. Several of his statements were challenged as untrue by Osgood Mackenzie and the other proposers of the purchase and Osgood duly bought the house, anticipating repayment.

As a 'solution' to the perceived problem Sir Kenneth offered land to build new offices free of charge. But he required information as to the nature of the building before deciding where this land might be. Clearly unhappy with this, the Parish Council refused to employ an architect until they knew which site was proposed. So there was an impasse.

Dr MacNaughton then tried to get the Parish Council to reimburse him for the legal fees he had incurred in this matter. Legal advice was sought, which concluded that both the refunding of the fees and the actual purchase were illegal. So, as the Valuation Rolls show, Osgood Mackenzie remained the owner of the doctor's residence at Moss Bank until all his property was passed over to his daughter and son-in-law in 1915. They retained responsibility for the now empty and derelict house.

The result of this episode seemed to be a final acceptance that the relations between the Gairloch and Poolewe sides of the parish had broken down with no hope of compromise. In 1900 the County Council had unanimously agreed to support the case for division, despite a telegram sent by Osgood Mackenzie and Angus Stewart against taking the matter to the Secretary of State for Scotland.[35] At a ratepayers' meeting in Achtercairn Public School in February 1901 the Rev. Mackenzie of Gairloch vowed he 'would not leave a stone unturned until the problem was solved', the parish was too large 'for practical parish purposes and division would conduce to the better management and supervision of parochial affairs'.[36] Whether Osgood Mackenzie liked it or not the Parish Council again voted for the split. Sir Kenneth wrote to the Local Government Board in February 1902 to request that they receive more money. Much evidence with respect to Poor Law provision was included to support the funding application, comparing the area, population, length of roads and number of paupers and lunatics in Gairloch parish with that of Glenelg, (further south on the west coast), though the issues were now much greater than this.

	Gairloch	**Glenelg**
Area in acres	200,466	134,778
Population 1891	4181	1503
Miles of county road	98m 389yds	33m 124yds
Average no of paupers (1900)	177	67
Lunatics	16	6

The case seemed convincing but the Board, not surprisingly, rejected his request (16 February). The move went ahead regardless. Sir Kenneth was determined to appoint a second doctor and wrote, on 6 June, to Dr MacNaughton informing him of the decision. He reassured the doctor that he would be guaranteed the £200 salary of his current contract for another year whilst he decided whether to continue in half the parish for £150 or seek a different post. Sir Kenneth considered his proposal 'would be of distinct advantage' to the doctor and asked him to write to his Edinburgh address with comments. The contract for 1902 shows that, for his £200, he was to

- attend to paupers at home and provide medicines and medical appliances
- certify whether applicants for parish relief are fit or otherwise to earn their livelihood
- make quarterly visits to lunatics in their homes and to certify new lunacy cases

Thus was brought to an end over fifty years of wrangling, though the decision he made is not known.

The wider problems of the provision of adequate medical cover were, at long last, taken into account as part of the welfare reforms enacted by the Liberal Government. Finally, in 1913, some of the key recommendations of the 1852 Report of the Royal College of Physicians were implemented when the Highlands and Islands Medical Services Board was established:

> A grant of £42,000 was made available to allow doctors in the region to charge fixed low fees. This was a recognition of the exceptionally high costs of delivering a medical service in sparsely populated and remote districts and the very poor health record of the western Highlands.[37]

State of health

There is considerable evidence as to the health and medical problems of the Gairloch population. Dixon reported, quoting the *Old Statistical Account,* that 'as a natural consequence of the proximity of middens to dwelling houses, and other unhealthy arrangements, cases of fever occasionally occur'. Further:

> Spring fever used to decimate the west coast. [...] Such outbreaks have happily become rare since the potato famine of 1847 led the people to depend more on imported meal for their sustenance in spring.
>
> Few of the crofters' houses are floored, so that the inmates stand on the natural ground, or put their feet on a loose plank. In wet weather the ground often becomes damp. From this and other local causes pulmonary consumption is common among the crofter class. [...] Smallpox is said to have been fatal in Gairloch in the eighteenth century. [...] Thanks to vaccination, it is now almost unknown.[38]

Charles Robertson, the Poolewe surgeon and medical officer for four years, 'no other medical officer residing in the parish', had been interviewed by Sir John McNeill on 20 March 1851 as part of his post-famine enquiry. He testified: 'The sanitary condition of the people is satisfactory. There has been no epidemic disease amongst them for about two years. The most frequent diseases are afflictions of the organs of respiration, and diarrhoea, especially during the last two years'.

Under the Public Health (Scotland) Act of 1867 the functions of removing nuisances, constructing sewers, water supply and the control of infectious diseases were added to the duties of the Poor Law Boards. In 1875 the national Government, at last, consolidated existing permissive legislation into a Public Health Act which required all county and town councils to appoint a Medical Officer of Health. These officers had to publish an annual report into the conditions within their areas and make recommendations for improvement.

The 1891 *Report of the General Medical Officer for Ross and Cromarty* gave a fascinating insight into the limitations of the public health conditions of the day. His priorities were for sanitation and personal cleanliness which must be taught to the young in their schools. Unfortunately many of the schools were 'sanitarily disgusting'. The prime need was for fresh good water and clean lavatories. He suggested that people could use the contents of 'dry' privies as manure on land. He was not so keen on wet privies and singled out Ullapool's public privies for condemnation. Other recommendations he made included: the improvement of roads; public scavengers to save building expensive underground drains and sewers; a pure water supply; good housing for poor people with internal walls, chimneys and proper middens.[39]

One of the main responsibilities of the Medical Officer for the County was to control the spread of infectious diseases. Inoculation was only available for smallpox. All others were greatly feared as there was no treatment. Leaflets had been distributed to advise on the most common, such as scarlet fever, typhoid and measles. Typhoid, he believed, could be avoided by proper disinfection. He highlighted the need to remove cases of infectious disease to designated places, giving himself credit for introducing an isolation ward into Dingwall hospital. He would have liked to have had more hospitals to supplement the two in Dingwall and Stornoway. He praised good local doctors but advocated a central nursing home, proposing it be based in Tain, where nurses would be trained and then available to be sent out to help wherever there was contagious disease.

There were some instances of typhoid outbreaks in the Gairloch area. One, ironically, was actually in Mossbank, the house of the Poolewe doctor, starting on 12 October 1899, just a few days after he died. Dr MacEwen's death had left a vacancy for a Medical Officer of Health so the County Medical officer took control. He made the house into a temporary hospital, employed nurses and attendants and was fortunate to have 'a sufficient quantity of good milk supplied, mainly owing to the kindness of Mr Osgood Mackenzie of Inverewe, so that all the patients made a speedy and satisfactory recovery'.[40]

The evidence proved that the largest cause of death in the County, consistently over the years, was consumption, also known as phthisis. There was information for each area. Thus, in 1891, for Gairloch:

> (N. and S., population 4,257.6) has –
> cancer, 6; pneumonia, 6; diarrhoea, 1; diphtheria, 3; erysipelas, 1; mumps, 1; rheumatic fever, 1; scarlatina, 1; typhoid, 1; consumption &c., 42. Total deaths, 304, out of which 200 are uncertified.[41]

In 1905 it was reported that several cases of phthisis in the Gairloch area 'of different form and at different stages, have terminated fatally'.

Diligently, in 1891, the Medical Officer had visited almost every school in his county to be able to write a section on their sanitary condition for his annual Report. He commented on the heating efficiency of the grates, ventilation, cleanliness and toilet provision. Ullapool was a 'model school' in this respect.

Others seen were very dirty. He stressed that boys must use privies, not squat at the first corner that they come to! Many schools were reported on in detail but he complained that the workload was unreasonable for just the one Medical Officer. So, unfortunately, there was only patchy and limited detail for those on the west coast:

> I have thus visited and carefully inspected from the public health point of view, almost all the schools on the mainland with the exception of a few in Gairloch and one or two in Lochbroom. [...]
>
> Gairloch school. – Ventilation sufficient. Privies little used. Water supply might be got nearby
> Poolewe School answers its purpose fairly well. Seems rather cold. No water supply, and no lavatories.[42]

The Log Book for Achtercairn School in Gairloch (probably the one noted above) recorded, 2 August 1895, that 'the offices [i.e. toilets] are considered by the Health Officer for the County to be too close to the master's dwelling and in view of their present condition the objections seems well founded'.

School log book records

The most common diseases nationally for young children were measles, diphtheria, (w)hooping cough, mumps, scarlatina and, (often a killer), cold and influenza. Tuberculosis, known as consumption, was rife but often disguised as 'coughing' at an early age. For none of these was there any inoculation. Pasteur proved that germs spread disease in 1860 but this was much disputed for many years and vaccines to prevent illnesses taking hold were not available until well into the twentieth century. Only from 1913, for example, was there a diphtheria vaccine and, of course, it was not free. The gravestone inscriptions in the local burial ground at Londubh, Poolewe, give telling evidence of infant and young child mortality. One of those who died young of diphtheria was Johanna, aged just three, the daughter of Mr James Packman, Manager of the salmon fishings.[43] The length of time that schools were closed once an outbreak of contagious disease was recognised showed how seriously it was regarded. In the big cities cholera and typhoid could also be major killers but neither reached the isolated north-west settlements. Though there was cholera in Inverness in 1849 it escaped the 1866 outbreak and Gairloch Parish was not affected on either occasion.

The log books of schools in the area show occasional outbreaks of all the expected children's epidemics.[44] The deaths of individuals were recorded. So, 'No 35 of the girls' of Opinan died on 27 October 1873 from a cold and another girl, from Achtercairn School, on 16 February 1876 from diphtheria. Particularly distressing was the death of the Schoolmaster's son and two others in his household in December 1882, again from diphtheria.

The School Board had the authority to sanction the closure of a school for an extended period to limit the spread of infection. Thus, for 4 August 1876, the entry for Achtercairn told that attendance had been low, 'the existence of hooping cough among the children is the cause as well as for the last two or three weeks.' By the 21 August: 'Attendance to-day so low owing to the prevalence of hooping cough, that, in accordance with the instructions of the School Board, the holidays are given at once, without waiting until the usual date'. Not until 13 October did the school re-open, 'hooping cough nearly gone'. Similarly, there was an earlier start to the summer holidays at Opinan on 16 August 1892 as there was diphtheria in the area and at Achtercairn, from 15 until 25 March 1907, 'school closed by order of the managers because of influenza'. At the same school on 21 September 1908 the 'headmaster turned up to-day intending to re-open the school but received an instruction not to do so until further notice on account of an epidemic of measles' and it remained closed until 16 October. The pupils of Opinan and Poolewe were no doubt dismayed to be told that, after nine weeks closure because of whooping cough in 1910, their summer holidays were cancelled!

Infectious illness could affect the school for many weeks, even months. From 20 March 1891 until 8 May the Achtercairn head recorded 'children affected with mumps'. Particularly noticeable though was the fear that resulted from just the rumour of disease. Children were kept away. The Opinan head noted for 6 April 1877: 'Some few of the children were taken ill during the week and it is rumoured they have scarlatina. The school in consequence was entirely deserted to-day, only 12 being present'; the Inverasdale head, 30 September 1887: 'One case of measles at Naast. Children from that district precluded from attending. People throughout the whole district alarmed'; and on 23 February 1904 the same school reported a Scarlet Fever scare: 'The local attendance manager was at once informed. He promptly went to the houses said to be infected and found there was no truth in the rumour. The children were asked to tell this at home and to request parents to send their children tomorrow'. There was a major epidemic of measles in the Gairloch area, 1905–1906, and the schools were closed. But it was several adults, not children who died. 'It was discovered that the disease was spread more from Churches and Meeting-Houses than from the Schools'.[45]

In May 1906 the attendance officer was himself the cause of a long-term closure at Inverasdale:

> 2 May: A rumour to the effect that the compulsory officer is suffering from measles brought down the attendance to-day to 35. The parents in the Cove district refuse to send their children to school for fear of infection.
>
> 3 May: It appears that the compulsory officer is suffering from measles and as he visited a number of houses only two days ago there is a fear that he may have infected some who have hitherto escaped.
>
> 4 May: School was closed until 21 May.

The local doctor would be called in to check suspected cases. Dr Black closed Achtercairn school on account of scarlatina on 18 April 1877 and Dr Robertson was rather uncertain when he was checking on possible whooping cough on 12 May 1880: 'He saw nothing to convince him that it is really hooping cough, though he suspected from descriptions that there is'. By 1 June 'there is no doubt now that there is'. The medical officer of health could be called in from Dingwall. In October 1912 there was a serious outbreak of scarlatina. The school managers visited the school, 8 October, 'and advised closure from this evening until 15 October, school to be disinfected'. This was then extended 'as fresh cases of scarlatina were reported'. By 24 October the school manager, Mr Mackinnon, was writing angrily in the Log Book:

> The managers can't keep the children in school but the authorities refuse to close it. [...] Managers have no legal remedy and in the circumstances cannot be responsible for the poor attendance and injury to the school.

Eventually, 26 October, '10 pupils put off roll by order of the Medical Officer of Health', so they were no longer to the detriment of the attendance percentages which helped determine the annual education grants.

As the Liberal government reforms of the pre-First World War years (1906–1914) took effect with medical inspections, school meals and more care for young children, the general health of school age children improved dramatically. They were now fitter and better able to fight infection – and for their country. Nonetheless, no risks could be taken when the influenza epidemic struck at the end of the First World War: both Poolewe and Inverasdale schools were closed from 27 February 1919 for seven weeks.[46]

Appendix

Replies from Gairloch Parish to the Questionnaire sent out in 1850 by the Royal College of Physicians of Edinburgh to the ministers, doctors and heritors of the parishes in the north of Scotland.[47]

	Dr Coldstream Poolewe March 18 1850 Dear Sir, This place is a clear proof that your object is a benevolent one. I am not at liberty therefore to conceal truth from any personal delicacy. Of course I write with the usual confidence in such cases. J S M	
Questions	***Rev*** ***The Minister of the Parish of Gairloch by Dingwall***	***Rev*** ***The minister of Shieldaig by Loch Carron (July 11 1851)***
1 How many medical men practise within the Parish of …	Poolewe. There is no resident Med'l man. The paupers pay one Robertson from Gairloch, and the others are presently only preparing to get a proper person. Dr Mackenzie of Eilenach lives in Poolewe but he does not commonly practise, tho' a very proper person for the purpose if other calls admitted of it	Gairloch One

2 The Names and Addresses of these	John Mackenzie Esq MD of Eilenach – Isle of Ewe – Poolewe by Dingwall. Charles Robertson Gairloch a surgeon and little Farmer, procured by Dr Mackenzie for the Paupers & crofters of the Gairloch property & other inferior purposes. We expect a Proper Person for Poolewe soon.	Charles Robertson, Auchtercairn. Gairloch by Dingwall
3 Has the number increased or diminished of late years?	There seems to have been no person till the Poor Law passed. Robertson is employed by Poolewe & Gairloch at present for the poor. Dr Mackenzie was always here. So it seems to be an increase numerically speaking. But we are worse than entirely wanting a medical man from all I hear and know	Increased – there were none a few years ago
4 Have any left the Parish since you became connected with it? If so, for what reasons?	Since early in 1849 when I came here no person of the Soc't either came or went. Only Dr Mackenzie came to reside in Poolewe this year to live on his Farm of Isle of Ewe. Robertson went from here to Gairloch to a little sheep farm called Auchtercairn. We are quite unprovided now.	None have left

5 Is there any complaint among the people of inadequacy in the supply of Medical Aid	They seem to have never known better but as death and every kind and degree of discomfort have ever prevailed in consequence. I need not say that our complaints cannot be too strong. Since I came here Robertson's chief work was to libel the Gairloch minister and that has him useless for his own work.	There is no complaint of inadequacy in the supply of medicine available. But there is certainly a complaint arising from the people being wholly unable to pay.
6 Do you know of any cases of protracted suffering, or of injury by Accident, such as might have been alleviated had proper advice been at hand?	Mrs Macrae of Aird House Poolewe is a case now in existence. Other such cases where the doctor refuses are almost numberless. A feeling of jealousy between the Parishes hurts. The Dr is said to presume on the Gairloch interest and not to regret any harm which Mr Bankes' people may incur on the Poolewe Bound. As there are near 100 miles to cover he might come occasionally about tho' he were better & be paid to be so.	I do

7 To what extent is the deficiency of qualified Practitioners made up by the efforts of other parties?	Mr Bankes the wealthy proprietor here had this month to send 80 miles to Dingwall for 2 doctors for his own uses as he could not employ Robertson. Several kind and generous parties give simple medicines both strangers & others. The place is healthy and we propose to get this serious blank in our comforts filled up by a subscription headed by Mr Bankes to get a conscientious and skilful medical man for Poolewe.	To no extent
8 Does your experience enable you to suggest any measure – of general applicability – such as would be likely to relieve to some extent the evils (if they exist) of deficiency in the supply of Medical Aid?	"Placing a man in each Parish at the least"– getting him from parties of authority as your College to check from petty and impertinent mischief as in Robertson's case to leave him as far as his respect and comfort admit to his own earnings from the people to check his indifference to pain. A committee in each parish would guarantee a sum for so vital a purpose. Poolewe is poor & still it can and will support a proper medical man if only folk agreed as to his qualifications	I cannot suggest any measure unless the Heritors joined & allowed a medical man a fixed salary for attending those who do not pay above £20 of rent

9 What heritors are resident, either generally or occasionally, in your Parish?	Mr Bankes lives here in summer & harvest. He lives on his English Estates in winter. Dr MacKenzie Factor for Sir Kenneth Mackenzie (a minor) & Sir Alexander M'Kenzie lives here at present. Lady Mackenzie Gairloch is in Poolewe at present. Mr Bankes is the only resident Heritor & his income is worth all the rest together.	Sir K Mackenzie Bart. Occasionally Meyrick Bankes Esq of Letterewe. Occasionally

	Charles Robertson. Surgeon	**John Mackenzie**
1 How long have you practised in the locality you presently occupy?	Five years	Seven years
2 What are the ordinary, and what the greatest distances which you have to travel in visiting patients?	Ordinary distances 10 or 12 miles. Greatest dist 20 miles	Ordinary distance about 12 miles and the Greatest about 40 miles
3 What means of conveyance do you employ in going long journeys?	A Pony. Riding	Riding, walking & Boating

4 What is the state of the roads in your neighbourhood?	There are still some parts in which there is merely a foot-track. This was generally the case until recently when roads were made by the Dest[itution] committee	The parliamentary roads are generally good but the country is intersected with district roads which are very indifferent
5 Is the position of medical men in general in your quarter improved, or otherwise, in later years?	The Position of Medical Men have not improved since I became first acquainted with this locality	Owing to the failure of the potato crop and consequent destitution together with the low price of cattle their position for several years back had been very much impoverished. Indeed it is in vain to expect any remuneration for medical attendance from the great body of the people
6 Supposing the people of the H and I were generally able to pay for medical advice, according to rates usually observed in other parts of the kingdom, what extent of country in your locality would you regard as sufficient to occupy a single practitioner fully?	One Medical Man might attend to the Parish except during the prevalence of epidemics	I consider two Parishes sufficient so as to make proper attention

7 **Mention, if you please, any special hardships incident to your situation, such as you think might be remedied by some general measure or enactment.**	The principal Grievance of which I have and which I think the generality of practitioners with just cause complain of is the inability of the people in general to pay. I have the Minimum allowance from the Poor law Board and the Govt Grant for Medical Relief for attending to the Poor- but when I mention that during the time I have been in this parish Private practise has not averaged five pounds per Annum that the population of the Parish is about five thousand and this will be sufficiently evident	The greatest hardship is the poverty of the parish and the fatigue that has very often to be encountered in providing them with the requisite medical attendance for which any remuneration can very seldom be expected besides being frequently obliged to supply medicine. The obvious remedy should be such as would enable a medical man to procure the requisite medicine for the sick poor who are not entitled to poor relief under the Poor law Act. And such remuneration as would enable him to pay proper attention to each case

References and Notes

1 *Inverness Courier*, 18 April 1922.

2 *The Scotsman*, 15 March 1876.

3 Until 1925 heritors had particular responsibilities for the maintenance of the church, manse and schools, and, in parishes like Gairloch, maintained their interest in poor relief, even though, from 1845, they legally no longer had to. Osgood Mackenzie was certainly involved in all these aspects of parish life. No mention of his local involvement is to be found in *A Hundred Years* but there is information in Dixon's *Guide to Gairloch,* occasional commentary by Dr John Mackenzie in his writings, a somewhat haphazard, but nonetheless revealing, range of medical information, a few local records in the Gairloch Heritage Museum and sporadic

newspaper evidence from letter pages and reports of Parish Council meetings, though these are very limited.

4 He had 76 votes with the three successful candidates polling 110, 105 and 89 respectively. This must have been a big blow to his standing in the community and was almost certainly owing to the publicity of his failed Appeal in the House of Lords, trying to divorce Minna.

5 See Chapter X for the County Council role.

6 *Report of the Poor Law Commissioners 1834*, Part II, 1.8.

7 Post-famine, Osgood's mother remained concerned about the plight of the poor and there are newspaper records, for example in the *Inverness Courier* of 4 January 1881, describing her generosity: 'A large quantity of warm clothing was sent by Lady Mackenzie of Gairloch to be distributed among the poor of Gairloch estate'.

8 See Chapter III for explanation of the consequences of the Potato Famine of the 1840s.

9 Dixon, p.296.

10 Peter Higginbotham, www.workhouses.org.uk, accessed 10 November 2008.

11 Gairloch Museum Archives ('Medical' file).

12 Poor Law organisation details from Jean Lindsay, *The Scottish Poor Law* (Ilfracombe: Stockwell Ltd, 1975), pp.222–224.

13 Byam Shaw, p.284.

14 Byam Shaw, p.398.

15 Dixon, p.115.

16 Dixon, pp.295–296.

17 Gairloch Heritage Museum Archives.

18 Draft letter to the Local Government Board. Gairloch Heritage Museum Archives.

19 Byam Shaw, p.365.

20 Byam Shaw, p.370.

21 *Northern Chronicle*, 13 March 1901. A similar notice in the *Inverness Courier*, same date, had typhoid, rather than typhus. Both terms tended to be used to cover general severe sickness and diarrhoea, rather than their modern, specific, attribution.

22 Mackenzie, pp.36–37

23 W.P. Alison, *Observations on the Management of the poor in Scotland (1840)* quoted in Dr Morrice McCrae, *The Case for State Medical Services for the Poor. The Highlands and Islands 1850*, www.rcpe.ac.uk/library/history, accessed 3 March 2006.

24 McCrae, www.rcpe.ac.uk/library/ history.

25 McCrae, www.rcpe.ac.uk/library/ history.

26 A full transcript is appended to the chapter.

[27] *Statement regarding the Existing Deficiency of Medical Practitioners in the Highlands and Islands* published by the Royal College of Physicians 1852, Royal College of Physicians Library. Queen St, Edinburgh.
[28] *Responses to the Inquiry of the Royal College of Physicians on the Supply of Practitioners of Medicine and Surgery* 1850. Royal College of Physicians Library.
[29] *Inverness Advertiser*, 21 April 1882.
[30] Unless otherwise attributed all the information in these sections on the 'Medical disputes in Gairloch parish', comes from documents and correspondence kindly donated by John Mackenzie of Conan House to the Gairloch Heritage Museum.
[31] *Scottish Highlander*, 22 October 1896.
[32] *Northern Chronicle*, 28 October 1896.
[33] *Scottish Highlander*, 29 October 1896.
[34] *Northern Chronicle*, 18 November 1896.
[35] *Inverness Courier*, 23 March 1900.
[36] *Inverness Courier*, 1 February 1901.
[37] Devine, *Clanship to Crofters' War*, p.239.
[38] Dixon, p.133.
[39] *1891 Report of the Medical Officer of Health for Ross and Cromarty*, pp.7–12. Highland Council Archives, Inverness.
[40] Report of the Western District Public Health sub-committee to the Ross and Cromarty County Council, 18 October 1900. Highland Council Archives, Inverness.
[41] *1891 Report of the Medical Officer of Health for Ross and Cromarty*, p.21.
[42] *1891 Report of the Medical Officer of Health for Ross and Cromarty*, p.33.
[43] *Inverness Advertiser*, 31 January 1860.
[44] Some log books are held in the Gairloch Heritage Museum Archives, others remain in the schools themselves.
[45] Report of the Western District Public Health sub-committee to the Ross and Cromarty County Council, 18 October 1906.
[46] Log Book records.
[47] This is a transcript of the original handwritten responses.

CHAPTER X

The Heritor – continued

'That Mr Mackenzie did what he no doubt believed to be right is not the point. The point is – was it a sensible thing for a member of one Church to go and take a formal part in connection with another Church?'

Church affairs: the Disruption

Ever since the Scottish Reformation of the sixteenth century, led by the indomitable John Knox, the Church of Scotland had been a strong force within the political as well as the religious spheres, both at national and local level. It had been 'established' by the 'Glorious Revolution' Settlement of 1690 and it was still extremely influential in rural Scotland in the nineteenth century. The landowners (heritors) in each parish took on responsibility for the parish church and the minister. They were assessed on the value of their lands and rents to provide several properties: a building large enough to accommodate two-thirds of the potential congregation over the age of 12 years; a manse for the minister together with provision in kind or cash for his livelihood; a school and a churchyard. It was the minister's duty, his material needs thus having been provided for, to give spiritual sustenance to the people.

The Presbyterian Church had often shown itself vulnerable to splits over issues of principle and policy and in 1843 came another. The 'Act of Separation and Deed of Demission' was the culmination of a 'Ten Year Conflict' which had started in the 1830s. This began as a debate about the rights, or otherwise, of landowners to appoint the ministers in their manses, irrespective of the wishes of the congregation. It escalated to become an issue of the fundamental relationship between the Church and the State.[1]

The 1712 Patronage Act had given a patron the right to 'present', or appoint, the minister to the church of his parish. A third of patronages were owned by the Crown, but the majority were in the hands of the landed aristocrats and gentry. This 'presentation' was supposed to be accompanied by a 'call', signed by the male heads of the family in the parish, showing that they agreed to the nomination. Over time this right to 'call' had often become but a formality and the views of congregations ignored. During the early decades of the nineteenth century, the 'Evangelical' party within the Church, which stood for a more direct preaching and was more focussed on the parish and ordinary people, became the majority in the General Assembly of the Church of Scotland. By 1834 its adherents outnumbered the 'Moderate' group which had long held sway. The leader of the Evangelicals within the Church was Thomas Chalmers. As a parish priest in a working class area of Glasgow (1815–1823) he had emphasised self-help, thrift and communal charity, before becoming Professor of Moral Philosophy in 1823 and then Chair of Divinity at Edinburgh University.

He campaigned within the Church against the landowners upholding their rights of patronage, believing that no minister should be appointed against the wishes of the congregation, so reasserting the rights of congregation members. The General Assembly soon passed a 'Veto Act', (which was, however, never ratified in Parliament), giving the male heads of family the right to gainsay their patron's choice, should they consider him inappropriate. Patrons were then supposed to make an alternative appointment, or accept the congregation's nominee.

Generally this seemed to be working well in practice, with only ten vetoes between 1834 and 1839 from one hundred and fifty settlements. However, three of these became causes célèbre. The first, at Auchterarder in Perthshire, saw Robert Young vetoed by all but two of the male heads of family after his nomination by the Earl of Kinnoul. The Earl was willing and able to make an alternative and acceptable appointment but Young appealed his case. The General Assembly upheld the veto, but the civil Court of Sessions, and then the House of Lords, insisted that Young be installed. They ruled that the patron did not need to take any notice of the 'call' and that the General Assembly was subordinate to the civil court.

Similar decisions were made with respect to the Crown's appointment at Lethendy in 1835 and, most well-known, (given the cartoons of the 'reel of Bogie' published in the satirical press), in the Strathbogie presbytery for the parish of Marnoch. The dispute lasted from 1837 to 1841. Here the local 'Moderate' ministers, who were minded to obey the civil court rulings, were suspended by the (Evangelical) Assembly but maintained in their position by the Court of Sessions. Ministers sent by the General Assembly to take services were refused entry to the churches and so held them outside in the snow. £8,000 was then raised, very quickly, by supporters of the Evangelicals to build a new church for their chosen minister there.

More money would have to be raised to pay the 'damages' being awarded by the civil courts to Robert Young of Auchterarder and a further thirty-nine cases by then (1842) in process. Debates had been held at Westminster throughout the controversies but, ultimately, none of the 'English' prime ministers of the period (Melbourne, Aberdeen and, from 1841, Robert Peel) wished to become involved, other than to confirm that the rulings of the House of Lords (that the General Assembly could not take precedence over the civil authority of the land) must be obeyed.

The Moderate ministers in the General Assembly were minded, often reluctantly, to accept the civil authority, but, since 1839, those who had the sincere conviction that the church was a spiritual institution under the sole headship of Christ saw the situation leading to just one conclusion: 'If the state was not prepared to honour its part in the compact', to preserve and protect the spiritual life of the Scottish people, then they could not remain within the Established Church. This became inevitable once, in January 1843, the Court of Session had ruled that the General Assembly had acted illegally in setting up *quoad sacra* churches in parishes – giving the minister and elder the usual spiritual rights, powers and duties, but without the responsibilities of poor relief and education. Poolewe's church, built in 1828, had been designated as one such. Most though had been built since 1834 following an incredible money-raising campaign by the General Assembly which had resulted in over 220 new churches being erected. Given that many of the ministers of *quoad sacra* churches were of the Evangelical Party, this decision of their illegality wiped out, at a stroke, its majority in the General Assembly.

So, on 18 May 1843, Chalmers led a pre-organised walkout from the chambers of the General Assembly. In the nearby Tanfield Hall some 451 ministers, of a total of about 1,200, constituted themselves as the first General Assembly of the Church of Scotland Free. In committing themselves to the Free Protesting Church of Scotland 'most of the ministers gave up secure incomes, comfortable manses and respectable social status for an uncertain future. They were prepared to sacrifice their worldly interests for a principle – that of the spiritual independence of the Church'. They dedicated themselves to the mission of spreading the gospel, reawakening concern for sin, grace and redemption and reclaiming the lost. Most then had to find somewhere else to live and worship as the great majority of landowners saw the new Free Church as a 'subversive force challenging both the rule of law and social hierarchy'.

Those 'coming out' generally received great support from the ordinary folk in the North of Scotland who saw the action as a stand against the autocracy of their often absentee landlords. The way in which many landowners had instructed their clergy to support the Clearances for sheep in the Highland glens had also not been forgotten. Although much of the money was raised in the industrial and commercial centres of lowland Scotland the 'central sustentation fund' was shared out amongst all ministers so they were not dependent on the relative wealth of their parish. In the first three years of its existence the Free Church built over 400 manses, organised its own parochial system, established a national system of schools, set up a college to train its ministers and still found resources to support missionaries abroad.

The churches in Gairloch Parish

For many ordinary folk the chapels and formal church buildings of the parish were impossible to reach on a weekly basis and there had long been a tradition of holding occasional mass communions for three or four thousand people 'packed tight one to one another' in the famous 'Leabadh' or 'Bed of the White Cow', a hollow which is now part of the Gairloch Golf course. Osgood Mackenzie quoted at length from his uncle, Dr John, about the Communion service which lasted for five days. It was then only held, perhaps, every three years as the journey was so difficult 'owing to the want of roads, wheels or steam'. The thousands of people, many of whom had spent days walking, could hear every word of the sermons and the Gaelic psalms. Uncle John recorded how he 'should be very much surprised if any one who once heard an old Gaelic psalm floating in the air, from the thousands of worshippers in the 'bed' could forget it in a hundred years'.[2] Afterwards they could enjoy 'very earthly-like tables, with penny rolls, cheese cebbucks, goodies, ginger-bread etc, to suit all hungry ideas'.[3] Osgood recalled: 'Those gatherings were much the same in my young days, and I regularly attended with my mother'.[4] School log books reported closures necessitated by the public communions in Gairloch or Aultbea well into the twentieth century.

The Church of Scotland had its 'mother' church in Gairloch, built in 1791, but in 1828 a new 'Parliamentary' church, on the 'standard' design of Thomas Telford, had been completed on land in Poolewe donated by Sir Francis Mackenzie, Osgood's father. He had been awarded a grant by the government as part of the scheme to provide more churches in the Highlands and Islands. So Poolewe had become one of the new *quoad sacra* parishes.

By 1847, just four years after the Disruption, the new Free Church had erected 730 places of worship, often despite the considerable and active opposition of landowners. The Duke of Sutherland, for example, refused it sites and building materials. At Loch Sunart, denied land access, the enterprising congregation had bought an iron ship to be a 'floating church'. However, in the parish of the Gairloch Mackenzies there was no such problem for the Free Church supporters. Poolewe became part of the new Aultbea parish. Although a complaint was published that there was 'No Church, No Manse, No School' in November 1848,[5] three years later there was better news:

> An excellent meeting house has been erected at Poolewe, where the worthy incumbent of the parish occasionally preaches. It is capable of containing a pretty large congregation, and when the internal arrangements are further completed, it will be a very comfortable place of worship.[6]

In *A Hundred Years* Osgood confirmed his family's untypical attitude to these events, incidentally highlighting the difference between resident 'local' and absentee landowners:

> The Disruption in the Church of Scotland took place about the time when I was born, and I never worshipped in the old Parish Church of Gairloch, as our family entered the Free Church. No wonder the people rebelled when worthless men were appointed to big parishes by lay patrons, quite regardless of their being suitable or unsuitable.

Osgood linked this with the matter of the Gaelic language, decrying the poor efforts of one minister who 'had hardly a word of Gaelic, tried to make up for his want of the language by the roaring and bawling he kept up in the pulpit while attempting to read a Gaelic sermon translated from English by some schoolmaster!' He compared this priest unfavourably with his mother. Lady Mary, from an English Quaker family, had taught herself Gaelic so effectively that 'she started going regularly to church when she understood only the one word *agus* (and), and she ended by understanding every word of the longest and most eloquent sermons'. Osgood told that his 'dear mother, when we lived at Gairloch, always went to her school at Strath, about two miles away, to teach her Sunday Class' and that he himself went to a Gaelic Sunday school class and 'thoroughly learned my Gaelic Shorter Catechism'.[7] One writer, remembering the 'late Mr Osgood Mackenzie of Inverewe' in 1922, 'had the honour and privilege of being one of the late Mr Mackenzie's scholars in the Poolewe Sabbath School many years ago, in which with his mother he taught the classes. The religious knowledge gained from the teaching has greatly benefited many in after years'.[8]

The Free Church was thus an integral part of Osgood's early life and he developed close links to the Aultbea Free Church.

> How well do I remember as a young lad, when living at Inveran Lodge on the Ewe, our Free Church Minister, whom we liked very much and whose manse was at Aultbea, coming every alternate Sunday to preach in the little old meeting-house at Poolewe. [...] At the yearly Communion-time at Aultbea how hospitable the minister and his wife were, and how the luncheon-table in the manse groaned with the very best of everything eatable and drinkable.[9]

Dr John also remembered fondly the 'agreeable pastor at Aultbea, Mr Noble, and the weather generally allowed us to cross to Church, and be paid by a glass of wine and a bit of famous cake in the manse ere returning to the Island (for I had not dreamed of abstaining for ten years after this part of the story)'.[10] In 1872 the Rev. Ronald Dingwall, born in Kingussie, took over the ministry there.[11]

Osgood went to the service in the Gairloch Free Church, escorting his mother, on his return from honeymoon in 1877. However, with his home at Inverewe, he more conveniently worshipped in Aultbea or Poolewe, particularly as his marriage difficulties led to rifts with the Flowerdale Mackenzies. He was critical of those lairds who 'are so unpatriotic as to have forsaken the Church of their forefathers. Instead of worshipping with their tenants and their servants in the Presbyterian Church in their neighbourhood, they motor great distances to some chapel where they can find ritualistic services and probably hear only a very poor sermon'.[12]

Religious controversies

Nonetheless, Osgood's views and actions with respect to two local religious issues suggest that he was somewhat ambivalent in his adherence to the Free Church, apparently seeing his position as a heritor within the parish as more important than his church affiliation. The first situation concerned his involvement in an Established Church scandal, the second brought down on him considerable criticism from his own Free Church minister and was referred on to the Free Church General Assembly.

From 1879–1881 there was much press comment concerning the Church of Scotland minister of Poolewe, the same Rev. John S. Mackay as had responded to the questionnaire of the Royal College of Physicians of Edinburgh in 1850 with strong words against the local doctor.[13] In October 1879 he became subject to an enquiry by the Established Presbytery of Lochcarron. A complaint had been lodged that he had fabricated his answers to questions on the official schedule returned to the House of Commons in 1878 with respect to the number of communicants in his church at Poolewe that year. It was claimed that the fictitious return, 'said to have been made for him or by him', counted 10 males and 15 females as communicants, whereas he had actually not even dispensed the sacrament of the Lord's Supper during that year, and only once in 1877. The initial hearing into the charge was held at Strome Ferry in November 1880. The Rev. Mackay's response was that he had never signed any such document and he disclaimed all knowledge of the Poolewe return. There were, he claimed, double that number of communicants, though when pressed he could only specifically identify himself, his wife and two schoolmasters! Further, when the Gairloch Church of Scotland minister, (another Mr Mackenzie), had been appointed by the Presbytery to take over the duties in Poolewe he had been refused the key to the church. So, given no option, he, along with 'one of his heritors, Mr Osgood H. Mackenzie, climbed the gate and read the edict at the door'.[14]

The matter dragged on with further concerns:

> Serious charge in Poolewe that the minister Rev. John Sutherland Mackay made up the number of communicants in the parish; that no roll had been kept and that he had neglected his pastoral duties by failing to administer the sacrament of the Lord's supper in 1871, 1876, 1878 and 1879.[15]

In July 1881 the 'Poolewe Case' continued.

> The first witness yesterday was Mr Osgood Hanbury Mackenzie of Inverewe who knew Mr Mackay for several years, though not intimately. He considered him decidedly eccentric, but quite responsible for his actions. He never heard him preach and therefore could say nothing of his pulpit oddities. [...] The tenor of Mr Mackenzie's evidence was in favour of the sanity of Mr Mackay.[16]

There was obviously some doubt about this though. His wife claimed that 'he was insane during that time and still was'.[17] The case was adjourned for medical evidence. The outcome was that Mr Mackay did retain his position but was provided with an assistant, the Rev. Cameron, to help him.

The second controversy arose when he died in December 1888. Osgood then became involved in a much more personal way. A 'requisition' was sent 'to the Established Church Presbytery, signed by a number of parishioners of both Free and Established Churches, requesting that Mr Cameron might be permanently settled in the vacant charge'. Osgood was one of those who signed. To his astonishment 'a special sermon was preached in the Free Church of Aultbea on the subject of this petition and against the Free Churchmen who had signed it. [...] My friend the Free Church minister distinctly told me that any one who had signed the petition had (by so doing) made himself a member of the Established Church, and as it was impossible to belong to both churches, these Free Churchmen who had put their signatures to the memorial could no longer be acknowledged as members of his church'.

Even more astounding was that the minister, the Rev. Dingwall, ordered those of his church who had signed the petition to go to the Free Kirk the following Monday, 'where absolution was granted only on condition that they signed a form of recantation, stating that they had sinned through ignorance'. Osgood was so outraged by all this that he wrote a letter entitled 'Free Church Intolerance on the West Coast of Ross-shire', sending it to three different newspapers. He insisted that the action he and others had taken, in signing the petition, was completely within the law as 'All inhabitants of a parish above fourteen years of age (being Protestant) have now the right to sign a call to a parish minister, quite irrespective of the Church to which they belong or which they may happen to attend'.

He fulminated at what he saw as completely unacceptable pressure by 'his friend', the Aultbea minister, and he made an accusation that Rev. Dingwall had only preached in Poolewe, on average, 'some seventeen times per annum' instead of on alternate Sabbaths as he was nominally to do. In these circumstances Osgood had even gone 'with my family to hear God's word read and preached in the Established Church. Should I not more resemble a heathen than a Christian if I did not do so?' Osgood demanded tolerance and co-operation between the sister churches and remonstrated with the uncharitable attitude, and the 'narrow and bitter spirit' that was evident:

> How far more Christian-like would it have been of my friend Mr Dingwall, when absent from home and not requiring his church, had he offered the use of it to Mr Cameron, instead of letting his brother minister officiate to his congregation close by in a cold, draughty boathouse. I am sorry to hear that Mr Dingwall has never even called on his brother clergyman at Poolewe.

Unsurprisingly, this was not the end of the matter. Following Osgood's letter the Free Church congregation met and passed two resolutions, one that the 'soliciting of names of the Free Church people' for the settlement of the Rev.

Mr Cameron was 'most reprehensible, an unwarrantable interference with the Free Church congregation', and a second:

> That Mr Mackenzie of Inverewe has inserted a letter in each of three newspapers, with Mr Dixon of Inveran reportedly in another, traducing our minister, that said communications are tissues of misstatements and misrepresentations [...] concealing the fact that [...] Mr Dingwall has been repeatedly away in the south collecting the funds for the erection of two churches, at much cost and discomfort for himself. The meeting considers Mr Mackenzie's action more aggravated from the fact that he has contributed nothing to the Church Building Fund, though a landlord, and a member in full communion in the congregation.[18]

(These two churches were a 'proper' church, opened in 1889, to replace the meeting-house on the Riverside in Poolewe, which had been used since the 1840s, and a replacement for the original one built in Aultbea about two years after the Disruption. This had originally been built facing east rather than to the south, and it was soon evident that, owing to the 'unrelenting wind and rain', this had not been a wise decision).[19]

Mr Mackenzie was cited to appear before the Free Kirk presbytery of Lochcarron and the case then went on to the General Assembly of the Free Church. A special committee had been set up to consider the issues. It concluded:

> The General Assembly dismiss the dissent and complaint, and affirm the judgement of the Presbytery in so far as it resolves that this case should now take end, and recommends Mr Mackenzie to do all he can to support Mr Dingwall and the interests of the Free Church in the parish, but, at the same time, for the guidance of members and adherents of the Free Church in similar circumstances, the Assembly takes this opportunity of declaring that it is not becoming or consistent with their duty to sign calls or take part in any formal congregational proceedings of another church.

Some understanding was expressed that Mr Mackenzie had acted in good conscience at the time, wanting 'to see a godly man set over the parish', but in the end the General Assembly concurred with 'the deliverance, which has been considered [...] in every word and [...] every letter by the committee.' The report of the discussion ended with the comment that 'this deliverance was not intended in any sense to be a censure on Mr Mackenzie. It is simply a common-sense judgement. That Mr Mackenzie did what he no doubt believed to be right is not the point. The point is – was it a sensible thing for a member of one Church to go and take a formal part in connection with another Church?'.[20]

What Osgood had to say on this point is not recorded. Rev. Cameron was, in fact, elected to be the minister, and Mr Dixon, 'even though a member of a different church', put the recommendation to the required formal meeting which confirmed the appointment. 'Even the poorest inhabitants would be able to come there to public worship, and hear the Gospel preached, and that without charge – no pew rents, no sustentation fund, nor other expenses. [...] In Mr Cameron they would find a capable and earnest minister'.[21]

Osgood Mackenzie maintained a somewhat flexible approach to the Sabbath-keeping expectations of the Free Church. He was concerned that the Free Church minister, visiting Inveran Lodge, would only be able to change his shirt after his energetic sermon on the Sabbath if he had sent it on ahead the previous day, 'for though he was driven to church in his own dog-cart, nothing would induce him to carry the smallest parcel in his trap on the Sunday'. An old servant had a similar problem, being unable to take a lamp with her for the journey home in the dark unless she had been able to organise getting it to the Church in advance.

Nor was it permitted to collect fresh drinking water for the Sunday lunch in the minister's own home: 'It would have been an unpardonable sin to go to the spring, which was quite near the manse, for a jug of fresh water; anyone guilty of doing so would render himself liable to undergo Church discipline and censure from the Kirk Session'. Furthermore, a Free Church elder, delayed on his fishing boat by storms, could not attend the Sunday service because he was unshaven, 'shaving on a Sunday being a quite unpardonable sin.' On occasion Osgood was quite outspoken:

> What a pity that such superstition should have been fostered and encouraged in the Highlands by the clergy. If the ministers would preach less about predestination and abstruse dogmas of that kind, and would take sometimes as their text that "a merciful man is merciful to his beast", and persuade their people to clean out their byres and stables on Sunday, they would be doing more good in my opinion.

and

> Even I can remember not so many years ago being present at an Aultbea Communion where a Free Church minister, when fencing the tables, forbade

> anyone communicating who was "a frequenter of concerts or dances"! It was said in Gaelic [...] which shows how very rigid and narrow is the creed of the Free Church, and also of the Free Presbyterians, even at the present day.[22]

The Kirkyard

In addition to their responsibilities for poor relief and education the parochial boards usually, though not compulsorily, provided and maintained kirkyards (cemeteries). The Burials Ground Act had given the Board the right to acquire exclusive rights of burial. The Local Government (Scotland) Act of 1894 allowed the landowners to transfer the property to the parish council. The need to extend the Gairloch graveyard was one issue of concern for some years. In 1885 the Churchyard Improvement Society reported that it had insufficient funds to keep the churchyard in proper order.[23] In 1894 space had run out inside the burial ground so interments were now having to be made outside. This led to the three local heritors, Sir Kenneth Mackenzie, Osgood and P. Bankes of Letterewe cooperating in a 'handsome gesture'. They agreed 'to make the necessary extension at their own expense'. The contract was given to Farquhar of Tolly Croft, Poolewe. 'The commencement of the work gives great satisfaction in the district'.[24]

Further to this, Osgood prepared a standardised letter which he signed, to be copied to all grave owners, offering each the opportunity to buy land, if interested, for a family burial area. He referred to the 'Proprietor', (presumably Sir Kenneth), who had offered extra land free, but there would still be the expense of laying it out and enclosing the land. A committee had been set up by the Parochial Board to investigate the likely costs – reckoning 30 shillings for a 10 ft by 4ft 6in grave. So if the families were interested in purchasing the plot for sole rather than "common burying ground for public use" they were asked to put it in writing.[25] On the western edge of the 'old' Gairloch cemetery Osgood secured a burial lair for his mother. He chose to be buried beside her, when his time came.

Justice of the Peace

Both the 1881 Census, which recorded Osgood Mackenzie as a 'proprietor-magistrate', and one of his obituaries confirm that Osgood was a Justice of the Peace but no evidence of his work in that role has been found. According to Dixon, 'several justices of the peace reside in Gairloch parish, but they seldom hold courts. When they have business they meet in Poolewe. Ordinary misdemeanours are tried by the sheriff at Dingwall'.[26]

One of the most common matters in which JPs became involved was that of the illegal distilling of whisky. Small stills for family use had been banned in 1786 and in 1822 the Illicit Distillation (Scotland) Act saw increased fines and penalties for those who allowed stills to be set up on their land. The Revenue men were given strong rights to search without needing a warrant. For the most part, these laws were ignored and bypassed by laird and crofter alike. As Sir George Mackenzie of Coul, (the previous owner of the Inverewe and Tournaig parts of Osgood's estate), pointed out, if JPs imposed fines on those caught then effectively they were fining their own tenants who would then not be able to pay their rent![27] The 'Revenue Men' were hated and watched wherever they went, though occasionally a reward was claimed for informing them of a pre-arranged 'find'.

According to Dixon, 'the principal intoxicating beverage in Gairloch is whisky', though he reported that 'the mania for illicit distillation did not reach the parish until the year 1800'. The first was 'made by a stranger' (alleged, but unlikely) at Mellon Charles and the isles of Loch Maree were 'the scenes of illicit distillation in the early part of the nineteenth century'. He admitted that the mania 'is not yet extinct'.[28] The *New Statistical Account* of 1836 suggested that smuggling was, by then 'very much on the decrease'. Further, 'it may be mentioned to the honour of one of the heritors, that he has erected a licensed distillery, for the sole purpose of giving a death-blow to smuggling on his estate', though said heritor is not named. It seems unlikely to have been a Gairloch Mackenzie.[29]

Osgood included a full chapter on the subject in *A Hundred Years*, quoting from his Uncle John's diaries about illicit drink. His grandfather (John's father) had 'never tasted any but smuggled whisky'. John himself took it for granted as a youngster that, when out shooting, he would come across a bothy where brewing was going on, so he could get a can of sweet 'barm' (yeast) for bread-making. Later in life, as a JP himself, he had to deal with smugglers and 'ended all my connection with smuggling'. As factor he 'warned the crofters that anyone convicted of smuggling would be evicted'.[30] Sir Kenneth's estate rules included some relating to the use of alcohol and being found drunk, or in breach of the excise laws. Eviction was the punishment stipulated.

There are a number of newspaper references to illegal distilling being uncovered in the local area. One, in 1886, concerned an Alexander MacLeod of Braes, Inverasdale. The Excise men found a drain in a field, which led to a pipe into the house, then to a fireplace, 'constructed for an illicit still, a stone stand constructed for a mash tub, and the plug used in the tub and a cask containing some draff. The window of the apartment was carefully covered over with sacking'. They did not find any liquor. What made it more newsworthy was that the uncle of the said Alexander was an elder in the Free Church. 'It was believed his influence will be exerted to induce his wayward nephew to return to more honest and respectable paths'.[31]

By chance, some letters have survived regarding an illegal still which was found on Osgood's own estate in 1887. On 2 November the Inland Revenue office at Loch Carron received a telegram from Osgood. The next day the Revenue men went to speak to him at Poolewe Inn, together with his shepherd, Kenneth Urquhart. This shepherd had followed a man on Osgood's land about a mile and half around the coast until they came upon a bothy which contained an illegal whisky distillery. Kenneth had taken the drink offered him but had then fallen asleep on the way back. As he had not arrived home his worried friends alerted Osgood at Inverewe. A search was set up which found the bothy. The shepherd turned up the next morning to find himself the centre of an investigation.

Following this initial meeting the Revenue Collector visited Inverewe on 22 November and spoke to Alexander Cameron, the Tournaig sheep-manager. Others willing to give evidence were John Matheson, Gamekeeper and Roderick Forbes, Gardener, both of Inverewe. Alexander Mackenzie, an ex-gardener now unemployed, was one of those thought to be involved. Unfortunately no evidence remains of the outcome of this case.[32] Osgood certainly could not, and would not, turn a blind eye to illegal distilling, though there was little chance that he would have had any impact on its practice.

Osgood made no mention of his own views on drinking alcohol in *A Hundred Years*. However, during the divorce case proceedings, there were several references to his disapproval. 'The pursuer is a total abstainer' was significant in the evidence.[33] Osgood's commitment to abstinence is demonstrated by his role as president of the local Temperance Society, which numbered fifty-seven members. John Dixon was another active member of the group. In 1883 there was a winter season of meetings. After a talk by Dr MacEwen, on the connection between the love of the beautiful and health, stressing the importance of keeping the skin clean and of sea-bathing, and the negative impact of superstition, bigotry and intolerance on the wellbeing of the communities, Dixon gave the formal vote of thanks and then delivered a Temperance address. In their last meeting that year Osgood read a lecture by

Rev. Mr Heywood Joyce of Harrow-on-the-Hill, near London, which was followed by a lecture in Gaelic by the Rev. Dingwall. The weekly meetings had been well attended and 'enthusiastically conducted'. There had been excellent addresses on temperance by the office bearers. The Aultbea police constable commended the 'highly edifying and moral tone'.[34]

County Duties

There were two ways in which Osgood Mackenzie served the county of Ross. He was a Commissioner of Supply, being thereby a member of the committee of large landowners, whose role initially had been to collect the land tax on behalf of the Crown (from 1667), to be responsible, along with justices of the peace, for county roads and bridges and, from 1857 to establish a county police force. In 1868 the commissioners of supply were authorised to levy a county assessment for other duties, such as public health, prisons and highways. However, although they were not abolished until 1930, most of their roles became redundant after the establishment of county councils by the Local Government (Scotland) Act of 1889. From then on the only duty they had was an annual meeting which appointed members to a committee that was responsible for the county constabulary. Osgood's name is on the roll of commissioners until at least 1913, by which time he was number one on the list (the longest serving member).

From 1898 Osgood was an elected County Councillor, replacing John H. Dixon as the member for the Poolewe ward. The Minutes of the meetings (held, usually, four times each year) show that he very rarely attended and even more rarely contributed to business. On 20 December 1898, during the only meeting he actually attended during his first three years as a councillor, he spoke on an issue dear to his heart: there really was no need to extend the list of so-called 'endangered' wild birds needing protection in the County, except to include the sea-eagle. Despite his ongoing lack of commitment (he attended only four meetings, and never recorded an apology for absence) he continued to be re-elected to represent Poolewe until 1913. As the war meant there would be no triennial election in 1916 a letter was read to the County Council on 19 October 1916: 'Mr Osgood H. Mackenzie has intimated his resignation of the office of County Councillor for this division. The Committee recommended the County Council to appoint Mr Robert John Hanbury, Tournaig, Poolewe, to fill the vacancy". Robert accepted the invitation.

The cultural life of Poolewe

Osgood frequently emphasised his commitment to the Gaelic language and presented himself as a dedicated Highland laird. A full length portrait shows him in old age, an upright man with full white beard, wearing his Mackenzie tartan kilt and every inch the Scot.[35] Having been banned after the battle of Culloden (1746) the kilt had become legal attire again in 1772. In the early part of the nineteenth century, 'the kilt was still the dress of many men in Gairloch, who never put on the trews until old age came, and in some cases not even then'.[36] Queen Victoria, particularly with her furbishing of Balmoral, had made tartan very fashionable in the second half of the nineteenth century, though this, for some, emphasised the way in which the kilt frenzy 'took on a life of its own, little related to the Highlands. It was a British, unionist, imperialist enthusiasm. [...] Tartan was Tory – worn above all by those connected to the army, pillar of a conservative social order, next by the upper class and only then by anyone else taking a fancy to it. Many Scots saw it as an affectation. Other leaders of society on the whole did not wear it – not judges, professors or moderators of the General Assembly of the Church of Scotland'.[37] Photographs of him in his daughter's albums, and elsewhere, suggest that Osgood actually wore plus-fours for everyday use. Generally the kilt was only infrequently worn.

> The Highland dress is now only worn in Gairloch by a few gentlemen, pipers, keepers and some of the better-to-do schoolboys. [...] The Gairloch company of rifle volunteers originally wore the kilt, but about the year 1878, in common with the majority of the battalion to which they are attached, they agreed to substitute Mackenzie tartan trousers. The change was made partly on the grounds of economy.

However, tradition died hard:

> After the review of the Scottish volunteers at Edinburgh on 25 August 1881, which was attended by the Ross-shire battalion, including the Gairloch company, a general wish was expressed that the example of the volunteer battalions of the adjoining counties should be followed, and the kilt resumed. The Gairloch company unanimously petitioned their gallant colonel to restore the kilt.[38]

Dixon, though not Osgood, became very involved with these local Rifle Volunteers. The 'volunteer' movement was an important part of Highland and social life in the second half of the nineteenth century. The first company in the Gairloch area had been established in 1867, with sections based in Achtercairn (Gairloch), Opinan (to the south) and Poolewe. From 1881 onwards they were linked with Regimental districts and became the "I" Regiment of the Ross Highland Rifle Volunteers. Their role was in home defence. Dixon attended the 'memorable Edinburgh Review before H.M. Queen Victoria' in 1881[39] and became its captain in 1883. He was very proud of his section: It 'is well supported, and is generally over its authorised strength. It has three pipers and the rank and file comprise a number of fine men'. Further: 'The right hand man stands six feet four inches in his stockings and a number of the rank and file are fully six feet in height'.[40] When the full Gairloch Volunteer Company mustered in 1886 it numbered two officers, six sergeants and eighty-four rank and file.[41] They wore 'scarlet Highland doublets' and marched along Riverside to Inveran, bringing back to local minds the story of 'companies of soldiers in red uniforms marching to and fro' which had been a 'second sight' vision fifty years previously.

Dixon was diligent in organising exercises and practices, hiring the Poolewe Hall for drill.

> The sections meet occasionally for combined drill during the spring months. [...] There are rifle ranges at each of the three sections. Each section has its annual shooting competition, the prizes being mostly provided by subscription, to which the gentlemen in the neighbourhood handsomely contribute.[42]

In 1886 there were knock-on effects of the severe Government action underway to suppress unrest by crofters on Skye, including the sending of warships and armed military. In protest a letter was sent by the 1st Inverness Rifle Volunteers, based at Portree: 'Taking into account the present military proceedings in Skye, we the undersigned members of 'H' company, beg to tender our resignations as members of the corps and to ask our discharges'. There were similar repercussions in Gairloch: 'A large number of the Gairloch volunteers put in their resignation on Friday and Saturday of last week and it is most probable that before this will appear in print the Gairloch corps will be known as an institution of the past'. The protest was against the 'present military of Skye, at the instance of the Secretary of State for Scotland and Sheriff Ivory "whose memory [...] will stink in the nostrils of all true highlanders for generations yet unborn"'. There were further reports that sixteen were dismissed from the service by Capt Dickson [sic] in an attempt to restore discipline to the ranks.[43] The matter must have been resolved though because, at the inspection in

May the following year, there were ninety-one volunteers present on parade, with eleven more absent with permission.[44]

Linked with the Rifle Volunteers were the Highland Games. There had been some 'athletic games' in March 1885, held at Inverewe, and the children were given a half-day holiday in order to attend.[45] The *Inverness Courier*, 2 April 1886, reported on the Athletic Sports held at Poolewe. 'Several years ago Captain Dixon, Inveran, instituted athletic sports and Highland games' for his Company of the 1st Ross-Shire Rifle Volunteers. On this occasion they took place in 'one of the Inverewe Parks kindly granted for the occasion by Osgood H. Mackenzie of Inverewe'. Osgood, accompanied by his mother and young daughter, attended and helped with the events. These included races of varying lengths, jumping long and high, throwing both light and heavy stones and light and heavy hammers, a hop, step and leap, three-legged race, swarming the rope and piping strathspeys and reels. Prizes were paid for and presented by Captain Dixon himself, with a vote of thanks: 'the liberality with which their commanding officer treated his company was unparalleled', comparing this to the 'parsimonious treatment it continued to receive from the government'.

Dixon wanted to extend his generosity in pursuit of Highland culture further. He proposed a range of prize-winning competitions to be held annually as a beneficial stimulus to the people of Gairloch:

> Home spun cloth, plaids, and carpets produced within the parish;
> Gairloch hose;
> Vegetables, fruit and flowers grown by Gairloch people;
> Highland games and athletic sports;
> Pipe music by local pipers;
> Gaelic songs by Gairloch bards.
>
> Perhaps boat races might be added to the list. Substantial prizes for merit in these competitions would unquestionably tend to encourage industry and develop excellence. If sufficient funds were forthcoming, a competent committee could readily be got together to work out the details. I earnestly invite the assistance of all who visit this romantic country towards a proposal designed to promote the advancement of its Highland inhabitants.[46]

There is no evidence that this ever came about.

Another interest John Dixon and Osgood Mackenzie shared was the patronage of Gaelic bards and artists. Close to Inverewe House, on the shore road, there is a cairn:

IN MEMORY OF
ALEXANDER CAMERON
THE TOURNAIG BARD
1843–1933
Who lived all his long, useful and highly
Respected life on the shores of Loch Ewe and whose
Gaelic poems and songs earned for him
A wide and honoured reputation
Throughout the North.

'Is Glormhor obair naduir fein
A'ghrian ag oradh neoil nan speur
Cuan 'na chomhnard boideach reidh
Torman seimh aig seis nan allt'
MOLADH THURNAIG

In 1886 Dixon printed one of Cameron's poems, *In Praise of Tournaig,* with translation from the Gaelic, and explained:

> Alexander Cameron, who may be called "the Tournaig bard", is a native of Inverasdale, on the west side of Loch Ewe. He was born about 1848. He has been manager of Mr Osgood H. Mackenzie's farm at Tournaig for some sixteen years, and has been on the Inverewe estate since he was a boy of fifteen. He is the author of a number of songs and poems of considerable merit. [...] He has the courteous manner of a true Gairloch Highlander.[47]

The cairn is fourteen feet high, on the shores of Loch Ewe, close to the bard's home. It was unveiled on 9 August 1952 by Osgood's daughter, Mairi, after an entirely Gaelic ceremony of prayers and psalms. Mr I.M. Moffat-Pender, a Gaelic scholar who lived for some time in the Gate Lodge at Inverewe, delivered the memorial address. He had studied under the Tournaig Bard and helped to produce a selection of his poems in 1926.[48] His poems showed his love of the simple things of nature and he was praised for never writing anything that was satirical or harsh.[49]

Osgood (and John Dixon) contributed to a memorial fund for another local Gaelic scholar who had died in 1848, at the early age of forty-two, at his parents' home in Londubh, Poolewe. This was the John Mackenzie, author of *Sar Obair; or The Beauties of Gaelic Poetry and Lives of the Highland Bards*, (published 1841), which 'went through eight editions and innumerable reprints, and is probably the most influential secular work ever printed in Gaelic'. The monument, a granite column more than thirteen feet high, is still to be found between the Gairloch churchyard and the road.

> In memory of John Mackenzie (of the family of Alastair Cam of Gairloch) who composed and edited the 'Beauties of Gaelic Poetry,' and also compiled, wrote, translated, or edited, under surpassing difficulties, about 30 other works. Born at Mellan Charles, 1806. Died at Inverewe, 1848. In grateful recognition of his valuable services to Celtic literature, this monument is erected by a number of his fellow-countrymen. 1878.[50]

Finlay Mackinnon, the 'Poolewe artist', benefitted considerably from the support of the heritors. He was born c.1864, lived with his mother at Moss Bank in the village and was educated at the local Public School. Dixon was first introduced to Finlay, just a 'little bare-legged lad' but even then intent on 'the drawing', in 1877. He started him 'in a course of instruction, and Mrs Mackenzie of Inverewe gave him great assistance' (presumably Minna). 'He progressed rapidly'. By 1883 he had been invited to London to study, his talents having been recognised by a Mr H.B.W. Davis, a visitor to the area. Finlay had more financial support from, amongst others, Osgood and Sir Kenneth. Dixon reported that some of his watercolour sketches 'already display considerable merit, and there is every prospect of his becoming an able delineator and interpreter of the beauties of Gairloch and Loch Maree'.[51]

This promise was to be fulfilled. Mackinnon spent some years in South Kensington, with his own studio. 'He was very Scottish in his dress and speech and was considered a character in the London art world'.[52] However, he always saw Poolewe as his home and built a house and studio there. This caused him some problems as, in 1894, he was sued in the Inverness Debt Recovery court by his architect who alleged not to have been paid in full for his work on the new house. The artist claimed that the plans were of such poor quality that they could not be used by the builders, but he lost the case.[53]

Many of his paintings were watercolours of the local area. Osgood continued to be his patron and (modest) benefactor, even sending him a salt cellar, with Mairi giving a butter dish, for his high society Scottish traditional wedding to Isabel Matheson of Lochalsh in London in 1898![54] In a letter of 1907 Osgood mentioned that the daughters of Sir Hector Munro of Foulis were coming to Poolewe to study under Finlay Mackinnon.[55] He was commissioned to paint for various Scottish noblemen and his illustrations were used in books such as Sir Hugh Fraser's *Amid the High Hills* (1923), which was a collection of articles on sport and natural history, and in Seton Gordon's *The Immortal Isles*, a natural history of the Outer Hebrides. He exhibited eighteen times in the Royal Academy between 1894 and 1929.

Finlay Mackinnon had been an active member of the Gairloch company of the 1st Volunteer Battalion of the Seaforth Highlanders[56] and when war came he joined up, as did so many local men, in their 4th Battalion. He was responsible for the watercolour sketches which illustrated the wartime history of the battalion. He died at home in Poolewe in 1931, being buried in the local cemetery.[57]

There were other ways in which Osgood and John Dixon helped to extend the cultural opportunities for local people:

> There is at Poolewe a building used as a public hall. It comprises a reading and recreation room, which is available for meetings, and though comparatively small is sufficient for the population. It was opened on 12 February 1884 by a meeting, at which Mr Osgood H. Mackenzie presided. It contains accommodation for a caretaker and it is intended to provide an additional recreation room. The profits, if any, of this book are to be devoted to this little institution.[58]

Osgood had musical interests also. In 1882 he supported an evening entertainment in the Poolewe School, organised by John Dixon, to recognise the good work done by Angus Ross of the Caledonian Bank in Gairloch in setting up a local Gaelic singing class. Dixon's piper played the bagpipes, there was tea, cake and buns for all and then 'Mr Mackenzie of Inverewe played a selection of scotch airs on the piano'. Alexander Cameron, sheep manager, Inverewe, sang two Gaelic songs and Osgood accompanied the choir on the piano. At the end of the evening Dixon thanked everyone, including 'Mr Mackenzie of Inverewe for the use of and presiding at the piano'. Dixon, in turn was thanked for being 'always ready, with his time and his means, to promote good works and conduce to the happiness of others'.[59] Together with daughter Mairi, Osgood attended a concert in Gairloch in 1895, at almost exactly the same time as he lost his final appeal to the House of Lords. There were also several instances of Osgood attending the Gaelic music evening school sessions. The Poolewe Junior Gaelic choir sang in January 1904 when the school treat took place at Inverewe and, on 19 July 1906, 'the choir performed at a concert at Inverewe last night'.[60]

References and Notes

1 Almost all of the detail in this section is taken from (Eds) Stewart J. Brown & Michael Fry, *Scotland in the Age of the Disruption* (Edinburgh: Edinburgh University Press, 1993), Chapter I.

2 Dixon, p.120.

3 Byam Shaw, pp.319–320.

4 Mackenzie, p.193. One obituary notice, in the *Northern Chronicle*, 13 March 1901, emphasised how the Dowager Lady 'was in all weathers a regular attendant at church, and a devout worshipper, and always thought most of those who followed her example in this religious duty'.

5 *Inverness Courier*, 23 November 1848.

6 *Inverness Advertiser*, 28 August 1851.

7 Mackenzie, pp.192, 34, 197–198, 58.

8 One of the obituary notices in a photograph album at Inverewe House.

9 Mackenzie, p.196.

10 Byam Shaw, p.227.

11 Angus Matheson Mackinnon, *Highland Minister. The Life and Poems of Rev Angus MacKinnon, Aultbea.* (Nova Scotia: Catalone Press, 1997), p.157.

12 Mackenzie, p.59.

13 As explained in Chapter IX.

14 *The Scotsman*, 6 October 1879.

15 *Inverness Courier*, 29 January 1881.

16 *The Scotsman*, 19 July 1881.

17 *Inverness Courier*, 19 July 1881.

18 *The Scotsman*, 28 January, 7 March 1889.

19 Mackinnon, p.158.

20 *The Scotsman*, 3 June 1889.

21 *Scottish Highlander*, 31 January 1889.

22 Mackenzie, pp.198, 195–196.

23 *Scottish Highlander*, 28 August 1885.

24 *Scottish Highlander*, 3 August 1894.

25 Undated letter. Gairloch Heritage Museum Archives.

26 Dixon, p.296.

27 Devine, *Clanship to Crofters'* War, pp.130–131, 125.

28 Dixon, p.134.

29 Quoted in Dixon, p.406.

[30] Mackenzie, pp.214–217.

[31] *Scottish Highlander*, 21 October 1886.

[32] Inverewe House Archive.

[33] See Chapter VI.

[34] *Inverness Advertiser*, 9 March, 6 April 1883.

[35] This may be the one referred to in an undated, untitled newspaper article in Mairi's collection about Andrew Paterson, photographer of Inverness. He had had a 'magnificent portrait photograph of the late Mr Osgood Mackenzie' accepted for the Professional Photographers' Exhibition in London. It was 'the second year running that he had had photos exhibited. This year's exhibition was really the first truly international one. He had been asked to allow the society to retain the picture for a permanent touring exhibition'.

[36] Dixon, p.128.

[37] Michael Fry, *Wild Scots* (London: John Murray, 2005), pp.184–185.

[38] Dixon, pp.129–130.

[39] *Ross-shire Journal*, 29 October 1926 (Obituary Notice).

[40] Dixon, pp.113, 297.

[41] *Scottish Highlander*, 20 May 1886.

[42] Dixon, pp.129–30, 172, 297–298. The rifle range used is still evident in fields to the north of the River Ewe.

[43] *Inverness Advertiser*, 25 November, 23 December 1886.

[44] *Scottish Highlander*, 9 June 1887.

[45] Poolewe School Log Book, 27 March 1885.

[46] Dixon, p.124.

[47] Dixon, p.194.

[48] There is a copy of the memorial service programme in the Gairloch Heritage Museum Archives.

[49] Article in *The People's Journal*, 16 August 1952. Gairloch Heritage Museum Archives.

[50] Ronald Black, *John Mackenzie of Sar Obair* (unpublished paper, March 2006). Gairloch Heritage Museum Archives.

[51] Dixon, pp.200–201.

[52] Quoted Wright, p.33 from Paul Harris and Julian Halsby, *Dictionary of Scottish Painters*, 3rd edition 2001, p.141.

[53] *Scottish Highlander*, 5 July 1894.

[54] *Scottish Highlander*, 7 April 1898.

[55] Letter from Osgood Mackenzie to Sir Hector Munro of Foulis, 17 September 1907. Inverewe House Archive.

[56] *Scottish Highlander*, 12 October 1893.

[57] Obituary in *Ross-shire Journal*, 17 July 1931.

[58] Dixon, p.298.

[59] *Inverness Advertiser*, 13 June 1882.

[60] Poolewe School Log Book.

'Work and Play'

OLD TIMES

NEW TIMES

17. Old Croft … New Croft, from Francis Mackenzie's *Hints for the Use of Highland Tenants and Cottagers by a Proprietor*, 1838

18. Crofter Family, Poolewe, *c.*1880

19. A Crofter's House, Loch Ewe, *c.*1889

20. Deer Stalking at Inverewe, 1890

21. Fishing on the Fionn Loch, from the Tournaig Visitors' Book

22. Osgood with his black -and-white setters outside Inverewe House

23. Excisemen finding an illicit bothy: Murdoch Mackenzie, customs and excise officer and two of his men at an illicit still near Gairloch, *c.*1900

24. The Aultbea Schoolhouse, Bualnaluib

25. Poolewe Village, with the bridge over the River Ewe, *c.*1893

26. Poolewe, the 'Telford' church and Inn, *c.*1906

27. Mr Cameron, Headteacher, with the staff and pupils of Poolewe School, *c.*1903

28. Red Cross nurse training on Tournaig Lodge Lawn, August 1914

29. On the way to War, November 1914

CHAPTER XI

Education Matters

'When my mother took charge of the property there was only the one parish school, but she started nine or ten. [...] What a success her schools all were, and what intelligent scholars they produced.'

Schooling before 1872

'In the great extent of this parish [...] there is no school but the parochial, by which means the rising generation suffer much and are wholly neglected, having no access to the benefit of instruction.' The Rev. Mr Daniel M'Intosh wrote despondently about education in the Parish of Gairloch in the 1792 *Old Statistical Account* but, sixty years later, the provision in the area was to be commented on much more positively, even at national level, thanks to the efforts of the Mackenzie family.

The Gairloch Parochial School had been founded in 1784 under the auspices of the Society for the Propagation of Christian Knowledge. This society had been created in 1716 to improve English teaching in the Gaelic speaking areas of Scotland. There was to be no national system of education until 1872 but considerable improvements, both in the quantity and quality of education available, had already been made by the time of the *Second Statistical Account* of 1836.

> The total number of schools in the parish is nine; the parochial school is one of that number; all the rest are supported by different religious societies. The branches of instruction taught at the parochial school are Greek, Latin, mathematics, arithmetic, writing and English, and Gaelic reading. The branches taught at the Society schools are arithmetic, writing, English and Gaelic reading. [...] From six to eight schools are still required in the parish; and some of the schools now in operation ought to be put on a more permanent and efficient footing. Not more than one in every ten of the population is able to read and write in English.[1]

As with provision for the poor, there was a fundamental change as a result of the Disruption in the Church of Scotland in 1843.[2] The Free Church committed itself to establish rival schools. Dr Mackenzie spoke of the twelve schools that were there when he left, rather than the one when he came, claiming that he had set up nine new schools, with teachers' houses, 'and Lady Mackenzie and Frankie each built and provided a smart school [...] all which the laird, Kenneth, when he came of age in 1853, approved of and continued, till the Education Act raised very superior schools all over the Parish. And as what costs nothing is seldom valued, we levied six shillings from every tenant on the estate, yearly, nominally to pay the school expences but of course that was a small item in the yearly bill for the schools'.[3] Osgood, on the other hand, gave his mother the credit for starting all these new schools: 'When my mother took charge of the property there was only the one parish school, but she started nine or ten. [...] What a success her schools all were, and what intelligent scholars they produced'.[4]

That the provision of schools in Gairloch parish was somewhat extraordinary was recognised far and wide. In 1850 an article in the *Scottish Highlander* stated that Captain Eliott, of the Central Board for Destitution, had commented in his final report of the almost universal apathy with regard to education, holding up 'the solitary but bright exception of Gairloch, with its many well-managed educational and agricultural schools – showing what may be accomplished by the zeal, ability, and activity of one individual, and that individual a female, and originally a stranger, though now conversant with their language and identified with their interests'.[5] Incidentally, in correspondence with respect to Dr John's farming reforms (which the writer criticised), Lady Mary was again given praise and the need to continue to pay for the schools emphasised:

> Lady Mackenzie has done a great deal on the estate of Gairloch towards the moral culture of the rising generation in the planting of schools in different localities, and the people owe her a debt that they can never repay. A certain portion of the expense of maintaining this invaluable machinery is borne by the proprietor, but I regret exceedingly to hear that there is a surmise in the country that the Doctor is to withdraw Sir Kenneth's bounty. I sincerely trust this is but a false alarm.[6]

It was. Osgood expanded that his half-brother, Francis, 'had built and endowed a beautiful Girls' School at Bualnaluib for the benefit of the daughters of the numerous surrounding crofters, and had placed in it as teacher a daughter of John Fraser, my grandfather's old gardener at Conon, who looked upon herself as one of the family retainers'.[7]

Schooling after the 1872 Education Act

The existing local 'voluntary' schools were absorbed into the new framework of the 1872 Education Act without apparent administrative problems. Responsibility for providing and maintaining the elementary, or 'public', schools lay now with the parish. Local rates were levied to pay the costs of the building, teachers and books.

As a member of the Parochial Board Osgood, therefore, had to consider the provision of local education. One source of 1892 listed the schools that were maintained. Money was paid out to schools at Kenlochewe, Opinan, Auchtercairn, Sand, Melvaig, Inverasdale, Poolewe, Bualnaluib, Mellon Udrigle, Slaggan, Isle Ewe, Letterewe, and Slatadale, with detail given of the cost of teachers, repairs, and equipment. The last four schools mentioned were, however, very small and only received a small grant, with no accounts for cleaning, repairs, sewing etc. At that time 2d in the pound was set for the school rate. The *Inverness Chronicle* of 26 October 1894 reported that 'The School Board requirement was £900 raising the rate from 3d to 9d per £1'. It is not clear why there was such an increase.

Head teachers had to keep a weekly record of attendance, the 'introduction of new books, apparatus, and courses of instructions, the visits of Managers, absence, illness or failure of duty on the part of any of the school staff'. Inspection reports (both secular and religious) were hand copied into the standard-issue, 'stoutly bound' school log books. No 'reflections or opinions of a general character' were permitted.[8]

Attendance

The 1872 Act had made school attendance compulsory for children from age five to thirteen. In 1883 this was raised to fourteen though pupils could opt for half time education from the age of ten. Until 1901 children could leave at a younger age if they proved their competence to standard in reading, writing and arithmetic, so there were always very few children in the top classes. To qualify for the full attendance grant, and avoid awkward enquiries by the authorities, there had to be 400 half days when at least a third of the pupils were present. Only then could an official opening be credited. If insufficient children came to school it did not count, as at Inverasdale:

> 1905. Feb 16: Another tempestuous day – wind and rain. By 10.30, 24 children reached school but as they were in a soaked be-draggled condition their home exercises were corrected, others given and then they were sent home to change. Attendance cancelled

and

> 1918. 21 Jan: The attendance was cancelled on 7th, 8th, 9th, 14th, 15th, 16th, 17th and 18th respectively as there were less than one third of the pupils present.

Sometimes there was a warming cup of cocoa to be enjoyed before facing the often lengthy trudge back home. In a year of bad epidemics or weather too many cancelled sessions would necessitate opening on Saturdays to ensure the 400 total was reached. It was only on rare occasions that the log book noted 'percentage this week is 100% the best for this session. This is not likely to be bettered'.

One significant deterrent to attendance was the cost of education. In both Poolewe and Inverasdale the fact that many children were not sent to school until they were at least seven was a cause of concern. The reasons were believed to be both the distance to walk and the payments for schooling. The Poolewe head was very pleased, in December 1884, when the School Board decided to encourage parents to send children aged five to school by making their education free. In January 1891 forms were made available for parents who could not afford the cost of books.

The endemic poverty was exemplified by frequent comments about the inability of children to attend school being 'ill shod and ill clad' and 'bare-footed and bare-legged'. 'Stormy weather this week. Most of the parents here are in poor circumstances and are unable to provide their children with proper clothing etc: the attendance therefore cannot be but irregular' wrote the Poolewe headteacher, 18 December 1874; 'All bare-footed children were absent' at Opinan School on 5 February 1875; 'On account of a heavy fall of snow with the temperature about freezing point the attendance is not quite to the mark. On making enquiry the reason in most of the cases is want of boots' was recorded for 15 November 1897 at Inverasdale. Even in the summer, (August 1892), there was the same problem: 'Several children who were in the habit of coming barefoot to school have sore feet and cannot attend'.

'Boisterous' weather, snow and storm were blamed, time and again, for large numbers of children being unable to get in to school, or having to be sent home early. Dire weather was reported both winter and summer. There was always the problem of getting across the unbridged rivers when they were in flood and when the bridge at Strath, Gairloch was washed away in September 1892 the head wrote of his anger that the consequent poor attendance would be counted against the school. Sometimes there was an agreeable surprise: 'The weather being very stormy and severe I am surprised to find as large a number having come several miles to school'. The dark winter nights meant that lunch breaks were shortened to enable the children from a distance 'to reach their homes before dark, the road in some places being dangerous'.

The lack of adequate heating in the schools was also bemoaned time and again. Children had to bring their own peat initially but this was not always possible. The Opinan head logged how 'Catherine Macauley has been detected for two successive days attempting to evade the bringing of peats'. The penalty for her omission is not mentioned. The inadequacy of heating arrangements, be they open fires or closed stoves, was a constant theme of inspectors' reports. Frequently 'working' classroom temperatures in the 40s°F were noted. The situation was not helped when, at Inverasdale in 1897, the paid cleaner and lighter of fires frequently arrived late to work:

> The young woman who is engaged by the Board to light the fires etc in this school has been repeatedly warned to have them lighted by 9 a.m. [but] she did not arrive until after 10 o'clock this morning. [...] Although the weather is most severely cold and the thermometer at 42° F the fires were not put on till nearly eleven o'clock.

When said cleaner resigned in protest at being reproved it took three weeks to appoint a replacement, possibly not helped by the fact that the pay for the work was but '£3 per annum with a bonus of 10/- at the end of the year if the work is satisfactorily performed, the cleaner to provide all requisite materials and utensils for cleaning'.

Good weather would also affect attendance because it afforded the opportunity to make progress with the harvest, planting and lifting potatoes, cutting peats, sheep dipping, fishing, and the collecting of seaweed or whelks which, as in 1883, 'they sell to get money to pay for books'. Parents would often see their own farming and housekeeping needs as a greater priority than schooling and excused, particularly, their elder sons so that they might help with the chores of 'spring work'. In bad weather, of course, the corn stooks must be secured. The crofting needs were recognised by the authorities: for a while 'for the convenience of parents gathering sea weed at Spring tides it has been usual to allow a week's holiday'. However, in 1899 things changed: 'This year with the consent of the chairman of School Board only three days have been allowed'. However, whether the School Board consented or not, the annual sheep market in July at Tollie would result in significantly reduced attendance. Even if the children themselves did not go they would be expected to stay home to mind the croft whilst their parents were away.

Inevitably the threat, and reality, of infectious illness resulted in schools being closed for weeks on end. The lack of immunisation, and the potentially deadly consequences, ensured that just the rumour of diphtheria, whooping cough, scarlet fever, mumps, measles and even typhus (January 1887 in Inverasdale) would bring education to a halt. 'Panic seized the people on account of the epidemic. No children presented themselves to-day'.[9] Rarely did a year pass without mention of serious contagions thwarting the best intentions of the local school teachers.

For a different reason Inverasdale school remained closed for a week in March 1899: 'The Headmaster's wife died in the School house last night and in consequence there will be no opening of the school until after the funeral. This is approved of by the attendance manager'. The cause of death is not disclosed.

One common reason for limited attendance during term time, or often for the school being closed completely for several days, was the holding of the local communion services, with their associated Fast Days, be they in Gairloch, Poolewe or Aultbea. In 1881 these were in late June and early October. When the New Free Church opened in Poolewe in January 1890 a holiday was given. Most heads seem to have accepted this practice as part of the usual routine, though the head at Inverasdale struggled, in 1901, to come to terms with discovering, by default, that church events would be to the detriment of his tally of 'openings'.

> The school was ready at the usual hour but no pupils appeared. At 10 a.m. five came and the teacher then knew that this was a Sacramental fast day with the Free Church folk. The school was closed.

He was clearly exasperated at the lack of consistent observance of religious festivals:

> 18 Dec 1900: The so-called "Free Church" had a harvest Thanksgiving service to-day and the children of people belonging to that sect were absent to-day. Only 43 children were present. Each of the other sects have their separate day for thanksgiving.

and

> 30 Oct 1901: Last night the HM knew that this was to be observed as a Harvest Thanksgiving day by one of the Sects here, and when school was opened at 9.30 this morning only 19 were present in both departments. They were at once sent home as in the interests of peace it was thought best to take that course as there seems to be much bitterness between the rival sects.

In the nineteenth century the pupils would usually attend school on Christmas Day but could then have the bonus of two celebrations for New Year. The 'new' New Year might be recognised, perhaps grudgingly, as a single day's holiday. Then there would be another break of several days for the 'Old New Year' on 13 January. Times changed and on 25 December 1903 the 'School was this afternoon closed for the New Year's holiday' until 4 January, though it still closed for the 'New Year's Day (old style)' on 13 January 1904.

The actual date of the long summer holidays varied considerably. Until the last decade of the century it usually started towards the end of August, resuming in October. In 1883 at Inverasdale School the annual long break was delayed from 31 August until 20 September, whilst they were 'expecting notice of the Government Inspection'. So the 'summer' holidays did not end until 9 November that year! However, in 1887 there was an early start:

> Aug 3: Received instructions from the Chairman, through the Clerk to close the School for the annual holidays in order as far as possible to prevent the spread of measles through the district.

In 1897 a further week was added to the annual six, starting on 2 September, 'as this is the Diamond Jubilee of her Majesty, Queen Victoria'. By the 1920s the dates were more likely to be from mid-July, but it remained a very flexible arrangement.

Non-attendance

Maintaining the laws on attendance was a continual struggle for the teachers. None of the local heads was complimentary about the effectiveness of the 'Compulsory officers'.[10] The Opinan head was particularly damming:

> 10 January 1888: Compulsory officer's visit seems to have no perceptible improvement on the attendance. His own son is running absent out of school, by no means a good example to other would-be-absentees.

The situation had not improved almost three years later:

> He sympathises more with Defaulting parents than with the teacher in the way of securing good attendance. In fact his general conduct does everything to discourage both teacher and attendance than to encourage both. The man being quite unlearnt is quite unqualified, though willing, for the post.

In 1901 the same complaints were still being made by the same Head about the same Compulsory Officer! 'It is earnestly hoped he may be either made to do his work or be dismissed'. In 1908 Mr Cameron of Poolewe School was reporting: 'The irregularity of attendance is as usual most disgusting. The SB [School Board] must take steps to have decent attendance, otherwise the case is a hopeless one'.

So, the School Board was often considered by the heads to be remiss in its duty of ensuring good attendance. One Inspection Report on Inverasdale agreed:

> At the visit paid on 24th July 1908 in the main room there were present 11 girls and 6 boys and absent 7 girls and 2 boys and this without any special reason. This is quite unsatisfactory. The School Board must give this matter their serious attention.

A year later the Board was still deemed to be failing:

> In spite of the continued irregularity of the attendance at this School, it appears from the School Board's Returns on Form 33(a) that no defaulting parents have been prosecuted or even summoned to appear before the School Board.

As a result the school grant for that year was reduced because of the unsatisfactory attendance, even after warnings. It was not unknown for the Heads themselves to go in search of absent pupils – though with respect to one errant individual this merely resulted in the offender taking off to the hills for a day or two. Fines could be imposed but were unlikely ever to be paid. The lack of support from some parents merited comment:

> Opinan School: 30 July 1890: Two boys from Point ran home to-day for being punished slightly for eating and breaking pens, breaking pointers and non-preparation of lessons. [...] Their parents seem to have disapproved of the teacher's firmness in the matter by allowing these boys to remain from school to-day. Parents are greatly at fault for their children's disobedience and lack of good breeding.

The same head, totally frustrated, noted on 18 December 1891: 'It's a hard pull for a single handed teacher to combat against weather, prevailing illness, irregularity and intellectual dullness on the part of children of illiterate and otherwise indifferent parents'. But he persevered in the post for ten years more.

Curriculum

Inevitably, the main priorities at these 'public' schools were the standard 'Reading, Writing and Arithmetic', together with a strong emphasis on Religious Knowledge. However, there was a considerable range of advanced subjects for those who did stay on at school beyond the minimum leaving age. Latin and French were taught in both Poolewe and Inverasdale. One of the older pupils at Inverasdale impressed the inspectors in October 1889 with his competence, turning 'passages from Caesar into English and Gaelic with much credit'. Extra-curricular lessons could broaden the subjects considerably. 'French, German, Geometry and Algebra have been taught for some time between one and two o'clock and after 4 o'clock', though it does not say how many gave up their lunch and home time to study these in Poolewe School in December 1888.

History and Geography were also regarded as supplementary subjects. In 1903 Inverasdale's syllabus included: 'The Empire, History, growth and trade during the period 1714–1820' and linked this with the 'Geography of our colonies, with particular reference to their productions, trade and the openings for enterprise which they afford'. Nature Study that year included coverage of 'Natural phenomena, water, evaporation, condensations, clouds, rain, hail, dew, mist, ice, water as maker of soil, tides. Illustrated by experiments and observations'. There was an unusual addition to the timetable when, thanks to the generosity of Mr Dixon of Inveran, the school was presented with some new apparatus in 1892:

> Sir Wm Thomson's Compass, Magnetic needle with Stand, Two Bar Magnets and one Horse-shoe Magnet, – all to be used in the teaching of Navigation.

The Inspectors expressed their approval:

> Latin, Mathematics and Navigation are taught with great care. I should hope that the last subject may be the means of encouraging boys to go to sea and of paving the way for them there to promotion in their profession.

Gardening had been added to the subjects taught at Poolewe by 1911 and the headteacher at Inverasdale went to considerable trouble, during the First World War, to establish 'horticulture instruction'. The inspectors found no fault with his teaching and the results of his efforts so he must have felt quite aggrieved when the Scotch Education Dept in Whitehall, London (sic) decreed that 'unless Mr Macleod take definite steps at the first available opportunity to improve his qualifications to teach School Gardening the department may be unable in future to allow payment of the special grant for this subject'.

Sewing lessons were expected (or variably, 'Needlework, Mending, Knitting and cutting out') and most schools had a regular 'sewing mistress' (often the wife or the daughter of the Head teacher) on the staff. Cookery and Laundry, though, were occasional, rather than regular, taught subjects, depending on grant availability and qualified staff to teach them.

Physical education usually took the form of 'School Drill', noted to be 'quite inferior' at Inverasdale in 1885. In the summer of 1897 it changed its format as the pupils 'received their first lesson in marching and counter-marching which is to form part of the Physical Drill for the ensuing year'. Dumbbells were used in the Physical Exercises for Standard III and upwards and 'Music drill bells for Infants and Standards I and II'. In 1903 it was Military Drill for boys and Bar bells and Ring drill for Girls. A different, and rather risky, activity was tried at Poolewe School from 1904: 'Swimming is now in full swing. The girls are taught by an expert lady swimmer and the boys are under the tuition of the Headmaster'. This was presumably in the sea. The necessary swimwear was provided by the school. An order was sent in 1913 for

> 7 mens bathing pants
> 13 women's costumes
> Had to order these sizes as the smaller sizes are so small, tight and inferior that they get torn in a week.

Once the 'new supply of pants and costumes' had arrived the children could begin bathing – but it was the first week of July and the 'weather is rather cold'.

The teaching of Gaelic

The Dowager Lady Mary, though English born, had learnt Gaelic as an adult when she came to live at Gairloch. She became passionately committed to a Gaelic-based education both for her own son and the local people. 'Her rule was that no child should be taught English until he or she could read simple Gaelic first' and this was what she required in the schools she established.[11] Reference was even made to her views in Osgood's obituary:

> Mary Hanbury was [...] one of the most remarkable women of her day in the Highlands. She was also one of the few instances of a grown-up person learning to speak Gaelic fluently. So her son Osgood was reared in a domestic atmosphere which was thoroughly Celtic.[12]

Such an attitude to the Gaelic culture and language was perceived as most unusual at the time. Gaelic was 'the language of everyday life, religion, poetry and song [...] but English possessed both prestige and status. [...] English was also the language of the future, of education, economic opportunity and social progress'.[13]

So, children in the Highlands were expected to learn to read and write in English as the way to self-improvement. The 1872 Education Act had made no provision for Gaelic in the classroom. However, passive resistance, and a desire to retain this part of their own culture, remained strong amongst the local people. It was a recurrent theme that the children were deficient in being able to read, write and even speak English. As late as 1900 one tactic tried was to induce the children to talk English in the playground, in the hope that 'the practice may spread so that the children may be able to express themselves in English with some degree of ease'. In 1905 English was given extra revision time at Inverasdale as it 'is the most difficult subject for the pupils' and even in 1915, 'the children, who are most Gaelic speaking, still experience considerable difficulty in expressing their ideas in English'.

Osgood Mackenzie took a particular interest in the teaching of Gaelic and was very supportive of the work of William Cameron, Headmaster of Poolewe School from 1901 to December 1915. Mr Cameron became a great champion of Gaelic music. His predecessors had provided some singing lessons for the pupils – in 1880 the Inspectors of Poolewe reported that singing was 'very vigorous but should be more tasteful' and in 1887 they still hoped it could be 'sweeter'. But, in 1889, it was only allocated fifteen minutes at the end of the day. Cameron gave it much greater priority in the curriculum and he started evening classes, which Osgood actively supported:

> 22 November 1901: Evening classes in Gaelic and English music were opened by me last night. [...] O.H. Mackenzie Esq. of Inverewe offers 2 prizes of £1 and 10/- for competition in Gaelic.

Osgood visited the classes again on 21 February 1902: 'At his request the children gave a number of Gaelic and English songs in 2 part harmony. He and some other visitors expressed great delight with the music'. He went back again in March and April, taking 'his manager, Mr Cameron, Tournaig', with him on the second occasion. Mr Cameron was 'better known as the Tournaig Bard'. When HMI came on their annual inspection in 1904 they commented very favourably: 'Quite a feature was the high class Gaelic singing which brings out the meaning of the songs and by its sweetness is listened to with pleasure'.

William Cameron became very ambitious with respect to entering the Poolewe Gaelic School Choir in local, and then national, Mod competitions. They were often highly successful:

> One of the outstanding features of the Mod at Inverness this year was the performance of the Poolewe Children's Gaelic Choir. [...] They carried away several valuable prizes. Praise is due to Mr Cameron, Teacher, Poolewe, to whose indefatigable efforts the success of the choir is mainly due. Mr Cameron is a hale, hearty good fellow of a strikingly Celtic stamp. He is enthusiastic on everything connected with the Highlands and Highlanders. [...]
>
> To see Mr Cameron leading his choir is an incident never to be forgotten. [...] As an example of Mr Cameron's enlightened methods in dealing with his pupils, it may be mentioned that he makes a practice of telling them historical facts and explaining to them some of the traditions of the Celtic race. These were things that not so very long ago were ostracized from Highland schools.[14]

In order for the children to attend these annual Mods the school had to be closed. That this was permitted suggests how highly their success was valued. The Head was therefore bitterly disappointed in September 1909 when they were unable to attend the Mod competitions because there had been so much illness in the School. The next year they were back to prize-winning, achieving trophies in Edinburgh for solo and choral singing and essay writing. 'Flora Macdonald, Inverasdale, even got 2nd for best web of cloth'. (Perhaps the 'Gaelic' emphasis was the reason this particular Inverasdale child attended Poolewe school.)

William Cameron's methods and experience led to him being invited to present his ideas to some prestigious meetings. He regularly attended meetings of the Gaelic Society and in 1905 was invited to give a ten-minute paper on his system of teaching Gaelic. He read there 'an excellent letter from O.H.

Mackenzie, Esq of Inverewe, Chairman of the Gairloch School Board, which was received with great applause'. The text was copied into his Log Book.

> 23rd March 1905
> Inverewe, Poolewe,
>
> Dear Mr Cameron
> You have my warmest wishes for the success of the cause which takes you to Inverness!
>
> How I wish the rule in this Parish were still the good rule made by my dear mother, (the late Dowager Lady Mackenzie of Gairloch) whilst she had charge of the Gairloch Estates between the years 1843 and 1853. She started some ten schools on the property and the rule for all of them was 'No English to be taught till the pupils can first read the Gaelic Bible fluently'.
>
> How often have I heard and how do I still hear it said in the Parish – that the men and women brought up under that system were and are still superior in intelligence and in every other good quality, to those brought up under the present School Board system, where they are crammed with what is to many of them a foreign language by teachers who cannot interpret and cannot therefore cultivate their pupils' intellects. You know I am all for Gaelic in our schools where Gaelic is the spoken language of the people-
>
> So wishing every success to those who are trying to keep up our grand old language.
>
> I remain
> Yours very truly
> Osgood H. Mackenzie

One ex-pupil was particularly successful:

> Miss C.P. Turner (Mod Gold Medallist 1910) a pupil of the School has had a very busy season singing at many high class concerts all over Scotland. She is to sing Gaelic songs at the opening of the Glasgow Exhibition on Wed 3 May and she is also asked to sing at the Investiture of the Prince of Wales at Carnarvon (a week's engagement). She has given some beautiful records for a Gramophone coy in London and Glasgow and for a young girl of 20 years she has done remarkably well.

The quality of local education

The imminence of the annual inspection of the youngsters' learning usually discouraged the examinees and dismayed their headteachers. It certainly did not help the continuity of education when a school had to remain closed for almost eight months because the old building had been taken over for housing whilst the new one was as yet under construction, as happened to Opinan School from 28 August 1874 until 13 April 1875. Yet another week's schooling was lost there when the new building had to be painted the following October.

The poor state and inadequate size of the school buildings was often commented on by inspectors, with classrooms frequently very overcrowded. Although a 'commodious classroom in which Secondary Instruction is to be carried on' had been added to Inverasdale in 1894, in Poolewe there remained only the one room, even when there were enough children for two teachers:

> 2 May 1902: We are greatly hampered in our work by the want of a class-room. It is impossible for 2 teachers to do good work in such a small room with over 50 on roll.

Three years later matters had not improved: 'The weather is extremely hot (during past few weeks) so that the work is not easily carried out in such a crowded schoolroom and the atmosphere of the room sometimes is of the vilest nature'. The Inspectors agreed and in October 1905 threatened not to pay the grant 'until the buildings have been improved and the staff increased'. It seems nothing was done though.

On the other hand, the poor fires at Opinan received specific criticism in the Inspector's Report of 1899:

> The heating of the room is quite inadequate. The grate is small and peat of an inferior kind is the fuel. At a distance of about 6 feet from the fire place the highest temperature shown by the thermometer during my stay was 41°F. [...] This serious deficiency of heat must be rectified without delay. I also have to report that the Master's dwelling house, built in great part by Government money, has been allowed to get into a surprising state of disrepair.

The result was that the working temperature was 'too cold when the pupils are ill fed and badly clad' and 'the pupils hands are so stiff with cold'. Ventilation was also often an issue of concern, as in 1909: 'Both chimneys smoke very badly. They should be attended to at once. The arrangement of the stove, in the middle of the fireplace in the Infant Room, is unsatisfactory and can no longer be approved of'.

Cleanliness was a further problem. It was obviously so unusual an occurrence in Poolewe School that a Log Book entry had to be made when, in 1883, 'the school room was washed and scrubbed on Sat 24th inst by two women'. More than twenty years later things were no better: 'The school walls were thoroughly cleaned and white washed and the floor scrubbed on Saturday. It badly required this overhaul as it had not been done for two years'.

The sanitary facilities were likely to be particularly unsatisfactory. When Poolewe was inspected in August 1881 it was stated: 'the offices are very little visited and are not sufficiently attended to. [...] Arrangements to be made for a grown up person to clean the school room and offices'. Yet again, forty years later:

> It is gratifying to learn that repairs to the school fabric are shortly to be undertaken. It would be well if, when these are being carried out, steps were taken to replace the present offices from which there was an offensive odour on the occasion of inspection by another and more hygienic system.

HM inspectors arriving at Inverasdale in 1881 were clearly shocked at one 'taken for granted' practice, with respect to the cleaning of the toilet facilities, but their views were not accepted by the local School Board:

> The Managers cannot agree with HM Inspector's that it is in any sense undesirable that the Offices should be kept clean by the male pupils. Their parents are all labouring men and the pupils as they grow up are all engaged in manual labour. Consequently then making themselves useful in this and other respects can have no other than a beneficial effect in training them in habits of industry and cleanliness.

Osgood's son-in-law, Robert Hanbury, became a School Manager in 1914 and was not very impressed with the 'state of the wcs at the back which ought to have been cleaner' on his first visit to Inverasdale School. He also quite frequently mentioned the need for painting and whitewashing of various parts of the building, some of which was carried out, even though these were the War years.

The actual standard of teaching and learning generally was deemed to have been at least adequate. Occasionally the inspectors reported deficiencies: 'The grant for Grammar and intelligences is well earned. History is fairly known but a fuller acquaintance with Geography is desirable. In both subjects less rote and more intelligence should appear'.[15] Most of the time, though, they were quite complimentary about the standard reached by the children in the range of subjects tested, which was remarkable given the limited staffing allowed. In 1888 there were 104 children on the roll of Inverasdale School, with only one teacher and two monitors. Sir Kenneth Mackenzie visited but was evidently well satisfied: 'The school was orderly and the work being conducted according to the time-table'.

Though evidence of open disagreement between the headteachers and school managers was not often manifested on the written page, a Mr McCaig, at Inverasdale School, was not at all happy with his employers. He complained when left in dire straits, as he saw it, by the slow response of the School Board in ordering the requisite supplies for teaching: 'all the copies, writing, Dictation and Drawing are used up'. He sent in the order form, in duplicate, that same day, 8 November 1897, in good time for the Board's session on 12 November. However, they decided to put off considering the order until their next meeting. 'This is most serious and will damage the work of the School as all the copies are now finished and many pupils are unable to write or draw as they have no copies'. The order finally arrived on ss *Claymore* at the end of the month.

McCaig also made frequent comment that being the only teacher was 'most damaging to the work and general tone' of the school, particularly after his wife's brief contract as an additional teacher was terminated. This dissatisfaction with his conditions of work continued right through the summer and at the end of October 1898 he resigned, bitter to the end at the lack of support from the School Board. 'The teacher's salary was only paid up till to-day, [4 November] although the resignation does not take effect until to-morrow – another example of the liberality of the Board'.

The tone of his comments was the exception rather than the rule. Generally the log books reported positively. There was a, perhaps surprising, lack of mention of poor behaviour and virtually nothing on the use of corporal punishment. In Poolewe the first head was deemed to have rather firm discipline, but it was judged 'remarkably good' by the 1877 Inspectors. In 1879 they recommended that 'discipline might be milder and sweeter'. By 1882 it was 'rising in geniality but should do so still more'. The Inverasdale Log Book does occasionally suggest that the children were not all little angels. One head had a particular concern about the wider behaviour of his pupils:

> 29 December 1890: I found that three boys had been rude to a little girl. This gave occasion for giving the whole school a lesson on the duty of being kind to one another.

He had cause to reprove the children on a number of occasions: 'a case of gross misconduct on the part of several of the scholars on Friday night had to be severely rebuked' (18 November 1892); he reprimanded his pupils 'against the use of bad language in the playground and on the streets' (30 October 1893); repeated a similar message 'against rude and unseemly behaviour, either before or after school hours towards some of their elders in the village' (8 March 1895); 'The children were specially warned to refrain from the rude acts of lawlessness that have been customary at this season of the year' (11 November 1895); 'No Bible lesson was given this morning but instead a lesson on politeness and courtesy. The pupils were shewn the advantages of shewing their respect to their superiors and of kindliness to all' (12 July 1897). But there is no record of the strap or tawse, or even of detention, being given during Osgood's lifetime and the Inspectors indicated that 'the general order is exceedingly good' at this period.

Overall, the respect for education increased so that the complaints about 'late starters' diminished, the opportunities it offered widened and gradually the young of Gairloch parish were confronted with the realities of the modern world. There had been much excitement at Opinan school in January 1877 because a new school clock had been put up on the wall, the cause of 'a great distraction and lack of concentration'. By the 1890s the excitements for the scholars of the Loch Ewe area were more likely to be visits to the warships which arrived on exercise:

> 26 July 1898: The Channel Fleet arrived in the Loch today at 2.30 pm and the scholars were allowed out for about 35 minutes to watch the fleet taking up its position … the school will be closed on Wed, and Thursday 27th and 28th to allow the pupils to visit the fleet with their parents

and

> 22 October 1902: Last night fourteen Battleships and torpedo boats belonging to the Home Squadron anchored in Loch Ewe off the School and to-day the children were taken aboard HM ship Nile over which they were shown.

In September 1904 the Head was somewhat less happy with the arrival of eight battleships and four cruisers: 'The presence of the Channel Squadron in the Loch has had an adverse influence on the attendance as some of the children are employed in selling eggs to those who provision the ships'. But he took responsibility in attempting to explain matters of world concern.

> 10 February 1904: To-day the matters in dispute between Russia and Japan were explained to the children in the Highest classes and an article on the subject in the World's Work read to them. They will now it is expected take a keener interest in reading the daily paper which is given them to read during the dinner hour.

Such entries were unusual. Progress was more usually measured by a note, such as at Opinan School in 1908, that slates were no longer being used, except by the infants, since jotters and pencils were now being provided.

Generous benefactors

Some very generous donations enabled the local schools to extend the opportunities for their pupils. In 1900 Mr Carnegie gave Inverasdale 50 volumes 'as the nucleus for a school library'. In 1905 much gratitude was expressed when Poolewe received 440 volumes through a donation by Mr Coats of Paisley (the sewing thread manufacturer) for use by classes VI and VII. In May of that same year Coats sent S.J.A. Holmes Esq. to deliver a lecture on 'Books' in Poolewe Hall 'to large and intelligent audience. The Poolewe Gaelic Choir interspersed the lecture with several Gaelic and English Songs. Tonight the Choir goes with Mr Holmes to Inverasdale P School where he is to deliver a lecture. Mr Coats most generously defrays all expenses'.

Nor was this the end of his generosity. In June 1906 he presented 'over 200 books (value £20) to the Poolewe School for the use of the Supplementary Course, Nature Knowledge Classes, pupil teachers and as text books and books of reference. Some of the members of the School Board called and saw the books and they were quite delighted with this splendid gift of Mr Coats'. A week later 'splendid wall maps of Scotland, Orkney and of Shetland' arrived. His 'liberality and kindly thoughtfulness' extended further, beyond the school walls:

> 17 May 1907: 300 pairs of excellent and suitable spectacles were given away at Poolewe, Inverasdale and Aultbea. The Headmaster of this school [Poolewe] acted as interpreter to Mrs Love, Optician, Greenock. The people are well pleased with the glasses and Mr Coats deserves the highest praise for his great kindness on this and former occasions to the people of the Highlands.

The Mackenzie family commitment

The importance of providing elementary education to the young of the parish was a clear commitment for all in the family and the log books frequently provided evidence of the keen interest shown by Osgood's mother and his two brothers in founding and actively supporting the local schools. It was a condition of the estate tenancy that crofters could be evicted if they did not pay the rates which supported these schools.[16] Mary Hanbury had shown considerable resolution, in difficult times, in ensuring that many more of the crofter children could benefit from education. In 1852 there were

> 7 schools on the estate of Gairloch, established through the exertions of Lady Mackenzie and in connection with the Free Church. Three of these are female schools, one of which, that of Strath, is supported entirely by Lady Mackenzie. Her ladyship was present at the examination of the schools and took intense interest in the proceedings. No doubt she experienced during the examinations of the school at Strath, that her labour in planting and carefully watching over this school has been even already amply rewarded.[17]

The same paper had earlier (9 October 1849) reported the examination and prize giving, for both the boys and the girls, held at the female school which was attended by the 'amiable Lady Mackenzie (who took a lively interest in the examination as she has done in the success of those institutions themselves, and to whom we are mainly indebted for their existence)'. Dr John was also present.

There were entries in both the Achtercairn Board School and Opinan Log Books referring to visits she made in May 1876 and August 1877, but the best proof of her long term commitment was shown in the Poolewe Log Books, with a first visit in November 1877 and the last in 1899. Sometimes the headteacher saw fit to comment. For example, the Dowager Lady examined many of the classes on a visit in January 1879 and 'expressed herself highly pleased with all the classes. She was much taken with the writing, said it was excellent'. She sometimes brought her grand-daughter, Mairi. Lady Mary examined several pieces of work and 'was much pleased with the skill of the pupils' in sewing in June 1893; 'heard two of the classes say their lessons, in reading, spelling and meaning' in May 1895 and came with her son, 'manager of this school and Mr MacIntosh, Clerk of the School Board' for the annual inspection in July 1895. Her last visit to the local school was in February 1899, when she, quite fittingly, 'remained during part of the sewing lesson'. In respect of her support the Poolewe school head teacher, Mr Cameron, logged on 15 March 1901: 'On Wed the school was closed owing to the funeral of the Dowager Lady Mackenzie'.

Sir Kenneth, the eldest of the three Mackenzie sons, was Chairman of the Gairloch School Board from 1871 to 1894. The log books of the various parish schools identified his visits, often accompanied by his wife, sometimes his mother or brother, Francis, and occasionally by his daughter and/or son. For example, he went to Opinan regularly from 1871 to 1882, mainly, but not exclusively, in July. Sir Kenneth did not just sign the register, a statutory requirement, but also showed an interest in the pupils' work. He accompanied inspectors, commented on the Reports of their examination, checked on the new buildings under construction, (July 1874), physically pursued a truant and met parents of defaulting attenders. On 10 April 1877 he sanctioned the school to close when scarlatina was rife in the area. Lady Eila showed a particular interest in the 'industrial' work and, on 24 July 1878, 'she left material for carrying on the industrial work of the school'.

There were fifteen visits to Poolewe School indicated between 1875 and December 1890. As well as the customary check on the Registers Sir Kenneth occasionally stayed a little longer. He 'heard the Bible lesson given', and 'examined the writing of the different classes' in 1875, 'looked at Dictation and Arithmetic of various standards and expressed himself highly pleased with all he had seen' in July 1871 and conducted the examination on religious teaching in August 1881. The laird remained an advocate of Gaelic throughout his life, though could only read and speak it 'fairly well'. He was particularly keen that Gaelic should not be seen as 'an obstruction' in highland schools, but rather 'a valuable instrument of education' following the passing of the Education Act of 1872.[18]

In 1894 he lost his seat on the School Board 'by a combination of peculiar circumstances', brought about by a 'church squabble' and 'plumping', at the time of a split within the Free Church. The result 'astonished and disgusted many of the ratepayers'.[19]

The middle brother, Francis, was also committed to the education of the local children. He had personally endowed the girls' school at Bualnaluib, on the north side of Loch Ewe and the Mackenzie estate. He showed interest in several local schools. Achtercairn (Gairloch) logged:

> 25 January 1875: Francis H. Mackenzie esquire, Kerrysdale and Dr Robertson, two members of the School Board, called to-day

12 February 1875: Francis H. Mackenzie esquire visited regarding the admission of children from the school district supposed to be infected on the 25th inst

15 February 1875: regarding the admission of children excluded to provide against infection

2 November 1877: presented a large number of apples for distribution among the children.

There were further entries for 10 February 1882 and 13 July 1883. Francis made three visits to Poolewe School (1874, 1877, 1881), once with Osgood, one to Inverasdale, (August 1885, the last record we have of him in the area), and the school at Opinan had entries from 25 April 1873 to 1879 when it was noted, on 29 October, that 'Mr Mackenzie of Kerrysdale called in [...] to pay [for] books he kindly ordered for Duncan Macrae, Eradale, so as to enable the same boy to attend school. He has left money with the teacher to supply him (the boy) with boots'.[20]

As was usual practice in the Mackenzie family, Osgood himself never attended any school, but was taught by his mother and tutors. He often expressed his gratitude for this and brought up his own daughter, Mairi, in like manner. Nonetheless, he often, though rather intermittently, visited the two 'public' schools quite close to Inverewe. The closest was less than a mile away, on the Riverside. The second, at Inverasdale, was about six miles distant. The first visit entered in the Log Book at Poolewe School was in November 1877, when he went with his new wife, the last in March 1913. He made 91 visits in total, with a particular concentration between 1887 and 1894 and again 1900–1905, for part of which time, at least, he was the Manager responsible for Attendance. Inverasdale Log Book first recorded a visit on 16 May 1879 and the final entry was 1 December 1913.

Poolewe School's entries show that, in addition to the routine Register, Attendance and Time-table checks required of a member of the School Board, Osgood examined classes in Geography (five times) and History; heard a girl's French lesson (twice); examined reading (sometimes in Gaelic) and listened to the pupils singing. He was sometimes party to the school's annual Religious Knowledge exam, helping the Rev. Dingwall to give out the resulting prizes in 1891 and 1893. He checked various aspects of the school's buildings and fabric (including the toilets or 'offices'), 'requested the Head to register twice daily the temperature of the School' in November 1891 and inspected repairs that had been carried out. Very importantly, he signed the Log Book after decisions had been made to shut the school because of an epidemic. For example, influenza in November 1887 and measles in November 1894 required sanctioned closures. He greeted several new headteachers and collected information regarding the staffing of the school. At the end of the summer term in 1903 he showed appreciation of one of the teachers leaving:

> 31 July 1903: an interesting function took place when O.H. Mackenzie of Inverewe presented Miss MacNaughton PT [pupil teacher] with a gold watch suitably inscribed. The watch was subscribed for by the pupils and friends of the Poolewe School on the occasion of her leaving.

On a couple of occasions (only) he 'took the names of those pupils whose attendance has been irregular and is to call upon the parents'.

There were 41 visits logged at Inverasdale, where Osgood appears to have been less actively involved. Almost always he merely examined and signed the registers. Very occasionally, as in January 1887, he made home visits to parents with respect to absentees, along with other School Board members: 'Their visit had a good effect in several instances. Several children induced to return to school'. Generally he seemed to have been satisfied with the numbers present, but once, in 1910, expressed his concern: 'Serious attention of attendance manager directed to this matter'. He had occasion to verify the 'moral character' of a pupil teacher and to help give out the prizes after the Religious Knowledge examination 'to the most deserving in all the standards'. He was present, and impressed, when the first drawing exam took place: 'the appearance made surpassed our expectations'. Twice he went with his mother, the Dowager Lady Mackenzie. In 1898, 'at his request the senior pupils sang two part songs with which he was well pleased.' But twice he arrived after 4 p.m., which was too late to see the pupils who were already on their way home. Only once, in 1900, did he appear to take much interest in the state of the buildings, arranging for some repairs to be carried out.

Osgood was chairman of the School Board for at least two terms of office, the first being at the end of the century after John Dixon had resigned and left the area. He seemed, though, not to have been particularly committed, with only one visit being recorded for each of the more distant schools in Achtercairn and Opinan, both in February 1899, and then only carried out the statutory attendance check. At Achtercairn: 'Attendance was still low when Osgood H. Mackenzie Esq. of Inverewe, now Chairman of the Board, visited the school on the 2nd of February'. At Opinan Osgood handwrote 'Visited the School and found Register correct' which was corroborated by the head on 24 February:

> Mr Mackenzie of Inverewe, the Chairman of School Board visited the School today, counted number present on roll and compared and found correct. Mr Mackenzie ascertained the cause of absence of so many scholars on inspection day and the reasons assigned by all was that they were ill.

The second stint as leader of the Education Board started in 1905 and continued until April 1909. Osgood tried, unsuccessfully, to be re-elected in May 1909: 'Gairloch School Board meeting. After a vote was taken Mr Angus Stewart of Aultbea was appointed Chairman, defeating Mr Mackenzie of Inverewe by 5 votes to 4'.[21] To his credit he continued to make school visits thereafter.

From time to time the pupils of Poolewe School were given a treat by their local 'heritor':

> 24 January 1890: Children invited to a 'Christmas Tree' to-day at Inverewe House. I, at the request of the manager of the school, let them away for the day at 2 p.m., giving no interval.

There was then a long gap until

> 20 January 1904: Poolewe School Treat – over 60 pupils of the Poolewe school, with some of the parents and others, were sumptuously entertained to a Xmas Tree, Supper and Dance last night at Inverewe House, by Miss and Mr Mackenzie of Inverewe. Each child received a handsome present and they went home laden with all sorts of good things. The Poolewe Junior Gaelic Choir discoursed a number of Gaelic Songs to the delight of Lord and Lady Fincastle who were present. Mr Cameron, in a neat Gaelic speech, thanked Miss and Mr Mackenzie for the unbounded generosity and unstinted kindness they showed to and the great interest they take in the Poolewe Children. Cheers were given for Lord and Lady Fincastle and Miss and Mr M.
>
> Mr Wm MacLennon, Poolewe who supplied pipe music deserves our best thanks.
>
> 20 July 1906: the choir performed at a concert at Inverewe last night.

However, there were no treats courtesy of Osgood at Inverasdale, even though he could have seen the school from the top of An Ploc Ard!

Mr John H. Dixon

The most benevolent provider of 'treats' for the children, without any doubt, was Mr John H. Dixon. Soon after he installed himself at Inveran he began to show that keen interest in the two local schools, Poolewe and Inverasdale, which he was to maintain throughout his years in Gairloch district and even after he moved away. As early as August 1875, long before he held any official position on the School Board, the Headmaster of Poolewe expressed his gratitude:

> J.H. Dixon Esq of Inveran Lodge kindly awarded prizes to the most deserving in the School. Monday following he gave the scholars an excellent treat and presented the School with all the articles belonging to Cricket.

A tradition was, perhaps, established: in June 1904, 'the boys are enjoying their game of cricket and the girls delight in skipping and various other pastimes', though generally the prevailing weather must have limited the use of the equipment.

Osgood had been present at one treat given in 1880. It was reported in the press that the 'usual bagpipes, tea, games and prizes' at Inveran were observed by various other local dignitaries, including Osgood and the Dowager Lady Mackenzie, and Mrs Mitchell and her party, the shooting tenants of Inverewe.[22] The treats for the Poolewe pupils usually entailed the children processing the mile along the Riverside, (where their school was situated), to Inveran House, with banners flying and a piper playing his bagpipes.[23] There would be a sumptuous tea and 'a few songs sung by the juveniles'. These occasions seem initially to have been in the summer with games being played. The prizes for the successful competitors in the sports in 1879, somewhat surprisingly, were 'knives etc'![24] Sometimes, as in 1883, it was a winter event:

> 12 Jan 1883: Yesterday, the 11th inst, the scholars marched up to Inveran House, the residence of Mr Dixon. They were entertained to a grand 'Christmas Tree'. Each one present received some useful gift as a memento of the occasion. [...] All the pupils who passed the Govt exam got excellent book prizes. [...] This is only an instance of Mr Dixon's kindness and liberality to Poolewe School.

At Inverasdale the 'treat', be it in summer or winter, and almost regardless of the weather conditions, took place on the fine sands of Firemore.

> 26 August 1892: School closed yesterday (at the usual hour) for the Annual Holidays. Today (Friday) Mr Dixon gave the children their annual treat. Though the day turned out very wet and stormy, the usual games were held on the Sands at Firemore. The day's entertainment closed with distribution of Attendance and other prizes.

> 31 December 1898: To-day (Saturday) the children met at 11.15 a.m. After tea they proceeded to Firemore Sands and after sports there they returned to School, were again treated to a substantial meal. Mr Dixon then presented each pupil who made the possible number of attendances during the past year with half a crown apiece and every child with either a dictionary or an atlas. After some singing Mr Dixon who bore the expense of the whole treat very suitably addressed the children for which at the request of the master the children cordially thanked him. The prize winners at the sports then received their prizes. A pleasant day's proceedings terminated at 4 p.m.

Special occasions, such as the Golden Jubilee in June 1887, were suitably recognised: 'Holiday granted by the Board on Tuesday to celebrate the Queen's Jubilee. Queens Medal in silver presented to the best scholar by Mr J.H. Dixon, Inveran. Winner Alex Kennedy Ex VI. School treat and games'. The Royal Marriage in 1893 brought a double benefit: 'Mr. Dixon, with his usual generosity, and desire to please the children, provided them with buns. School was not held in the afternoon'.

Dixon was extremely wide-ranging in his prize-giving:

> 17 August 1877: Almost all got prizes. [...] Great credit is due to Mr Dixon for the great interest he has taken in the welfare of Poolewe School. There were about 40 prizes given, some very valuable books indeed. This is the second time that Mr Dixon has shown his liberality, and seeing the results of it he is intending to continue the practice. He is a gentleman in every sense of the word.

In 1878 he promised 'handsome prizes' for those in Poolewe School doing well in the exam, having gone in specifically to send 'for a catalogue that a selection might be made'. 'Doing well' was interpreted as being present and passing the annual HM inspection of the 3Rs. 'There being no failures in the school, all obtained prizes'. According to the *Inverness Advertiser*, at the evening presentation credit was given to the 'smartness, intelligence and application' of the scholars. His 'kindness and liberality' were this time recognised by the Rev.

Chisholm of the Free Church.[25] In 1879 Dixon was rewarding good attendance which 'has more effect than a defaulting officer'. He was very concerned, as he wrote in the Log Book on 5 November 1888, that children were being kept at home 'to assist in lifting potatoes: it is a pity since parents are so short-sighted'.

He also supported the musical activities of the school:

> 5 June 1882: concert of sacred and secular music had taken place on 29 May.
>
> 6 June: a soiree given to the Singing Class and other friends in Poolewe School by J.H. Dixon Esq., Inveran House.

Although willing to stand for election to the Gairloch School Board in 1879 Dixon, still a relative newcomer to the area, withdrew his candidacy to avoid an expensive competition[26] but by 1888 he was a member, elected with the most votes of all eleven candidates. As Chairman from October 1895 he made visits to schools throughout the area, checking registers and attending prize-givings. He presented medals to all the parish schools to commemorate Queen Victoria's Diamond Jubilee in 1897. However, visits to his 'local' schools were a priority. Between 1888 and 1898 the log books noted 51 separate visits to Poolewe School, as often as three times a month, and 63 to Inverasdale.

John Dixon frequently wrote entries of his own, particularly verifying the attendance numbers and often adding a comment. Usually these were positive. He was especially complimentary, and, on a number of occasions repeated his amazement, about the good attendance at Inverasdale, considering how far the children had to travel to get to their school and the prevalence of bad weather.

> Found 87 present this morning out of 98 scholars on the roll. This seems to me to be as good as can be expected the weather being very stormy and severe. Indeed I am surprised to find as large a number, having come several miles to school.

Sometimes there were very serious matters to record. The death of an HMI, en route to his inspection visit to Inverasdale in August 1889, was one sad tale, but even more to regret was 'the melancholy death of Mr Donald Macrae, the highly respected headmaster of this school' in March 1897, which necessitated a week's unplanned closure. His replacement proved to be rather a thorn in Dixon's side. Mr McCaig entered many criticisms of the School Board directly into the Log, being most dissatisfied with: the slowness of the School Board in ordering the required stock; the time it took to appoint a replacement for the tardy cleaner/lighter of school fires; the insufficient staffing for the number of pupils on roll; the inadequacy of the heating in the school; over-tolerant acceptance by the School Board of the poor attendance record of a pupil-teacher 'in delicate health'; its acceptance 'with eagerness' of 'frivolous and false' excuses by pupils for absence from school; not providing a woman 'to be present during the hours of instruction of the PT [pupil teacher] as required by Art 10 (c). Such instruction has therefore been dispensed with'. The final contretemps was with reference to how long the head was absent from the schoolroom when Dixon arrived, exacerbated by the 'fact' as Dixon saw it, that there was a discrepancy between the number of children in the room, compared to the number marked in the Register. With respect to this last occasion, Dixon actually wrote in the Log Book, December 1898, to refute the Head's accusations.

> I feel that it is necessary to contradict the statement in a minute made by the late teacher on 3rd Nov last to the effect that he was absent from the school that afternoon for a few minutes only. I was in the school much more than a few minutes and twice went to the house enquiring for him.

It particularly grieved him because he had just resigned as Chairman and member of the Board, prior to moving away.

Sometimes he came in to the schools with other members of the Board, quite often with Osgood Mackenzie, but also, for example, a number of times accompanying Rev. Dingwall to both schools, to distribute prizes for Religious Knowledge and regular attendance. As there is only one mention, he may not have been so keen on what should have been another of his duties – the inspection of the toilets, which 'seemed to be in sanitary condition' at Poolewe on 14 October 1895.

In 1898 Dixon resigned as a member of the Gairloch School Board and left in 1899 to live in Perthshire, taking with him his locally born manservant, Hector Mackenzie, but leaving a Gaelic bible with every household. Though he frequently travelled abroad, to Japan and even Australia, yet he retained an interest in the elementary schools which he had supported for twenty years, continuing to provide money so that the children could have their annual treats, as in 1901:

> The School was closed to-day.
> In the evening the children had their annual treat provided chiefly at the expense of Mr Dixon Ex-Chairman of the School Board. The school was decorated with holly and ivy and was crowded with parents and friends. The

> children gave an exhibition of jingle, and Bar-bell drill, sang a number of school songs and recited some pieces. Friends present sang several songs. Leaving and merit certificates were presented. Rev. Mr Cameron Poolewe presided.

Similarly in 1903. Perhaps expectant of more generosity it was noted, in June 1904, that 'the children were told last night that it was the intention of Mr Dixon, ex-chairman of the School Board, to visit this school to-day. As a result of this intimation every scholar on the roll is present to-day'. They were not to be disappointed:

> To-day the children had, on Firemore Sands, a pic-nic provided for them by the kindness of J.H. Dixon Esq Ex-Chairman of the Gairloch School Board. After games and tea on the sands the children returned to school where they got prizes for regularity of attendance and proficiency.

Poolewe's headteacher added another detail: 'The school was visited this afternoon by Mr Dixon of Pitlochry (late of Inveran, Poolewe) and a young Japanese gentleman. They expressed great satisfaction with the singing'.

Despite the cost of this visit, Dixon still donated funds so that the children could have their Christmas treat that year: 'This afternoon the children with their parents and friends were entertained in the school at the expense of Mr Dixon, Pitlochry. The children sang a number of their songs and acted a scene from Julius Caesar. Several of the visitors also sang'. This was the last reference to Dixon's contributions to school pleasures in Gairloch Parish, though he was to continue to exercise a benevolent interest in the wellbeing of young people until the end of his life.[27]

References and Notes

1 Quotations from the two *Statistical Accounts* are from Dixon, pp.401, 407.

2 See Chapter x.

3 Byam Shaw, p.282. In his 'Letter to the Gairloch Crofters' of 1856 Dr John suggested that 'Frankie' was just then building his girls' school in Bualnaluib so his recollection of the dates may be awry here.

4 Mackenzie, p.35.

5 *The Scottish Highlander*, 24 January 1850.

[6] Letter from Colin Munro in the *Inverness Courier*, 28 November 1850.

[7] Mackenzie, p.122.

[8] Log books for the period still exist for several Gairloch area schools, including those of Poolewe, Inverasdale, Achtercairn and Opinan. From all these come some fascinating insights into the running of the schools and, sometimes, of the way of life at the time. All references are to the Log Books of Poolewe or Inverasdale School unless otherwise stated.

[9] See Chapter IX for more on health-related issues affecting local schools.

[10] Also known as the 'Enforcement' or 'Defaulting' officers.

[11] Mackenzie, p.35.

[12] *A Veteran Highlander*, the Obituary for Osgood Mackenzie, in the *Northern Chronicle,* Wednesday 19 April 1922.

[13] Devine, *Clanship to Crofters' War*, p.117.

[14] *People's Journal*, 25 September 1903, pasted into the Poolewe School Log Book.

[15] Opinan School Log Book, 6 August 1894.

[16] *Scottish Highlander*, 27 November 1885.

[17] *Inverness Advertiser*, 23 March 1852.

[18] *Inverness Courier*, 13 February 1900. Sir Kenneth had presided at the inaugural meeting of the Inverness Gaelic Society in 1872 and was its chief for many years. He also wrote several papers for its 'Transactions' and a well-researched article on the military roads of the Highlands was due to be printed in the Inverness Field Club journal when he died.

[19] *Scottish Highlander*, 22 March 1894.

[20] This generosity to provide clothing extended more widely: following the example of his mother 'upwards of £200 is given yearly towards the same object by Sir Kenneth's brother, Mr Mackenzie of Kerrysdale', according to the *Inverness Advertiser*, 31 December 1878.

[21] *Ross-shire Journal.*

[22] *Inverness Advertiser*, 10 September 1880. This was only a month after Minna left him for good.

[23] *Scottish Highlander*, 28 August 1885.

[24] *Inverness Courier*, 11 September 1879.

[25] *Inverness Advertiser*, 2 August 1878. John Dixon proved himself to be very concerned about the physical and moral well-being of the adults, as well as the children, of the local community. In 1878–1879 he chaired a series of lectures for 'mutual improvement'. The *Inverness Advertiser* reported on one held on Friday 14 February entitled 'History, Use and Abuse of Money'.

[26] *Inverness Advertiser*, 14 March, 28 March, 1 April 1879.

[27] Dixon settled for the last years of his life at Dundarach House, Pitlochry in Perthshire. Here he developed a garden which was influenced by Japanese and Italian styles. He even had a miniature Fujiyama, with snow covered peak made out of the local white spar stone. He extended the house, adding a west wing to accommodate his Japanese landscape gardeners and staff, and entertained the great Japanese author Natsume Soseki when he was staying in Britain 1900–1902. (Details from www.dundarach.co.uk, accessed 09 January 2007). He died, aged 88, in October 1926. His obituary in the *Ross-shire Journal*, 29 October 1926, concluded with 'He was the oldest Boy Scout Master in Great Britain'.

CHAPTER XII

The Big, Wide World

'1914: Aug 15, Our men were called out
Sept 12, The Fleet came in again.'

Osgood Mackenzie's 'home' was always in the Highlands. He had spent much time on the continent as a child and young man and travelled quite widely, both in the United Kingdom and abroad, as an adult. He stayed frequently with members of the wide-flung Hanbury family and certainly was well acquainted with both the English and Scottish capitals. It is therefore surprising that he very rarely wrote of his response to the, often tumultuous, national and international events of the nineteenth and early twentieth century. It was as if they did not intrude on his long life though they certainly had significant effects on the daily routines of the local people.

The Highland Railway

The road building of the destitution years (late 1840s) opened up the west coast to visitors, game shooters and, increasingly, 'tourists'. Nonetheless, the distances to be covered and the time this took using horse-drawn vehicles still meant that a major expedition was required to come from the south of Scotland, let alone England. By the mid-1860s the first Macbrayne's steamers, linking the islands and west coast harbours, also helped to open up the area but it was the development of the railway that made the biggest difference.

The first major railway enterprise in the north of Scotland was the construction of the Perth to Inverness route which was completed in 1863. In the same year it was proposed to take a track from Dingwall west to Strome Ferry, it being considered impossible to build a railway line through the rock face along Loch Carron to the better harbour at Kyle of Lochalsh. This route was eventually completed in 1870, thus creating a link between the north east of Scotland and the Hebrides. The extension to Kyle was finally opened in November 1897.[1]

There were two trains daily in summer, one in winter, but never any on a Sunday. When, in 1883, a Sunday 'fish special' was planned there was a near riot. The people of Strome Ferry organised a takeover of the harbour and the railway until midnight on the Sabbath to stop fish being transferred from the ship to the train. The crowd prayed and sang in the railway station. Ten men, arrested for mobbing and rioting, were initially jailed for four months each. They were freed after questions in the House of Commons led to the Home Secretary ordering their release.[2]

Passengers for Gairloch would leave the train at Achnasheen, which became the postal station. Plans for branch lines to Gairloch and Ullapool were mooted several times in the 1890s and early twentieth century. The Great North of Scotland Railway and the Highland Railway were both interested in exploiting the potential for customers, be they trade (fishing) or tourist. Detailed plans were drawn up and the parliamentary approval, required for each and every separate line, applied for. A thirty-five mile route from Achnasheen connecting Gairloch, Poolewe and Aultbea with the Highland Railway line (Dingwall to Strome Ferry, and beyond to Skye) was promoted from 1889 by local landowners including Sir Kenneth Mackenzie, the Hon. Liot Bankes of Gruinard and Letterewe, Mr Mackenzie of Inverewe and John H. Dixon of Inveran.

Dixon wrote to *The Scotsman* on the 'great public question' of the intended North West Highland Fisheries Railway: 'Individually I should deprecate a railway down the romantic valley of Loch Maree were it not that [...] I am convinced that it would do more to benefit the struggling fishing populations than any other measure that has been selected'. He referred to the difficulties of the Minch and access to Ullapool and argued that Loch Ewe would provide a much better sea access, especially to Stornoway: 'Lochewe is the natural and fittest mainland harbour for the Lews' [Lewis]. He believed that the money spent trying to make Ullapool one of the four 'model' villages established by the British Fisheries Society in the north of Scotland in the 1790s would not have been 'uselessly expended' if Aultbea had been chosen. So Dixon urged support for an Achnasheen to Aultbea railway, in preference to the one also being proposed from Garve to Ullapool, in a 'desire to raise the fishermen of the northwest Highlands and Islands from their present miserable condition'.[3]

In April 1890 the West Highlands and Islands Commission visited Aultbea, which, as yet, had no telegraph office, to investigate the viability of any such railway. The commissioners were greeted on their arrival by Osgood Mackenzie, John Dixon, Meyrick Bankes and Duncan Darroch, owner of the Torridon estate. They visited the 'fine harbour with good anchorage' and considered its potential to be a 'centre for west coast fish traffic'. They were informed of the large number of tourists visiting Gairloch and were then addressed by Dixon in the Free Church. He stressed the benefits of fishing both for the mainland and the Lews. It was estimated that the cost of the railway might be £290,000, a 'large sum', and proposed that Parliament initially guarantee 3% annually of this until the line was making a profit – though he did not anticipate this being necessary for long.

Duncan Darroch, (who was also the laird of the Gourock estates near Glasgow), spoke of the four thousand tourists who would come to Gairloch each summer, of the need for local fishermen to have a ready outlet for their plentiful catches which currently they could not sell on, except in May and June, and of the benefits the railway would bring to the crofters, who would thus be 'better served than by agriculture, even though they got their crofts for nothing'.

The following day the Commission went to Gairloch, where they discovered that the fishermen there were not at all enamoured with the idea that the railway terminus be in Aultbea. Then they embarked for Lewis, accompanied by Osgood, the journey being undertaken in a north-westerly gale and in heavy seas. The debate as to whether the railway should go to Aultbea or to Ullapool was continued.[4]

Further detailed planning took place, with the survey of the proposed route paid for by the local landowners. Initially the cost was estimated at £325,000. Revised plans said it could be done for £200,000 using the Irish model of platforms at road junctions and with steeper gradients than originally planned. Given the high charges proposed by the Highland Railway company, if they were to run the service, the sponsors aimed to have a private line. They believed that passenger traffic, from tourists and locals, would generate sufficient revenue to pay the working expenses and provide a moderate dividend but they requested that the government make a contribution for the first thirty years.[5] Not surprisingly, Parliament did not support the bid when it was debated in 1893. Further proposals by the Highland Railway in 1897 met with another negative response and the revival of the idea in 1921 was similarly rejected.

Queen Victoria's visit to Loch Maree

So, even today, Achnasheen is the nearest railway station to Gairloch and Poolewe. In September 1877 it was the stopping-off point for the most prestigious visitor to come to the area during Osgood's life-time – Queen Victoria. However, there was no mention of him at any stage of the planning of her visit, which took place soon after he returned from his honeymoon, though the laird, Sir Kenneth Mackenzie, was instrumental in the arrangements. He corresponded frequently with the Queen's personal secretary, General Ponsonby, to advise that the Loch Maree Hotel, at Talladale, was a more appropriate lodging than the other possibilities of the Kinlochewe Inn or the Auchnasheen (sic) Hotel. The Queen had made privacy and the ability to control public access a priority. Her party occupied all twenty-three rooms, 'together with all the available accommodation at the crofters' homes in the district'.[6] Mr. Hornsby, the owner of the hotel, (he also owned that at Gairloch), was willing to block off some doors and to create the necessary new openings.[7] Victoria rated it 'a very nice little house, neatly furnished'.[8] Newspaper journalists arrived but were obliged to base themselves in Gairloch.

The Queen left Balmoral on the morning of Wednesday, 12 September. At Ballater she embarked on the train, with a number of ladies-in-waiting, other personnel and an injured John Brown – he had hurt his leg. Passing through Aberdeen and Inverness, she arrived at Dingwall at 4.20 p.m. where 'Sir Kenneth and Lady Mackenzie of Gairloch met us with their three children, two boys and a girl. He is a pleasing, courteous person, and wore the kilt'. They accompanied the Queen as far as Achnasheen station 'where there were a Gaelic inscription and some plaids arranged in festoons'. *The Scotsman* reported on a 'profuse display' of heather, evergreens and ferns on either side of the station and about the doorway and at the Station Hotel. Here there were also Union Jacks and banners of welcome.[9] Then came the twenty-mile drive through Glen Dochart, Kinlochewe (where horses were changed) and along the shores of Loch Maree to the hotel, passing through several heavy showers and seeing a rainbow, finally arriving a little after seven.

The Queen stayed until Tuesday 18 September. The weather was typical with many heavy showers but also sunny spells. Her Majesty commented several times that she found it quite 'hot and oppressive', 'the weather is very warm and muggy'. She experienced the inevitable midges, 'dreadful, and you cannot stand for a moment without being stung', and even a plague of wasps. Despite this, she was out walking every day and frequently took her sketch book with her. She also went for drives, in all directions. Travelling west along the river Kerry she remarked that the scenery was like Switzerland. She returned the same way another day, continuing further, on to Shieldaig and Gairloch. This village, she wrote in her diary, 'consisted of only a very few houses dotted about, the kirk, manse, bank, and on the highest point, the hotel'. There were banners and Union Jacks, and, again, decorations with heather. Bunting had been put up at the bank and numerous flags at the residence of Dr Robertson, the public school and the Hotel.

On the Saturday the Queen drove to Torridon, again changing horses at Kinlochewe. She was impressed with the mountain scenery: Ben Liarach (Liathach) 'is most peculiar from its being so dark, and the rocks like terraces one above the other'. She had her luncheon at 2.40, and sketched. 'We were nearly an hour sitting there, and we got down unwillingly, as it was so fine and such a wild, uncivilised spot, like the end of the world'. She saw the newly built school and went into the local shop, buying 'some very good comforters, two little woven woollen shawls and a very nice cloak'. Money did not pass hands but the shopkeepers received ample payment after she had left.

Both on this trip and on some excursions nearer to the hotel, Victoria was interested to find that many of the local people could not speak or understand English, only Gaelic. At Torridon she commented on the row of five or six wretched hovels, 'before which stood barelegged and very ill-clad children, and poor women literally squatting on the ground'. Her aides were always generous in donating money to the poor people and she herself gave 'biscuits and sandwiches out of the luncheon-box' to 'three or four very poorly dressed bairns'. On the visit to 'an old man who resides in a hut on the hillside [...] she handed him a sum of money sufficient to enable him to procure a large store of his favourite weed, tobacco'.[10]

Her activities on the Sunday attracted considerable adverse comment. The minister, Rev. Mr M'Kenzie, had prepared his kirk in Gairloch. It had undergone 'renovation, in anticipation of the Queen's attendance at it on Sunday'.[11] Many people made the journey to church expecting to join their Monarch there. She had even seen them passing the hotel early in the morning. 'At Gairloch parish church the attendance yesterday was between forty and fifty, the largest number which have worshipped in it since the Disruption. This was, of course, owing to the expected visit of the Queen'. However, she decided not to go, giving as reason 'the distance she would have to drive', and instead had herself rowed across the Loch to Isle Maree. The boat, a six oar 'gig', had been specially brought up from Glasgow. She saw the old gravestones and some modern ones and hammered her pennies into the wishing-well tree. Returning to the mainland she went on to visit some nearby waterfalls. Here the trees had been cut down, after she had passed the previous night, to allow her a view from her carriage. Surprising the programmers, she preferred to get out and climbed up to the water![12]

That the Queen should engage in such leisure pursuits on a Sunday was unacceptable to many. A strong letter of protest, from R.S.A., was published in the *Ross-shire Journal.*

> I presume such a profanation of the sacred day of rest has not been witnessed there in the present generation. [...] It is really very sad that the Queen, who holds such a warm place in the affections of her people and deservedly so – should manifest such disregard for the sentiments of her Scottish subjects regarding the Sabbath; for whatever may be her own views as to the sanctity of the day, she cannot but know that a fast majority of the inhabitants of Scotland believe that travelling and pleasure seeking are utterly inconsistent with the duties required upon it; and it is surely not too much to expect even rulers to pay some deference to sentiments held in such reverence by the best portion of their subjects. [...] If something is not to be done, we need not be surprised to find that the pernicious example that has been set by Royalty is followed by other strangers visiting Loch Maree.[13]

No response from Royalty is recorded. For her last full day, Monday 17 September, Victoria drove again towards Gairloch, and at Kerries Bridge met 'the good people who had asked permission to come over from Stornoway, in the *Isle of Lewis,* to see their "beloved Queen". [...] They sang "God save the Queen" with most loyal warmth. [...] It took them three hours to come over, and they were going straight back. There were two hundred and fifty of them of all classes, from the very well dressed down to the poorest, and many fishermen amongst them'.

She started her return journey on the Tuesday, a 'wet, misty morning. [...] We left with regret our nice cozy little hotel at Loch Maree, which I may hope I may see some day again.' She never did return. The Gairloch Estate factor, Donald MacKenzie, wrote to Sir Kenneth to report that the Queen had told him that she had 'not expected to be half as comfortable at Talladale' as she was. She was well pleased with the solitariness of the place and that the Loch was kept clear of boats. The London police had told him that they were amazed that there were so few people to keep away from the Queen.[14] This time she was met at Achnasheen by Mr Matheson, MP and about two to three hundred people. Sir Kenneth afterwards corresponded again with Gen. Ponsonby. The waterfalls she visited at Talladale were to be renamed after her, so they had to agree the wording, in Gaelic only, on a commemorative plaque. Unfortunately, despite his hospitality and more than satisfactory service, Mr Hornsby, the owner of the Loch Maree Hotel, was to fail in his business enterprises and be declared bankrupt in 1886.

Events of national significance 1848–1913

Though Osgood Mackenzie was very involved in the religious, political and social life of parish and County his political affiliations and views on national and government issues are not known. His mother did participate in the electoral campaign of 1848. She 'was of a Quaker family herself, and like most of her people, a strong Whig' who supported Sir James Matheson, standing as a Liberal against the sitting Conservative Member, 'old Mackenzie of Applecross'. Sir James 'had just before this come back as a very rich man from China, and had bought the Lews from the Seaforth Mackenzies'. Lady Mary campaigned 'heart and soul' on his behalf.

On the day of the election he 'sent a steamer (one of the first, if not the very first to enter the loch) with my mother and all the voters in the parish of Gairloch, to the poll at Ullapool [...] and back to our homes that night. Still more wonderful, the same steamer took a number of us over the following day to Stornoway with the latest news of the poll and back in the evening. [...] My mother got, I believe every voter on the Gairloch estate to vote for Sir James, and Sir James' majority in the county exactly equalled the number of Gairloch voters'.[15]

The local school children were kept informed of some of the more important events of their day, especially those relating to the Royal Family. Queen Victoria's Golden and Diamond Jubilees were recognised and celebrated by the presentation of medals, school treats and (no doubt, best of all as far as the children were concerned) extra holidays – a whole week on the occasion of the Diamond Jubilee.[16] Schools were also closed on days of national mourning, as with the death of the King (Edward VI) in May 1910.

Osgood made little reference to the major wars of the period, other than a passing comment about the Crimean War in 1853.[17] Though he wrote nothing about it, the Boer War did have an impact on his family. Ronald Sawyer, a Hanbury cousin, had bought himself a farm in Natal, which produced oranges, after his work as a mining engineer was ended by silicosis. He volunteered to serve in the Transvaal Mounted Rifles which helped to crush a Zulu native uprising in 1906 and was to be on active service during the First World War.[18] Remote as it was, this 'War to end all wars' was to have a big impact on the lives of the folk of Wester Ross.

Naval manoeuvres

Though better known as the base for the Arctic convoys of the Second World War, Loch Ewe, with its deep waters and shelter from the prevailing storm-winds, proved to be of considerable strategic importance to the defence of the Realm in the earlier twentieth century. The Admiralty, forced to respond to the considerable expansion of Kaiser Wilhelm's navy from 1898, used the north-west coast of Scotland for major exercises. The incidental evidence of the Poolewe School Log Book indicated how the strength, speed and armaments of the improved British battle squadrons were often tested here in the years leading up to the 1914–1918 War:[19]

> 15 September 1904: The Channel squadron of eight Battleship and four cruisers came into Loch Ewe on the 13th and this afternoon the children were taken out and shown over the Mars and the Jupiter.
>
> 1 April 1908: Great disappointment prevails in the district that the visit of the Channel Fleet to Loch Ewe on 1st April has been postponed for some unexplained reason. Six Torpedo boats lay at anchor here for 2 days and were visited by some of the natives and most courteously received.

The seriousness of the situation was perhaps not always fully understood:

> 22 July 1913: All the children in the school with their friends visited the fleet this afternoon on the invitation of Admiral Sir J. Hamilton, HMS Queen. The children thoroughly enjoyed themselves.

This may well have been the same admiral as Osgood took round his Garden:

> Well, I was showing one of the admirals of the big fleet we had in Loch Ewe this summer round my shrubberies, and telling him how disappointed I was with my Drimys, when his sharper and younger eyes detected a fine truss of its sweet smelling bloom just expanding.[20]

On 24 April 1914 Poolewe School's headmaster, Mr Cameron, wrote: '2 battleships are lying in the Loch'. The next day there was much more to record, sadly.

> A military funeral (or rather naval) took place this morning to Londubh Churchyard from "Zealandia". Great numbers turned out to see this sad and impressive cortège. The music was sad and the English Church Service was

> very impressive. Haskell was the name of young blacksmith who was severely injured in lowering of anchor and he died next morning after a serious operation.[21]

All that remains of his burial marker is the upright of a wooden cross. He was not entitled to a Commonwealth War Grave stone because he died in service before the outbreak of war. However, the young man was remembered by his friends, who had the following memorial placed on the wall of the chancel in Christchurch Priory in Dorset:

In Memory of
Albert Haskell
Who was killed in the execution of his duty on board
HMS *Zealandia*
*April 24*th *1914*
Aged 22 Years
This Tablet is erected by his messmates and friends

Loch Ewe and the First World War

At the outbreak of war in August 1914 Loch Ewe played an important role in the naval master plan. As expected, and fearfully anticipated by the commanding powers of the British Navy, the Germans immediately deployed submarines. On 1 September a periscope was sighted peering out from the waters of Scapa Flow in Orkney, the home base of the British Grand Fleet. Somewhat panic stricken, the battle-fleet ships weighed their anchors in poor weather and left that night. Admiral Jellicoe, Commander-in-Chief, kept it at sea, using Loch Ewe as his main base for refuelling and taking on stores. Extracts from his memoirs gave a glimpse into the events of that time.

> Aug 11th Orders were given to establish Loch Ewe as a secondary coaling base, and Rear Admiral Richard P.F. Purefoy was appropriated to take charge of the base
>
> Aug 12th The 3rd battle squadron went to Loch Ewe to coal and to test the suitability of this base and its capability for defence against submarine attack
>
> Aug 13th The dreadnought Battle fleet was coaling at Scapa during the day, and the 3rd battle squadron coaling and storing at Loch Ewe. My object in providing this alternative base was to expedite entry into the bases for fuelling and also to be prepared for a second base in the event of Scapa Flow becoming untenable (submarine attack)

Aug 14th All battle squadrons rejoined the flag, and battle exercises were carried out until 7 p.m. At midnight the whole fleet passed through the Fair Isle channel on its way to carry out a sweep in the North Sea

Aug 17th A telegram was sent to the Admiralty requesting that new condenser tubes might be sent at once to Loch Ewe together with dockyard workmen to assist with the retubing (of HMS Orion)

Aug 18th The Dreadnought battle fleet arrived at Loch Ewe to fuel early in the afternoon; it was accompanied by the 1st light Cruiser Squadron, which was without the Falmouth and the Liverpool. The attached cruisers were anchored in suitable positions for defending the entrance against submarine attack, so far as they were capable of doing it, and the armed steam boats of the Fleet patrolled the entrance [...] The Assistance arrived at Loch Ewe as base repair ship and was connected to the shore telegraph system

Aug 19, 20, 22 The battle Fleet and the 1st battle cruiser squadron remained in harbour during the 19th, coaling, storing, cleaning boilers and taking in additional ammunition up to a maximum storage. With the exception of the Orion, these ships left on the 20th at 6.30 p.m. for an area to the westward of the Orkneys to carry out target practice on the 21st. The battle Cruiser New Zealand was ordered to the Humber to join the Invincible

Aug 30th During the day the Assistance returned to Scapa from Loch Ewe as baseship

Sept 1st The Assistance was ordered to Loch Ewe

Sept 5th The Dreadnought battle fleet arrived at Loch Ewe at 4 p.m. on the 5th to coal; two mine sweeping gunboats having been previously detached to that base to search the entrance for mines

Sept 7th The Dreadnought battle Fleet remained at Loch Ewe until 6 a.m. The Orion was left behind to complete work on her condensers and rejoined the fleet at sea on Sept 9th

Sept 12th The Dreadnought battle Fleet proceeded to Loch Ewe. The DBF remained at Loch Ewe coaling, storing and cleaning boilers from 5 p.m. on Sept 13th to 6 p.m. on Sept 17th. [...] Advantage was taken of the stay at Loch Ewe to make arrangements with the Admiralty for the defence of that base, and on Sept 17th the 1st Lord of the Admiralty (Churchill) with the Chief of War Staff, the Director of the Intelligence Division Commodores S & T arrived at Loch Ewe to confer with me.[22]

In the burial ground at Londubh, Poolewe there are three War Commission gravestones. Two of these are of men who died, for unexplained reasons, during these first war months.

J. HIGGINS, STOKER 2nd CLASS,
RN, SS/114640
HMS "NEW ZEALAND"
18th AUGUST 1914

S. GORDON, STOKER 1st CLASS
RN, SS/113752,
HMS "LION"
20th AUGUST 1914

Admiral Jellicoe continued his account:

> 5 a.m. Oct 7th a submarine was reported inside Loch Ewe, being sighted by a collier and by the Assistance; she was fired at by the latter ship, in misty weather. On receipt of that report I ordered all vessels to leave Loch Ewe at once, and sent a division of destroyers there from Scapa Flow to search for the submarine.

On 16 October another U-boat scare drove the Grand Fleet to distant Lough Swilly in Ireland. But, evidently, some ships returned after their October departure, as another sad occasion was noted in the Poolewe Log Book:

> 19 November 1914: A very sad accident took place late last night whereby 3 young officers were drowned at "An Corran dubh" 200 yds from the shore. The names of those drowned are Lieut. Ellis of Technical College, Glasgow (a brother of Dr Ellis, Prof of Botany and Bacteriology, Technical College.) He was buried in Londubh Churchyard on Saturday. The others drowned were Lieut Burrell, Glasgow and Sublt. Longton, Paisley and Sublieut. Malquinn, a graduate of Toronto University, was saved by Mr U. Maclean, Merchant of Poolewe.

Osgood Mackenzie's son-in-law, Robert Hanbury, also made notes at the time: 'Three officers of the volunteer fleet of patrol boats were drowned at Poolewe, they had dined at the Inn and then went out in a small boat to get to their launches'.[23] So the third official gravestone in the Londubh burial ground reminds of

LIEUTENANT
A. ELLIS
ROYAL NAVAL VOL. RESERVE
18th NOVEMBER 1914 AGE 36

DIED IN THE SERVICE OF HIS COUNTRY

Throughout the war years the fleet continued to come and go. Once there were 'large armed cruisers', and naval officers were transferred to and from the main Aultbea base. Robert Hanbury saw 31 War Fleet vessels and a hospital ship in August 1914 but they soon left. Many of the ships were 'dummies' and recognised as such. One such, the HMS *Queen Mary*, struck a rock which holed her as she left Loch Ewe on 11 February 1915. She had to put back for repairs.[24] But there was relatively little real action: Robert commented in 1915 that 'nothing much happened here in the early part of the year' except 'German submarines were seen in the Minch'. In 1916 there was a 'loud explosion' one night (13 February) which 'must have been a mine gone on the rocks' but little else of significance.

A tantalising glimpse of visiting ships is evident through a full page of 'ship cards', some annotated with 'thank-yous', for the 3rd and 5th Battle Squadrons in Loch Ewe, which Osgood's daughter pasted into her photograph album:

HMS Hindustan
HMS Dominion – Capt A. L. Prynne. Royal Marine Artillery
HMS Prince of Wales
HMS Irresistible
HMS King Edward VII
Rear Admiral Reginald Tupper
Lt-Gen Sir Alfred Codrington

Only one was dated:

HMS Marlborough. First Battle Squadron. 19/8/1914.

Heroes all

There had long been an active and strong volunteer regiment of the Seaforth Highlanders in the Gairloch and Poolewe areas.[25] So, although their lives had been spent beside the sea, it was the army, rather than the navy, which recruited the volunteers of the district most successfully. In August 1914 'our men were called out'. Robert Hanbury and Finlay Mackinnon went with them to Dingwall for the medical examination, and 'some were sent to Nigg to guard the coast'.[26]

> 6 November 1914: Word has come yesterday that the Poolewe Section of Territorials proceeds at once to the Front with their regiment 4th Seaforths. Poolewe has sent 26 men (22 in 4th Seaforths) in all to Army which is excellent for such a small place of 240 inhabitants. About 11%, 20 of these have recently been pupils of Poolewe School.

The pride suggested by this Poolewe School Log Book entry was replaced by shock and sadness when, just four months later, news came through of the realities of trench warfare:

> 17 March 1915: Word has reached Poolewe last night that D Coy 4th Seaforths suffered severely on March 10 at Neuve Chapelle, N France. The following were pupils of this school and of mine (Wm C)
>
> Killed – Simon Urquhart, Carnmore
> Wm Ross, Riverside
>
> Wounded – Sergt Finlay MacIver, Londubh (seriously in stomach)
> Alex Ross, Riverside – arm
> John Cameron, Londubh – side
>
> The sad news has caused a deep sensation in the West, Over 160 casualties in 4th Seaforths. Several of their officers killed and wounded.
>
> [A side comment was added]
> 5 April: The sad news by wire reached Poolewe today that my good friend Finlay MacIver succumbed for his wounds 14th March.

An unexpected consequence of the war was the reduction in the money being paid to run the school. On 12 November 1915 the HMI (Inspector) wrote, 'The grant has been reduced by 1/20 [...] on account of the failure of the Board to secure the requisite number of School openings'. Mr Cameron explained: 'The closing above referred to took place in April owing to all the young men 'being away' at this awful war.'

The names of those who fell were inscribed on the war memorials in Aultbea, Poolewe and Gairloch. The *Third Statistical Account*, (not compiled until 1955), reported that about a hundred local men died. The War had given 'a rude shock to the economy of the parish and deprived it at the same time of many valuable lives. Nearly every fit man under 50 was on military or naval service. A company of 100 men, almost wholly Gaelic speaking, mobilised with the Seaforth Highlanders. Many fell in France. A group of horse, chiefly from Aultbea, mobilised with the Lovat Scouts and several fell at Gallipoli. Very few returned unwounded from the army'.

Having been designated a strategic war zone, travel restrictions were imposed across the area. There was a drastic reduction in the number of public trains through Achnasheen, with only one permitted each day, because of the demands for war traffic. Then, with the arrest of two enemy spies at the Station Hotel in Inverness, in August 1916, the north of Scotland was declared a special military area. Railway passengers were not allowed to continue beyond Inverness without a permit. In 1915 Mairi Hanbury was issued with her own *Defence of the Realm Local Pass*, which 'may be used only by a person resident in the county of Ross and Cromarty'.[27]

From the end of 1917, when the USA came into the war, there was a big growth in material and human transport. Kyle was used to land materials to be sent across country to Dalmore, near Invergordon, and Inverness. Starting in January 1918 the plan was to lay a huge mine cordon around the north of Scotland (and stretching to Norway). The whole railway west of Dingwall, together with the Pier at Kyle, was commandeered by the Admiralty and trains could no longer be used for domestic goods or passengers bound for Skye or the Hebrides.[28]

Although there were many more casualties to record, and ships to view, there were no further records related to the war in the Poolewe Log Book until 15 March 1918: 'Owing to there being practically no stores at Poolewe the senior children visit the shops at Inverasdale and Gairloch on arrival of steamer – consequently attendance suffers'.

Osgood Mackenzie himself wrote little about the War effort. He might have been forced to give up his beloved setters in 1914[29] but he would not be thwarted in his endeavours to acquire new plants: 'In spite of these hard times, and in spite of great new difficulties in the way of transport, I have got a nice lot of new things from my favourites nurseries in Ireland and Cornwall, which, if I live a few more years, I shall have such interest in watching'.[30]

Peace

The Poolewe School Log Book announced the 'armistice':

> 11 Nov 1918: today news has come by wire that hostilities have ceased on the continent. The armistice had been signed at 11 o'clock to-day. Naturally we spent the rest of the day in discussing some of the outstanding events since 1914 and paid special attention to details re the generals and advisers which brought our troops to victory.

The Peace treaties were eventually signed six months later – after the school had broken up for the summer holiday. The Log Book recorded: 15 Sept 1919, 'School was opened to-day after seven weeks' holidays. An extra week was given for Peace Celebrations'. In July 1919, Robert Hanbury wrote, 'We gave all the returned soldiers and their fancy ladies [sic] a day on Loch Maree. They had bonfire at Poolewe on Peace night which was very wet'. At Inverewe, now an elderly, though still very active, gentleman in his mid-seventies, Osgood Mackenzie commemorated the occasion in a most appropriate way:

The Peace Shrubbery
PLANNED BY OSGOOD H. MACKENZIE
OF INVEREWE
TO COMMEMORATE PEACE AFTER THE GREAT WAR 1918.

Lloyd George's visit 1921

After Queen Victoria's visit of 1877 there is no record of any 'official' prestigious guests until 1921 when the Prime Minister, David Lloyd George, came to stay in Gairloch for a much-needed longer period of rest and recovery.[31] Business could not be left entirely undone though and some important political visitors travelled north to consult with him whilst he was staying at Flowerdale. These included Patrick McGrath and Gerry Boland, representatives of Sinn Fein, who came to negotiate at a time of sensitive and significant decision-making about Ireland. The Irish republicans had declared their independence from Britain in 1918 and the British Army (Black and Tans) had been fighting in bloody and brutal confrontation since. On 9 September the two Sinn Fein leaders spent an hour with the Prime Minister before returning via Inverness to Dublin, taking with them messages for de Valera, the Irish Prime Minister. On 22 September a number of Cabinet ministers, including Winston Churchill, who was then Colonial Secretary, came to Gairloch and a full Cabinet meeting was held in Inverness. Other official visitors were several Labour London mayors who travelled all the way, with much publicity, to put on the pressure over problems of unemployment.

It wasn't all work though. Lloyd George managed an interrupted but 'exhilarating' round of golf on the Gairloch links course, where the vigour of his swing was noted.[32] A film evening was organised, with two Charlie Chaplin films on the bill. It apparently took the presenting company sixty hours of travelling to and from London for the pm's three hours of entertainment. One 'friend' arrived unannounced by yacht which caused a great panic. Clearly security was inadequate and a destroyer had to be ordered to Gairloch to ensure this could not be repeated. Time was also made to go fishing: 'The Prime Minister, Lloyd George, was angling on the Kerry River at Gairloch. He caught nothing on the fly and the ghillies advised a change to the worm. He caught a 20oz brown trout'.[33] Robert Hanbury recorded that he hooked a salmon on the River Ewe. Unfortunately, whilst he was at a local fair, he got soaked and caught a chill and he also had to have an abscessed tooth extracted. Whether Lloyd-George's visit to Poolewe School on 29 September 1921 was pain or pleasure was not recorded.[34]

References and Notes

1 H.A. Vallance, *The Highland Railway* (Dawlish: David and Charles, 1st pub 1938. Revised and extended 1963), pp.38–39, 45.

2 Vallance, p.86.

3 *The Scotsman*, 6 June 1889.

4 *The Scotsman*, 7 April, 8 April 1890.

5 Gairloch Heritage Museum Archives.

6 *The Scotsman*, 12 September 1877.

7 Correspondence between Sir Kenneth Mackenzie and General Ponsonby, August and September 1877. Gairloch Heritage Museum Archives.

8 Unless otherwise attributed, all quotations and evidence are from Queen Victoria's own diary, published as *'More leaves from the Journal of a life in the Highlands'*,

1884. A booklet, *'The personal account written by Queen Victoria of her visit to Gairloch Parish'*, which is a selection from '*More leaves*', is in the Gairloch Heritage Museum Archives.

[9] *The Scotsman*, 12 September 1877.

[10] *The Scotsman*, 16 September 1877.

[11] *The Scotsman*, 13 September 1877.

[12] *The Scotsman*, 16 September 1877.

[13] *Ross-shire Journal*, 21 September 1877.

[14] Letter from Mr Mackenzie, Gairloch Estate factor, to Sir Kenneth Mackenzie, 15 September 1877. Gairloch Heritage Museum Archives.

[15] Mackenzie, pp.209, 211.

[16] Inverasdale School Log Book, 24 June 1887, 28 June 1897, 2 September 1897.

[17] Mackenzie, p.113.

[18] Personal communications from Peter Hanbury, the nephew (by marriage) of both of Mairi's husbands. Ronald's medal for that expedition is still in Inverewe House. He was to marry Osgood's daughter, Mairi, in 1935.

[19] Entries from the Inverasdale School Log Book. There are further examples in Chapter XI.

[20] Osgood H. Mackenzie 'Floral Notes from the West Coast of Ross-shire', *The Scotsman*, 18 November 1913.

[21] Poolewe School Log Book, 25 April 1914. This is the only record of how Arthur Haskell died – and had there not been the funeral that day the famous photographs of Inverewe House burning would never have been taken. (See Chapter XIII). The *Zealandia*, of the King Edward class of pre-dreadnought battleships, was built in 1904 as the *New Zealand*. It was captained by Admiral Sir Walter Henry 'Tich' Cowan, and was one of the Third Battle Squadron of the Grand Fleet.

[22] Admiral Viscount Jellicoe, *The Grand Fleet 1914–16* (1919), quoted in *Poolewe – the Londubh Burial Ground and Pictish Stone*, a booklet published by the Loch Ewe Heritage Group, 2006.

[23] Robert Hanbury's *Game Book*.

[24] Web site: www.Norwayheritage.com, accessed 6 December 2006. This HMS *Queen Mary* had started life as a merchant ship, the *CEVIC*, built in 1894 by Harland & Wolff at Belfast as a livestock carrier. She sailed from Liverpool to New York until 1908, moved onto the Australia route, initially via the Cape of Good Hope, and then, as an experiment, through the Suez Canal. She was converted into a dummy battleship in December 1914.

[25] See Chapter X.

[26] Robert Hanbury's *Game Book*.

[27] Original in one of the photograph albums in the Inverewe House Archive.

[28] Vallance, pp.103, 105.

[29] Mackenzie, pp.118–119. The importance of these is explained in Chapter VII.

[30] Osgood Mackenzie: 'A Year in a Garden on the North-West Coast of Ross-shire'. *Journal of the Royal Horticultural Society*, 1917.

[31] The great-granddaughter of Robert Campbell, Osgood's Head Gardener at the turn of the twentieth century, is convinced that David Lloyd George visited Inverewe, as a house guest, before the First World War, though whether it was to visit Osgood himself or as a shooting tenant is not clear. No evidence has been found to corroborate this stay and when, as Prime Minister, Lloyd George returned to the area in 1921 he did not meet with Osgood as far as is known. Reference was made to Osgood Mackenzie's Inverewe House being in the neighbourhood and (erroneously) having burnt down in the early months of the War in an article entitled "*Some notes on the countryside the PM has brought into the public eye*" published at the time of his visit. Some correspondence and newspaper cuttings relating to Lloyd George's visit are in the Gairloch Heritage Museum Archives.

[32] *The Scotsman*, 28 September 1921. He had been offered free use of the course by the Gairloch estate factor!

[33] *Inverness Courier*, 5 August 1921.

[34] Only the fact that he visited is recorded, without comment.

CHAPTER XIII

Osgood's Inverewe

'His gardens at Inverewe were famous all over the country for the rarity of many of the species of plants and shrubs which he succeeded in growing year after year in a region in which it had not been believed possible for them to exist.'

Inverewe House

In 1862 and 1863, in two separate transactions, Osgood's mother had bought him the adjoining estates of Kernsary and Inverewe respectively. Building a house seemed to have been neither a priority nor of particular interest to him. The location chosen was not far from the public road, on the seashore, across the bay from the village of Poolewe. 'After taking about two years to settle where we should make our home, we finally pitched upon the neck of a barren peninsula as the site of the house. The peninsula was a high, rocky bluff, jutting out into the sea'.[1] The outlook was stunning – across the waters of Loch Ewe, with views to the mountains of Torridon and, more especially, to his favourite hunting grounds of Aridh Charr.

Osgood was happy to leave the 'whole trouble of house-building' to his mother.[2] After much excavation of rock, a well-sized baronial-style mansion was set on a raised terrace, framed against the hillside. An avenue of shrubs was soon planted between the wall to the garden and the edge of the drive, reinforcing the sense of impressive 'arrival' as the House came into view around the bend. 'The head dyke curves round creating an amphitheatre, following the natural landform'.[3]

The house was almost certainly designed by the architect Andrew Maitland of Tain, who also worked on Assynt Lodge and on John Fowler's house at Braemore in the 1860s. He is not known to have been involved previously in other Mackenzie family building projects. Eventually the substantial house was completed, probably by 1865. The general building sandstone would likely have come from the quarry on Isle Martin, close to Ullapool, but the better quality, 'blonde' stone which was used for the dressings to window and door openings, corner stones and more ornate work, is believed to have been brought by sea from the Glasgow area. The most distinctive feature of the design was the 'three-storey round tower, marking the principal entrance, surmounted by a tall, slated conical roof'. The roofs 'were finished with the usual West Highland slate, laid in diminishing courses'.[4] The house originally comprised '3 public, 6 bedrooms, servants' hall, butler's pantry, kitchen, six servants-rooms etc. There are also stables, kennels and garden'.[5] The Valuation Rolls gave it a rental value (for rate purposes) of £35 between 1868 (the earliest entry, not necessarily when the house was completed) and 1875.[6]

John H. Dixon was most impressed with the Mansion House:

> It is beautifully situated in a northern recess of the bay at the head of Loch Ewe, in the shelter of a rocky headland called Ploc-ard. The house has a Highland character; it faces due south, and commands a fine view of Beinn Aridh Charr. [...] From the village of Poolewe the house – surrounded as it is with planted woods now well grown – is a pleasing object. There are walks in these woods, and separate sea-bathing places for ladies and gentlemen. There is the best anchorage for yachts of the largest size close to the house.[7]

Inverewe House was not, however, entirely to the satisfaction of Osgood's wife. Minna wanted improvements. He would not allow, and could not afford, some of the, quite substantial, cosmetic changes she wanted. However, he did grant one to improve her comfort: 'I wanted hot water introduced upstairs at Inverewe and that was carried out'. The money came from the rental her father paid for the 1878 Shootings.[8]

The 1877 catalogue of the photographic company of George Washington Wilson, based in Aberdeen, included two aspects of the house and walled garden. A conservatory was visible on the west wall.[9] A terrace was built on the loch-facing front of the house, and 'a short flight of stone steps led to a lower level which was laid out as a well manicured lawn sloping gently towards the shingle beach. [...] The stone wall to the front of the terrace had received plants trained to create a decorative effect, as though they were garlands draped over the wall'.[10]

For some seasons in the 1870s, and almost every year from 1880, Inverewe House was rented out to shooting tenants. Minna had been surprised to find, when she returned to Osgood from Otterspool that summer, that she had to stay at Tournaig, her mother-in-law's residence, rather than Inverewe. Osgood was not 'at home' when *The Times* reporter visited in 1883, nor at the time of the 1891 Census. In the court case evidence with respect to Minna's access to her daughter it was stated that her visits were almost invariably to the nursery at Tournaig.

There were some prestigious guests amongst these 'shooting tenants'. Asquith, then Home Secretary, definitely stayed in 1894, one of a party hosted by his brother-in-law, Edward Tennant.[11] Among prominent businessmen taking the shooting lets were Andrew Coats of Ferguslie, Paisley (1895–1896) and E.E. Cook of Thomas Cook and Sons (1902–1903). Sir John Gilmour of Lundin and Montrave (later to be appointed Secretary of State for Scotland 1924–1929) stayed on three occasions between 1906 and 1909.[12] His wife, Lady Henrietta, is considered to be one of the first women photographers in Scotland and she included Inverewe in her collection.[13] Winston Churchill, Lloyd George and Thomas Lipton (of tea fame) are all said to have been visitors at Inverewe in the early years of the twentieth century, but whether Osgood was the host of such 'grand parties' or they were house guests of a tenant is not known. They arrived, apparently, by steam yacht.[14]

Over the years, substantial alterations had to be made to the original Mansion House to meet the requirements of the increasingly large family parties and their accompanying servants. Some had been carried out by the time of the 1902 Second Edition Ordnance Survey map, but there were significant extensions to the rear of the house thereafter. With rock-bank and hillside directly behind, room for extensions was at a premium. The expanded servants' quarters, facilities such as a gunroom and kitchen larder, and additional bedroom space did not fit comfortably into the limited space available. 'The short wing to the rear of the lodge on the northwest side must have been taken down, and then rebuilt, so as to connect with the 1½ storey wing to the rear'. It is likely that the firm of Andrew Maitland and Sons was responsible for the unavoidably rather 'unresolved changes'.[15]

It is not known what caused the fire on Saturday, 25 April 1914, which started early in the morning and destroyed all but the back rooms, the so-called 'New Wing', of Inverewe house. None of the Mackenzie family was in residence at the time and the fishing tenant, Capt. Beckwith, had left the previous week. As luck would have it, a naval exercise was taking place in Loch Ewe at the time, just months before the outbreak of the First World War. Albert Haskell, aged 22, the young blacksmith's mate on the battleship HMS *Zealandia*, had been killed in a 'terrible accident' on board. 'Just as funeral was over, Inverewe beautiful Mansion House took fire and was burnt to the ground. The bluejackets and marines did noble service all day in saving furnitures and goods etc'.[16] There were no casualties. Vice Admiral Humphry Hugh Smith remembered the occasion vividly:

> We landed very early one Saturday morning to bury him at Poolewe, and just as we were re-embarking after the funeral we noticed that a large house on the opposite side of the harbour was on fire. We dashed across the harbour, and as the water was too shallow for the boats to reach the beach we had to jump overboard and wade on shore, although we were all in our best clothes. The water supply of the house was so scanty that we were not able to quench the fire before a great deal of damage had been done, but we managed to save most of the furniture. The chief boatswain's mate, Grant by name, performed prodigies of valour in going up a ladder, smashing a window, climbing into a bedroom, both the floor and ceiling of which were blazing, and rescuing a Pekinese dog. My full-dress uniform never really recovered from the effects of that morning. Captain Walter Cowan, who had been terribly distressed by the death of the poor blacksmith's mate, really enjoyed the fire. It provided him with several opportunities of risking his life, and of these opportunities he took the fullest advantage – and he most unselfishly insisted on my accompanying him.[17]

A newspaper article (undated) reported that the Marines used several hoses and blew up part of the house with charge of gun cotton. Robert Hanbury recorded that 'about 800 bluejackets', including the Admiral, Sir Lewis Bailey, arrived about 8.30 a.m. Osgood returned on the Sunday afternoon.[18] A different version of events was told by Dawn Macleod, possibly based on the memories of his daughter, Mairi:

> Lady Mary did not live to see the conflagration; and her son and granddaughter (Mairi) with her first husband were away from Inverewe at the time. Luckily the leaping flames were spotted from a warship anchored in Loch Ewe, and a party of sailors rowed ashore. Hampered by lack of water and appliances, they were unable to extinguish the fire; but they did manage to bring most of the antique furniture and other family treasures out to the surrounding terraces and lawns. These were soon moved to the shelter of the one-storey lodge beside the gates, and when Osgood returned he enlarged it to make the rather straggling bungalow which became the family home for a number of years.[19]

(Osgood wrote, in a letter of 1922, that three rooms had been added to the Gate Lodge, giving him more space than at Tournaig.[20] This new wing was started towards the end of 1920 and completed in the summer of 1921.[21])

The gutted, burnt ruins of the original Inverewe House were left standing. Photographs show that the courtyard became a 'walled garden' in its own right, with trellis for climbing plants on the walls, and flowers in pots. The back rooms of the house were still habitable, and were used by young family visitors, though not thought suitable for paying guests.[22] Mairi and her first husband, Robert, used the Gate Lodge when their home at Tournaig, in its turn, was rented out to shooting parties. A 'new' Mansion House was not to be built until 1935.

Inverewe – the Garden

Only tantalising glimpses are to be found of the story of the creation and development of Inverewe Garden. From 1887 Osgood wrote occasional newspaper articles, which were published in *The Scotsman* and *Glasgow Herald*.[23] The relevant chapter in *A Hundred Years* is but nine pages long. No garden notebooks, planting, purchase and expenditure details now survive but in his articles Osgood sometimes quoted from what were clearly meticulous records, as in 1899: 'I see from my diary that the first azaleas expanded with me on the 18th of May, and they did not finish till the 24th of July, so that they lasted more than nine weeks'. He kept accounts of his spending on estate labour and garden equipment, and lists of plants that he had collected on journeys with his daughter. They were still to be read in 1952.[24]

Osgood wrote of his first memories of the pleasures of a garden:

> We were not very expert at flowers in those days in the Baile Mor garden [...] but the Kerrysdale garden was more up to date, my grand-uncle, being, like most of the Gairlochs, keen on flowers and trees. I shall always remember the smell of *Daphne* and *Ribes* there, and the big clumps of *Gladiolus cardinalis*, which was not common in those days, and the lines of Christmas roses, which flourished and bloomed in winter and early spring and formed edgings to the garden walks.

Osgood visited this same uncle, Kenneth, by then over 90 years old, in 1861 or 1862. The young man discussed his proposed purchase and was given a guarantee that, if he made a garden at Inverewe, he would undoubtedly grow good raspberries in it.[25] In a later chapter Osgood acknowledged another inspiration: 'I had all my life longed to begin gardening and planting, and had, I fully believe, inherited a love for trees and flowers from my father and grandfather'.[26] Dr John Mackenzie concurred with this suggestion of a family tradition: 'The uncles and aunts, as well as my Father, were devoted to gardening – as are most of their descendants. A harmless vice'.[27]

He evidently wished to make a feature of a walled garden from the very beginning. This was his '"kitchen garden" as my English friends always take care to call it. As is often the case with us Highlanders, I possess only the one garden for fruit, flowers and vegetables'.[28] It was not to be hidden away out of sight behind the house. Extensive engineering works were needed to take the drive to the house on its elevated route ensuring, as the 1870s photographs show, there would be a good view down, with the wall closest to the house being 'splayed out dramatically in an arc to provide shelter for espalier fruit trees supported on an elaborate, eye-catching framework of wires'.

> It appears that the walled garden had been constructed in two stages; the first of these being the larger section closer to the house, and the second for the greenhouses and nursery area, but both phases had been completed by the time that the fieldwork for the First Edition Ordnance Survey of the area was undertaken in 1874. The map shows a glass house within the eastern compartment.[29]

Massive sandstone walls were constructed to provide shelter from the prevailing south-westerlies and to reflect sunshine and warmth onto the soil. This was brought in from estate lands near at hand and 'from afar', transforming what had been the old sea-beach. Local lore has it that Ireland was the source of much of this earth, unloaded from ships in the bay, though there is no evidence to support this. Possibly Osgood had to demolish the original dwelling house of Lochend which is believed to have been there.

The Valuation Rolls show liability for rates on a 'garden', as distinct from just the House itself, from 1874/5, adding £10 in value to the property. Dixon, writing in 1885, described the garden as 'wonderfully attractive, yielding [...] exquisite flowers nearly all the year round', then quoted from a letter in *The Times* in the autumn of 1883:

> The garden was laid out by the proprietor, Mr Osgood Mackenzie, whose taste must be as unimpeachable as his knowledge of flowers. The gardens form a terraced amphitheatre, shelving gently towards the Loch, and backed up by the hanging woods, which have only been recently planted. Fruit-trees, but a very few years old, are already loaded with plums, pears &c. The low stone walls that front the earth banks are covered with many of the rarer creepers, some of them almost semi-tropical, with luxuriant myrtles just bursting into flower, and with clusters of roses of wonderful size. But what is most remarkable is the marvellous vividness of the colours in such brightly

> tinted flowers as crimson roses and scarlet gladioli. The warm damp seems to give a brilliancy to the tints which I have never seen either in England or in southern Europe.[30]

This article made reference to the fact that the House was rented out 'to a Lord Fitzwilliam'. It is rather ironical that Osgood very rarely stayed in his own house, to enjoy his own garden, during the summer months. It is also inexplicable that, when his 'interests' were considered during the Divorce proceedings in the 1890s, there was but one passing reference to his gardening concerns. Nor did Minna, Osgood's wife, make comment on the grounds of Inverewe House, though by the time she was living there (1877–1880) considerable progress had been made with planting the trees and creating the walled garden.

Osgood's interest in tree planting was also influenced by his family. His grandfather 'was a great planter of trees and all the big hard-wood trees scattered about the Baile Mor policies were planted by him'. So, the new landowner 'started work in the early spring of 1864, by running a fence across the neck of the peninsula from sea to sea, to keep out the sheep' and then waited for the trees he had planted as a shelter belt to grow: 'For four or five years my poor peninsula looked miserable [...] but at last we could see some bright green specks appearing above the heather'.

The two original dwarf willows and barren hillsides were transformed into a wooded landscape, already evident in the mid-1870s photographs. In retrospect, Osgood considered he had not made the best choices initially. In particular, he was disappointed with the native Scots pine. Corsican pines, he repeated many times, were 'far and away better doers in this locality than the Scotch fir, which, like the native birch, is a very poor subject to stand the Atlantic gales'. He had seen them in Corsica, 'in their own island on mountains 9,000 feet above sea-level [...] growing to an enormous size [...] and here, at the same age, they make nearly double the amount of timber compared with the Scots fir', which had turned out to be a 'dreadfully delicate tree when exposed to Atlantic gales'.[31] He was pleased, after a visit there, to see that his recommendations had helped the Earl of Dunmore to establish his own shelter-belt on the west side of South Harris, 'which had always been considered about as hopeless a subject, as regards tree growing, as Shetland'. [1909].

Osgood's articles, written for *The Scotsman* and *Glasgow Herald*, date from 1887 until the week he died in April 1922.[32] They were full of information and advice for the reader, supportive and encouraging, as in 1909:

> Last year I read a paper at one of the April meetings of the Royal Horticultural Society, my text being 'How an Apparently Impossible Subject on the North-West Coast of Scotland was made to Produce Good Trees, Shrubs, Fruit and Flowers', and as soon as my paper appeared in print in the "Transactions of the Royal Horticultural Society" I received so many letters [...] asking endless questions and advice, especially about planting trees and making them grow under unpropitious circumstances, that I have been induced to recast and shorten my lecture, and try to make it suitable for newspaper publication in the hope that it may be a help to others who may be struggling, as I struggled so many years, against difficulties of soil and situation.

Over the first fifteen or twenty years the pines and the hardwood trees, such as oaks, (somewhat to his surprise), created 'good shelter'. Other varieties, especially rowan and birches, did not flourish in the middle of a wood and had to be cut out. It was not until the early 1880s that Osgood began to risk planting a wider range of deciduous trees, including beeches and horse-chestnuts, and also many kinds of conifers, such as *Abies nobilis*, the Douglas fir and cypresses. He had allowed himself four *Wellingtonias* early on, as they were 'then the rage', and they did well. 'It may interest some of my readers to know how tall my first planted trees are and what their growth has been in over 40 years. Well, I measured some of my silver firs, Wellingtonias and Douglas spruces last winter [1908], and they were from 65 to 70 feet'.

He could then begin to cut out some of the 'commoner stuff' and fill the cleared spaces with a wide variety of trees and shrubs, increasingly becoming more exotic. One of the first of these was mentioned in his last article, published alongside the 1922 obituary notice in the *Glasgow Herald*. Osgood remarked that Darwin's Barberry was 'a great feature in the scene here in early March. [...] How well do I remember in the early sixties of the last century, getting my first small plant of it, as a great treasure, not so very long after its discovery somewhere in Southern Chile [...] and it did not take long before it seeded itself freely'. His big bushes of it were now as high as 16 feet and birds took the berries, with the result that it sowed itself in 'all directions, even in precipitous rocks; so that they become, like a good many other exotics here, quite thoroughly naturalised'.

It is not known exactly when, or why, Osgood took on the challenge of trying exotic plants. In *The Scotsman* in 1913 he wrote, following a return visit to the garden of Mr Robert Birkbeck, 'I always feel grateful to Kinlochhourn, with its wonderful collection of rare plants, as it was there I was first bitten with the desire to grow exotic shrubs and trees'. It seems most likely that many 'eucalypti, tree rhododendrons, Arbutus, Griselinas, Cordylines, and clumps of bamboos and Phormiums', which have become the symbol-plants of the Garden, were planted in the last decade of the nineteenth century. In 1915 he wrote of his pride in these Australian trees:

> My Eucalypti are, I think, very successful. [...] I asked my forester the other day to count them, and he reported that I possessed, all told, sixty-one big ones in seven or eight varieties. [...] I have them from fifteen to twenty-five years old, averaging from twenty-eight up to forty inches in circumference six feet above ground and I consider them exceedingly ornamental among Conifers in winter, especially the very glaucous ones, such as coccifera and cordata.

He also had many younger specimens as he was sent sixteen different ones from the Edinburgh Botanic Gardens in 1905.[33] The 1920 Gairloch area guidebook made specific comment about them:

> The road from Poolewe to Aultbea measures seven miles, and is tortuous and rough, with little of interest by the way-side. In passing the plantation at Inverewe the great variety of trees to be seen should prove particularly interesting, and it may perhaps be a hard mental exercise for the passer-by to recall a place anywhere in Britain where the Eucalyptus grows to such a size, and unprotected during the whole year, as it does here.[34]

By 1898 Osgood had created a long, sunny, terraced border 25 foot by 2 foot 'with the best of soils we could find' and was developing three small enclosures within his policies to suit particular plant varieties.

> My "fantasie" is hard and gravelly, and does the genista and citisus tribes very well. My "Riviera" is very sunny, and with good soil, and in it I grow my rarest exotics; and "America", my latest creation, being more peaty, damp and shady, like a wee bit of the backwoods, has been given over to the so-called American plants – rhododendrons, azaleas, andromedas, kalmias, heaths, and besides these, magnolias, bamboos, and very many other things; so many indeed that besides the sixty azaleas which fill a bed in the centre, there are a hundred and seventy kinds of rare plants in it, gathered from most of the temperate portions of our globe.

The Inverewe rhododendrons are well renowned. Osgood frequently remarked on the pleasure they gave him, both large and small varieties. He was amazed how they thrived so far north, how tall they grew and was particularly thrilled by their flowering well outside the expected season. Several times he commented on the joy of having *R. nobleanum* blooms in October or November, but best of all, they were often decorating his Christmas dining table. He knew that 'if a truss is cut just as it is beginning to show the crimson tint, and before it is liable to be injured by hail or snow, it will expand to perfection in a warm room, and last nearly a month'.

Patience was certainly a necessary virtue and Osgood promised his readers that their wait, as his, would be well worthwhile.

> I hear people complain sometimes that their big-leafed Rhododendrons, such as Falconeri, Hodgsoni, Argentium, and Exinium, do not flower with them, or, at least, do not flower freely. Doubtless these Rhododendrons, which grow into what might be termed trees, do not often flower in their early stages. [...] I have just two middle-aged Falconerii, and though they do not bloom quite every year, they do not often disappoint me. For instance, the smaller one of these two had no blooms in 1914, in 1915 it had two great trusses of white blossom, and in 1916 it will have twelve, as its flower buds are so distinct that there is no mistaking them, even nine or ten months before they expand, and twelve trusses will be an ample crop for the size of this bush.

In 1921 Osgood wrote an article in celebration of having succeeded, at long last, in finding rhododendrons in bloom in his garden all the year round. It illustrated also his great enthusiasm for his plant collection – so evident in all his newspaper articles.

> I was always aware that the great ambition of the owners of those wonderful collections of trees and shrubs in Cornwall was to have rhododendrons in bloom during the twelve months of the year; and I am proud to be able to say that in the past year I have been fairly successful in accomplishing this achievement. [...] From February to the end of June there are, of course, rhododendrons galore, of both species and hybrids, of almost every conceivable shape and colour, but the trouble comes in July and on to November. Well, last year, I was never without rhododendrons in blossom during all these months, as Waterer has invented some new very late hybrids which carried on into July, and Rhododendron Keysii (whose brilliant little blooms are unlike any other rhododendron of my acquaintance) opened that month, and then that most lovely Rhododendron Maddeni followed it all through August, both in 1919 and 1920; but, alas, though its foliage is hardy enough, its bloom buds are not so if there is much winter frost, and I consider it a great

> feather in my cap that I am able to do it all up so far North. [...] How well it repays one for bestowing a little extra pain on it, as its palest of pink flowers are so beautifully shaped and so deliciously fragrant.
>
> Then came September, and just as I was wondering if I should have any rhododendrons during that month I suddenly noticed one of my three big bushes of Rhododendron Zelanicum was full of buds and just ready to expand, and they kept opening all through the month. Its blossoms (or rather its trusses of bloom) are not particularly fine in shape or size from a florist's point of view, such as the spring-flowering barbatums and fulgens and the wonderful Cornubia; but its colour is quite the equal of any of them – viz., an intense scarlet – and how it did set off the otherwise colourless beds of rhododendrons in September! [...] October came, and most seasons I should have been beaten that month for rhododendrons in blossom, but up here, north of the Caledonian Canal, we had an exceptionally good sunny autumn, which started the Nobleanum tribe more than a month before their usual time, and that saved me, and all November and December, besides the old kind, I had the two new varieties – viz., Nobleanum Venustum and Nobleanum Coccinium – blooming profusely.

Hydrangeas are another iconic Inverewe plant. These were an early success: 'In the middle of November [1898] my hydrangea bushes were quite mounds of bright blue. I counted the blooms upon one and they exceeded one hundred, and a lady who saw them said she had never seen the like of them for brilliancy of colour except once in Cornwall and I have not given them iron filings nor any special treatment'.

In 1909 he boasted that he could grow many species at least as well as gardeners hundreds of miles further south.

> Yet here I am, in the happy position of being able to say that I can really grow almost anything that can be grown in Cornwall, and that is undoubtedly the British paradise for rearing rare and beautiful exotic trees, shrubs and plants. Many people (indeed most people) have no idea what they could do on this West Coast of Scotland if they would only protect! I am growing palms, Cordylines, and trees ferns most successfully, and New Zealanders are so kind as to tell me that they never saw more magnificent New Zealand flaxes (Phormiums) in their own islands.

Osgood appreciated strong and brilliant colours, such as *Rhododendron thomsonii* in bright April sunshine, 1915, 'ablaze with blossom [...] one of which had on it some fifty trusses of its heavy waxy blooms, and was so dazzling when the sun shone on it that it made our eyes smart to behold it'. He mixed colours in a way that might not be considered so fashionable today:

> I am sometimes flattered by being told that I have one of the finest crinodendrons in the British Isles; at any rate, we calculated that it had something like 10,000 blooms on this year in June, and with a big embothrium on one side of it, with some 250 of its dazzling scarlet flowers, [...] and tall Himalayan blue poppies in front, they formed a wonderful floral picture, which would have been something worthy on which to try this new coloured photography of which one hears so much.

One example of the several plants from Chile which flourished in the garden was *Crinodendron*, about which he wrote many times, as in 1911: 'Truly no country I think quite comes up to Chile as regards the brilliant beauty of her floral products and their suitability to our mild, wet, west coast climate'. However, despite evident pride in his achievements, he did acknowledge, in 1913, that not everything succeeded:

> There are several other charming shrubs [....] which I do not succeed with. One is Caesalpinia Japonica, which I have seen so flourishing in Sir Harry Veitch's nursery at Coombe Wood, and which is by no means what would be called a warm situation; and another failure with me has been the so-called New Zealand Broom, Notospartium Carmichaeliae. I had not seen it doing really well anywhere, and had lost heart and caring for the one or two miserable specimens I possessed.

He cultivated a wide range of relatively tender flowers as well. Most of these were probably planted within the protection of the walls of his 'kitchen' garden, though he seemed to have liked to intersperse bulbs amongst the trees and shrubs. Borders would not have been maintained in any formal way. He waxed lyrically on many occasions about exotic flowers, such as *Agapanthus*, lilies and *Schizostylis coccinea* which dazzled in their profusion, unprotected out of doors all year round. In 1909 he challenged his readers with respect to a *Lilium giganticum* (Himalayan lily), 'which I have grown up to 10 feet high with 19 blooms on it. Can anyone beat this my lily record?' He had a long memory as that had actually been in 1896 and a visit to Kew the following year had ascertained that the best they could manage was sixteen or seventeen flowers! He also liked to have cut flowers indoors: 'our dining room table was decorated with schizostylis, winter-flowering Rhododendron nobleanum and Gloire de Margotin roses' in December 1897.

The final aspect of the garden of which Osgood was extremely proud, though he wrote about it less frequently, was of fruit growing. (Vegetables were never described, though the walled garden must surely, originally, have been built to provide the household with fresh produce?). He referred, in 1898, to an earlier article on the topic of fruit but that has not yet come to light. He mentioned in 1909 that 'nothing, I believe, astounded my hearers in London more than that in the long period from the early sixties up to now I had never failed to have a crop of apples – and, I might add, pears and plums also. [...] So much for the good old Gulf Stream'. He then addressed the subject in great detail in a very long newspaper column in 1915. The list of plums grown is astonishing: Rivers Prolific and yellow Myrobelle, Victorias, small Prince of Wales, Belle de Louvain, Prince Engelbert, Pond's seedling, Czar, Monarch, Cox's Emperor, River's late orange (a big, yellow plum) and, the latest of all, the Yorkshire Wydales, 'the better of a touch of frost'.

Over the years Osgood compared his results with much satisfaction to those of the most prestigious botanic gardens, such as Kew and Edinburgh. He was delighted when he could show round Mr Bean of Kew in about 1906. 'When I visit that charming collection in the temperate house in Kew [I] assure myself that I can grow a great many of its contents better in the open air, in the far north, than can be grown at Kew under glass'. Further, 'nothing would give me greater pleasure than to have a visit of inspection from some of the members of the Royal Horticultural Society'.[35] His generous friend, Professor Bayley Balfour of the Edinburgh Botanic Garden, had, in 1898, identified a *Scilla chinensis* (or *bernardia*) which had taken years to flower. In gratitude, Osgood gave him some and also *Fabiana imbricata* which they did not actually have there. He 'felt it quite a feather in my cap to be able to supply the Royal Botanic Gardens of Scotland with anything from my humble kailyard'.

Osgood's writings demonstrated a never-ending curiosity and willingness to accept the challenge of his west coast location.

> [1915] Though I am now more than three years past the allotted span of human life, I am still as keen as ever on trees and shrubs, and having gained a good deal of knowledge in the fifty years I have been prosecuting my hobby [...] I think I must once more tell of my successes and failures for the benefit of those who may not have experimented on exotics as long as I have done.

He was always prepared to try something new, particularly if it concerned a specimen which did not grow happily elsewhere. He explained which plantings had flourished and occasionally mentioned those which had not done so well. He provided lists and details, never hesitating to use the Latin names, with commentary about where they did best. For example, he planted *Iris stylosa* according to the 'special recipe kindly given me by the famous florist, Mr Peter Barr, – viz., at the foot of a hot south wall, on little else than gravel, and be both starved and baked' [1907]. Above all, he recognised the need for patience, waiting years for plants to flower, and encouraging his readers, as in 1915, never to give up:

> Occasionally disappointments do occur, such as the sudden withering up of some favourite tree or shrub from no accountable reason; but knowing there can be no forest without its withered tree, I console myself by repeating that good old proverb in its original Gaelic, "Cha neil coille gun a crianaich", and so I cheer up, and order another living plant immediately to replace the dead one.

Plant sourcing

Much has to be left to conjecture as to where Osgood sourced his plant collections. From the last decade of the nineteenth century he ventured afield more often, and surely used these journeys to observe, and acquire, more plants. Lady Cunninghame Graham, a niece of Osgood's first son-in-law, Robert Hanbury, told in an interview in 1988 how Osgood and Mairi travelled together, especially before she was married (1907) and 'always brought back something interesting'. A cousin of Mairi's confirmed that father and daughter went on long plant-collecting trips abroad, almost every year – 'where there was warm water to swim in and interesting plants to collect to bring home'.[36] At some stage he and Mairi went to the Drakensberg mountains in South Africa.[37] It is possible to identify nurseries and seedsmen incidentally from his newspaper articles and he mentioned a number of interesting plants given to him by friends.

Not surprisingly, the first source of plants was his own family. 'I at once dibbled a lot of the good old single *Narcissus Scoticus*, which I had got from my great-uncle at Kerrysdale. How they still bloom there every spring, though I planted them nearly sixty years ago'.[38] From his brother, Sir Kenneth, he obtained pines, 'one hundred plants of the right breed from his old native fir-wood of Glasleitir, on the shores of Loch Maree, which [...] are as different in growth and constitution from what are too often sold nowadays as Scots firs as Scots kale is from cauliflower'.[39]

It is also probable that Osgood sourced plants from the Hanbury Garden on the Italian Riviera. Known as La Mortola, it was established in 1867 by Sir Thomas Hanbury, a distant maternal relative. He was a Quaker philanthropist who had prospered as a Shanghai silk and tea merchant. 'His family were also building a garden at their home on the French [sic] Riviera and he, I believe, was able to bring plants from there'.[40] Osgood travelled to the Italian Riviera and lakes at least three times: once before 1898 when he saw *Ixia*; then from April to June 1905, driving on from Venice to the Konigsee and the Bavarian Highlands, 'one continuous Alpine garden', where he 'feasted on flowers', and again, in 1907, including a visit to the Glacier garden at Lucerne. As always, he compared what he could grow at Inverewe with what he had observed in distant parts: 'In a good July I have seen the tea-roses on my lower terrace wall almost as good as on the Riviera'.[41]

There are records of visits to Ceylon in 1906, Madeira in 1907,[42] Germany 1908 and Algeria and Spain in 1913. Comments in articles also made it clear that he had spent time, no date given, in Corsica (well before 1898) and the Pyrenees where he saw *Epipactus ensifolio*. His time in Corsica was particularly interesting in the horticultural sense. He saw his favourite Corsican pine in their native habitat and heard, 'in the ship-building yards at Savona that old Laricio timber was as good as the best Baltic redwood'.[43] He also saw a hillside covered with *Erica arboria*, 'in full bloom, and at first sight for a moment some of us thought a heavy shower of snow had fallen on those braes', which he then determined to buy and plant. Less innocently, he revealed in 1922 that he had had no compunction about grubbing up 'a tall, pale lemon coloured *orchis*, whose name I knew not' from the top of a hill in Corsica, 'while its neighbour, *panacratium illiricum* – also dug up in the same island – took some years to recover its temper', but did flower in 1896 and 1897. 'It grew in Corsica on the sandy beaches, where the waves of the tideless sea all but reached it, as well as in chinks in the limestone rocks quite inland, and thousands of feet above the Mediterranean Sea level'. He could not take it with him but he did get cuttings of the shrub *Fabiana inbricata* sent by post from Agaccio. It 'had flowered beautifully in June' in the garden of his hotel.

In Ceylon (1906) he particularly admired *Andromeda* or *Pieris formosa*. A fellow traveller, believed to be James Arthur Campbell, the creator of Arduaine, offered to give him a cutting from his own garden in Argyll to save him the trouble of bringing one back. He also supplied the unusual *Rhododendron zeylanicum* which Osgood had first seen in the highlands there, 5,000–8,000 feet above sea-level.

> They grow singly and in clumps on the grassy plains of Newera Eliya, which form the most perfect and most popular golf courses in the East; they have stems twelve to fifteen feet high, with heavy round tops like old orchard apple trees, only, of course, evergreen; the blooms are crimson, and very handsome they look among tree ferns and giant lobelias fifteen feet high.

He planted his specimen in Bamboosalem, and in 1919 placed the Peace Stone next to it.

On his travels, Osgood went to the Berlin Botanic Garden in 1908, where he saw *Cercidiphyllum japonicum*, 'which is about the best autumn coloured small tree I have ever seen; it turns the most gorgeous pink, carmine, and crimson, and grows like a willow'. In 1917 Osgood commented on flowers he had seen in the Middle East, though the date of his visit is not known: 'I noticed in Palestine that *Cyclamen persicum* throve to perfection in holes and chinks in pure limestone rocks, and what a sight they were in Galilee in early March'.[44] On the whole he appears to have admired plants *in situ* and not to have brought them back in quantity from his travels. Nor did he commission Victorian plant-hunters to add to his collections.

Closer to home, he travelled quite extensively within the UK. He certainly went to Cornwall before 1909 where he was particularly impressed with Caerhays Castle. The whole back was 'covered from top to bottom with the white and the red *Lapageria*, just as if it were covered in ivy'. He travelled in the county again in 1915, when he saw New Zealand *Dicksonias* 25 feet high. In his very last article he reported that he had seen a hedge of *Rhododendron ciliatum* in Cornwall, and 'I so lost my heart to the effect of the pinky white against the deep scarlet that I must needs copy it in a small way'. He spent time in Dorset in 1913 and 1916, being particularly complimentary about Lady Ilchester's garden at Abbotsbury, where he saw 'huge mounds of philesia' and various kinds of mimosa, 'almost like forest trees', and evergreen azaleas in rows and masses everywhere. However, he was 'left not a little elated' because his *Crinodendron* were 'far bigger and better' and he could grow *Embothrium* whereas they 'almost refuse to grow at all' at Abbotsbury. In 1921 he reported having flowers of *Convolvulus cheorum*, 'which was really at its best on the shortest day', on his table with Christmas roses besides it. He had acquired a bush of this shrubby, not climbing, plant at Ilchester. Norfolk was another part of the country that he visited more than once. He was delighted when, being away in June 1913, his gardener sent him 'a tin-box full of rarities blooming in my absence'.

Osgood seems to have been a fairly frequent visitor to the Botanic Gardens of Kew and Edinburgh and was keen to try shrubs which flourished in those prestigious places. When he created the 'Riviera' enclosure within his policies, from 1898 on, he planted 'a number of things of which I know little or nothing [...] such as [...] Aristotelias, Pittosporums, Rapphiolepsis [...] &c., and in spite of their names I must say they look happy; these I got mostly from my friend, the Regius Keeper of the Edinburgh Botanic Gardens, who so kindly allows me to experiment on some of his spare plants, and, in fact, to make my little enclosures regular Jardins d'Essai on a small scale'. This was somewhat disingenuous, as, between 1899 and 1922, Osgood received ten separate despatches of select plants, 146 in all, from these Botanic Gardens.[45]

On a visit to Kew in January 1916 he was 'very much struck' by *Rhododendron macronulata* seen flowering out in the open and 'though it is not easily got, I have managed to procure two plants of it!' There are several indications that Osgood attended some of the big horticultural showpieces. He went to the Chelsea Show in 1913 where he ordered fourteen hybrid 'Waterer' rhododendrons and, in the same year, saw *Caesalpinia pinnatifolia* in the famous Veitch garden at Coombe Wood near Kingston, Surrey.

Only towards the very end of his life did Osgood begin to weary of travel. In 1921 he turned down the opportunity for a floral tour of Cornwall by car because it was so far away and 'I am very old' and had had flu in the winter though, only the previous year, he had written to his friend, Mrs Wayne, who lived at Badentarbert, near Achiltibuie, to say he had a young friend with car who was planning to visit and who might drive him north to visit her there.[46]

Osgood was willing to search far and wide for the nurseries and seed catalogues from which he bought his specialities. Thousands of bulbs were purchased from Messrs. Anton Roozen of Overween, near Haarlem. He was appreciative, in his earlier gardening years, that they delivered for free and that each bulb was considerably cheaper than he could have bought it in UK, 'so who could find fault with me for dealing with a foreign house?' He had, for example, a monster *Campanula 'ostrowskya magnifica'* of Bokhara and *Ixias, Tigridias* and *Platycodons* which grew well in 1896. From M. van Houtte of Ghent, an explorer and nurseryman, he sourced the azaleas which formed the centre-piece of his 'America' area:

> Sixty plants in sixty different varieties or species. There are single and double hardy Ghent azaleas, and single azalea mollis, and double hybrids of mollis. [...] I can truly say there was not a bad plant or a bad variety among the lot, and every one of them was full on arriving.

In a series of three articles published in 1917 Osgood credited some of his favourite nurseries. One in France which provided him with some marvellous rhododendrons was a firm originating in the sixteenth century, founded by Philippe Victoire, Louis xv's botanist:

> I possess a Rhododendron of a very different style, gifted to me by M. de Vilmorin of Paris – viz., a new and as yet uncommon species from China, Rhododendron chartophillum. It is snow white, and has this peculiarity, and, I think, great merit about it that the delicate pale green young growths push up through the centres of the loose bunches of inflorescence and this takes away all stiffness, and makes the trusses of bloom, from a little distance, look as if they were a most tasteful combination of green and white. I do not know of any other Rhododendron with this quite peculiar and charming habit, and it is such a good doer here.

Another French supplier was Lemoine of Nancy, from whom he purchased a number of *Philadelphus* varieties. The company was world famous at the time for developing superior forms of lilac, cultivating about two hundred different selections.

From Ireland he had bought some of the plants which he was later to praise loud and long. Osgood acquired a *Solanum crispin autumnale* from Glasnevin, the National Botanic Garden in Dublin. He appreciated its 'masses of lavender blooms' and that 'it was such an easy thing to grow anywhere and its flowering season lasts such a long time'. The 'rare and beautiful' *Crinodendron hookeri*, (which he planted in his 'Riviera' in Spring 1897), *Abutilon vitifolia* and *Carpentaria californica*, which 'has a great name now, especially in Ireland, for hardiness and for its beautiful blossoms' all came, 'along with many other rarities, from Newry', as did his *Mitraria coccinea*. Osgood was also pleased to find, 'after considerable trouble', that Mr Smith's nursery was able to provide him with 'some good plants of *Erica arboria*, which we had so much admired on the hill-sides of Corsica. They seem to do very well here, and two of them bloomed this summer, but whether they will grow into trees in my 'Riviera' as they do on the shores of the Mediterranean I cannot yet tell'. All in all, Osgood was very satisfied with Mr Smith who 'keeps so many charming rarities'.

Osgood 'started for a trip to Ireland' on 28 April 1919 but whether this was his only visit is not known.[47]

Quite a long list can be made of British seed and plant suppliers: from Messrs. Wallace of Colchester he bought *Calochortus* and *Brodeas,* having seen them at the firm's stall at the 'last May Temple show'; from Veitch of Chelsea 'a delightful dwarf rhododendron'; from Amos Perry of Winchmore Hill '*linaria repens alba* along with several other good things'; from Mr Carter a 'wonderful batch' of seedling *Penstemon*, though he had subsequently been able to get better from the (unnamed) 'greatest horticulturalist' in Britain, together with *Lobelias* which were 'simply superb'; from Messrs Gauntlett, (late of Redruth), came a 'treasure', the *Eryngium pandanifolia*, which 'was only planted in April, and by October it had grown to an immense size, the foliage something like a glorified pine-apple, and the two flowering stalks were each ten foot high. [...] This year it has eight blooms, and it stood the winter perfectly', and from Messrs. Dobbie of Rothesay he got 24 cactus dahlia plants.[48]

In addition, Osgood was sent and given cuttings and seeds from friends and contacts near and far. 'According to the scant records of Osgood Mackenzie which still survive, some of his seeds and plants from around the world arrived at Inverewe by letter post, 130 years ago'.[49] These included those of the *Wellingtonia*. A *Dicksonia*, or tree-fern, planted in the new 'Riviera' in 1898, 'was raised from spores actually produced on its parent in Arran'. Seeds of *Cordyline australis* came from Scourie, in Sutherland.[50] A Norfolk friend gave him sixty little seedling plants of *R. ciliatum*, which, by 1922, had become 'a hedge 60 feet long in front of some tall crimson rhododendrons and it has been a great success and is now a solid mass of blooms from end to end'. As with all good gardeners he reciprocated. In addition to the donations he made to the Edinburgh Botanic Garden, he sent a sample of fragrant berries of *Eugenia ugni*, a kind of myrtle, to a friend in Switzerland.

Gardening influences

Osgood's lectures and newspaper articles were written in the spirit of encouragement and he willingly shared his practical knowledge and experiences. He had connections with some other local gardens. He visited, and certainly had an influence on, Lady Alice, wife of John Fowler, who bought Braemore Lodge in 1867, about forty miles away. Robert Hanbury attended Lady Alice's funeral and her obituary notice made reference to her friendship with the late Osgood Mackenzie of Inverewe, both being students of Highland lore and having knowledge of the botany of Ross-shire.[51] Dundonnell House, the home of Mr Hugh Mackenzie in the 1840s, and the Vaughan Lees by the late 1870s, was 25 miles away. Mairi told of her father purchasing an old camellia which had failed to flourish at Dundonnell but which 'flowered and lived a good while longer' at Inverewe.[52] It is very likely that much more plant interchange took place.

In 1920 Osgood signed his name in the Visitor Book of Baron von Shröder of Attadale House, Strathcarron, more than forty miles to the south. Mairi and Robert were there on at least three occasions, 1919–1923. It may well have been there that Osgood met C.W. Murray, owner of another renowned Wester Ross garden at Courthill, Loch Carron. He referred to visiting Courthill before 1899, admiring the bamboos and *Choisyas*.

There were several west coast gardens with which Osgood had useful contacts. James Arthur Campbell had started to develop his, at Arduaine, from 1903. After they had met in Ceylon in 1906 there were reciprocal visits. The Tournaig House visitor book shows that Campbell visited in 1908 and again in 1921.[53] In 1917 Osgood mentioned having seen *Dierama* at Arduaine and also 'several interesting new plants which are in course of being tried for their hardiness here-viz the *Gevuina,* which has so far proved itself quite hardy at Arduaine in Argyllshire for the last two or three winters'. In 1926 Campbell wrote a list, still extant, of the 'Rhododendrons at Inverewe'.

Craignish Castle, Ardfern, the Scottish home, since 1832, of the Trench-Gascoigne family, was another Argyllshire garden with which Osgood had links. Gwendolyn Gascoigne stayed at Tournaig 2–3 August 1921. The family would sail up the west coast to visit Inverewe. It was either at Arduaine or Craignish that Osgood saw *Abelia grandiflora,* a 'nice pink October-flowering shrub' which did quite well at Inverewe, though 'flowering much more profusely against a hot terrace-wall in Argyllshire'. In 1907 he praised a type of *Veronica* that he had got from Craignish Castle, 'whose special name I do not know, but which is, I fancy, a garden variety, is bright sky-blue, and is quite a feature in the present rather dreary December landscape!' Later he wrote of 'a Eugenia or Myrtle, which I got from Craignish, in Argyll; it flowers profusely in September and October'. Towards the end of October his *Eryngium pandanifolium,* 'just manages, (more or less), to perfect its steely-blue sea-thistly flowers'. He had seen one 'at Craignish lately, with a big sheaf of blooming stalks ten feet high'. Osgood Mackenzie was both the adviser and helper when Mrs Gascoigne made a 'wild, exotic hill-side garden, in the spirit of Inverewe at their Scottish home in Argyll'.[54] It was called the Mackenzie Garden after him. Research on Lotherton Hall, Leeds, the Gascoigne's English home, has suggested that the Edwardian Garden that Gwendolyn laid out there was also influenced by Osgood, despite the differences in climate and soil.[55]

Crarae was the third Argyllshire garden with which the Mackenzies were associated. George Campbell, whose mother began planting woodlands there, 1912–1925, stayed at Tournaig for over a week in April 1921. He extended her work into a 'Himalayan style' rhododendron paradise from the mid-1920s. Through his acquaintance with Lady Gascoigne at Craignish, Osgood is believed to have met Ellen Willmott, (1858–1934), the famous gardener of Wardley Place, Sussex. It does not though seem that John H. Dixon took with him many ideas from Inverewe when he developed an Italian and Japanese garden at his new home of Dundarach, Pitlochry, though it is believed that Osgood did pay a visit.

The weather

All gardening is weather-dependent and, for most local would-be gardeners, the rain, wind and lack of sun of north-west Scotland prove to be too daunting. It is the wonder of Inverewe that exotic trees, shrubs and flowers flourish at a latitude of almost 58° North.

> The exposure [...] was awful, catching, as it did, nearly every gale that blew. With the exception of the thin low line of the north end of Lewis, forty miles off, there was nothing between its top and Labrador; and it was continually being soused with salt spray. The braes above the site of the house were somewhat better, but even they were swept by the south-westerly gales, which are so constant and so severe in these parts.[56]

The worst did not always come from the south-west. 3 October 1860, just before Osgood acquired his estates, there was a sadly memorable 'Great Storm':

> A day that will never be forgotten by those who witnessed its terrible events. A number of open boats with their crews were at the head of Loch Ewe near Boor, Cliff House, and Poolewe, setting nets for herrings, when a storm suddenly came on, far exceeding in violence any other storm before or since, so far as those now living remember. A hurricane sprang up from the west-north-west, of such extraordinary force as actually to lift boats and their crews from the water, and in one or two cases to overturn the boats. Happily most of the men clung to their boats, and were soon washed ashore. One boat was carried rapidly past the point called Ploc-ard, by Inverewe House. As she was

> passing close to some big stones one of her crew jumped out on to a rock, but was washed off and drowned. In another boat, opposite Cliff House, there were four men; the boat was capsized and three of the men were drowned; the fourth had tied himself to the boat which came ashore by Cliff House. [...] The bodies of the drowned men were recovered, and were buried in the Inverewe churchyard, where the date of this memorable storm is recorded on a gravestone over the remains of two of the men named William Urquhart and Donald Urquhart.[57]

In his writings, Osgood did not make frequent reference to the 'usual' challenges of the climate, only to extremes. Wind, frost, rain and, sometimes, drought are mentioned in passing in some of his articles. In many respects wind can be the most damaging of all as it destroys the work of years. In November 1920, after an exceptionally sunny and frost-free autumn, Osgood must have been heartbroken. On 15 November there was a cyclone and '2,600 of our trees were torn up by their roots or their stems snapped right across, all of them from 50 to 56 years old, and from 60 to 70 feet high, and all, I may say, planted with my own hands'.

Frost also could be destructive. All the winters from 1866 until 1871 were harsh, as was 1875. However, 1876 and 1877 were very mild. He made no mention of the blizzard recorded in the Poolewe School Log Book: '3 Dec 1878: 15 inches of snow on ground. There has not been such a snow storm since 13 years, such is the general report', though he does concur with the School record with respect to 1881: '15 Jan: New Year Holidays. Heavy fall of snow last week. It was reported that there was not the like of it for the last 30 years – the frost was most intense'. This 'exceptionally severe' month saw trains becoming lost and buried in the snow. In 1894–1895 there were five weeks of blizzards and storms, cutting off Dingwall and Skye through much of January and February.[58] 'One of the most severe storms ever experienced in the west has been raging for the last few days. The roads are blocked and the cold is most intense' was noted in February 1902.[59]

1909–10 was a very hard winter:

> The worst and most deadly time of frost and snow I have ever encountered since I started growing all those less well known exotics. We had 18 to 20 degrees of frost, [...] consequently I lost a few things, such as a fine young Acacia dealbata, which had stood out four or five winters, which was a good height. [...] I lost one of my two lomatias [...] and two out of seven of my Ericas arboria, about 8ft. high, a good height for heaths to grow in the far north.

In November 1912 there came a 'night or two of hard frost [...] at a time of year when severe weather is most unusual on this coast, and unfortunately for us, in this case the West Coast suffered as much as the East. Nearly every rambler rose was cut down here. [...] Till then I thought ramblers were as hardy as willows. [...] I do not know what came over the Phormiums, as I have grown them for many a long year with such success, and only very occasionally have I seen the more delicate variegated ones touched a little; but last November the whole lot of them [...] were injured'.

Even worse was an unusual late spring frost in 1915 which 'did a lot of harm to the young growths of various species of the rarer Rhododendrons, and when I returned [mid-June] many of them looked badly, but, in spite of the awful drought of last summer, they have managed to repair their losses wonderfully by starting entirely fresh growths'.

More often, Osgood could comment on the mildness of the season and the benefits this brought. He recognised that the prevailing influence was the Gulf Stream. This, plus 'lots of peat and shelter' allowed, as he was pleased to point out when visiting the Isle of Wight, plants like *Agapanthus* to be left outdoors all year round, without any protection even in winter.[60] From 18 October to 11 November 1897, 'we had neither rain, wind, frost or fog, and hardly even a cloud. Under these most unusual circumstances, flowers bloomed as they had hardly ever bloomed before. [...] We imagined ourselves in California, or in some such wonderful clime'.

The winter of 1897–98 remained very mild. November and December 1916 were also remarkable in this respect:

> No frost as yet (November 25th). [...] The thermometer goes up sometimes to 50 and even one day to 55 and this, together with the great blessing of having usually an early Spring here, makes the much dreaded winters pass so easily and quickly; and how different it must be where in many Scottish and English homes the gardens are dreary deserts, the effect of some cruel frost in September. [...]
>
> 9th of December, and there has not been as much as one degree of frost at Inverewe yet!

The pleasing consequence of this was that, as in 1915, 'we are generally full of flowers through the most, if not the whole, of November, and thus can rejoice in the prolongation of the time of flowers by about two months, which shortens the winter so'.

Osgood did not consider the rainfall to be a problem: 'This is supposed to be a very wet part of the country, but, according to my gardener, who keeps his rain-gauge very carefully, we had under 55 inches in 1907, whereas there are places in Britain where the fall is 130 and even 140 inches'. To make the point, Robert Campbell, the gardener, sent a letter to *The Scotsman* with all the details, though it did actually rain on 210 days in the year![61] The 1920 Guide to the area commented positively how 'the rainfall of the district has long been over-estimated' and that 'the average for the months of May, June and July – the months always most strongly recommended for visitors – are the lowest for the year, and next comes the month of September'.[62]

Even if the weather did get bad, Osgood had, over the years, learned that he could cope: 'January [1916], I was told, was something awful up here in the way of hurricanes and floods, but there was next to no frost, so my tenderest exotics did not mind the weather in their snug corners'. In 1914 there was a drought, but even that brought its advantages. The *Rhododendron falconerii* did extremely well because of 'the very great ripening it got during the past hot and dry summer' and the following 'grand sunny year' brought with it the best crop of plums 'we ever had since the garden was first made over fifty years ago. [...] Some branches broke with the weight of fruit'.

Pests

In addition to the weather, Osgood obviously had to contend with some of the common pests and threats to gardening. He knew he had to fence his land against sheep from the very beginning if he wanted to grow anything. Grouse were not a problem, though black game carefully picked 'all the leading buds out of the little Scots firs' to do 'their level best to make them like the bushy *Pinus montana.* Brown hares and blue hares cut some of the fat young shoots of the Austrian pines and oaks; but, on the whole, my young trees fared well in comparison with the way young plantations here would fare now from the rabbit plague, and the roe, and the red deer'.

By the time he wrote his book he was having to enclose his spaces with six-foot fences to make them safe.[63] His recipe, provided in 1915, 'for having patches of brilliant colouring and flowers for cutting from December to the end of March' was to make 'a rabbit-proof enclosure, large or small, which must be on a slope facing due south and very sheltered, surrounded at back and side with tall trees, in fact a sun trap, with a wind break in front of from twelve to fifteen feet high to keep out the south-west gales'. Rabbits, ironically, had been introduced to the north of Scotland by his grandfather who had deliberately brought them from England to his Dingwall estate, the 'darling, lovely little pets' and 'dear little innocents'![64] Osgood discovered that the Corsican pine, which he so strongly recommended, was 'proof against cattle, sheep, deer, and rabbits, which no other tree is that I know of'[65] and the native crowberry he gave, in 1909, 'the very highest character in every way; for, though it is rather slow of growth, it eventually reaches 20 feet or more, and luckily it is not much eaten by rabbits and still it makes excellent woodcock cover'.

Once, but only once, in 1898, he mentioned slugs as a problem, which he dealt with by putting down slices of potatoes and turnips as counter attractions. But nowhere is there reference to midges, the greatest deterrent of all to the enthusiastic west coast gardener. Perhaps he was not the weeder-in-chief! His daughter, Mairi, was much more of a 'hands-on' gardener and certainly appreciated the unpleasantness of the 'wee beasties'.[66]

So, Polson's 1920 guide-book, could comment on the 'wonderful gardens' of Inverewe House, 'reclaimed from a rocky hillside, and laid out with exquisite taste by the proprietor, Mr O.H. Mackenzie, who has proved that with a little care and forethought almost any plant between the tropics and the Arctic circle can be got to grow here; and a walk through the place, with Mr Mackenzie as guide, is a liberal education, as he can point out shrubs from North and South America, from Germany, France, Corsica, Northern Africa, China, Japan, New Zealand and Australia flourishing side by side, some of them growing to a size which is simply marvellous in our climate. All the year round there is a wonderful profusion of flowers, whose peculiar vividness of colour is accounted for by the warm moist climate'.[67]

Staff

In the Peace Shrubbery area of Bamboosalem there is the one and only engraved stone to be found in Inverewe Garden. Commemorating the end of the First World War, the dedication reads:

The preparation and planting were all done
By Donald Grant aged 77
His faithful friend and servant
For over 50 years

When he was about sixteen, Osgood told how 'we had a favourite sailor and fisherman in our employ at that time and for many years after, William Grant.

[...] Three or four of these Grants have served me faithfully and devotedly all through my long life, and one of them (Donald) is still serving me, aged seventy-nine'.[68] Donald outlived Osgood to serve Mairi also.

The story of Donald Grant and his family was typical. Generations of the same family served first Osgood's mother, then him and then his daughter.[69] Some stalwarts were recognised in *A Hundred Years*, though more in connection with Osgood's pursuit of game than his garden. Two estate staff had tombstones erected in their honour in the Old Burial Ground. One was for George Maclennan of Londubh, who was *'foreman of works, Inverewe Estate for 40 years. Died 15/4/1903 aged 84.'* Osgood recalled 'my old faithful servant, George Maclennon, telling me a story which shows how scarce anything in the form of bread was even in comparatively modern times'.[70] The other was for John Grant:

> *Erected by Osgood as a token of his great regard for John Grant who served him and the Gairloch family faithfully all his life. He died at Strondubh House 27th September aged 66 years. An cuimhna air Iain Granade etc.*

Osgood remembered how 'big boy, John Grant, came over to us at Gairloch with the bread and the letters once or twice a week. How well I can remember him standing, usually dripping wet, shivering in the Tigh Dige kitchen, while the cook expressed lively indignation because the bread-bag was soaking wet. That lad served me as a man very faithfully for many years as grieve after I bought Inverewe in 1862'. John had met the packet steamer which came once or twice each week from Stornoway. He was known as "Big John" and once carried the fat Post Office official, as well as the post, for several miles after he fainted.[71]

Osgood took him onto his estate staff and recounted how 'my good and faithful grieve John Grant, when at the head of his squad (long before mowing machines were ever thought of) used to be quite annoyed at the continual hindrance to the scythe work through men stopping to raid bees' nests in the grass, and losing time in eating the honey. [...] My old sheep manager, Alexander Cameron, better known to his many friends as the Tournaig Bard on account of his being such a good Gaelic poet and improvisatore, owned a collie dog in the 'sixties which learned to point at bees' nests'.[72]

This Alexander Cameron, the 'Tournaig Bard', was another loyal worker, based at the farm where 'the road bends to the left and passes the Tournaig farm buildings'.[73] He remained sheep manager for over thirty years and his son, Murdo, worked with the trees and shrubs of the Inverewe estate for more than forty years.

One of Osgood's first servants was 'My dear old foreman of works, [...]

George of Rory Merchant, who was at the head of everything, and who did everything for me at Inverewe when I began there in 1862'.[74] At much the same time he took on John Matheson. Osgood was clearly very fond of his 'late faithful friend and gamekeeper, John Matheson, who came to me when he was sixteen and I was nineteen, and lived all his life with me'.[75] In court in 1892 John testified that he had been gamekeeper at Inverewe for nearly 30 years and was aged 46.[76] The man loyally repaid his master by giving evidence on his behalf on several issues. Matheson was the skilled 'dog-breaker' whose death, shortly before the First World War, resulted in Osgood gave up breeding his beloved setters.

'Our present stalker, Donald Urquhart, who has also been all his days with us' was another valued servant.[77] He was highly praised in Osgood's book for his hunting of both foxes and eagles.[78] Donald accompanied Osgood on his winter stay at the Roxburgh Hotel in Edinburgh 1920–1921.[79]

Robert Campbell was the one Inverewe 'gardener' credited as such in the Valuation Rolls. He was first recorded as having an estate house in 1892/3 but had been working for Osgood before then as Robert Hanbury recorded his death in 1921: 'poor old Campbell, end of July, after an operation in Inverness and was buried at Poolewe. He had been at Inverewe 33 years'.[80] His family recall that Robert's wife continued to be allowed to live in a 'staff house' for the rest of her life and was given free coal.[81] The work in the wider policies would have been undertaken by estate men as required, but they were not nominated as 'gardeners'. Mairi also mentioned a Kenneth John Urquhart as having worked for the family for over forty years.[82]

There are two incidental mentions of other staff. The first was in a letter of 1922 to his friend, Mrs Wayne. Osgood informed her that he had had flu in Edinburgh and that 'our Tournaig ploughman's wife, his dairymaid, died of it. She had 7 children'. This was the wife of the younger John Matheson.[83] The second, in a memoir by a locally born man, told that his father was the chauffeur/ handyman employed at Inverewe after being demobbed from the army in 1918. 'In those days Kenny-John and my father were the only outdoor staff permanently employed at Inverewe, both of them remaining there until they eventually retired after the nts took over ownership of the garden'.[84]

The domestic staff employed followed the same pattern of continuity and commitment to the Mackenzie family. Osgood told of Kate Archy, housekeeper at Tigh Dige. She was 'widow of Fraser, our gardener, and mother of a daughter who succeeded her and remained with the family all her life'.[85] Jane Macgregor had been parlour maid to Lady Mackenzie since 1863 and held the same position with her son before his marriage. She stayed with the family until September 1877. The wife of Alexander Cameron, Jessie Macpherson or Cameron of Tournaig, was a parlour maid at Inverewe the year before Osgood married and then became maid to Mrs Mackenzie. Christina Mackenzie was then the cook and Margaret Packman the housemaid. Other servants were Mrs Johanna Bethune and Mrs Isabella Maclean. Almost all testified in Court to support Osgood's kindness to, and concern for, his wife. It was his personal tragedy that he failed to win her affection and loyalty in the way he appeared to have gained that of his staff.

Appendix

Osgood's Known Travels 1862–1922

DATE	EUROPE and BEYOND	UK
Before 1877	Brazil	
1878		Isle of Wight
1897		Kew
? but before 1899	Italian Riviera; Corsica	Torridon; Ord in Skye; Scourie; Courthill, Loch Carron; Norfolk
1905	Venice, Italian Riviera, Konigsee, Bavarian Highlands (one trip)	
1906	Ceylon	
Before 1907		Tour of Argyll, including Poltalloch ('lately')
1907	Italian Riviera, Glacier Garden (Lucerne); Madeira	South of Scotland: Perthshire, Midlothian and Fife
1908	Germany (including Berlin Botanic Garden)	West side of Harris (autumn)
1913	Algeria and Spain	Chelsea Show; Norfolk (June); Abbotsbury Gardens, Dorset; Veitch Nursery at Coombe Wood; from Skye to Loch Hourn (August)
1915		Cornwall (Spring); Sussex, Norfolk
1916		'The South'; Kew (January); Abbotsbury Garden, Dorset; Monreithin, Galloway; Arduaine
1919	Ireland	
1920		Edinburgh
1922		Edinburgh
Unknown	South Africa – Drakensberg; Palestine, Galilee (March)	

References and Notes

Osgood Mackenzie wrote the following articles. All quotations are from these unless otherwise stated.

DATE	TITLE	SOURCE
1887 1 October	Exotics Hardy on the West Coast	*The Scotsman*
1898 25 January	Floral Notes from the West Coast of Ross-shire	*The Scotsman*
1899 13 January	Floral Notes from the West Coast of Ross-shire	*The Scotsman*
1907 15 January	Floral Notes from the North-West of Scotland	*The Scotsman*
1908	Gardening in the Western Highlands	*Journal of the RHS.* Vol 34, pp.47–53
1909 27 March	A Garden in the North	*Glasgow Herald*
1911 7 October	Floral Notes from West Ross	*Glasgow Herald*
1913 18 November	Floral Notes from the West coast of Ross-shire	*The Scotsman*
1915 30 November	Floral Notes from the North	*The Scotsman*
1917	A Year in the Garden on the North-West Coast of Ross-shire	*Journal of the RHS.* Vol 43, pp.79–95
1917 2 January	Monthly Floral Notes from the North-West Coast of Ross-shire I, March-May	*The Scotsman*
1917 9 January	Monthly Floral Notes from the North-West Coast of Ross-shire II, June-August	*The Scotsman*
1917 16 January	Monthly Floral Notes from the North-West Coast of Ross-shire III, September-December	*The Scotsman*
1921 7 February	Rhododendrons All the Year Round	*The Scotsman*
1922 9 March	Early Spring Flowers in the North	*The Scotsman*
1922 19 April	March Flowers in the Far North-West (published posthumously)	*Glasgow Herald*

[1] Mackenzie, p.245.

[2] Mackenzie, p.247. Lady Mary's direct involvement in this 'home-making' was to pose significant problems when Osgood came to marry.

[3] Wright, p.23.

[4] Wright, pp.25–28.

[5] *The Highland Sportsman*, 1882.

[6] Thereafter the 'gardens and offices' were included so it is not possible to see if the value changed.

[7] Dixon, p.318.

[8] He had not actually intended to take them that year, but did so to help Osgood's finances after the failed Loch Dubh court case. See Chapter VII.

[9] *George Washington Wilson Photographic Archive*, Aberdeen University. Early print at Inverewe House.

[10] Wright, p.27. A photograph taken in the mid-1880s showed the markings of a tennis court on this front lawn. Gairloch Heritage Museum Photographic Archive.

[11] Herbert Asquith, *Moments of Memory* (London: Hutchinson, 1937), p.88.

[12] Ross-shire Valuation Rolls, Highland Council Archives, Inverness.

[13] Wright, p.29.

[14] Personal communication from E.R.C. Mouat, grandson of Robert Campbell, Osgood's 'kitchen' gardener.

[15] Wright, pp.31–32.

[16] Poolewe School Log Book, 25 April 1914.

[17] Vice-Admiral Humphrey Hugh Smith, *An Admiral Never Forgets* (1936). Gairloch Heritage Museum Archives.

[18] Robert Hanbury's *Game Book*.

[19] Macleod, p.31.

[20] Correspondence with Mrs Wayne, 11 March 1922. Inverewe House Archive.

[21] Robert Hanbury's *Game Book*. When the Gate Lodge was built is rather a mystery as it does not appear on the 1905 Six Inch Ordnance Survey map, nor in any of the older photographs.

[22] Butler, *Memories*.

[23] These articles became more frequent, though never regular, in the last decade of his life. The section in *A Hundred Years* (1921) was based on a paper given to the Royal Horticultural Society in London as early as 12 May 1908.

[24] Macleod, p.130. These note-books were not found after Mairi's death in July 1953.

[25] Mackenzie, p.62.

[26] Mackenzie, p.247. Osgood Mackenzie had no formal horticultural training. Though he used botanical Latin with ease it was not always correct – and

nomenclature has changed considerably in the past century. All plant names in quotations are as he wrote them.

27 Byam Shaw, p.78.

28 Mackenzie, p.253.

29 Wright, p.23.

30 Dixon, pp.318–319.

31 Mackenzie, pp.247–249.

32 He also referred to one he had written in 1897 on growing fruit but this has not been found.

33 In 2004 Duncan Donald, then Property Manager at Inverewe, compiled a list of the plants which Osgood Mackenzie had had sent from the Edinburgh Botanic Gardens between 1899 and 1922.

34 Polson, p.20.

35 Mackenzie, p.252.

36 Transcript of an interview 'Memories of Inverewe' by Margaret Cuthbert, c.1990. Inverewe House Archive.

37 Macleod, p.40.

38 Mackenzie, p.232.

39 Mackenzie, p.249. Scottish Natural Heritage also found, when they first started planting trees in the Beinn Eighe Reserve, that not all Scots Pine will grow successfully in the area. They have had to source 'the right breed' of *Pinus sylvestris* locally.

40 Jeremy Laing, undated, unattributed magazine article, quoting Prof. Henderson, then property manager of Inverewe, c.1992. Inverewe House Archive.

41 Mackenzie, p.257.

42 Letter from Osgood Mackenzie asking for a letter of introduction as he was going to Madeira for two weeks, 28 January 1907. Inverewe House Archive.

43 Mackenzie, p.248.

44 The visit must have been pre-war as no foreign travel was undertaken by Osgood, or his daughter and son-in-law, between 1914 and Spring 1919.

45 As per Duncan Donald's listing.

46 Letter, 25 May 1921, in Inverewe House Archive.

47 Robert Hanbury's *Game Book*.

48 Interestingly, most of these purchase attributions are in the earlier articles.

49 Laing, c.1992. Inverewe House Archive.

50 Mackenzie, p.200.

51 Undated newspaper cutting in one of the photograph albums, Inverewe House. John Fowler designed much of the London Metropolitan Railway, (forerunner of

the underground railways), later served as an engineer in the development of the London subway system and then designed and built the Forth Rail Bridge (1882–90) in Scotland, the first major structure made of steel. A prototype for this, a small suspension bridge, was built over the Corrieshalloch Gorge at his Wester Ross home. Lady Fowler's 'Fern Walk' is all that remains of her garden. It was estimated that about six million trees were planted on the Braemore estate.

52 M.T. Sawyer, 'Inverewe: A Garden in the North West Highlands', *Journal of the Royal Horticultural Society*, Vol. LXXV Part II, 1950, pp.436–444.

53 Inverewe House Archive.

54 Nancy Boydell, 'The Gardens at Lotherton Hall' *Garden History*, Vol. 6, No. 2 (Summer, 1978), pp.11–15.

55 Mette Eggen's dissertation on Lotherton Hall is held at the University of York. There is correspondence from her in the Inverewe House Archive.

56 Mackenzie, p.246.

57 Dixon, p.171.

58 Vallance, p.116.

59 Poolewe School Log Book.

60 Mackenzie, p.257.

61 Letters Page, *The Scotsman*, 6 January 1908.

62 Polson, p.14.

63 Mackenzie, pp.246–252.

64 Mackenzie, pp.64–65.

65 Mackenzie, p.248.

66 Macleod, p.21.

67 Polson, p.18. Polson made good use of Dixon's *Guide to Gairloch* as his reference book. Although he published in 1920 the reference to Inverewe House makes it clear that he had visited before the House burnt down in April 1914. Perhaps the War delayed printing.

68 Mackenzie, p.143.

69 The Valuation Rolls provide names of staff who were living in estate properties worth £4 per annum but not those who lived independently or in estate accommodation of lesser value. Census information is not specific about which local people worked at Inverewe. There were other local proprietors who employed 'gardeners' and farm labourers. The Divorce papers and newspaper accounts referred to some employees, in particular to the domestic servants. Great loyalty to the Mackenzie household was proven through their testimonies to the courts. Mairi Sawyer referred to three long-serving staff in her chapter in *A Hundred Years*.

70 Mackenzie, p.181.

[71] Mackenzie, p.32–3. '1862' should, as always, be 1863.
[72] Mackenzie, pp.47–48.
[73] Dixon, p.194. There is more on the Tournaig Bard in Chapter x.
[74] Mackenzie, p.39.
[75] Mackenzie, pp.165–166.
[76] *The Mackenzie Case*, p.133.
[77] Mackenzie, p.166.
[78] Mackenzie, p.150. See Chapter viii.
[79] Robert Hanbury's *Game Book.*
[80] Robert Hanbury's *Game Book.*
[81] Personal communication from Katriona Lloyd, great-grand-daughter of Robert Campbell. A photograph, sent by his family, showing them all standing outside the house known as Tigh an Uilt, (still there as staff accommodation), is in the Inverewe House Archive. One of Robert's children, Annie, became a pupil teacher at Poolewe School in 1903 and was then helped financially to go to college in Edinburgh to qualify. (She eventually returned to the area to teach.)
[82] 'Kenny-John' outlived Mairi Sawyer, and was the first 'head gardener' once Inverewe was taken over by the National Trust for Scotland in 1953. He finally retired in 1964.
[83] Letter to Mrs Wayne, 11 March 1922. Inverewe House Archive. Robert Hanbury's *Game Book* provided the name of the deceased.
[84] Kenneth C. Mackenzie, *Yesterday's Poolewe* (Booklet published privately, 2002).
[85] Mackenzie, p.108.

People

30. Family and Staff outside the Mansion House, *c.*1885

31. Mairi Mackenzie, exquisitely attired

32. 'An accomplished young woman'

33. The proud father

34. John H. Dixon, author of *Gairloch and Guide to Loch Maree*

35. Robert Hanbury, who married Mairi in April 1907

36. Osgood, Mairi and Robert on a family outing

37. Osgood in his garden at Inverewe

38. Robert Campbell, Osgood's 'gardener', with his family in the Walled Garden at Inverewe

39. The 'Peace Stone', Inverewe Garden

40. Osgood was buried with his mother in the Gairloch burial ground

CHAPTER XIV

Mairi Mackenzie of Tournaig

'Miss Mackenzie is held in high esteem in the district.'

Tournaig

With the purchase of the Tournaig lands in 1863 Osgood Mackenzie had acquired a farmhouse, out-buildings, grazings, with sundry 'biggings yeards orchyards tofts crofts outfield lands infield lands loanings grasings shealings woods' and it was here that he set up his farming enterprises.[1] He had agreed, before his marriage in May 1877, that his mother should not live with him and Minna, but no arrangements were made to provide her with another home. She stayed with her step-son, Francis, at Kerrysdale for a while, clearly hoping that her absence from Inverewe would be short term. However, Minna, her father and Sir Kenneth all insisted that the promised separate provision must be made for her. Although Minna would much have preferred that she left the area completely, it was decided that the Dowager Lady would have a house built for her at Tournaig, financed by a loan from Sir John Moss. It was less than two miles north along the road.

This lodge was designed by the architects Matthews and Lawrie, of Inverness – a different company from that engaged for Inverewe but one which had been involved in other Mackenzie house-building in Easter Ross.[2] Lady Mary moved in June 1879 'rather before it was finished' and 'from that time forward Tournaig was my home. [...] I had my furniture put into Tournaig, and that was my home entirely after it was finished'.[3]

It was not a small house, but certainly had not been built in the expectation that the married couple, and eventually family, would also be living in it. The first time Osgood rented out Inverewe House to raise some income his mother went away so he could have use of her home. When Osgood, with baby Mairi, came to stay in the spring of 1880 the assumption seemed to have been that Minna had left for good. When she arrived, anticipating a return to Inverewe and finding that not possible, there were considerable accommodation problems. Probably there were five bedrooms in all, as well as public rooms, but this was insufficient for mother, the married couple – who now required separate bedrooms – the various servants and the young lad visiting. Once Minna had left, Inverewe remained the nominal family home, but circumstances and the financial imperatives combined to make Tournaig the main residence of the Mackenzie family for much of the year for the rest of Osgood's life.[4]

In 1886 John H. Dixon wrote in glowing terms:

> The highroad now takes an easterly course, and passing young plantations, soon comes in sight of Loch-nan-Dailthean. Here is Tournaig, [...] described in the *Times* letter just quoted, as follows:-
>
> "Even more noteworthy, perhaps, is the less pretentious garden at Mr Mackenzie's pretty cottage of Tournaig. [...] There, a mere pit in the heather, which must have originally resembled a stone quarry, has been turned, chiefly by blasting, into a little fairyland of leafy luxuriance and gorgeous colouring, though where the plants find soil to strike their roots is a puzzle. As for the cabbages, in their swelling proportions they are rather like balloons than ordinary vegetables. And it must be a piquant experience to stroll of a morning among flower-beds that recall the beauties of Bellagio or the Isola Bella, and afterwards to go out ptarmigan shooting or deer-stalking on some of the most storm-beaten hills in the whole breadth of the Highlands".[5]

An accomplished young lady

It was here that Osgood's only child was brought up. It is difficult to judge how Mairi was affected by the acrimonious relationship between her parents throughout her formative years. Nurse Bain, the Gaelic-speaking servant, (appointed by Osgood without discussion with his wife in March 1879), stayed with the family until March 1883 but Mairi's chief carer was always her grandmother. The Dowager Lady Mary certainly took the responsibility of supervising her grand-daughter's upbringing very seriously and seemed to have remained active and healthy well into old age. Her parlour maid, Jane Macgregor, said she was 'a lady of extraordinary activity ... I should not say great strength, she was very hearty'.[6] According to Osgood's testimony in the 'Access' hearings in 1887, his mother was implementing such a regulated course of instruction that there was no opportunity for Minna to visit her daughter during the week.

Mairi never attended any school and, as consistently advocated by her grandmother for all local children, was said to have spoken only Gaelic until she was seven years old. The one and only reference Osgood made to Mairi in his autobiography was when discussing the family custom of speaking in Gaelic at home: 'To-day my daughter and I do the same'.[7] This early concentration on Gaelic was the explanation given later for her reluctance to write in English, her poor handwriting and idiosyncratic spelling. Letters to her Hanbury relatives at Green End, Hertfordshire, had to be left on the kitchen table for days whilst members of the family worked out, bit by bit, what was written.[8] Nonetheless, in 1887 it was claimed that Mairi was 'exceptionally far advanced for her age'.[9] In the early 1890s Tournaig was extended, apparently to provide accommodation for a governess for the child.

Mairi may not always have been a diligent pupil though, preferring the outdoor life. She liked to walk barefoot, particularly if in a hurry, which was attributed to her rather tomboyish upbringing.[10] One governess 'would often toil down from the house to fetch her in (from the Cuddy Rock) to do her lessons. [...] This governess had been youngish and interested in gardening. In fact she had helped to plant Mairi's very first rhododendrons, on an island in the lochan opposite another home of the family – the house of Tournaig, a mile or two north of Inverewe'.[11]

Mairi did pay occasional visits to the local school in Poolewe. She went with her grandmother and Philip Ogilby, (a young relative), in April 1889 'and stayed from three to four'; accompanied her father, grandmother and a temperance lecturer, who 'made a short speech to the children', in February 1891; returned in June 1893, when she 'remained during the greater part of the sewing hour', this time with her grandmother and Governess; in March 1894 a record was made that 'Dowager Lady Mackenzie and Miss Mackenzie visited the school. Miss Mackenzie invited the scholars to their annual treat', (the first mention of a 'Mackenzie', rather than 'Dixon', treat for the village children), and finally, at the end of October 1896, 'scholars examined in RK today. Prizes were distributed by Miss Mackenzie of Inverewe'.[12]

The headteacher at Poolewe School logged two further visits several years later:

> 17 October 1902: The school was visited this afternoon by Miss Mackenzie of Inverewe, along with two other ladies. They inspected the drawing and heard several Gaelic and English songs – two part harmony and they expressed themselves well satisfied.
>
> 13 May 1904: Miss Mackenzie and the Kembles of Knock visited.

Osgood obviously concurred with his mother's decision to educate Mairi at home, as was the family tradition. He criticised the local schools for not providing a curriculum fit for purpose, (though as a School Board manager it might have been thought that he had some influence on the matter): 'I am afraid that education, when it takes the shape of drawing, French and music, has made the present generation of girls very unsuitable as wives for young west-coast crofters'.[13] Echoing her father's views, Mairi herself, as an adult, expressed the same lack of confidence in public education, considering people had mostly been far happier, a good deal wiser and worked much better before 'all these grand lessons made girls despise domestic chores, and so many boys want more money and excitement than they can get working on a croft'.[14]

Osgood clearly made a distinction between the education of 'crofter children' and his own daughter, given the wording of a newspaper advertisement placed by the Dowager in 1894. A German lady, with drawing and painting skills, was required as holiday governess for a girl of fifteen.[15] The evidence from Mairi's sketchbook and some surviving paintings shows that she used watercolours quite skilfully.[16]

In addition to her artistic talent, Mairi was a very competent spinner. The wool came from her own sheep.[17] She also had a keen interest in outdoor pursuits, encouraged and tutored, no doubt, by her father. In an undated photograph she was standing outside the front door of the Mansion House, one hand in her father's and the other clutching a gun, mirroring the one her father was holding. She must have been about eight at the time![18] She played a full part in hunting expeditions with her first husband and the shooting tenants of Inverewe and Kernsary and was fully capable of doing her own stalking and shooting, just needing help to lift the deer carcase onto the pony. She readily skinned and butchered the venison. She was also an enthusiastic and 'very fine fisherwoman' all her life, maintaining boats at both the Fionn Loch and Loch Kernsary. Fortunately, she was able to complete the process, being renowned for her cooking.[19]

Despite her upbringing in the remote Highlands, Mairi had a wide social life. In 1898 she attended the Northern Meeting, and again in 1906.[20] Posed photographs of her as a young woman show her immaculately and expensively dressed. She was reputed to be very attractive to men.[21]

Mairi's marriage

The Scotsman, 29 December 1906, announced the engagement of 'Maire Thyra, only daughter of Osgood Mackenzie of Inverewe, to Robert J. Hanbury, second son of George Hanbury of Burnham, Bucks.' He was her cousin. William Cameron, Headteacher at Poolewe School, recognised the occasion:

> 5 April 1907: Tonight the School Board Clerk, Mr W.B. MacRae and I and a few local gentlemen are to wait upon Miss Mackenzie of Inverewe and to present her with a fruit service (£25) on behalf of her friends and the public of Gairloch parish on the occasion of her forthcoming marriage on 18th inst. Miss Mackenzie is held in high esteem in the district. Her father is the respected Chairman of the Gairloch School Board.[22]

On 18 April 1907 they married, 'very quietly, on account of mourning', (Robert's grandmother had died the previous November), in Holy Trinity Church, Brompton, London.[23] Mairi pasted the Service programme of R.J.H. and M.T.H. into her album. Given the photographs and postcards of Lago Maggiore, Firenze and Milan which follow immediately, it seems likely that the honeymoon was spent in northern Italy. A conservatory was added to Tournaig house the following year.[24]

On 2 May 1908 Mairi gave birth to her first child. Two newspaper snippets were added to her photograph albums, without comment. One read: 'On May 2nd at 26 Connaught-square, London, the wife of Robert J. Hanbury, a son'. (This was the Hanbury family's London residence). The other (undated) recorded the birth of a son to Mrs Robert Hanbury, at their London residence, and described celebrations held in Poolewe, where Miss Buchanan, the daughter of the fishing tenant at Inverewe House, hosted the celebrations. Mr Cameron, the 'well known Tournaig bard', proposed some Gaelic toasts and a bonfire was lit.[25] He also gave three hearty cheers and 'dancing on the hillside to the strain of pipers was indulged in. Inverewe House and others in the vicinity were brilliantly illuminated'. The Poolewe school children joined in the celebrations: 'On Monday the 4th inst all the children attended a bonfire on Meall an Doire in honour of the birth of a son and heir to Mr and Mrs Hanbury of Tournaig'.[26] But just a few weeks later, on 1 July, the child, named John Rolf, died. He was buried in Robert's family graveyard at Hitcham in Hertfordshire.

Six years later another cutting was pasted into an album. From *The Times* births column, it announced 'on 11 December [1913] at 8 Athole Crescent, Edinburgh to Mrs Robert Hanbury of Tournaig, a son'. Then the Poolewe Log Book, 27 February 1914, recorded:

> A splendid treat of apples, oranges, cakes, sweets and crackers as well as several useful articles and numerous good toys were given to the Poolewe children this afternoon by Mr and Mrs Hanbury, Tournaig. The treat was to have taken place at Tournaig, but for the unfortunate illness of the kind donors' young

> son. Mr K Urquhart, Riverside, Manager and Mr K Mackenzie, Chauffeur, distributed the gifts. About 40 children were present.

Sadly again, the death was then announced, in Edinburgh 8 March 1914, of Roderick Mackenzie, 'infant son of Mr and Mrs R.J. Hanbury of Tournaig, Poolewe.' This infant was buried in the cemetery at Poolewe. No reason has been found for the death of either child, though it has been suggested that the younger boy died of a 'childhood illness'.[27]

Socially, the Hanbury couple moved in high-class circles. In March 1910 'Mrs Robert Hanbury and Miss Marjorie Thyra Mackenzie were presented at court to their majesties the King and Queen by Lady Marjorie Mackenzie of Gairloch'.[28] In 1923 Mairi and her husband regretted 'they were unavoidably prevented from obeying their Majesties command to attend the afternoon party at Holyrood Palace on 11 July.'[29] At a more local level, they were on good terms with the owners of the Dundonnell, Letterewe and Gruinard estates and visited Baron von Schröder at Attadale House, Loch Carron, several times (1919, 1920, 1923), joining in successful fishing and stalking expeditions.[30] The Baron and his wife stayed at Tournaig House on a number of occasions between 1918 and 1926.[31] There were also frequent and quite lengthy visits to members of the extensive and far-flung Hanbury family, many of whom returned to spend part of their summer holidays at Inverewe or Tournaig.[32]

After the death of the Dowager Lady in 1901, Mairi and Osgood travelled abroad more often. The Inverewe albums contain postcards and photographs of foreign places, some showing Mairi accompanying both her father and her husband, for example in southern Spain and North Africa. Egypt and Italy can be recognised in others. In 1914, just before the outbreak of war, Mairi and Robert spent almost two months on their own fishing in Norway, with great success.[33] One Christmas (at least) they went to Switzerland, taking Donald, an old ghillie with them,[34] although they usually selected places 'where there was warm water to swim in and interesting plants to collect to bring home'.[35]

Public duties

One obituary told how Mairi and Robert 'both took a keen and beneficent interest in the welfare of the Gairloch district and in public administration, an interest maintained by Mrs Sawyer until the end'.[36] Occasionally mention of her 'public' role can be found. In 1906 Mairi, who 'came of good Highland stock and was descended from a lady famed for her knowledge of Gaelic literature', was appointed Convener of the Ross and Cromarty stall for the Great Gaelic Bazaar in Edinburgh.[37] She was said to have 'enthusiastically fostered' Highland Home Industries in Poolewe, together with Lady Marjorie Mackenzie.[38]

Though she is only recorded as having paid one further visit to the local school, (in September 1910, with two friends, when they 'heard the choir for over an hour'),[39] she occasionally gave them a 'treat' as in 1908: '25 December: The children were entertained last night at Inverewe House by Mrs and Mr Hanbury and Mr Mackenzie to a tea, magic lantern and a Xmas Tree. Nice presents were given to each child'. At Christmas time, 1914, Lord Mackenzie of Inveran (no relation) paid for a party for the children of Poolewe. 'Mrs Hanbury of Tournaig kindly sent a few dozen crackers, with which the children greatly amused themselves'.[40]

Robert did take on some local responsibilities. In 1913 'a strong committee under the chairmanship of Mr Hanbury, Tournaig, has taken over for a year the transhipment of goods and passengers on their weekly call at Poolewe'.[41] He also became involved in the local elementary education and was a member of the Gairloch School Board.[42] He first visited Poolewe School in October 1910, again in October 1914 and then more frequently during the war years. He wrote just one comment himself in the Log Book:

> The attendance has not been good but the weather has been fearful and made it very difficult for the children to get to school. The parents have also been compelled to keep the children to help them with the potato crop which has been most difficult to secure this year.[43]

The first note in the Inverasdale Log Book was on 25 May 1914. On subsequent visits he commented on various aspects of the state of the buildings: the WCs at the back, 'ought to have been cleaner', the need to repair broken windows urgently, and, several times, on the repairs and painting necessary, both of the school itself and of the school house. He also made reference to the improved quality of the children's exercise books (twice), how well the younger children were answering questions, their attendance and general appearance.[44] His last known school visit was in April 1919 to Poolewe, though he was to live until 1933.

Mrs Hanbury of Tournaig and Inverewe

In 1901 Mairi had become the liferentrix of Tournaig, following the death of her grandmother. Further legal papers, dated 18 December 1910, recorded:

> Lease by Osgood Hanbury Mackenzie of Inverewe and Kernsary with a consent to his daughter, Mairi Thyra Mackenzie or Hanbury, wife of and residing with Robert John Hanbury at Tournaig, Poolewe for 31 years from Martinmas 1910 and from year to year thereafter during her lifetime and on her death, to said Robert John Hanbury, should he survive her, for the remaining period (if any) of 31 years and thereafter from year to year during his lifetime of the Dwelling House and offices known as Tournaig situated on and bounded by the Estate of Inverewe and Kernsary, with the old Garden, the old and new plantations, [...] extending in all to 20 acres, in Parish of Gairloch, with exclusive right of fishing in Loch nam Dailthean and in the burn running out of said Loch down to the sea.[45]

Then, on 15 February 1915, Osgood, aged seventy-three, made his will and put all his property in her name, giving Mairi Thyra, the wife of Robert John Hanbury, the estate valued at £7,538 14s 10d.[46] As the house at Inverewe had burnt down in 1914 Mairi took ownership of the 'Home Farm' at Kernsary, the deer forest, grouse shooting and fishings of the estate. Her husband, Robert, was, from then on, recorded as the occupier of Tournaig House and Garden.[47]

Tournaig had always been Mairi's primary residence. Sometimes, after the 1914 fire, it was rented out to shooting tenants and then she and Robert stayed in the Gate Lodge at Inverewe. Wherever she stayed, it is evident that Mairi was very committed to the garden her father had developed over half a century. She clothed the walls of the ruins with rambling roses and clematis, calling it her 'Burnt House Garden'. Her family remember her very much as a 'hands-on' gardener.[48] Mairi had become 'the Lady of Inverewe'.

The Hanburys' war efforts

A newspaper cutting, dated 8 February, in one of Mairi's photograph albums, (on the same page as a funeral notice for 1912), reported that 'Lieut R.J. Hanbury had resigned his commission from 4th Ross Highlander battalion, Seaforth Highlanders'. Nonetheless, in the first days of what became the First World War, Robert went to Dingwall intending to sign up. However, 'everyone has to be medically examined, I did not pass so returned home on Aug 8th'.[49]

Thereafter, Robert was to become heavily involved both in supporting the administration of the war effort and in social activities with the locally-based military and naval officers. He immediately offered Tournaig as the base for a training course for the Red Cross.[50] He became a member of the regional Food Control committee, which usually met at Kinlochewe, and was concerned with the unregulated high price of goods. He continued to visit local schools, fitting in twenty-one attendances at the two nearest ones, though the only comment that he himself made with respect to these visits was that, whilst lunching with the clerk, he 'saw a great number of salmon jumping in front of the house'!

Although unfit to serve himself, he organised the signing up of local people. 'Robert J. Hanbury, Tournaig, Poolewe' was named as the Recruiting Officer on an undated Recruitment poster for the 4th Battalion, Seaforth Highlanders which 'still had a number of vacancies'. One incentive offered was that 'Wives of married men enlisting would get 'Separation Allowance' of 1s 1d per diem + 2d per diem per child under 14 years'. Many of the wider Hanbury family served as officers in the trenches and Mairi collected cuttings, greetings and postcards, photographs and other momentos of their wartime experiences. A number were seriously injured.[51] There are also several articles in her albums about local men who served and suffered during the war. One of these was an illustrated cutting about 'the late Pte. J. Mackenzie, Mellon [who] died from effects of severe wounds received in the battle of Arras [...] until Aug 1914 employed by Mr R.J. Hanbury of Tournaig and mobilised with his regiment the 1/4th Seaforths immediately on the outbreak of hostilities'. A whole page of cuttings and photos was devoted to the death of Sgt. MacGillivray who lived at Poolewe.

From the very start of the war the Hanburys were supportive of those who were in the Armed Forces. Unfortunately, it was not possible to take charge of the 160 German prisoners, as Admiral Browning requested in August 1914, as 'we had no arms' but they did help to 'arrange the burial of two men from the fleet'. In February 1918 'Mairi found a wounded soldier on the road. We kept him for a week or more and then he bolted'.

One 'thank you' to Mairi and her husband accompanied a photograph of HMS *Dominion*, and on the same page was another, dated 1914:

> Dear Mrs Hanbury,
> Very many thanks for your most kind message and your vegetables etc.
> I hope when the war is over to come and pass the time of day with you.
> I am afraid your prices have all gone up, with such an enormous fleet here.
> Lewis Bayley

Two notes, placed closely together, are expressing gratitude for providing cigarettes to men serving in the War. The notes are on cards obviously from inside the packet: 'The smokes sent with this postcard were supplied to the Tobacco Fund by Martins Ltd. 210 Piccadilly, London'. The first, headed 11 January 1914 (an error for 1915), to R.J. Hanbury from 'Hugh Ross, Sgt, 4th Seaforths. Maxim Gun Section, late painter' had the comment in brackets, 'perhaps you recall having met me in Tournaig'. The second, with the accurate date, 15 Jan 1915, came from Pte. J. Traynor. 2339 D Coy. 4th Batt. Seaforth Highlanders. There are other cards and notes which suggest more social occasions. Thanks came from 'The Fort' March 26 (no year given): 'Madam, on behalf of the marines at the fort, to tender our best thanks for all the marks of kindness we have so often received from you during our long stay here.'

The demands of organising the war on the home front did not detract from the appeal of outdoor sports and locally based officers often joined the Hanburys on their stalking and fishing expeditions.

> (1914) Dec 23 A lovely frosty day. Admiral Purefoy came to shoot. We saw a nice lot of woodcock.
>
> Dec 24 [...] Capt Goldfinch came to shoot. We had lunch outside – in the time it was like Switzerland.
>
> (1915) Nov 16 A lovely day, snow and hard frost. Capt Nugent, Capt Watson and Surgeon Thatcher and self. Mairi came out to lunch, found a good many birds out on the hill.

The hospitality was reciprocated. On 5 June 1917 they attended 'a farewell dinner at the base for Capt Truman' and Vice Admiral Reginald Tupper, invited them to 'dine on board'. His card, from the 'United Services Club, London sw.', was pasted in an album, with Robert's handwritten comment '9th June 1917'. Officers from Aultbea came for Christmas lunch in 1917.

Family members often came north for the pursuit of game during their wartime leaves, including Mairi's future husband, Ronald Sawyer, at the end of September 1917, who 'arrived from France for 4 days'. The venison was often distributed to the local people who were struggling to cope with the high prices and shortages, as in January 1918: 'Things are getting very difficult. Food of all kinds very scarce and no herrings for the people. We gave hinds to our work people and the people of Poolewe'. Perhaps the 6,000 cabbages which Robert planted on Inverewe land in May 1916 were also destined for the Poolewe lunch tables?

Mairi was involved in fund-raising. In her own hand there is list of monies, the names being both of people and places, (such as Badachro, Bualnaluib/ Aultbea), which she signed as Mairi J. Hanbury, Tournaig, Poolewe. These were subscriptions for GMCA huts, though precisely what and where these were is not evident. One entry in the Poolewe School Log Book gave another insight into the Mackenzie war effort: '22 July 1918: All the children were up at Inverewe Moor on Sat the 27th collecting sphagnum moss. 6 bags collected – afterwards Mrs Hanbury gave us all a splendid tea and a service of fruit'. Sphagnum moss, so abundant on the Wester Ross bogs had been found, (ironically in Germany), to be most useful to dress war wounds.

> The growing plant, with its underlying layers of withered stems and leaves, is collected, picked clean from other plants, pineneedles, etc., and dried. It is then lightly packed in bags of butter-muslin which are sterilised before being placed on the wound. Sphagnum Moss has important advantages (as an absorbent) over cotton-wool. Many materials, including other kinds of moss, are equally soft and light, but none can compare with it in power of absorption, due to its sponge-like structure. [...] The wounds of our men at the front were of such a suppurating character as to require specially absorbent dressings, and overworked doctors and nurses constantly expressed themselves thankful for a dressing that lasted longer than cotton-wool. Time and suffering are saved, as well as expense: the absorbent pads of moss are soft, elastic and very comfortable, easily packed and convenient to handle.[52]

Almost at the very end of the war, on 30 October 1918, Osgood H. Mackenzie, (of Tournaig), Mairi and Robert Hanbury, who were accompanying Captain H.G. Alston, the Senior Officer, Aultbea, Comd. J.H. Goldfinch, RN, Lieut C.W. Amers, PNVR, all officers of the Royal Navy, signed the Visitors' Book of the now dismantled lighthouse at Ruadha Reidh, beyond Gairloch.[53] Four days after the Armistice, Robert and Mairi 'were asked to lunch at the base by the officers still there. After some speeches they presented us with a lovely silver Rose Bowl from the men and officers who had been there'. Further

> On Dec 1 Captain Alston took us over to Loch Broom to see the Canadian and German prisoners cutting the woods. The Canadians had very good log huts and entertainment Huts, all lighted by electricity. The German prisoners had also been put in huts and looked well and nearly all of them had sealskin coats on.

The naval base at Aultbea was closed during the first week of April 1919.

Though they undoubtedly made the best contributions they could to the war, and Robert's *Game Book* showed a keen interest in world-wide events throughout the conflict, it was not that difficult a time for the Hanburys. There is no evidence of any billeting for either residence, even though there were still some habitable rooms at the back of the ruined Inverewe House.[54] Nor is there any suggestion of wartime requisitioning with respect to the walled garden or front lawn there. Guests were still able to stay with them at Tournaig. One was the painter, William Leadbetter Calderwood, responsible for the well-known (1912) head-and-shoulders portrait of Osgood. They went fishing together in 1916.[55] Robert and Mairi still travelled quite frequently and quite far afield, to visit relatives and friends, staying several times in Edinburgh, London and with the family at Hitcham, particularly during the winter months. In 1917, after Christmas there, they went on to Bath for a month, returned to London and then moved on to Suffolk where they did plenty of hunting. Fishing tenants, such as Lord Cunliffe, Governor of the Bank of England, still arrived to contribute to their income.

Once the war was over the Hanburys helped to show the appreciation of the area to those who returned safely from the Front. A newspaper article (undated) was glued into one of Mairi's albums. It reported that Robert J. Hanbury was Chairman of the Presentation Committee which honoured Coy Sgt-Major Alex McKenzie in a function on Friday at Poolewe Drill Hall. He had been awarded the D.C.M. for 'his part in the titanic struggle against the Kaiser and his hordes'.

At the end of 1919 Mairi and Robert left Inverewe to go abroad for several months. They travelled through North Africa and then returned via France, where they toured and took many photographs of the desolate battlefields and ruins of Noyens, as well as visiting Versailles palace. They stayed for a while with the same Salovèze as Osgood had visited for hunting in the Compiègne forest back in 1903 and who had been recalled from a stay at Inverewe the week war broke out. But by now Mairi's father was too frail to accompany them.

Osgood's death

He died quite unexpectedly. Robert Hanbury wrote in his *Game Book* in 1922:

> On April 9th Osgood went to see Donald Grant who was ill and slipped up and hurt his leg, he was brought home in a cart and got him to bed. An

> operation was found necessary as he had ruptured the large muscle. He decided to have this done and Dr Duke came from Inverness he came through splendidly and had no pain. On April 13 he had a heart attack but this passed off. His leg healed and the stitches were taken out and he seemed doing splendidly sleeping well. On April 15 he was reading and writing and said he never felt better and then just before 8 had another heart attack and passed away in a few minutes...
>
> 19 April 1922 ... It was a most glorious day.
> Snow on all the hills but like a summer's day. We had a service here at the House which Mr Macleod did in English and then carried him to the foot of Croft Brae and then motored to the Gairloch Hotel and then carried him to the grave where Mr MacKinnon did the service in Gaelic, it was most impressive. Kenneth Mackenzie, Capt. Hanbury, Major Mitford and Major Thumble were present and a very large number of people from the district. W. Macrae played the pipes beautifully.

Osgood had decided not to be buried in the local cemetery at Londubh, Poolewe, but rather to be interred next to his mother and close to Flowerdale, his childhood home.[56] Mairi herself, when her time came in 1953, chose to be laid between her two husbands and next to her baby, Roderick, in a family lair at Londubh, in sight of Inverewe.[57]

References and Notes

1. 1863 Disposition re Inverewe Purchase. Inverewe House Archive. See Chapter VII for details of the farming enterprises.
2. Wright, p.26. The notice to tender for the jobs created by the erection of this new Lodge was posted in the *Inverness Courier*, 27 December 1877.
3. *The Mackenzie Case*, p.106.
4. Detailed in Chapter VI.
5. Dixon, p.319.
6. *The Mackenzie Case*. p.122.
7. Mackenzie, p.59.
8. Butler, *Memories*.
9. *The Scotsman*, 8 July 1887.

[10] Butler, *Memories.*

[11] Macleod, p.43.

[12] Poolewe School Log Book, 19 April 1889, 13 February 1891, 8 June 1893, 23 March 1894, 30 October 1896.

[13] Mackenzie, p.186.

[14] Macleod, p.126.

[15] *The Scotsman*, 2 June 1894.

[16] One sketch book, mainly of drawings made in South Africa but including three local scenes in watercolour, is to be found in the Inverewe House Archive. Further paintings are in the ownership of Mairi's nephew, Peter Hanbury.

[17] Two photographs were taken of her, as a young woman, at her spinning wheel which was still in Inverewe House in 2009.

[18] Gairloch Heritage Museum Photographic Archive. Osgood himself was always proud that he was only eight when his mother gave him his first gun. Was this photo taken to recognise the same significant milestone in his daughter's life?

[19] Butler, *Memories.*

[20] *The Scotsman*, 24 September 1898, 21 September 1906.

[21] Butler, *Memories.*

[22] Poolewe School Log Book, 5 April 1907.

[23] *The Scotsman*, April 1907.

[24] Wright, p.26.

[25] In a photograph album at Inverewe House. No date or attribution.

[26] Poolewe School Log Book, 7 May 1908.

[27] Butler, *Memories.*

[28] *Ross-shire Journal*, March 1910. Inverewe House Archive. Lady Marjorie was the daughter-in-law of Osgood's half-brother, Kenneth. Perhaps Mairi had reconciled the two sides of the Mackenzies. The King was Edward VII, who died only a few weeks later on 6 May.

[29] *The Scotsman*, 18 July 1923.

[30] A photograph, showing Mairi at the dinner table, was discovered on a visit to Attadale House, September 2007, in the Visitors' Book belonging to Baron von Schröder, the owner at the time of these visits.

[31] Entries in the Tournaig House Visitors Book, June 1918, 7–8 June 1919, 31 March-2 April 1921, 30 June–2 July 1923, 7 June–8 July 1926 and mentioned in Robert Hanbury's *Game Book*. Another notable guest to sign the Tournaig Visitors' Book, August 1926, was the couturier Norman Hartnell.

[32] Butler, *Memories.*

[33] Precise dating of these photos is rarely possible, but, as with this trip to Voss in

Norway, June/July 1914, the pictures in the Inverewe photograph albums can occasionally be cross-referenced with entries in Robert Hanbury's *Game Book.* A 38 lb. salmon was caught.

34 Macleod, pp.182–183.

35 Typescript of an interview with Margaret Cuthbert, a cousin of Mairi's, whose memories of Inverewe were recorded in 1990. Inverewe House Archive. But Margaret Cuthbert had not met Mairi until 1948 so this was based on family hearsay. Her nephew recalled that she would also happily swim in the very cold water of Wester Ross, diving in from a boat on the loch. (Butler, *Memories).*

36 *Ross-shire Journal*, 31 July 1953.

37 An undated newspaper report of a meeting in Dingwall was pasted into Mairi's photo album.

38 *The Scotsman*, 29 August 1906.

39 Poolewe School Log Book, 30 September 1910.

40 *Inverness Courier*, 25 December 1914.

41 *Ross-shire Journal*, November 1913. Inverewe House Archive.

42 1915 Ross-shire 'Roll of Honour' and *Souter's Directory.* Gairloch Heritage Museum Library.

43 Poolewe School Log Book, 9 November 1917.

44 Inverasdale School Log Book, 22 February 1915, 21 October 1915, 23 November 1915, 30 May 1916, 27 June 1916, 10 May 1918.

45 Sasines Record, Inverewe House Archive.

46 Copy held in Inverewe House Archive.

47 Ross-shire Valuation Rolls, Highland Council Archives, Inverness.

48 Butler, *Memories* and photographs in Mairi's albums. Ed. Elizabeth L. Ewan, The *Biographical Dictionary of Scottish Women* (Edinburgh: Edinburgh University Press, 2006) does give her credit: 'History has tended to paint her in his [Osgood's] shadow but Inverewe Garden is her life's work as much as his'.

49 The information in this section, unless otherwise indicated, has come from Robert Hanbury's *Game Book* and Mairi's photograph albums.

50 There are a number of photographs in Mairi's album of women in very pristine-looking nurses' uniform practising their skills on the lawn there. August 1914.

51 The 'Uncle Bob' who contributed a number of fascinating 'souvenirs', including the 'Happy New Year booklet for 1919', a commercial production in French, with pictures, was almost certainly R.H.O. Hanbury, Robert's cousin. It was definitely not Robert himself as was once believed locally. Local rumour also told that Mairi's husband was gassed during the war. This is not correct. Robert Hanbury's *Game Book* included mention of many family injuries in war service and Mairi's second

husband, Ronald Sawyer, was one of these. He was invalided home to South Africa, but the nature of his injuries is unknown. Nor is it clear who sent her a 'post-card' photograph of a large group of war-injured soldiers, (in wheelchairs and waving crutches), entitled "*Fragments from France and elsewhere meet the future full of Faith and Hope" Roehampton 1916.*

[52] *A Modern Herbal* by Mrs M. Grieve 1931, www.botanical.com, accessed 28 November 2008.

[53] Rudha Reidh Lighthouse Visitors' Book. Gairloch Heritage Museum.

[54] Personal communication from Peter Hanbury who stayed there himself with his siblings and a nanny in the 1920s.

[55] Calderwood was born 1865 in Glasgow. The portrait is dated 1912.

[56] 'He was taken from Inverewe at 2.45 p.m. on 19 April 1922, and proceeded at 4 p.m. from the Gairloch hotel to the burial ground'. *Inverness Chronicle*, 18 April 1922.

[57] Robert Hanbury died in 1933.

CHAPTER XV

The Legacy

Osgood's reputation in the Poolewe area was undoubtedly tainted by his personal life. Public sympathy was with his wife, Minna, particularly once it was evident that Kenneth, laird of Gairloch, supported her rather than his own half-brother. Though the 'good deeds' and reforms of his mother, the Dowager Lady Mary, and his Uncle, Dr John, are still given credit, Osgood's involvement in so many aspects of public life, as JP, Parochial Board chair, or School manager, have not been recognised or remembered. Folk memories of him recall not how he fulfilled his duties as a heritor but that he was a difficult and often inhospitable man. Dr Kenneth Mackenzie of Dundonnell and his son, Murdo, made an expedition by boat to Aultbea in 1874. 'The crusty old clearance landowner Meyrick Bankes' offered 'dinner at the Inn'. Also present was 'Osgood Mackenzie who was not at all entertaining'.[1]

A story, not substantiated but passed on through the generations, illustrates how local people regarded him. An old woman lived on the land that became part of the Walled Garden. She was evicted from her home for not paying her rent. The house had been set on fire but she took some roof timbers with her and set up a shelter against the walls of the Londubh burial ground. When Osgood forced her to move on from there she put a curse on the family to the effect that there would never be a male heir at Inverewe whilst a Mary reigned. Both Osgood's mother and daughter bore that name and both Mairi's sons died in early childhood.[2]

He strictly enforced what he saw as his rights to prevent public access to his land and fishing lochans, he was self-righteous with respect to religion and drink, he did not often open his house and grounds for public entertainment or school treats. Despite his commitment to speaking Gaelic, the encouragement of local artistic and poetic talent and practice of wearing the kilt, his English ancestry and income seemed to keep him somewhat of an outsider.

Yet, though the respect of the locals was limited, his fame further afield grew as his trees, shrubs, flowers and fruit – gathered from throughout the world – flourished. The first article in a national newspaper was published in 1887. From 1897 he contributed frequently to the two major Scottish papers. His contributions to the Royal Horticultural Society came in 1908 and 1916. For the last twenty-five or so years of his life, once the final, failed divorce hearing was concluded, it seemed that his garden at Inverewe took on a more equal importance with his passion for sporting pursuits.

In one of these articles, written in 1915, Osgood reflected back on his horticultural interests: 'What an amount of real pleasure I have had from forestry and gardening during my long life'.[3] Such writings indicated an enthusiasm and enjoyment that was not reflected in the short chapter in *A Hundred Years in the Highlands*. He was somewhat surprised at how successful his book had been. Initially he had had to persuade the publishers to get it printed 'in these bad times' (and before he died) but the first edition sold out in a fortnight at the end of April 1921. A further 9,000 copies were to be printed. Osgood reckoned he still had sufficient material to write another fifty to hundred pages for a second edition: he had a 'lot more stories in my old head and in my Uncle's manuscript note-book'.[4] However, a second book was not to be.

Clearly, by the time of his death in 1922, he had won much respect for his horticultural expertise. Even after he died he was still contributing to garden wisdom: those attending The Royal Caledonian Horticultural Society's monthly meeting in October were to hear 'a reading of a Paper on Exotic Plants, written for the Society by the late Mr Osgood H. Mackenzie'.[5] His daughter, Mairi, never seemed to have considered leaving the isolated Wester Ross life, much though she enjoyed travelling and visiting at home and abroad. She remained in Poolewe, dedicating herself willingly to maintaining and enhancing her garden inheritance and selling other parts of the estate to ensure its upkeep.[6] She is more fondly remembered by local people. In 1935 Mairi remarried. Her second husband was another cousin, Ronald Sawyer, the nephew of her first husband, Robert. Ronald had often stayed at Tournaig and he was to spend much money and effort trying to improve the fishing and farming there. He is best known though for building a new villa on the site of the ruins of the original burnt-down Inverewe Mansion House. He and Mairi returned to live at Inverewe in 1937.

Nonetheless, had Osgood not prepared the ground, literally, there would never have been the abiding legacy of Inverewe. 'He made barren ground bring forth flowers, shrubs and trees'.[7] In 1922 one obituarist wrote: 'His collection of plants from all parts of the world in the Inverewe gardens and policies is one of the most interesting in the Kingdom'.[8] For tens of thousands of visitors every year, (themselves coming from all parts of the world), this remains the case.

References and Notes

1 David Iredale, *Dundonnell of the Mackenzies* (West Sussex: Phillimore Press, 2007). Osgood had failed to impress this Mackenzie family by his apparent rudeness on a visit he made to their Dundonnell home at about the same time. There were some Australian relatives staying which (according to letters written afterwards) was unfortunate because Osgood was "one of those who looks down on Australians as a low set … thinking that we were an ignorant set and knew nothing". This Murdo Mackenzie considered Osgood's random shooting expeditions made him 'next to a poacher', pp.147–148.

2 Re-told in Ian Crawford, *Held in Trust, The National Trust for Scotland* (Edinburgh: Mainstream Publishing, 1986), p.98.

3 *The Scotsman*, 30 November 1915.

4 Letter in reply to Mrs Wayne, 25 May 1921. Inverewe House Archive.

5 Advertisement in *The Scotsman*, 30 September 1922.

6 Most notably, Tournaig in December 1943.

7 *Ross-shire Journal*, 21 April 1922.

8 *The Scotsman* Obituary Notice, 18 April 1922.

Who's Who

Name	Information
Bain, Nurse	Mairi's first nanny. She was present at the incident on 4 August 1880 and gave evidence in the divorce proceedings.
Bankes, Meyrick	Owner of the Letterewe and Gruinard estates from 1835. He evicted many of his tenants to introduce sheep farms. His legal victory in the Loch Dubh 'fishing rights' case, 1877–1878, cost Osgood dearly.
Cameron, Alexander	Osgood's farm/sheep manager at Tournaig. Known as the 'Tournaig Bard', he was a fellow promoter of Gaelic culture.
Cameron, William	Headteacher of Poolewe School 1901–1915. His promotion of Gaelic music was actively supported by Osgood Mackenzie.
Campbell, James Arthur	Creator of Arduaine Garden. He met Osgood Mackenzie in Ceylon 1906, donated plants to Inverewe and stayed at Tournaig.
Campbell, Robert	Osgood's 'only gardener', who worked at Inverewe for 33 years. His daughter was a pupil-teacher at Poolewe. Local sponsorship enabled her to undertake full teacher training.
Chalmers, Thomas	The leader of the Evangelical Group during the 'Ten Year Conflict' (1833–1843) within the Church of Scotland which led to the 'Disruption' and the setting up of the Free Church.
Darroch, Duncan	Born 1836, died 1910. Owner of the Torridon estates from 1873. Collaborated with Osgood Mackenzie in the unsuccessful efforts to bring the railway to the Gairloch/Aultbea area in the 1890s.
Dingwall, Rev.	Minister for the Aultbea and Poolewe Free Church. He raised the funds to build the churches in both villages (1889) and came into dispute with Osgood in the late 1880s when he, as a heritor, signed a 'call' nominating a new minister for the Poolewe Church of Scotland.

Dixon, John H.	Born 1838, died 1926. Lived at Inveran, on the shores of Loch Ewe, 1874–1898. For much of the time he was a good friend of Osgood's and they had similar cultural and public service interests. Author of the *Guide to Gairloch and Loch Maree* (1886) which revealed so much of the 'Records, traditions, inhabitants and natural history' of the area.
Eliott, Capt.	Inspector General of Highland Relief. He kept in close contact with the landowners of Wester Ross during the famine years.
Fowler, John, Sir	Owner of the Braemore estate. He was the engineer responsible for the Forth Rail Bridge amongst other achievements. His wife, Alice, was connected with Osgood in respect of botany and gardening.
Grant, Donald	Osgood's 'faithful friend and servant' to whom the Peace Stone (1919) was dedicated.
Grant, John	'Big John': Osgood's 'good and faithful grieve'.
Hanbury, Robert	Born 1867, married Mairi in 1907, died 1933. Local 'recruiter' during the First World War, School Board Manager and County Councillor. His *Game Book* revealed details of local happenings, (especially during the First World War), estate management and family events, including those leading to Osgood's death in April 1922.
Harris, Annie	Maid to the Dowager Lady Mary. Accompanied Minna to Conan in January/February 1880 and revealed to Osgood the alleged 'Plot' to take Mairi to England.
Haskell, Arthur	The young blacksmith's mate who died after an accident with the anchor chain, 25 April 1914. During his funeral his ship-mates noticed that Inverewe House was on fire.
Hornsby, James	Proprietor of the Loch Maree Hotel (and Gairloch Hotel) who hosted Queen Victoria during her visit in September 1877.

Jellicoe, Admiral	Commander-in-chief of the British Grand Fleet which was based in and around Loch Ewe in the early months of the First World War.
MacEwen, F. Dr	Poor law doctor at the centre of a dispute about medical provision in Gairloch parish in the 1880s and 1890s.
MacIntosh, James	Inspector of the Poor and Clerk to the School Board for Gairloch Parish for more than 50 years.
Mackay, John S. Rev.	The 'Poolewe Minister' (Church of Scotland) who contributed to the 1850 Enquiry of the Royal College of Physicians of Edinburgh. By 1879 his sanity was in doubt and his management of the parish under scrutiny by the Loch Carron Presbytery.
Mackenzies of Coul	The relatives, with estates near Dingwall, from whom Osgood rented sporting land in the 1850s. Osgood's mother purchased the Tournaig and Inverewe parts of her son's estate from them in 1863.
Mackenzie of Ord	The second trustee (with the Dowager Lady Mary) of the Gairloch estate during the minority lairdship of Sir Kenneth. 1843–1853.
Mackenzie, Donald	Factor to Sir Kenneth Mackenzie's Gairloch estate. Involved in supporting the laird during the 1880s' period of agricultural unrest and during the long-running disputes within the parish as to whether there should be one or two doctors for the poor.
Mackenzie, Eila, Lady	Wife of Kenneth, 13th laird. Supportive of Minna throughout her marriage.
Mackenzie, Francis Alexander	Born 1798, married (1) Kythé Smith Wright 1829, (2) Mary Hanbury 1836, died 1843 in a mental institution in London. 12th laird of Gairloch. Father of Kenneth, Francis and Osgood. Attempted to improve the quality of crofting on the Gairloch estates during the 1830s.

Mackenzie, Francis Harford	Born 1833, died 1895. Half-brother of Osgood. Strong supporter of local 'public' education. Lived at Kerrysdale until he went to Serbia in the 1870s where he spent the rest of his life, though returning to visit his family most years.
Mackenzie, John of Eileanach, Dr	Born 1803, died 1886. Uncle of Osgood, brother of Francis 12th laird. As factor of the Gairloch estates, 1841–1853, he instigated and managed the reform of land holding to create the 'crofting' pattern still to be seen today. Lived on Isle Ewe until he returned to the Inverness area 1856.
Mackenzie, Kenneth, Capt.	Great uncle of Osgood. Lived at Kerrysdale. Advised Osgood on gardening in Wester Ross. Wife was 'Aunty Flora'.
Mackenzie, Kenneth, Sir	Born 1832, died 1900. 13th laird of Gairloch. Half-brother of Osgood. Member of the Napier Commission 1884. Lord Lieutenant of Ross-shire, County Councillor and strong public servant. Lived mainly at Conan. Supported Minna, not Osgood, during the troubled marriage.
Mackenzie, Kythé Smith Wright	Wife of Francis, 12th laird of Gairloch. Mother of Kenneth and Francis. Died in childbirth 1834.
Mackenzie, Mairi Thyra	Born 1879, married (1) Robert Hanbury 1907, (2) Ronald Sawyer 1935, died 1953. Daughter of Osgood and Minna. Two children (John Rolf and Roderick) both died as infants. Gave Inverewe House and Garden to the National Trust for Scotland in 1952.
Mackenzie, Mary, Dowager Lady	Born c.1812, married 1836, died 1901. Second wife of Sir Francis, 12th laird. Mother of Osgood. Purchased the lands to create the Inverewe estate. She lived at Tournaig after his marriage and brought up Mairi once Minna had left.

Mackenzie, Osgood	Born 1842, married Minna Moss 1877, died 1922. Third son of Francis, 12th laird. Brought up at Flowerdale, given his own lands by his mother 1862/1863. He created the estate of Inverewe where he lived for the rest of his life. One daughter, Mairi. Held many public offices in Gairloch parish and Ross-shire County. Created the world-famous Inverewe Garden.
Mackinnon, Finlay	Born c.1864, died 1931. Poolewe-born artist, specialising in landscape water-colours. Supported in training and then patronised by Osgood Mackenzie and John H. Dixon.
Macleod, Charles	Manager of the Gairloch crofts during the destitution years.
MacNaughton, Dr	Appointed as the parish doctor after the death of Dr MacEwen 1899. Became involved in further difficulties concerning medical issues and the role of the 'poor law' doctor.
Matheson, John	Born c.1845, died before 1914. Osgood's gamekeeper for more than 40 years who was also renowned for his skill with the dogs.
McNeill, John, Sir	Born 1795, died 1883. Chairman of the Board of Supervision of the Scottish Poor Law 1845–1868. Visited Gairloch parish and interviewed Dr John Mackenzie as part of the preparation for his *Report to the Board of Supervision on the West Highlands and Islands* (1851).
Moss, John	Elder brother of Minna. Spent much time in the Highlands hunting, shooting and fishing.
Moss, Minna Amy, (Mackenzie)	Born 1852, married Osgood 1877, separated 1880, died August 1909 at Birdingbury Hall, near Rugby. Lived in Pool House, Poolewe 1881–1897. Fought for 'Access' rights to daughter, Mairi 1884–1891. Successfully defended herself in Osgood's three attempts to divorce her.

Moss, Thomas, Sir	Born 1811, married Amy Charlotte Edwards, c.1849, died 1890. 1st bart. Father of Minna. Wealthy banker and merchant.Lived at Otterspool, Liverpool, with a second home at Ennismore Gardens, London.
Moss, Tom Cottingham	Second brother of Minna. Took her back to Otterspool in February 1880 and tried to reconcile the couple in 1882.
Mulock, Thomas	Outspoken journalist who campaigned against landowners in the early 1850s. Was briefly editor of the *Inverness Advertiser* and then the *Northern Ensign.*
Murdoch, John	Radical journalist. Supported the H.L.L.R.A. and the cause of crofters in the mid-1880s, particularly during the evidence-collecting of the Napier commission.
Napier, John, Sir	Chairman of the commission investigating the 'Condition of the Highlands and Islands of Scotland' in 1883. His *Report* helped influence the 1886 Crofting Act. Then became Chairman of the Crofting Commission.
Pine Coffin, Edward	Born 1784, died 1862. Military officer sent to the north-west highlands and islands by the Central Board of Management for Famine Relief (Destitution Board) to ensure that funds were appropriately distributed and spent.
Pirie, Alexander	Aberdeen paper merchant who became owner of the Lechmelm estate, near Ullapool, from 1879. He soon initiated a wide-ranging eviction policy to enable him to convert the crofted land to deer forest. The resulting public outcry helped generate support for the H.L.L.R.A.
Plumridge, Annie	Maid to Lady Moss. She accompanied Minna when she returned to Poolewe in July/August 1880.
Robertson, Charles	The Gairloch Parish Medical Officer who contributed to the Royal College of Physicians of Edinburgh's enquiry into the Case for Medical Services for the Poor, 1850 and also Sir John McNeill's *Report.*

Rose, Capt	Inspector for Central Board for Famine Relief in Wester Ross area.
Sawyer, Ronald	Born 1883, married (2) Mairi 1935, died 1945. The nephew of Mairi's first husband, Robert, he often came to Wester Ross on visits from his farm and mining interests in South Africa (early 20th century). Was on active service, and wounded, during the First World War.
Scrope, Poulet	MP. Visited and wrote on the post-famine Highlands praising Dr John's reforms.
Speight, James Sir	The shooting tenant at Inverewe 1882. He tried and failed to reconcile Osgood and Minna. In 1884 took Osgood to court over misleading shooting claims.
Trevelyan, Charles, Sir	Under-secretary of State at the Treasury. Responsible for famine relief to Highlands and Islands from 1846. Then became the Chair of the Highlands and Islands Emigration Society (early 1850s).
Urquhart, Donald	Osgood's stalker, with remarkable shooting abilities. Another long-serving family retainer.
Victoria, Queen	Stayed at the Loch Maree Hotel 12–18 September 1877, visiting local places of interest.

Bibliography

Anderson, George and Peter, *Guide to the Highlands and Islands of Scotland,* Adam and Charles Black, Edinburgh, 1851

Asquith, Herbert, *Moments of Memory,* Hutchinson, London, 1937

Barron, James, *The Northern Highlands in the Nineteenth Century, Newspaper Index and Annals.* Vol. 3, 1842–1856, Carruthers and Sons, Inverness, 1913

Brown, Stewart J. and Fry, Michael (Eds), *Scotland in the Age of the Disruption,* Edinburgh University Press, Edinburgh, 1993

Butler, Pauline, *Memories of Inverewe,* (the recollections of Peter Hanbury), Author for NTS, 2007

Byam Shaw, Christina, *Pigeon Holes of Memory,* Constable, London, 1988

Campey, Lucille H., *After the Hector. The Scottish Pioneers of Nova Scotia and Cape Breton, 1773–1852,* Natural Heritage Books, Toronto, 2004

Camshron, Alasdair, *Am Bard,* Archibald Sinclair, Glasgow, 1926

Cowan, May, *Inverewe: A Garden in the North West Highlands,* Geoffrey Bles, London, 1964

Devine, T.M., *The Great Highland Famine,* John Donald, Edinburgh, 1988

Devine, T.M., *Clanship to Crofters' War. The Social Transformation of the Scottish Highlands,* Manchester University Press, Manchester, 1994

Dixon, John H., *Gairloch and Guide to Loch Maree,* Co-operative Printing Co Ltd, Edinburgh, 1886

Fairrie, Angus, *The Northern Meeting 1788–1988,* Pentland Press, East Lothian, 1988

Fenyo, Krisztina, *Contempt, Sympathy and Romance,* Tuckwell Press, East Linton, 2000

Fry, Michael, *Wild Scots,* John Murray, London, 2005

Haldane, A.R.B., *The Drove Roads of Scotland,* Birlinn, Edinburgh, 1997

Hanley, Cliff, *History of Scotland,* Gallery Books, New York, 1986

Hawkins, Marjorie, *Gairloch, Pictou County, Nova Scotia,* Macquarrie, Pugwash, 1977

Hunter, James, *The Making of the Crofting Community,* John Donald, Edinburgh, 1976/2000

Iredale, David, *Dundonnell of the Mackenzies,* Phillimore Press, West Sussex, 2007

Lindsay, Jean, *The Scottish Poor Law,* Stockwell Ltd., Ilfracombe, 1975

Macdonald, Murdoch, *Old Torridon* (Notes on the History of Torridon), Torridon, Evanton, 1997

Mackenzie, Alexander, *History of the Highland Clearances,* A. & W. Mackenzie, Inverness, 1883

Mackenzie, Compton, *My Life and Times. Octave Three. 1900–1907,* Chatto and Windus, London, 1964

Mackenzie, Kenneth C., *Yesterday's Poolewe,* Author, 2002

Mackenzie, Osgood, *A Hundred Years in the Highlands,* Edward Arnold, London, 1921

Mackie, J.D., *A History of Scotland,* Pelican, London, 1964

Mackinnon, Angus Matheson, *Highland Minister. The life and poems of Rev Angus MacKinnon, Aultbea,* Catalone Press, Nova Scotia, Canada, 1997

Macleod, Dawn, *Oasis of the North,* Hutchinson, London, 1958

MacRobbie, William, *Gruinard and Letterewe: Lairds and Clearances,* Author, Laide, 2001

Orr, Willie, *Deer Forests, Landlords and Crofters,* John Donald, Edinburgh, 1982

Polson, Alexander, *Gairloch (The book of Gairloch),* Souter, Dingwall, 1920

Prebble, John, *The Highland Clearances,* Secker and Warburg, London, 1963

Richards, Eric, *The Highland Clearances,* Birlinn Ltd, Edinburgh, 2000

Shaw, Donald, *A Hundred Years in Wester Ross 1900–2000,* D. Shaw, 2000

Thompson, Francis, *Crofting Years,* Luath Press, Edinburgh, 1984

Thompson, Francis, *Victorian and Edwardian Highlands,* B.T. Batsford Ltd, London, 1976

Vallance H.A., *The Highland Railway,* David and Charles, Dawlish, 1938/1963

Victoria, (Queen), *More leaves from the Journal of a life in the Highlands,* 1884

Wright, Andrew P.K., *Inverewe House Conservation Plan,* National Trust for Scotland, 2008

Primary evidence in archival collections

Gairloch Heritage Museum

Transcripts of the evidence given to Sir John McNeill when he visited Poolewe in 1850

Transcripts of the evidence given to Napier Commission (*Royal Commission of Inquiry into the Condition of Crofters and Cottars in the Highlands and Islands of Scotland*) when it visited Poolewe in 1883

The Mackenzie Case, John H. Dixon's bound copy of the legal documents from the 1892 Court of Sessions hearings for the divorce petition of Osgood H. Mackenzie

School log books for Achtercairn and Opinan schools (those for Poolewe and Inverasdale have remained in the schools)

Photographic collections

Highland Council, Inverness

Ross-shire Valuation Rolls, 1868–1923

Minutes of the Ross and Cromarty County Council Meetings and various Reports included therein, 1890–1916

Inverness Reference Library

Transcripts of the evidence given to the Royal Commission on Highland Pastures and Deer Forests when it visited Aultbea, 1894

Inverewe House (National Trust for Scotland)

Sundry documents, including letters, newspaper cuttings, Osgood Mackenzie's *Game Books*, and Mairi Mackenzie's photograph albums

Family Archives

The manuscript diaries of Dr John Mackenzie of Eilenach (10 volumes), kindly lent by John Mackenzie of Gairloch and Conan Estates

The *Game Book* of Robert Hanbury, kindly lent by Nigel Hanbury, his great-nephew

Newspapers and Journals

Glasgow Herald

Inverness Advertiser

Inverness Courier

Journal of the Royal Horticultural Society

Northern Chronicle

Northern Ensign

Ross-shire Journal

Scottish Highlander

The Scotsman

The Times

Articles

Balfour, Rodney A.C., The Highlands and Islands Emigration Society', *Transactions of the Gaelic Society of Inverness*, Vol. LVII 1990–2

Caird, J.B., 'The Making of the Gairloch Crofting Landscape', Baldwin, John R. (Ed), *Peoples and Settlement in North-West Ross*. The Scottish Society for Northern Studies, 1994

Macphail, I.M.M., 'The Napier Commission', *Transactions of the Gaelic Society of Inverness*, Vol. XLVIII 1972–1974

Internet References

Higginbotham,Peter: Information on Highland workhouses
www.workhouses.org.uk

History of the Highland and Island Emigration Society
www.angelfire.com

Report of the Poor Law Commissioners
www.econlib.org

Royal College of Physicians of Edinburgh:

i) Report: The Case for State Medical Services for the Poor. The Highlands and Islands 1850

ii) Responses to the Enquiry of the Royal College of Physicians on the Supply of Practitioners of Medicine and Surgery 1850

iii) Statement regarding the Existing Deficiency of Medical Practitioners in the Highlands and Islands 1852

iv) McCrae, Dr Morrice, 'The Case for State Medical Services for the Poor: the Highlands and Islands 1850'
www.rcpe.ac.uk/library/history

The Royal Commission of Inquiry into the Condition of Crofters and Cottars in the Highlands and Islands 1884 (Napier Commission):
www.highland-elibrary.com